It is impossible to emphasize how important Cl
However, much of the content accessible for C
ed in Western epistemologies and, as a result,
Christianity in the African context. The apologetic endeavour that will effectively appeal to Africans must take into consideration the social, economic and political situations of Africans, given the apparent problems of injustice, poverty, insecurity, social inequality, human trafficking, malnutrition, physical and sexual abuses, exploitation, war, political uprising and bigotry on the continent of Africa.

African scholars, lay people and marketplace theologians can all benefit from this book, which does a fantastic job of taking these African realities into account and engaging with them contextually. The book's unique contributors are African theologians with experience grappling with African realities and the contextual realities of apologetics from an African perspective. I offer this book my best recommendation and am confident that it will have a significant impact on the development of apologetics in Africa.

Rev. Nathan H. Chiroma, PhD
Principal,
Africa College of Theology, Kigali, Rwanda

Apologetics in Africa: An Introduction, edited by Kevin Muriithi Ndereba, brings together reflections and responses, written almost exclusively by young African theologians and apologists, that reflect a clear understanding of the contemporary African situation and reality. The chapters of this book address biblical, philosophical and cultural issues that are of special concern in the African situation and respond to many of the questions often asked by African believers and students. The book adopts a multi-disciplinary perspective and offers critical, contemporary and relevant responses to the issues tackled. The approach is practical and down-to-earth. Clearly and simply written, this book will be warmly welcomed by younger African readers, as well as others.

Aloo Osotsi Mojola, PhD
Professor, Philosophy and Translation Studies,
St Paul's University, Kenya
Formerly Translation Consultant and Africa Translation Coordinator,
United Bible Societies

To say that I'm concerned about the present spiritual state of the church in Africa is an understatement. This church faces many challenges, the primary being false teachers and their heretical teachings. These false teachers teach a different gospel that denies the gospel of our Lord Jesus Christ and the result is not only a distorted Christianity, but a distorted salvation. When the apostle Jude warns us about false teachers in his short letter, he says this is also about our salvation because when faith is at stake, our salvation is at stake. If the truth is lost, salvation is lost. And that is why the central message of the book of Jude is that every Christian should contend for the faith.

This book, *Apologetics in Africa: An Introduction*, equips us to do just that – contend for the faith. Here, various African apologists provide a gospel-centred apology to critical questions most African Christians grapple with. Questions about the reliability of the Bible, the resurrection, natural evil, the Christian faith and the practice of dowry, etc. These questions require a gospel-centred apologetic in a manner that avoids the burden of "selling Christianity to non-Christians." This book provides a solid foundation for African Christians to explain their faith to non-believers while confronting heretical church teachings. Here you will find pertinent gospel responses to often confusing matters. Read it so that you're prepared to defend the gospel to anyone who calls you to account for the hope in you.

Victor Nakah, PhD
International Director for Sub-Saharan Africa,
Mission to the World

This book, under the guidance of Dr. Ndereba, is a long-awaited contribution to Christian apologetics specifically addressing issues in Africa, written by authors who are familiar with our continent. It focuses on key aspects such as whether God has a direct relationship with creation or is distant and must be sought through the living dead. Opposite to fear of demanding ancestors, salvation in Christ includes assurance and peace with God, who cares and knows our pain.

This book includes important advice on apologetic approaches to occultism, Islam and Eastern religions in Africa, as well as more ethical matters such as *lobola* (bride-price) and domestic violence. There is also a much-needed focus on cults in Africa.

Henk Stoker, PhD
Professor of Apologetics and Ethics,
North-West University, South Africa

Christians in all ages have had to consider how to be "prepared to give an answer to everyone who asks you for the reason for the hope" they have in their particular context, and how to do so "with gentleness and respect" (1 Peter 3:15). In *Apologetics in Africa*, Dr. Kevin Muriithi Ndereba has brought together a team of African scholars working in various disciplines to produce a collection of essays, which will be valuable for thinking Christians in Africa and beyond as they wrestle with challenges to Christian faith. The contributors demonstrate familiarity with arguments and literature by thinkers and authors from Africa and elsewhere, and engage with them in a constructive manner. This book has the potential to make a significant contribution to the way in which Christians understand their own faith and engage with other views, in Africa and throughout the church worldwide.

Alistair I. Wilson, PhD
Lecturer in Mission and New Testament,
Coordinator of the ETS Centre for Mission,
Edinburgh Theological Seminary, UK

Apologetics in Africa

Apologetics in Africa

An Introduction

General Editor

Kevin Muriithi Ndereba

Published 2024 by HippoBooks, an imprint of ACTS and Langham Publishing.

Africa Christian Textbooks (ACTS), TCNN, PMB 2020, Bukuru 930008, Plateau State, Nigeria
www.actsnigeria.org
Langham Publishing, PO Box 296, Carlisle, Cumbria CA3 9WZ, UK
www.langham.org

ISBNs:
978-1-83973-662-9 Print
978-1-83973-967-5 ePub
978-1-83973-968-2 PDF

British Library Cataloguing-in-Publication Data
A catalogue record for this book is available from the British Library

ISBN: 978-1-83973-662-9

Cover & Book Design: projectluz.com

Contents

List of Figures

Foreword

The book you hold in your hands is important. Indeed, it is unique. Some of the issues covered are pertinent outside of the African continent. They would include issues of biblical criticism, the historicity of the resurrection and the like. But many, while possibly not unique to Africa, are tied into the history and the culture of the continent. They would include eldership, the dowry, African gods, witchcraft, etc. Other issues, while not uniquely African, are germane to a number of dealings outside of Africa, such as confronting Islam and counseling for domestic violence.

Why Africa? Several reasons. First, the good news has a long and noble heritage there. Going back at least to the waters of life in the garden, then the Queen of Sheba and possibly the biracial prophet Zephaniah, including the role of Egypt, the Ethiopian eunuch, and then through Athanasius, Tertullian, Felicita and Perpetua, and of course to the great Augustine, so much prodigious thinking and great theology has been generated here throughout the centuries down to the present. Africa is the imminent context, often ignored, for some of the most extraordinary disclosures of God's ways. As this book shows, this reality has often been unjustly hijacked by Western views.

A second reason is the need to revisit and repair the horrors of exploitation, from slavery to the theft of natural resources, to manipulative outsourcing of cheap labour, and the like: injustices are rampant. There is widespread poverty on this continent, much of it caused unnecessarily. The world's nations bear considerable responsibility for this condition, and thus for its remedy. Awareness of the cruelty of exploitation is only slowly making its way into Western consciousness. This book does not limit itself to these tragedies. There is much more.

A third reason is the wealth of African religious thinking. Africa is a vast continent, encompassing many different local histories and cultures. It is no surprise, then, that theological production, even from a more evangelical standpoint, varies considerably from society to society. Among the most important fruits of this theological thinking is that which resulted from movements of independence, such as the revolt against apartheid, and the break away from overbearing missions as well as commercial ventures. Independent christologies have been particularly influential. The African Christian analysis of various religions is prominent. Here, we could think of the work of John Mbiti, Kwesi Dickson, Charles Nyamiti and others. A number of Africans, such as Lamin Sanneh and Kwame Bediako, have persuaded Westerners to reevaluate church history in the light of the reality on this continent.

An increasing literature exists on the African way to read Scripture.[1] Hermeneutics are at least in part determined by the cultural context of the interpreter. While there should be no radical departure from the Reformation principle of perspicuity and the accessibility of the Bible to all readers, there can be an awareness nurtured by one's place of origin. The African perspective on the parables, for example, brings out features of these tales from the vantage point of story-telling, which is a lively tradition in Africa. Local readings are also growing. For example, there is a significant output coming from Ghana.[2]

Finally, I have a personal reason for stressing an African awareness in matters of theology and ethics. I have spent a lifetime studying and enjoying the music of sub-Saharan Africa. While, sadly, much of the music is derived from Western pop, the countries I have visited have lively local music-making traditions. When these are "redeemed" and used for worship, there can be a depth, sometimes an exuberance, sometimes laments, which are fresh to our ears. The powerful music of the Negro Spiritual has its distant origins in African ways of singing.

Why Christian apologetics for Africa?

First, and hardly unique to Africans, many Christians do not see the importance of apologetics. Their spiritual life is emotional, with little respect for ideas or the importance of the mind. The technical term for this approach is "pietism." It is true that there is extraordinary growth of a zealous Christian experience in common with the advance of the gospel in the majority world. But with this explosive growth often comes a need for more depth. As Sipho (the discipleship training manager for African Enterprise) has said, often the Christian faith on the continent is "miles wide and inches deep."[3] Apologetics is not just a discipline for answering unbelievers, but it also reinforces the reasons to believe for Christians.

1. See the *Africa Bible Commentary*, Tokunbah Adeyemo, ed. (Grand Rapids: Zondervan, 2010).

2. See Sarah Fretheim, *Kwame Bediako and African Christian Scholarship* (Eugene: Wipf & Stock, 2018).

3. [https://aesouthafrica.wordpress.com/2011/10/11/lets-make-christianity-in-africa-miles-wide-and-miles-deep/].

Second, as mentioned earlier, there are questions and issues which come from the African context, which are not emphasized in the West. Unless one is familiar with such matters as animism, polygamy, the health and wealth gospel, or the problem of evil in the African grain, then a simple application of Western apologetics is not likely to be effective. This extraordinary book addresses those issues head-on. Years ago, an Apologetics conference in Kenya showcased the need for a truly African and biblical approach. Here, the debate was led by atheists who argued for the removal of the Christian faith from educational institutions on the continent. Some of the Christian answers were inadequate, to say the least. They were not *ready* to give the reason for their hope (1 Pet 3:15).

Finally, this remarkable book is both a manual for answering specific questions and a guide to the proper spiritual disposition for one's arguments. The second part of the classical text from 1 Peter 3 says, "yet do it with gentleness and respect, keeping a clear conscience." This text from Peter actually addresses persecuted believers: "asking for a reason" is often from hostile people. While growth in the church here is extraordinary, persecution is widespread. Answering that requires special godliness. The tone of this book is exemplary. It neither shies away from the issues, nor dissolves into inoffensive relativism. I have learned immensely from it, both its content and its attitude. I believe every reader will.

William Edgar
Professor Emeritus of Apologetics,
Westminster Theological Seminary, Pennsylvania, USA

Acknowledgements

Writing a book is similar to the process of birth. It takes the agency of God, the input of the village and remarkable strength of spirit. For all these reasons, I write from a deep sense of gratitude for God's leading in my own life. Having grown up in a Christian home and nurtured in the church, I still had questions in my undergraduate years as I was studying electrical engineering and leading a student-run organization in our campus, which exposed me to various religious and philosophical viewpoints. Unfortunately, I received the response "just believe." It was in these years that I first interacted with apologetics through the writings of C. S. Lewis, and later, the ministry of Hugh Ross, Reasons to Believe. Through them, I came to see that the Christian faith is not a leap in the dark, but has rational justification. However, while I had intellectual questions, I remained in spiritual darkness. It was through reading the book of 1 John that I saw the grace offered to sinners through the person of Jesus Christ. Afterwards, I knew part of my service to Christ was to walk alongside those who have questions. So this book is a testament to God's agency throughout the years.

The village is rather vast, in both African settings and in the writing of this book. Sensing a call to prepare for ministry, I undertook an M.A. in Biblical and Theological Studies at the then Nairobi International School of Theology (NIST), now International Leadership University. From my cursory research on the internet on Kenyan universities offering apologetics, NIST appeared at the top. The only problem was that apologetics was a concentration in the M.A. program, and so I was utterly shocked to report to campus and sit for Hebrew for my first class! By God's grace, I made it through. Prof. Elizabeth Mburu was an initial encourager when she saw that I had both the passion and ability to pursue apologetics. I took critical thinking with her, in addition to classical apologetics, cultural apologetics, and worldview studies with other lecturers such as Prof. Bernard Boyo and Prof. Jonghun Joo, which strengthened my other studies in biblical and theological studies. This created a good basis for my eventual doctoral work in the Department of Philosophy, Practical and Systematic Theology at the University of South Africa, where I researched youth cultures and sub-cultures and their role in holistic discipleship, that engages young people in African cities intellectually, spiritually and vocationally.

Through God's leading, I met a group of friends, including Bill Dindi who has served in evangelism and discipleship ministries in many capacities. Our dream of creating a space where people could ask questions and explore answers eventually took the form of Apologetics Kenya, a ministry that has grown since 2017. To this band of brothers and sisters who have continued to serve in apologetics out of a genuine desire to serve God, I offer my deep gratitude. I would also like to thank the good people at Biola University, Talbot School of Theology who were generous in supporting me in undertaking a short course in Christian apologetics, offered by renowned apologists. I especially thank Kailyn C., Matthew Strawsburg and Whitney Spradley. The pioneering Kenyan apologists, mentors and friends, Reuben Kigame and Dr. John Njoroge, did a lot of explicit and implicit "hand-holding." To them, I am thankful. I register my appreciation to our other apologetics education and ministry partners – Danson Ottawa and Rodgers Atwebembeire (and Paul Carden) of Africa Center for Apologetics Research, Simon Brace and Daniel Maritz of Ratio Christi, South Africa and Ben Clifton, Doug Anson and Dr. Kristen Davis of Apologetics on Mission – who continue to labour in apologetics ministries the world over. I am grateful as well to my colleagues in various academic and professional societies that I am involved in, including the International Association for the Study of Youth Ministry (IASYM), Africa Society of Evangelical Theology (ASET), the Society of Practical Theology in South Africa (SPTSA), International Research Network for the Study of Science and Belief in Society (INSBS) and the International Society of Christian Apologetics (ISCA).

The need for apologetics has remained clear through my pastoral ministry in the Presbyterian Church of East Africa, and in my speaking engagements in various academic and church gatherings far and wide. In my teaching role initially at Pan Africa Christian University and currently at St. Paul's University, where I am a full-time lecturer in practical theology, I noticed a gap for resources in apologetics that could not only engage the classical questions in apologetics – such as the existence of God, the problem of evil and suffering, faith and science, and the like – but that could also engage African realities. These include questions such as the traumas of the colonial enterprise, the salient problems around gender-based violence, the question of African traditional gods and cultural practices such as dowry and sacrificial practices. Clearly, such a task would need pastor-scholars engaged both intellectually and ministerially in these important areas. So, I would like to thank the contributors to this book – Prof. Elizabeth Mburu, Dr. Robert Falconer, Prof. Samuel Waje Kunhiyop, Dr. Mihretu Guta, Prof. Joseph Okello, Prof. Kyama Mugambi,

Primrose Muyambo, Dr. Seyram Amenyedzi, Joseph Byamukama, Dr. Daniël Maritz, Rodgers Atwebembeire and Dr. Judy Wang'ombe. These contributors work in a variety of academic and ministry settings both within the continent and abroad, and they have done a great service in writing thoughtful, thorough, biblical, critical and culturally sensitive chapters for the church and academy. For believers desiring to deepen their faith and those training for various types of Christian ministry, these contributors have done a great service.

Given such a focus in the book's aims and approach, Langham Publishing were a perfect fit. However, before approaching Langham, Colette Owens, now Executive Editor and Executive Director of The Gospel Coalition Africa, reached out and asked me to serve as a guest editor for the apologetics series on their blog.[1] It was through these initial pieces that we saw the need to develop this further. She has been kind enough to allow for the inclusion and expansion of my articles on "Atheism in Africa" and Muyambo's "A Christian Response to Dowry Practices" in this book project. Together with The Gospel Coalition Africa team, I am grateful to Dr. Nelson Jennings, editor of the *Global Missiology* journal and Dr. Annette Potgieter, editor of the *African Theological Journal for Church and Society* for allowing us to reproduce my previous publications with them – "Apologetics in a Digital Age" and "The Supremacy of Jesus Christ: A Theological Response to *Mburi cia Kiama*" respectively.

Following through the "birthing" imagery of this book project, Langham have served as remarkable midwives. Mark Arnold was kind and gracious enough to consider the book manuscript, and to steward it along the contracting, manuscript development, manuscript review and final publication stages. The copy editors and design editors have produced an aesthetically pleasing book, in a way that covers any blemishes that could have been attributed to the book editor. Prof. William Edgar, Professor Emeritus of Apologetics at Westminster Theological Seminary, was kind enough to write a gracious and hospitable Foreword. He represents a tradition of apologetics that has anchored the church through shifting cultural times and one who has produced a great body of work, and so I am grateful. Thanks also goes to my academic colleagues at St. Paul's University.

To my extended family – particularly parents and siblings – who created an environment for the nurture of Christian faith and a space for my intellectual curiosity, I am grateful. My parents Eng. James Ndereba and Angela Ndereba, and my siblings Ann Mweha and Alex Kaguti, together with your spouses, thank you. Lastly, I would be remiss not to mention my wife Jessica – I am

1. See https://africa.thegospelcoalition.org/series/african-apologetics/.

living out the adage, "saving best for last." She is more than a pillar of support. Her prayers, understanding and down-to-earth nature continue to inform how I see the Christian life and ministry. If the spirit and tone of the book have such a character, then my wife's influence will have played a central role. My son Noah reminds me that being a follower of Jesus and being a servant of Jesus is not just in talk but also in deed. These dear ones remind me that Christian ministry and academic ministry must flow downstream to everyday life. I am grateful to God for them, and hope that Noah's generation would find this resource of help as they face the questions of faith of their time. As such, we are accountable to others, not only in birth, but even beyond death.

For Christ's service and kingdom,
Kevin Muriithi Ndereba, PhD
Lecturer and Head of Department,
Department of Practical Theology,
Joshua and Timothy School of Theology,
St. Paul's University, Limuru, Kenya

Introduction

African Apologetics through a Multidisciplinary Perspective

Kevin Muriithi Ndereba, PhD

Lecturer at St. Paul's University, Kenya and Research Fellow Department of Practical Theology and Missiology, Stellenbosch University, South Africa

Apologetics is no stranger to the African continent.

Yet we should rather say, "ought not to be" a stranger to the African continent. Missiologists continue to observe how Africa, and much of the global South, is growing not only as a center of gravity, but even now, as a mobilizer of the Christian mission to the rest of the world.[1] While this has been interpreted in many ways, the question still looms: in what ways can Christianity in the continent grow in its depth so that as it grows numerically, it also positions itself as a faith that can coherently encounter the intellectual challenges of rising generations?

This question immediately invites the concerned Christian and ministry leader into the foray of Christian apologetics. Apologetics, the discipline that is concerned with the rational justification and defence of Christian truth claims as well as its communication to a sceptical world, has been envisaged within the contemporary world as a stranger to a largely emotive expression of Christianity in the continent. While Christian expression in Africa has been described as vibrant, the authors in this project seek to explore the intellectual foundations of the Christian faith in Africa. More specifically, these authors seek to answer the questions that people of faith and also sceptics of the faith are asking within the continent.

1. James V. Spickard, and Afe Adogame, "Introduction: Africa, the New African Diaspora, and Religious Transnationalism in a Global World," in Afe Adogame and James V. Spickard, eds. *Religion Crossing Boundaries* (Leiden: Brill, 2010), 1–28.

In the history of the global church, apologetics was the default mode of Christian faith and mission, to the extent that the early church's theologians are usually referred to as "the apologists." These apologists gave robust responses to the challenges posed towards Christianity as it grew from a Jewish "sect" to a global faith. Athanasius, Augustine, Tertullian, Felicita and Perpetua are key figures who have been hijacked and molded into Westernized caricatures, implicitly silencing, ignoring or re-envisioning them outside their African villages, towns, cities, cultures, languages and contexts. Take for instance Tertullian, the Carthaginian theologian and apologist who wrote in Latin. While it is true that these early figures of the Christian faith were influenced by Western cultures, Tertullian himself being an insider in "Greco-Roman culture,"[2] their African heritage is often silenced – Osborne for example in his book on Tertullian, adds the description "the theologian from the West."[3] Noting the complexities in the socio-cultural and historical setting of Tertullian, Wilhite appreciates Tertullian's African heritage despite the Roman imperial rule and cultural superiority of the time.[4] Wilhite for example considers Tertullian's complex identities and cautions against an anachronistic reading of Tertullian as an "African theologian," given how that term in contemporary usage is defined through various postcolonial struggles.[5] Nonetheless, I argue that remembering Tertullian, and these early church fathers, as Christians in an African continent – which continues to be a complex continent – is part of retrieving a subtle silencing on the part of their contemporary interpreters. In fact, Bediako observes that the apologetic significance of Tertullian against the Roman empire and Greco-Roman thought, was an "African inspiration," one that has been foundational to the contribution of the Latin Christian tradition to the history of the global church.[6] Following Thomas Oden's provocation to the global theological world, it is important for us to consider their African influences and their contribution to the shape of global Christianity through the ages.[7] This realization quickly beckons Christian believers and thinkers in

2. Kwame Bediako, *Theology and Identity: The Impact of Culture upon Christian Thought in the Second Century and in Modern Africa* (Akropong-Akuapem, Ghana: Regnum, 1999), 100.

3. Eric Osborne, *Tertullian, First Theologian of the West* (Cambridge: Cambridge University Press, 1997).

4. David E. Wilhite, *Tertullian the African: An Anthropological Reading of Tertullian's Context and Identities* (Berlin: De Gruyter, 2011), 8.

5. David Wilhite, *Tertullian the African*, 191.

6. Kwame Bediako, *Theology and Identity*, 117.

7. Thomas C. Oden, *How Africa Shaped the Christian Mind: Rediscovering the African Seedbed of Western Christianity* (Downers Grove: InterVarsity Press, 2007).

Africa to interpret the contributions of these key figures and their significance in shaping Christian mission. This mission is inevitably God's mission and activity in the world, to save a people, from different tribes, languages, ethnicities and nations to himself, to the glory of his name. Apologetics should not be a stranger to the continent but should be an enterprise that every ordinary Christian believer takes up, particularly during a time in which Africa is at the forefront of God's activity in the world.

Why is Apologetics Important?

Apologetics remains central to the mission of Christianity in the world. Christianity, as a faith that is translated across different languages, cultures and religious worldviews, often meets different belief and cultural systems.[8] Thus, Christians are called to be ready in all seasons to "give a reason for the hope that [they] have" (1 Pet 3:15). This passage is a *locus classicus* in the study of apologetics, as it reveals the what, the who and the how of apologetics. This passage unfurls the task of apologetics as the aspect of giving a defence or an *apologia* to those who ask questions concerning the hope that the Christian has in Christ. *Apologia* was a term used in Greco-Roman cultural context, particularly as part of court-room language, for people who were called to give a rational justification to charges made against their conduct. Peter's context is not far removed as it speaks of Christians who have been dispersed as a result of persecution (1 Pet 1). Apologetics therefore has to do with making a defence or giving a reason for the hope that a Christian has in Christ (see the exposition of hope in 1 Pet 1). This "living hope" has to do with the new birth that believers have through Christ, and which provides assurance in light of present sufferings in the Christian life as well as a forward-looking expectation of "the revelation of Jesus Christ" (1 Pet 1:3–9) in his second coming. In an elementary sense therefore, apologetics is primarily about the hope we have in Christ, the hope "that is in you" (1 Pet 3:15) as the ESV renders it. Christian apologists have noted this connection between apologetics and evangelism, by saying that apologetics is the handmaid of evangelism. Construed this way, apologetics is not a preserve of specially gifted Christians, even though they have a key role, but apologetics is part of everyday Christian life and witness.

This central text of apologetics also supports this claim that apologetics is for the everyday Christian as it is addressed to "the elect exiles" (1 Pet 1:1),

8. Lamin Sanneh, *Translating the Message: The Missionary Impact on Culture* (Maryknoll: Orbis Books, 2015).

in other words Christians set apart from the world and set apart for God. This implies that Christians are to live in light of this unique calling as God's people, that is, "in your hearts, honour Christ the Lord as holy" (1 Pet 3:15 ESV). Apologetics is therefore foundationally a Christian calling. But lastly, with all the nuanced discourses on apologetic methodologies, such as classical, presuppositional, evidential, cumulative-case approaches among others as discussed by Steven Cowan,[9] a summative posture of apologetics is gentleness and respect (1 Pet 3:15b). I fear that much "popular apologetics" is oftentimes engaged in an adversarial approach, that is far from the Christian calling to apologetics. Perhaps this is a reason many prematurely surmise that apologetics is for certain personalities and for certain experts, especially the more extroverted or argumentative kinds of people. This could not be further from the truth, especially when we think of this central mandate in terms of the "how" of apologetics. A parallel passage, one that is well known, is Acts 17 when Paul makes his *apologia* in Athens. What is striking is that Paul's motive is driven by a genuine concern regarding the plight of the Athenian people and their philosophers in their lack of personal knowledge of God. What drives Paul into his apologetic engagement is this concern for the people and their idol-shaped and idol-filled city.[10] Apologetics therefore begins on the foundation of a concern for those who have no personal knowledge of God.[11]

The African Challenges that Necessitate Apologetics

But lest we think that apologetics is mainly for non-Christians, the task of apologetics is also for Christians. By knowing the "why" behind the "what" of the Christian faith, Christians are more confident in their witness, they are more grounded in the face of evil and suffering and they grow in their maturity concerning the love of God. The love of God is both a command and an expectation of growth in the Christian life.[12] In this sense, apologetics serves

9. Steven B. Cowan (ed.), *Five Views on Apologetics* (Grand Rapids: Zondervan, 2000).

10. Andrew M. Mbuvi, "Missionary Acts, Things: Modeling Mission in Acts 17:15–34 and a Concern for Dialogue in Chinua Achebe Things Fall Apart," *Ex Auditu –Volume 23: An International Journal for the Theological Interpretation of Scripture* 23 (2008): 140–56.

11. While all people in all cultures have some knowledge of God, personal knowledge of God comes from regeneration through the Holy Spirit. Here, I follow the reformed theologian John Frame's thinking. See John Frame, "Unregenerate Knowledge of God," *IVP Dictionary of Apologetics* (Downers Grove: InterVarsity Press). https://frame-poythress.org/unregenerate-knowledge-of-god/.

12. Voddie Baucham Jr, *Expository Apologetics: Answering Objections with the Power of the Word* (Wheaton: Crossway, 2015).

both an inward and an outward function, as it serves not only the Christian but also serves the world that she seeks to engage. Within the African context, various challenges towards the gospel of Jesus Christ exist.

On one hand, the apologist in Africa must be able to engage the scepticism of the contemporary culture that wishes Christ were another option among many other religious teachers. Our technological age has only increased the options available, and with increased globalization, young Africans who have been educated physically or digitally, through secular Western worldviews, have imbibed the best of postmodern thought and secular humanism. This was made very apparent during a public debate organized by Apologetics Kenya between Christian apologists and members of the Atheist in Kenya society, which has in the past, pushed for the removal of Christian religion from the public education system (similar reforms have been pushed in the area of sexuality and gender, most recently, in the 2019 petition on Gay, Lesbian, Bisexual, Transgender and Queer identification in Kenya).[13] Present in the debate was a group of Kenyan students who had studied at an Ivy League University and had raised several counterarguments at the end of the debate. One of them said something to the effect that "I think Christianity has messed us [Africans] up and we need to go back to our traditional religion." I happened to be sitting next to one lady, who identifies as a "progressive Muslim," who claimed that the arguments from both sides were logical, but she could not come to a coherent conclusion. Additionally, the phenomenon of churched youth leaving the church has birthed various responses.[14] At the heart of the solution is the need to offer solid biblical teaching in light of popular culture.

---

13. National Gay and Lesbian Human Rights Commission (NGLHRC), the Gay and Lesbian Coalition of Kenya (GLACK) and NYARWEK network combined to petition the court to declare sections 162 (a) and (c) and 165 as unconstitutional because they violate various constitutional [sexual] rights, gaining traction on Twitter with the hashtag #Repeal162. On the 24th of May 2019, the High Court, led by a three judge bench Lady Justice Roselyn Aburili, Justice Chacha Mwita and Justice J. Mativo, dismissed the petition that was seeking to decriminalize gay, lesbian, bisexual, transgender and queer sexual acts according to the website of "Love is Human." An article, posted by HIVOS on February 2019 and updated after the May ruling, bemoaned the ruling as a failure to let everyone to freely be themselves and participate in society. The question of sexuality and gender is poised to be a significant issue for the next generations as it challenges Christian anthropology, and more specifically, the biblical teaching that humans are image bearers of God (*imago dei*). Our response must be based on a robust biblical worldview, that helps the African church not to go the way of some of the churches in the West that have embraced sexual liberal values even to the point of ordaining ministers or pastors who identify as LGBTIQAA+.

14. Kevin Muriithi, "Youth Worldviews among the De-Churched and Implications for Ministry," MA Thesis, International Leadership University, Nairobi (2015); Kevin Muriithi

The second challenge is one from within. Conrad Mbewe notes the correlation between *excessive* charismatic Christianity – meaning here the excessive type that focuses only or overbearingly on health, wealth, healing and gifts, without biblical discernment – and African traditional religion. For instance, he notes that many of such Christian adherents have merely baptized African traditional ideas with Christian verses.[15] The prosperity preacher, who is elevated by his followers, is merely a replacement of the witchdoctors of the old religious superstructure, who attracted an unrealistic sense of reverence. Christians in Africa have also been gullible to these teachers of a false gospel, who through their reading of biblical texts mishandle various Scriptures leading to errant doctrines that take people away from God and draw them towards personalities.[16] Thus, we could summarize this problem as one of clarifying what the Christian faith is for Christians in Africa. In other words, the second challenge is one of discerning the cultural or popular Christianity and weighing it with the timeless Scripture, God's revelation to humanity.

Demystifying Apologetics

These two challenges fall squarely within the purview of apologetics. As a Christian discipline, it is far from apologizing, but has the following elements which can be distilled from those who have studied and practiced apologetics:

1. Understanding why we believe what we believe (Voddie Baucham).[17]

Ndereba, "Engaging Youth Worldviews in Africa: A Practical Theology in Light of John 4," *Conspectus: The Journal of the South African Theological Seminary* 32 no. 1 (2021): 187–98.

15. Conrad Mbewe, "Why Is the Charismatic Movement Thriving in Africa?" Banner of Truth Trust, 2015. Accessed here https://banneroftruth.org/us/resources/articles/2015/why-is-the-charismatic-movement-thriving-in-africa/.

16. In the Kenyan context, the "Shakahola massacre" is a phrase referencing the 2023 discovery of more than 400 graves in the south of Kenya in Malindi of adherents of a cultic leader by the name of Pastor Mackenzie of the Good News International Church. Among other teachings, Mackenzie taught that fasting to death was a path for his adherents to reach to God. These sad events have generated several discussions around the role of the state in regulating churches, doctrinal issues and the need for counter-cult apologetics. See a panel discussion by NTV Kenya featuring Kevin Muriithi, Sammy Wainaina and Kimathi Kamencu "A Cult above the Rest: False Doctrine, Regulating Religion and Freedom of Worship" (25 April 2023). https://ntvkenya.co.ke/wadr/a-cult-above-the-rest-false-doctrine-regulating-religion-and-freedom-of-worship-wadr/.

17. Voddie Baucham, *Expository Apologetics.*

2. Defending what we believe in (R. C. Sproul).[18]
3. Confronting unbelief with the truth (John Frame).[19]
4. Communicating the truth with gentleness and respect (Dallas Willard).[20]

Part of growing in our apologetics is learning from others who have thought about, and hopefully practiced, these things at length. But apologetics is ultimately about the gospel. It helps to break down the barriers that people have raised towards the gospel based on their ignorance or "suppression of the truth" as per Romans 1:18–20. Geisler and Turek have thus argued that it takes more faith to reject the evidence for God as opposed to assenting to the clear evidence of God from nature.[21] R. C. Sproul commenting on Romans 1:19 goes on to say that atheists don't really exist.[22] The canon of Scripture assumes the existence of God and his claim on our lives (Gen 1:1; Ps 19:1–6; Rom 1:18–32). A robust biblical worldview takes as its core foundation the reliability, authority and sufficiency of Scripture, even in the task of apologetics. Thus, we must always begin with biblical presuppositions if we are to do apologetics for the sake of the gospel. The place of logic, philosophy, cosmology, rhetoric, intercultural studies, Western and African thought, fields that are indispensable to the apologetic task, must be subservient to the Scriptures and the gospel of the Lord Jesus Christ contained therein.

Holistic Apologetics is for the Head, Heart and Hands

Further, apologetics is not merely intellectual boxing to get our enemies on the floor. Belief and unbelief are realities that influence the whole human person – head, heart and hands. For the Christian, loving God with our heart, mind and soul is oftentimes interconnected. For the unbeliever, the same is true – "They [Gentiles] are darkened in their understanding, alienated from

18. R. C. Sproul, John Henry Gerstner, and Arthur Lindsley, *Classical Apologetics: A Rational Defense of the Christian Faith and a Critique of Presuppositional Apologetics* (Grand Rapids: Zondervan, 1984).

19. John Frame, *Apologetics: A Justification of Christian Belief* (Phillipsburg: P&R, 2015).

20. Dallas Willard, *The Allure of Gentleness: Defending the Faith in the Manner of Jesus* (New York: HarperOne, 2015).

21. Norman L. Geisler and Frank Turek, *I Don't Have Enough Faith to Be an Atheist* (Wheaton: Crossway, 2004).

22. R. C. Sproul, *The Consequences of Ideas: Understanding the Concepts that Shaped Our World* (Wheaton: Crossway, 2018).

the life of God because of the ignorance that is in them, due to their hardness of heart. They have become callous and have given themselves up to sensuality, greedy to practice every kind of impurity" (Eph 4:18–19 ESV). Paul traces the same argument that the head, heart and hands are connected. This is why the gospel, and theology at large, is helpful in forming us as disciples of Christ. We live out of the convictions we hold about particular things. As we engage in apologetics, understanding the relationship between the intellect, the emotions and the will is foundational. In more recent times, Paul Gould argues that today's cultural climate necessitates an apologetics approach that engages the cultural fragmentation of postmodern culture through arousing the conscience and imagination.[23] This may be particularly helpful for the post-Christian West, and specific African urban contexts.

Apologetics in the Power of the Spirit

The ministry of the Holy Spirit in the life of the Christian apologist cannot be ignored. The task of engaging with unbelievers is an arduous one similar to a journey that one takes to a far-off and perilous land – one needs an engine that is well-oiled. Similarly, because ultimately the work of making a defence consists of various interrelated issues, the ministry of the Holy Spirit is critical in:

1. Convicting those who the Christian apologist engages with the truth of the Christian claims (Acts 2:37).
2. Encouraging the Christian apologist as she makes a defence to the culture and the religious and political classes of the day (Luke 12:11–12; 21:15; Acts 2:14; 4:8, 31; 13:9).
3. Leading the Christian apologist to those who need to hear our defence (Acts 13:4) – Barnabas and Saul sent by the Spirit to Cyprus.

A Movement for African Apologetics and Apologists

Many have marveled at and noticed the tremendous growth of the early Christian church. Acts is a foundational book for the task of apologetics in Africa. Our audiences involve the political classes, "nominal Christians" or other religious adherents, and lastly those who like new and novel ideas, much

23. Paul M. Gould, *Cultural Apologetics: Renewing the Christian Voice, Conscience, and Imagination in a Disenchanted World* (Grand Rapids: Zondervan Academic, 2019).

like the Greek philosophers in Acts 17. Like our African context, the task of apologetics requires a firm grounding in biblical worldview and gospel, a Spirit-empowered witness and a love for those who are trapped in the deceptions of the world. This was certainly the pattern of the African apologists who have gone ahead of us in the early church period, such as Athanasius and Augustine, and also the apologetics of the Reformation period as well as in the modern period that has born much fruit. We will also do well to pay attention to some of the findings from archeologists and other Christian scholars, for their findings have often confirmed what is already true – for example, the reliability of the Scriptures, the resurrection of Jesus Christ through the "minimal facts" approach and the geographical places in the Bible.[24]

In Kenya, there is a growing ministry of apologetics. As part of other Centers for Apologetics Research globally, the African Center for Apologetics Research is equipping believers for the task of cult engagement.[25] Apologetics Kenya equips believers and engages sceptics with the Christian worldview through monthly fora, public lectures and debates (with Atheists and Muslims).[26] They are running the first Certificate in Apologetics programme that addresses the questions within the African continent and are currently working on a contextualized apologetics curriculum to enhance their campus engagement. In 2018, Reuben Kigame, a renowned gospel artist, published *Christian Apologetics through African Eyes*. Saturday PM is also a local church ministry (Christ is the Answer Ministries) that engages the big questions of life through biblical expositions.[27] In South Africa, Ratio Christi, the international apologetics ministry that is specifically aimed at campus students, has local chapters in five campuses namely North-West University, KwaZulu-Natal, Rhodes, Stellenbosch and Pretoria.[28] They have also been organizing annual symposia, to equip and engage interested people. Daniël Maritz, University of Pretoria Chapter President at Ratio Christi summarizes the situation:

> The apologetics landscape is truly diverse. Since universities tend to be a melting pot of ideas, we have secularism and some

---

24. See for example William L. Craig, *The Son Rises: Historical Evidence for the Resurrection of Jesus* (Eugene: Wipf & Stock Publishers, 2000); Michael Licona, *The Resurrection of Jesus: A New Historiographical Approach* (Downers Grove: IVP Academic, 2010); Gary Habermas, *Risen Indeed: A Historical Investigation into the Resurrection of Jesus* (Bellingham: Lexham, 2021).

25. http://www.acfar.org/.

26. https://www.apologeticskenya.org/.

27. http://www.thesaturdaypm.com/.

28. https://www.ratiochristisymposium.co.za/.

> of its progressive ethics flowing in on the university campuses, especially in Cape Town. We are also confronted with some of the major cults like the Jehovah's Witnesses and the Mormons who are also doing their evangelism on and around some of the campuses. Prosperity Gospel theology also infiltrates some of the churches and it has devastating consequences. One last challenge that is worth mentioning is Islam. As an apologetics ministry, Ratio Christi comes beside the local church to equip young Christians to better be able to defend their faith against these challenges.[29]

The Gospel Coalition Africa has also developed a section on apologetics articles, which engage with some of the questions that Africans are asking in light of the Christian faith and colonial missionary enterprise. On special invitation, I attended an apologetics leaders' summit in Entebbe Uganda on 29th April to 1st May 2022 organized by Benjamin Clifton, of Adventurous Apologetics. Bringing together those involved in apologetics in the East African region, this conference highlighted the issues facing apologetics ministry within the context of local church, para-church, and higher education institutions. One of the key issues is the lack of apologetics resources that capture not only the perennial questions in apologetics, but also the emerging questions in Africa.

Why a Book on Apologetics in Africa?

As a pastor-scholar engaged in both practical ministry and theological education, I have realized that there is a gap in books on apologetics written to specific African issues. In my teaching, I have had to gather material from a combination of eclectic sources. With the cultural and spiritual changes happening in this century, there is need for robust apologetics resources that include not only the classical issues in apologetics (e.g., philosophy, existence of God, theodicy) but also some of the cultural issues within the African context (e.g., cultural practices such as dowry, eldership rites, traditional witchdoctors), and which arouse most interest in the global South. Further, there is need for a regionally representative and multi-disciplinary resource, that represents the diversity in the continent. While this book has engaged the eastern, western and southern regions and contextual issues in Africa, there is need for engaging the north of Africa. This book will enable the majority world (global South)

29. Personal email correspondence.

to continue with the needed work of contextualizing biblical and gospel ministry as it meets cultural, theological and philosophical challenges to the faith in Africa. The aim is a biblically robust, contextually relevant, ministry-oriented, and accessible resource that is beneficial to the life and ministry of African Christians.

This work brings together multi-disciplinary perspectives within the continent in the important areas of apologetics research, education and ministry. They are written by scholar-practitioners, thereby linking the gap between education and practice. Since the Bible is foundational for Christian life and ministry, the first section surveys the issues surrounding the Bible including reliability, the biblical case for apologetics, resurrection apologetics, and apologetics in the early church. The second section explores the philosophical issues including theodicy, logic, epistemology, and ethics. The third section deals with cultural issues that ministry leaders, missionaries and educators deal with including dowry practices, gender violence, eldership rites and African traditional religions. The fourth section deals with practical apologetics issues that people engage, including new age movements, African public life, Christian-Muslim engagement and digital youth cultures. What unifies these chapters is the biblical and theological engagement with African thought and issues.

What to Expect

Prof. Elizabeth Mburu, Africa regional coordinator of Langham Literature, is a respected New Testament scholar. In her chapter, she reveals why her work has been beneficial to both her students and scholars alike. She covers significant ground in New Testament critical scholarship and interpretation approaches, in a way that is both scholarly while at the same time accessible to the student who is entering the biblical world for the first time. Critical approaches to the Bible are not a reserve of contemporary pan-Africanists, or modern-day liberal theologians. Mburu's first section covers the important historical ground that has been the source of contemporary criticisms of the Bible. Her first section considers the Enlightenment and post-Enlightenment periods. For instance, she observes Hume's rejection of the supernatural, building on John Locke's and George Berkley's thinking that was characteristic of the "Age of Reason" and was the soil in which biblical higher criticism flourished. This sceptical approach, anchored in Hegelian philosophy, gave way to deism and eventually to atheism, with its encroachment into the development of Christian doctrine, including the doctrine of Scripture. Mburu eloquently captures the sceptical approach when she notes: "since the Bible was not regarded as an authoritative, infallible book, but rather was understood as the subjective writings of the experiences of others, it had no dogmatic value. Being subjective in nature, it denied the existence of any absolutes either in truth or morals."

Mburu helps us to see how this Enlightenment marriage of secular philosophy and biblical criticism gave birth to neo-liberalism and post-liberalism in the 1980s. While the neo-liberals accept the divinity of Christ, they reject key biblical doctrines such as the substitutionary atonement of Christ, which is central to Christian orthodoxy. Having covered this historical ground, and its impact on postmodernist approaches to the Bible, Mburu seamlessly moves to questions surrounding the canonization of Scripture. This section helps the reader to respond to questions surrounding the role of the Apocrypha, the relationship between canon and authority and the place of the church in the confirmation of the canon of Scripture, among others. Mburu then moves to the questions surrounding transmission and translation of the biblical text, while foraying into some of the popular level questions around seeming contradictions of biblical passages.

After attending to these classical questions surrounding the Bible, Mburu progresses to the question of interpretation – particularly in response to the African challenge that the Bible was used as "a tool of oppression." This last half of the paper echoes her expanded work on *African Hermeneutics*, and intermediate-level readers will do well to consider this key supplementary text.[30] She reveals that part of the response to this African challenge is to read the biblical text in a way that facilitates dialogue "between biblical cultures and assumptions and African cultures and assumptions." By exploring hermeneutical approaches in Africa, Mburu implicitly answers the question surrounding missionary cultural baggage in view of the colonial enterprise. This grants African readers the confidence to make use of the interpretive tools bequeathed to us while at the same time allowing the Bible "to speak powerfully to the present" and thus correcting excesses from our African heritage. By noting various African hermeneutical approaches such as Ethiopian hermeneutics, African Independent hermeneutics, liberation and black hermeneutics, womanist hermeneutics, contextual Bible study, Pentecostal hermeneutics, reconstruction hermeneutics, postcolonial hermeneutics, mother-tongue hermeneutics, and inculturation/intercultural hermeneutics, Mburu helps us to appreciate how Africans have engaged in the struggle to read the biblical text within the socio-cultural contexts that they find themselves

30. Elizabeth Mburu, *African Hermeneutics* (Carlisle: HippoBooks, 2019).

in so as to participate in the "transformation of all of life." Most instructively, Mburu explores the strengths and weaknesses of these approaches, and helps us consider ways in which Africans have dealt with some of the apologetic challenges surrounding the reading and the interpretation of the Bible.

In the second chapter, Robert Falconer, an academic at South Africa Theological Seminary, explores the doctrine of the resurrection in the biblical text, beginning in the Old Testament and moving to the New Testament. This reveals the strength of this book in taking the biblical text seriously, even while moving on to the apologetic and philosophical issues at hand. He notes the biblical narratives of resurrection in the stories of Zarephath's son (1 Kgs 17:17–24), a Shunammite woman's son (2 Kgs 4:18–37), and an Israelite man (2 Kgs 13:20–21) in the Old Testament. In the New Testament, he focuses on the widow of Nain's son (Luke 7:11–17), Jairus's daughter (Luke 8:49–56), Lazarus (John 11:1–44), Tabitha, also called Dorcas (Acts 9:36–42), and Eutychus (Acts 20:7–12). Yet, he also contrasts these with the resurrection of Jesus Christ by noting that while they were raised to life, they eventually died. Contrastingly, "Jesus's body was raised in glory at his resurrection, and so too will be the bodies of believers, that is, in glory and immortality."

Secondly, Falconer not only foregrounds these important passages but through careful biblical exegesis, he explores their nuances in dialogue with African commentators, revealing their important work visible in biblical scholarship in the continent. Yet, to reveal the global significance of the topic of the resurrection, Falconer also significantly engages the key works of scholars such as Gary Habermas and Mike Licona. What is more interesting in Falconer's chapter is his consideration of resurrection in African theology, where he explores the significance of the resurrection apologetics within the African context. While he engages with contemporary African theologians such as James Kombo, Elias Bongmba and Matthew Michael, he also re-reads the church fathers (such as Tertullian and Origen) and their resurrection treatises through African eyes, revealing that apologetics, as many other contributors argue, is germane to the African continent. Thus, offering an apologetic for the resurrection in African worldview, Falconer engages the classical approaches while exploring their significance for African society and life. As Falconer concludes,

> . . . the resurrection has implications in many parts of African life. Yes, we have the future hope that we too will enjoy bodily resurrected life as in Jesus' resurrection, but it also calls African Christians to participate together in the eschatological community,

> a community that actively seeks restoration, reconciliation, and harmony in the ecclesiastical, social, cultural, political, economic, and ecological realms.

Much of the pushback against apologetics is that it is seen as a foreign activity that is only tailor-made for people who like to dabble in philosophical argument. What my chapter "Apologetics in the New Testament and Church History" does is to reveal how apologetics is part of the church's ministry throughout the ages. What is interesting to note for the contemporary African church is that the earliest apologists of the church were actually part of the Roman church in Africa. Beginning with the apologetic engagements of Jesus Christ in the gospels, I move through some key passages in the New Testament letters, particularly showing how apologetics has always been a handmaid of the evangelistic witness of the church. Having set the stage from the New Testament, I survey the important figures, events and turning points in church history, dividing the apologetics engagement into the early church period (AD 0–500), the early medieval period (AD 500–1000), late medieval period (AD 1000–1500), reformation period (AD 1500–1700) and finally surveying the modern period (AD 1700–present). While this survey is not exhaustive, it helps the reader to appreciate the role of apologetics in dealing with the unique historical settings and ideas of each time, through engaging the writings of the church's apologists. The chapter explores the role of apologetics, in the New Testament as well as in the post-New Testament period, as taking four key functions: internal apologetics (or polemics), external apologetics, evangelistic apologetics and public or political apologetics. The other chapters in the book supplement these functions and situate them within their unique contexts. This first part of the book functions as a foundation for the entire book by exploring the biblical issues surrounding the apologetics task. Following the protestant principle of the authority of Scripture for life and doctrine, beginning with the Bible within the African context is a logical starting point.

The second part of the book deals with philosophical issues. Joseph Okello, professor of Christian philosophy at Asbury, engages with the free will defence offered by Christian philosophers in their grappling with the problem of evil and suffering, and observes that in African thinking, moral evil and natural evil are synonymous. The strength of this philosophical argument is showing how within the African worldview, supernatural metaphysics leads to a more comprehensive approach when it comes to offering a theodicy. In his theodicy, he also employs the narrative of Job to make a case for his argument. The second essay in this section deals with the challenge of religious pluralism, and the discussion about whether there are many paths to God. Mihretu Guta is an academic at Biola University, whose research has engaged with the contemporary developments surrounding the interface of faith, science and philosophy. His first chapter engages the various proposals of inclusivism, pluralism and particularism, through a logical framework. Moving beyond easy answers to the questions, he shows how these various proposals seek to answer the question "Do all religions lead to the same God?" by considering their strengths and challenges, while leaving the reader to make an informed argument. Philosophy also entails the exploration of the faith-science dialogue, which is a growing concern among intellectuals in Africa and usually proceeds from worldview presuppositions. With recent developments in the physical and natural sciences, the usual caricature in the faith-science dialogue is one of conflict. Sceptics continue to suggest that the two are incompatible, thereby challenging people of faith. However, important networks and research agenda increasingly debunk this "incompatibility thesis" from scientific (sociology, cognitive science, psychology, cosmology, biology etc), philosophical and theological grounds. Within the scientific field, the growing research on the scientific theory of Intelligent Design (ID) continues to make a case for the presence of design within scientific fields such as cosmology, biology and paleontology.[31] Within other sciences such as sociology and psychology, the International Research Network for the Study of Science and Belief in Society is an example of the growing research in the nexus of faith and science.[32] Researchers in this network explore the stereotypes that are often entrenched in the faith-science dialogue among both religious and non-religious people.[33] Finally, the philosophical and historical arguments in favor of compatibility have been mounted by a range of scholars. Alvin Plantinga in philosophy and Thomas Dixon in the history of science and religion are only two examples

31. See the work of Discovery Institute https://www.discovery.org/ and the work of figures such as William Dembski, Stephen Meyers and Michael Behe. An introductory guide is William A. Dembski, Casey Luskin, and Joseph M. Holden, *The Comprehensive Guide to Science and Faith: Exploring the Ultimate Questions about Life and the Cosmos* (Eugene: Harvest House Publishers, 2021). Others are more critical of the movement, seeing it as "ideological." See for example Gregory R. Peterson, "The Intelligent-Design Movement: Science or Ideology?" *Zygon* 37 no. 1 (2002): 7–23.

32. See their website here https://scienceandbeliefinsociety.org/.

33. See for example Howard Ecklund, *Science vs. Religion: What Scientists Really Think* (Oxford: Oxford University Press, 2010).

of scholars working in these fields.[34] These scholars continue to debunk the "incompatibility thesis."

Samuel Waje Kunhiyop is no stranger to the theological enterprise in Africa, being one of the theologians active in writing and providing the church and academy in Africa with his two books *African Christian Ethics* (2004) and *African Christian Theology* (2012). In his chapter, he covers the ethical foundations of the Christian faith, which undergird the apologetic enterprise that is often conducted in the context of Islam, African Traditional Religions and Christianity in the continent. Ethical foundations in apologetics, particularly within the contemporary apologetic literature, primarily engage Western secularism and atheism. While helpful, apologists in Africa often have to develop their own ethical positions in the practice of ministry. Fortunately, Kunhiyop assists both academics and ministry practitioners, to navigate the ethical questions related to the apologetic task. Readers will benefit from his engagement with the original texts and scholars in the three contrary worldviews and explore how the doctrine of the Trinity is the ground of Christian ethics. His argument that morality is universal, is a refreshing reality for African Christians navigating a sea of fragmented worldview ethics. As he argues, "the triune God is the ontological grounding of the Christian faith and consequently of morality. Proper Christian faith must subscribe to an unambiguous assertion in God the Father, the Son, and the Holy Spirit." This is the only coherent position in dealing with the ethical challenges that the Christian encounters in their everyday life and ministry.

The third part of the book focuses the apologetic task on the cultural challenges against the Christian faith. Since African cultures are at once similar, yet varied and divergent, this chapter only handles specific cultural issues that Christians encounter in their life and ministry. A foundational issue, often proposed by postcolonial thinkers, is that the Christian faith is a Western import that is at odds with African traditional cultures (and religions). Kyama Mugambi, currently Assistant Professor of World Christianity at Yale Divinity School, offers us a critical response to this charge by surveying the history of Christianity in the continent. Moving beyond the usual colonial baggage imposed on African Christians and her theologians, he helps the reader understand other indigenous expressions of the Christian faith, revealing how

34. See for example Alvin Plantinga, *Where the Conflict Really Lies: Science, Religion, and Naturalism* (Oxford: Oxford University Press, 2011); Thomas Dixon, Geoffrey Cantor and Stephen Pumfrey (eds.), *Science and Religion: New Historical Perspectives* (Cambridge: Cambridge University Press, 2010).

African Christians have innovatively expressed the Christian message in their own terms while following Christian orthodox beliefs.

I follow up with an examination of a localized practice within Kenyan Christianity among *Agĩkũyũ* Christians. Among the *Agĩkũyũ* or *Kikuyu* (a Bantu ethnic community concentrated in Central Kenya, East Africa) Christians, there has been a push from the traditional council of elders to "return to our roots." Part of this return is the call to give away a goat or goats, called *mbũri cia kiama*, which is usually given to the council of elders as part of the progression of a man into the status of eldership. Some churches and church leaders have taken the position that this practice has no bearing on one's faith in Jesus Christ, and that *Gĩkũyũ* men should see no harm in doing this. Further, it would be a sign of celebrating the *Gĩkũyũ* or African identity of Christian men. Utilizing Bevan's contextualization methods, I make use of an integral approach to theological reflection by engaging christology in the book of Hebrews with the anthropological findings of the aforementioned practice. I argue that while there are some positive elements in such practices including the African values of communality, mentorship and respect for elders, the covenantal underpinning of the practice obfuscates the new covenant in Christ and should therefore be repudiated. I therefore show how the continuities and discontinuities of *Gĩkũyũ* culture and Christianity impacts African Christianity and African theology and suggest implications for Christian ministry.

Primrose Muyambo adds another voice on the cultural questions that African Christians are concerned with. She is a Zimbabwean emerging scholar with a Master's in Theology from George Whitefield College, in South Africa. Her chapter looks at the intersection of gospel and African culture, through the exploration of *lobola*. The practice of lobola (or dowry practices) is a germane part of African cultural life, in the initiatory rite of marriage. Hospitality is a central concept of African worldview and is evident in how Africans view the institution of marriage. However, Muyambo notes how this good practice has been commercialized in contemporary African practice, through a material focus on money, as well as the subtle way in which some modern practices of lobola devalue women. As a response, Muyambo engages the biblical text moving from the dignity of women in Genesis as well as the New Testament passages on the proper attitudes on money, as a way of legitimizing the practice in view of healthy biblical principles on this important cultural practice. She also notes the excesses, which sometimes leave Christians struggling with the gospel-culture question.

Gender and domestic violence issues remain protracted within African societies. Younger Africans question the validity and even "goodness" of the

Christian faith to speak, in a meaningful way, to societal injustices such as gendered violence as well as abuse in the church. This is especially fostered within discussions surrounding the growth of feminist movements in the continent.[35] What might a biblically and theologically balanced approach look like in light of domestic violence? Seyram Amenyedzi is a Ghanian Academic working as a postdoctoral scholar at the University of Western Cape with a passion for the missiological implications of Christian theology for women, children and persons who are differently abled. In her chapter, she utilizes empirical data to reveal the salience of domestic violence. She broadens the understanding of domestic violence, from merely the physical, while noting its emotional, psychological, and religious expressions. On the same front, she explores the gendered aspect of domestic violence, while also speaking to how domestic violence is not restricted to husband-wife relationships but also among parents and children (and adolescents) as well as towards house-helps. Through this socio-cultural approach, she grounds the reader in reality when it comes to this prevalent yet minimally reported and researched issue. The last half of her paper considers how specific Christian passages have been interpreted to support the devaluing and harming of women and children, not only in the domestic set-up but also within the church's ministries of preaching and counseling. As part of her recommendations, Seyram suggests a more sensitive application of biblical texts to this specific context, the place of pre-marital and post-wedding counseling in the area of abuse and domestic violence, and the place of church discipline and policy when it comes to how it handles domestic cases. She concludes "as Christians, we must allow the unconditional love of God to rule in our hearts and homes while we follow Jesus's model of servant-leadership. If these recommendations are considered closely, there is the possibility to reduce domestic violence in our homes." This may be a healthier view of the gospel's intersection within domestic and ecclesial spaces, in a way that commends the faith to watching and sceptical young people.

An emerging scholar, Joseph Byamukama, a PhD Candidate in New Testament at Ridley College, takes on a topic of abiding interest within the

---

35. Within theological scholarship, approaches that centre women's experiences have been termed feminist or womanist, with different nuances. For an overview of these types of theologies, see Teresia M. Hinga, "African Feminist Theologies, the Global Village, and the Imperative of Solidarity across Borders: The Case of the Circle of Concerned African Women Theologians," *Journal of Feminist Studies in Religion* 18 no. 1 (2002): 79–86; and Daniel Kasomo and Loreen M. Maseno, "A Critical Appraisal of African Feminist Theology," *International Journal of Current Research* 2 no.1 (2011): 154–62.

continent – what do we do with our traditional gods? Many pan-Africanists see the Christian god as white and foreign. For some, embracing Christianity seems to intrinsically entail a rejection of our traditional gods and, to an extent, African-ness. Thus, the clamor to return to nativity concerns more than traditional herbalists and folklore. It regards a return to the gods of the land, the guardians of our ancestral clans. And those who advocate this anticipate either a total rejection or redefinition of Christianity. But one must wonder about the nature of the African Traditional gods and their place in our African traditional and ancestral praxis. Byamukama engages with the postcolonial philosophers of religion including Mbiti and Olupona, among others, exploring the concepts of God in African traditional religion. Surveying important texts in the Bible, he then unpacks the revelation of Yahweh, in his nearness (immanence) and in his incarnation, thereby distinguishing him from the polytheistic conceptions of God in our traditional religions.

The last part of the book explores practical areas of apologetic involvement and ministry. Daniël Maritz, an apologist and pastor, takes on the task of exploring new age movements in Africa, and in South Africa in particular. He guides the reader in understanding the postmodern angst in exploring divergent spiritualities without the coherence of the Judeo-Christian worldview. Most illuminating is his dissection of the new age movement in its over-reliance on subjective experiences rather than on objective reality, which is found in the created world and anchored in the truth that is expressed in and through Jesus Christ. Rodgers Atwebembeire leads a ministry called Africa Center for Apologetics Research, affiliated to other global centers, that specifically tackle the emergence of contemporary cults and cultic practices. He offers us a global survey of cults, but also considers present day cults in Africa and how Christians can engage with them.

Judy Wang'ombe's chapter engages in Christian-Muslim apologetics from within an inter-religious dialogue perspective. She is an academic at Africa International University focusing on the Christian-Muslim interreligious dialogue. While much of the apologetic engagement comes from within a comparative and doctrinal approach on God and Allah, Wang'ombe's chapter uniquely traces Christian-Muslim apologetics in history, and in East Africa in particular, and offers a practical engagement that is attuned to scholarship as well as bearing the marks of one who has had the practical experience of Muslim outreach.

My final chapter follows up on my own research in youth culture, by paying attention to how digital youth cultures pose a unique challenge to the Christian faith among African youth.[36] The chapter conceptualizes young people in their worldview divergences as well as their socio-economic and cultural uniqueness. Specifically, it locates young people within the digital media culture that shapes them as persons in three major areas. First, digital media culture leads to a shift in the area of knowledge and certainty. Consequently, young people are sceptical of claims to authority or pursuit of objective truth, as is found in the person and work of Jesus Christ for instance. Second, digital media culture leads to isolation and attendant mental health issues. The apologetic implications are that engagement with young people must be a holistic approach, that is both cognitive and affective. Third, digital media culture provides a bridge for engaging popular culture's philosophical and religious ideas that are propagated by new media. This chapter proposes that, to counter digital isolation or assimilation, Christian leaders are called to "wise-engagement" modelled after Paul's apologetic in Acts 17. The chapter offers practical considerations for engaging in the apologetic task among Africa's next gens.

I am aware that such a book cannot handle all the nuances involved in the gargantuan apologetic task comprehensively. Given the complexities of the continent, and the diversity of the issues, this book serves as an introduction. In my view, what this book helps to fill is a gap which provides a contextual apologetics resource that can supplement the fastest growing Christian continent with growing depth in Christian mission.

Following Augustine, I invite the reader to "take up and read."

Bibliography

Agang, Sunday Bobai, Dion A. Forster, and H. Jurgens Hendriks, eds. *African Public Theology*. Carlisle: HippoBooks, 2020.

Baucham, Voddie. *Expository Apologetics: Answering Objections with the Power of the Word*. Wheaton: Crossway, 2015.

Bediako, Kwame. *Theology and Identity: The Impact of Culture upon Christian Thought in the Second Century and in Modern Africa*. Akropong-Akuapem, Ghana: Regnum, 1999.

Cowan, Steven B., ed. *Five Views on Apologetics*. Grand Rapids: Zondervan, 2000.

Craig, William L. *The Son Rises: Historical Evidence for the Resurrection of Jesus*. Eugene: Wipf & Stock, 2000.

36. Kevin Muriithi Ndereba, "The Role of Youth Culture in Holistic Faith Formation of Youth in Nairobi: A Practical Theological Approach" (PhD Dissertation, University of South Africa, 2021).

Dembski, William A., Casey Luskin, and Joseph M. Holden, eds. *The Comprehensive Guide to Science and Faith: Exploring the Ultimate Questions about Life and the Cosmos*. Eugene: Harvest House Publishers, 2021.

Dixon, Thomas, Geoffrey Cantor, and Stephen Pumfrey, eds. *Science and Religion: New Historical Perspectives*. Cambridge: Cambridge University Press, 2010.

Ecklund, Howard. *Science vs. Religion: What Scientists Really Think*. Oxford: Oxford University Press, 2010.

Frame, John. *Apologetics: A Justification of Christian Belief*. Phillipsburg: P&R, 2015.

Geisler, Norman L., and Frank Turek. *I Don't Have Enough Faith to Be an Atheist*. Wheaton: Crossway, 2004.

Gould, Paul M. *Cultural Apologetics: Renewing the Christian Voice, Conscience, and Imagination in a Disenchanted World*. Grand Rapids: Zondervan Academic, 2019.

Habermas, Gary. *Risen Indeed: A Historical Investigation into the Resurrection of Jesus*. Bellingham, Lexham Press, 2021.

Hinga, Teresia M. "African Feminist Theologies, the Global Village, and the Imperative of Solidarity across Borders: The Case of the Circle of Concerned African Women Theologians." *Journal of Feminist Studies in Religion* 18, no. 1 (2002): 79–86.

Kasomo, Daniel, and Loreen M. Maseno. "A Critical Appraisal of African Feminist Theology." *International Journal of Current Research* 2, no. 1 (2011): 154–62.

Licona, Michael. *The Resurrection of Jesus: A New Historiographical Approach*. Downers Grove: IVP Academic, 2010.

Mbewe, Conrad "Why Is the Charismatic Movement Thriving in Africa?" *Banner of Truth Trust*, 2015. https://banneroftruth.org/us/resources/articles/2015/why-is-the-charismatic-movement-thriving-in-africa/.

Mburu, Elizabeth. *African Hermeneutics*. Carlisle: HippoBooks, 2019.

Mbuvi, Andrew M. "Missionary Acts, Things: Modeling Mission in Acts 17:15–34 and a Concern for Dialogue in Chinua Achebe Things Fall Apart." *Ex Auditu – Volume 23: An International Journal for the Theological Interpretation of Scripture* 23 (2008): 140–56.

Ndereba, Kevin Muriithi. "Engaging Youth Worldviews in Africa: A Practical Theology in Light of John 4." *Conspectus: The Journal of the South African Theological Seminary* 32, no. 1 (2021): 187–98.

———. "The Role of Youth Culture in Holistic Faith Formation of Youth in Nairobi: A Practical Theological Approach." PhD dissertation, University of South Africa, 2021.

———. "Youth Worldviews among the De-Churched and Implications for Ministry." MA Thesis, International Leadership University, Nairobi, 2015.

Oden, Thomas C. *How Africa Shaped the Christian Mind: Rediscovering the African Seedbed of Western Christianity*. Wheaton: InterVarsity Press, 2007.

Osborne, Eric. *Tertullian, First Theologian of the West*. Cambridge: Cambridge University Press, 1997.

Peterson, Gregory R. "The Intelligent-Design Movement: Science or Ideology?" *Zygon* 37, no. 1 (2002): 7–23.

Plantinga, Alvin. *Where the Conflict Really Lies: Science, Religion, and Naturalism*. Oxford: Oxford University Press, 2011.

Sanneh, Lamin. *Translating the Message: The Missionary Impact on Culture*. Maryknoll: Orbis Books, 2015.

Spickard, James V., and Afe Adogame. "Introduction: Africa, the New African Diaspora, and Religious Transnationalism in a Global World." In *Religion Crossing Boundaries*, edited by Afe Adogame and James V. Spickard, 1–28. Leiden: Brill, 2010.

Sproul, R. C. *The Consequences of Ideas: Understanding the Concepts that Shaped Our World*. Wheaton: Crossway, 2018.

Sproul, R. C., John Henry Gerstner, and Arthur Lindsley, eds. *Classical Apologetics: A Rational Defense of the Christian Faith and a Critique of Presuppositional Apologetics*. Grand Rapids: Zondervan, 1984.

Wilhite, David E. *Tertullian the African: An Anthropological Reading of Tertullian's Context and Identities*. Berlin: De Gruyter, 2011.

Willard, Dallas. *The Allure of Gentleness: Defending the Faith in the Manner of Jesus*. New York: HarperOne, 2015.

Part I

Biblical Issues

1

Is the Bible Reliable?

Biblical Criticism and Hermeneutics in Africa

Elizabeth Mburu, PhD

Langham Literature Regional Coordinator Anglophone Africa and Associate Professor of Greek and New Testament at Africa International University, Kenya

Abstract

The Protestant tradition has historically offered the church a high view of the Bible. Yet in different periods of the church's history, different movements have challenged the reliability of the Bible. This chapter will approach the reliability of the Bible from within two perspectives. The first will consider the classical questions within the discipline of apologetics such as the canonicity of the Bible and its uniqueness among other sacred texts. The second section will approach it from a hermeneutical perspective. Within the continent, prominent pan-Africanists have claimed that the Bible was used as a tool of oppression. The hermeneutical approaches to the Bible will help the African ministry leader to develop confidence to engage with the Bible for the transformation of individual lives and communities in Africa.

Keywords: Canon, Hermeneutics, Historical Criticism, Liberal and Post-Liberal Theology, Translation

1. Introduction

Although the Protestant tradition has historically offered a high view of the Bible, its reliability has been questioned by different movements throughout church history. This chapter will consider the question of the reliability of the Bible from two perspectives – classical and hermeneutical questions. Among the questions asked could be termed "classical questions." Is the Bible reliable? Can we be certain that it is ultimate truth? Do we have confidence that the text was faithfully transmitted and that our translations accurately reflect what the authors originally wrote in Hebrew, Aramaic and Greek? The first section will consider the classical questions within the discipline of apologetics such as the canonicity of the Bible, its transmission and translation, and its uniqueness among other sacred texts. It will begin with a brief Enlightenment and post-Enlightenment overview of the development of sceptical readings of the Bible. It will then address the issues of canonicity, transmission and translation of the Bible. The second approach will be from a hermeneutical perspective. Several prominent pan-Africanists have claimed that the Bible has been used as a tool of oppression in Africa. The various African hermeneutical approaches to the Bible will help the African ministry leader to develop confidence to engage with the Bible for the transformation of individual lives and communities in Africa.

1.1 A Brief Historical Overview of Sceptical Approaches to The Bible

There are two ways of reading the Bible. The first views the biblical witness as reliable and therefore true. Scholars like Augustine, Calvin, Luther, Bengel and Wesley struggled to interpret the Bible in a reasoned and intellectually responsible fashion. The second way in which we can read the Bible is with a "modern" sceptical reading that focuses on doubts about the reliability of the biblical message. This is reflective of historical criticism. For instance, many scholars have suggested that large blocks of material in the Gospels lack historical credibility. Hence, the Gospel records of the words and deeds of Jesus are judged to be unreliable. This arises from the tensions resulting from different versions of certain events in the different Gospels, and the alleged "fabrications" that surface at some points. This scepticism has grave implications for the interpretive task. This first section of this chapter is focused on Western theological movements since the Enlightenment and how these have shaped Christianity. Moreover, while sceptical readings are not generally an issue in the church in Africa, such trends have begun to grow and must therefore be understood.

1.2 The Enlightenment Roots

The age of scepticism was ushered by the period known as the Enlightenment, or the "Age of Reason." A major characteristic of the Enlightenment was the distrust of all forms of authority and tradition where matters of the intellect were concerned. Instead, there was an emphasis on scientific inquiry, reason and observation. It emphasized the elevation of human reason, which was seen as sufficient to "penetrate the mysteries of the world,"[1] as well as a passion for human welfare. Because of the influence of scientific discoveries, such as those made by Sir Isaac Newton, people believed that all life could be understood with reference to itself.[2] The Enlightenment stressed an overwhelming optimism about the human ability to achieve understanding through reason unattached and unaccountable to any ancient authority.[3] It greatly affected the way theology was approached in the church, especially because reason played such a prominent role. This renewed interest in the ability of human reason, as opposed to divine revelation, set the foundation for religious liberalism. In addition, pluralism gained ground in this age since all religions were understood as leading to the same ultimate reality. While some of the great thinkers of the Enlightenment were opposed to the church, the fact that most were deists made it possible for many of the ideas of the Enlightenment to be incorporated into theology.

Many deists evolved into pantheists and atheists. Men like John Locke,[4] and men like George Berkeley,[5] who denied special revelation, and David Hume,[6] who built on both Locke and Berkeley, concluded that miracles did not exist since objective truth could not be known.[7] They exemplify the agnosticism and the scepticism that characterized the theological arena during this time. Reason was elevated above faith, tradition and biblical authority found themselves out

1. Alister E. McGrath, *Historical Theology: An Introduction to the History of Christian Thought* (Oxford: Blackwell Publishing, 1998), 220.

2. Niccolò Guicciardini, *Isaac Newton and Natural Philosophy* (London: Reaktion Books, 2018).

3. McGrath, *Historical Theology*, 221–222.

4. John Locke, *The Reasonableness of Christianity, as delivered in the Scriptures*, ed. John C. Higgins-Biddle (Oxford: Clarendon Press, 1999).

5. George Berkeley; Colin Murray Turbayne, *A Treatise Concerning the Principles of Human Knowledge* (n.p.: Forgotten Books, (1710) 1957).

6. David Hume, *Enquiries concerning Human Understanding and Concerning the Principles of Morals,* reprinted from 1777 edition, 3rd ed., ed. L. A. Selby-Bigge (Oxford: Clarendon Press, n.d.)

7. Roger E. Olson, *The Story of Christian Theology: Twenty Centuries of Tradition and Reform* (Downers Grove: InterVarsity Press, 1999), 531.

of favour, such that the only natural outcome was the rejection of the Bible and everything supernatural. This was enhanced through the writings of the secular humanists.

According to Enlightenment leaders such as Immanuel Kant, thinkers in previous centuries had been confined to an intellectual nursery by several harsh spinster nannies.[8] These were the church, the Bible, creeds, tradition, old scientific theories, the emperor and the pope. But now humanity had grown up and could think and explore on its own. This kind of thinking had a tremendous impact on Christian doctrine. First, this thinking denied the doctrine of original sin, stressing that this was an oppressive idea. Second, this thinking denied that humanity was fallen and that both humanity and the world were affected by sin. Natural disasters revealed that God did not exist or was not involved in the world. Third, this thinking denied the divine inspiration of the Bible and relegated it to the realm of human literature. Fourth, this thinking denied the deity of Jesus Christ, claiming that he was not the incarnate Son of God but merely a superior moral teacher. Fifth, this thinking denied Christ's atoning, sacrificial death on the cross, arguing that he did not die in our place but rather as an example of self-sacrifice.[9]

1.3 Liberal Theology

Liberal theology, one of the most crucial developments within Protestantism, was the natural outcome of the Enlightenment and can be traced back to the developments in human knowledge that took place during this period. One such example is Darwin's theory of evolution. Liberalism tended to be flexible in that it aimed to bridge "the gap between Christian faith and modern knowledge."[10] As Olson notes, "[l]iberal theologians were convinced that human culture had taken a quantum leap forward with the Enlightenment and that the very existence of Christianity as more than a privatized folk religion depended on updating it to square with the best of Enlightenment's 'modernity project.'"[11] Modern cultural norms defined the shape of Christian beliefs and attitudes to Scripture. This meant that some beliefs were abandoned (e.g. the doctrine of original sin) and others were reinterpreted (e.g. Christ was seen as

8. Immanuel Kant, *An Answer to the Question: 'What is Enlightenment?,'* trans. Hugh Barr Nisbet (London: Penguin Books, 2010).

9. McGrath, *Historical Theology*, 223–26.

10. McGrath, *Historical Theology*, 232.

11. Olson, *The Story of Christian Theology*, 539.

an exemplar and not divine in any sense). Liberalism called for a grounding of faith in common human experience. While Immanuel Kant, Friedrich Schleiermacher, Albrecht Ritschl, Adolph Von Harnack, and Horace Bushnell, all contributed in various ways to liberal theology, the household name in liberalism is Paul Tillich. He was an American theologian who emphasized the need for interaction between the Christian faith and culture.[12] He recognized that existential questions arise from culture, and that these must not only be heard, but dealt with as well through theology.[13]

Liberalism, in general, held that reason and experience were paramount in religion, such that any beliefs had to be tested against both reason and science. Hence, miracles and the supernatural, falling into the category of things that cannot be proven, had to be rejected. This naturally meant that the core doctrines of the Christian faith found no place in liberal theology. The Bible was not regarded as inspired but was seen as an ordinary book that reflected high ethical standards and that displayed the evolution of human religion through the Old and the New Testaments. Consequently, liberals "saw modern thought as a necessary tool of interpretation and most of them gave it a guiding and even controlling authority in determining the essence of Christian truth."[14] Since the Bible was not regarded as an authoritative, infallible book, but rather was understood as the subjective writings of the experiences of others, it had no dogmatic value. Being subjective in nature, it denied the existence of any absolutes either in truth or morals. Hence, rather than the world conforming to biblical standards, liberal theologians taught that Christianity must be relevant and hence must be adapted to the modern world, to the world of human reason and science. Liberalism denied sin and its highly optimistic worldview meant that humankind was not only basically good, but also capable of doing good.[15] Because of this essential goodness, human beings were thought to have the ability to better the world through their efforts. Thus, the kingdom of God was not to be found in some distant future, but in the here and now, and was to be achieved through the application of biblical principles (social gospel). For liberal theologians, Jesus was not God, but merely a good teacher and the ideal man.

Another direction in which liberalism went, and that eventually influenced how the Bible was read, was that of Georg Hegel. His philosophy attempted to

12. Paul Tillich, *The Courage to Be* (New Haven: Yale University Press 1952, 2008).

13. McGrath, *Historical Theology*, 234.

14. Olson, *The Story of Christian Theology*, 539.

15. McGrath, *Historical Theology*, 233.

bring the concept of evolution into history and religion. For him, history should be defined as the meeting of two opposing movements whose contradictions must be integrated or unified.[16] Christian doctrines were to be understood not literally, but as symbols. In their higher criticism of the Bible, both F. C. Baur and Julius Wellhausen were strongly influenced by this Hegelian philosophy. They questioned the previously accepted authorship of biblical books. Baur, in particular, had a great influence on biblical criticism.[17] He denied the historical accuracy of the biblical accounts, seeing them more as myths than anything else. The documentary hypothesis, which questioned the authorship of the Pentateuch, finds its roots in Hegelian methodology.

1.4 Neo-Liberalism and Post-Liberalism

Liberalism evolved in two major ways, that is, neo-liberalism and post-liberalism. Neo-liberalism (with proponents such as Harry Fosdick who was strongly opposed to fundamentalism) rejected the subjectivism and the idealistic philosophy of older liberalism.[18] While higher criticism and the denial of inspiration continued to be a major tenet of their theology, the Bible was taken more seriously. Humans were still regarded as basically good (the doctrines of original sin and total depravity were rejected) but the optimism that dominated the older liberalism was dropped. Neo-liberals accepted the divinity of Christ, but this was not at the level of orthodoxy. In addition, while Christ's death was important for humankind, it was in no way understood in terms of substitutionary atonement.

Post-liberalism, a movement that gained popularity from the 1980s, has also raised various issues against liberal theology. Proponents of this school of thought have objected to the Enlightenment concept of a universal rationality and the liberal presupposition of a common religious experience. Thus, it strives to return to tradition, emphasizing historical and social continuity. It is characterized by an anti-foundational approach, as well as a communitarian

16. Georg Wilhelm Friedrich Hegel, *The Science of Logic*, trans. George Di Giovanni (Cambridge: Cambridge University Press, 2010). Note that some scholars have pointed out that explaining Hegel's dialectic in terms of thesis-antithesis-synthesis is not strictly accurate and that this terminology was actually developed by Immanuel Kant.

17. John Barton, *The Nature of Biblical Criticism* (Louisville: Westminster John Knox Press, 2007), 119.

18. For some of Fosdick's works, see *The Living of These Days* (n.p.: Harper Chapel Books: 1967), and his famous sermon "Shall the Fundamentalists Win? Defending Liberal Protestantism in the 1920's," http://historymatters.gmu.edu/d/5070/ retrieved 13 June 2022.

and historicist emphasis. The major theologian associated with this movement is George Lindbeck, the proponent of a cultural-linguistic approach to theology.

An early reaction to liberalism was neo-orthodoxy, also referred to as "New Reformation Theology" or "dialectical theology."[19] As a result of the loss of faith in liberal theology (catalysed by World War 1), neo-orthodoxy begun to take over from liberalism. Karl Barth, a Swiss theologian trained in liberalism, is generally heralded as the father of neo-orthodoxy.[20] He was an advocate of Søren Kierkegaard, a Danish philosopher and theologian who emphasized the value of experience as opposed to the cold orthodoxy of creeds and doctrines. Barth rejected his liberal training and developed Kierkegaard's views. He taught that God was transcendent, and hence an objective knowledge of him was impossible. However, to him, God could be known subjectively, through one's personal experience. For Barth, the Bible was to be understood as a witness to the word, as opposed to the objective word of God. Barth spoke of the revealed word, the written word and the preached word. Most importantly for him, it was only as one encountered the word of God through the Bible that it became the word of God.[21] Since Jesus was the only revelation of God, Barth rejected general revelation and emphasized the centrality of Christ in theology. Many critics of Barth note a strong sense of universalism in his theology.

Another household name as far as neo-orthodoxy is concerned is Rudolf Bultmann. He is famous for his insistence on the demythologization of the Bible and the irrelevance of history.[22] For him, the Bible was unreliable since it consisted of the subjective views of the early church as opposed to objective, factual truths about God and Christ. He used form criticism, approaching the Bible as he did any ordinary piece of literature. Form criticism (German *Formgeschichte*) focuses on the earliest stage of the origins and transmission of the Gospels, that is, the stage during which various portions that later became part of the written Gospels were transmitted orally. The term "form criticism" was first coined and used by Old Testament scholars such as Herman Gunkel.[23] Later it was adapted for New Testament studies by scholars such as Karl Ludwig Schmidt, Martin Dibelius, and Rudolf Bultmann. Form critics argue that the

---

19. Olson, *The Story of Christian Theology*, 570.

20. McGrath, *Historical Theology*, 237.

21. Olson, *The Story of Christian Theology*, 571.

22. Rudolf K. Bultmann, *History of the Synoptic Tradition* (San Francisco: Harper San Francisco, 1976); *The New Testament and Mythology and Other Basic Writings* (Augsburg Fortress Press, 1984).

23. Hermann Gunkel, *Genesis: Translated and Explained*, trans. Mark E. Biddle, 3rd ed. (Macon: Mercer University Press, 1997).

laws of transmission that apply to the oral transmission of other folk and religious traditions in general, can also be applied to the Gospel material. Hence, historical reliability and age of the various pericopes can be determined using these laws. Other key theologians in the neo-orthodox school included Emil Brunner (crisis theology), who reacted to the liberal view of christology, and Reinhold Niebuhr, with his work on social ethics.[24]

Neo-orthodoxy holds that the Bible is not to be regarded as the objective infallible word of God – it is not revelation, but a witness to revelation, and hence fallible. Since Jesus Christ is the focal point of God's revelation, humans do not meet God in words (Scripture), but in an experiential encounter with Christ. Events of Scripture, particularly the resurrection, should not be understood as history, which is itself verifiable and without error, but as story. Because of this approach, it is not necessary to insist on the historicity of the biblical accounts. Many of the biblical accounts are therefore mythical in nature, but this does not affect their validity and higher meaning. Transcendence is emphasized over immanence, such that we can only know God by an act of faith that is wholly subjective in nature. These were some of the views in the school of neo-orthodoxy.

1.5 Modernism and Post-Modernism

Modernism, first applied to Roman Catholic theologians, runs parallel to liberalism. However, in modernism, the findings of science as well as the importance of history are stressed. Modernists tended to have a highly sceptical attitude toward traditional Christian doctrines and hence leaned in the direction of Enlightenment thinking. They "fostered a positive attitude toward radical biblical criticism, and stressed the ethical, rather than the more theological, dimensions of faith."[25] Unlike other theological movements, modernism tended to incorporate a wide range of ideas and hence the term should not be seen as referring to a particular school of thought. Within the Protestant arm of the church, modernist attitudes were also changing the shape of theology. Hastings Rashdall, and his particular brand of an exemplar or moral approach to the

24. McGrath, *Historical Theology*, 238.
25. McGrath, *Historical Theology*, 235.

atonement, is one representative of modernist thinking in England.[26] In the United States, reactions to liberal thinking pushed many to re-emphasize a conservative approach to theology. While modernism waned after the first world war, it resurfaced and gained momentum, probably reaching its peak in the early 1970's.

With the fall of modernism, postmodernism gained prominence. Postmodernism is a pluralistic movement that is mainly characterized by relativism with regard to truth. It is a reaction to the modernist rationalism so prominent in the early part of the twentieth century. Postmodernism holds that one's knowledge and understanding of truth cannot be confined to any one idea. Moreover, truth is what proves to be good and beneficial to one's community. Of great importance is the fact that this movement has little regard for history, believing that history is created by the historian. For postmodernists, language is understood as being referential and hence does not mirror any external reality. Since language is arbitrary, it can and should be deconstructed. Unfortunately, what this means for postmodernists is that every ideology that is part of their movement also finds itself with no grounding. The most important aspect of postmodernism in terms of biblical interpretation is their emphasis that authorial intention and the worlds behind the text are not important to the understanding of a text. Since it is a reader-centred approach, all interpretations have equal validity. Hence, they challenge the historical-critical approach as being in error since it emphasizes authorial intent and the specific historical contexts in which texts are found. Having looked at the various movements that gave rise to sceptical readings of the Bible, we now turn our attention to those aspects that engender confidence in its reliability.

2. Canonicity of the Bible

One of the major issues when it comes to the reliability and integrity of the Bible is the question of canonicity. Scholars have not always agreed as to which books constitute the Bible. For instance, do the Apocryphal books (i.e., the extra books found in the Roman Catholic Bible) qualify as Scripture? If the lost letters of Paul were to be found, do they belong in our Bible? What is the relationship between the canon and the authority of the books?

---

26. Rashdall Hastings, *The Idea of Atonement in Christian Theology* (London: Macmillan, 1919). From an earlier generation, across a wider range of intellectual life, including the new critical approaches to the Bible, see *Essays and Reviews* (London: J. W. Parker, 1860), a collection of essays by 7 scholars in England.

2.1 What is the Canon?

The word "canon" is derived from the Hebrew *qāneh* and the Greek *kanōn*. It denotes a straight rod or rule. It later came to be used for "list" or "table."[27] Since the first century, certain books had been recognized as inspired and authoritative. The terms "Old Testament" and "New Testament" began to be applied by Christian writers to collections of Scriptures in the second and third centuries. The earliest Christian lists of the Old Testament and the New Testament were those of Melito and the Muratorian fragment from the 2nd century AD (twenty-two of the twenty-seven documents later listed as canonical are included) and the earliest Jewish list of the Hebrew Scriptures found in a primitive tradition or Baraita quoted in the Babylonian Talmud is probably older. The creative and historical process by which the twenty-seven books came to make up the New Testament at the Council of Carthage in AD 387 is known as canonization.

2.2 The Canon and Revelation

Questions surrounding the canon are greatly influenced by the issue of revelation. A foundational presupposition of Christianity is that God has revealed himself in two main ways. The first is general revelation which is "God's communication of himself to all persons at all times and in all places."[28] This knowledge is available through nature, history and human beings. This has often resulted in debates as to whether one can truly know God and construct theology on the basis of general revelation alone. General revelation has at least five significant implications.[29] First, everyone has a knowledge of God. This is a common point of contact between Christians and everyone else. Second, one can obtain some knowledge of divine truth without special revelation. Third, because all have access to this general revelation, no one can claim that they are completely without opportunity to know God. Consequently, God is not unjust in condemning those without access to the gospel. Fourth, general revelation is an explanation for the worldwide phenomenon of religion and religions. There is harmony between creation and the gospel. And lastly, all truth is God's truth.

---

27. D.A. Carson and Douglas J. Moo, *An Introduction to the New Testament* (Grand Rapids: Zondervan, 2005), 726.

28. Millard J. Erickson, *Introducing Christian Doctrine*, 2nd ed. (Grand Rapids: Baker Academic, 1992, 2001), 42.

29. Millard J. Erickson, *Introducing Christian Doctrine*, 49–50.

The second way in which God has revealed himself is through special revelation. This is "God's particular communications and manifestations of himself to particular persons at particular times, communications and manifestations which are available now only by consultation of certain sacred writings."[30] Special revelation is personal, it is communicated in human language and generally in forms that were part of ordinary human experience (i.e., anthropomorphic), and it uses meaningful analogies to communicate heavenly realities.[31] The modes of special revelation include historical events, divine speech and most fully, in the incarnation of Jesus Christ. A major implication of special revelation is that "God has taken the initiative to make himself known to us in a more complete way than general revelation and has done so in a fashion appropriate to our understanding."[32] The preservation of this revelation is what is known as inspiration.

The question of inspiration has often produced controversy. Four main theories have been proposed to explain it.[33] The first is the neo-orthodox theory. Modern readers of the Bible experience God through the accounts of the ancient writers, which may have contained paradoxes or errors. This theory fails to consider those portions of the Bible that clearly state that the Bible is the word of God (2 Tim 3:16–17; 2 Pet 1:20–21). The second is dictation theory. This theory proposes that God dictated word for word what he wanted the biblical writers to communicate. Unfortunately, this does not account for the personalities of the different writers. The third is limited inspiration theory which argues that while God inspired the thoughts of the biblical writers, the words they used were their own. This freedom may have resulted in some errors in the historical details, but the doctrinal portions were protected by God. This theory does not account for the emphasis that various portions of the Bible place on historical detail. The fourth is plenary verbal theory. This theory argues that human authors were supernaturally superintended by the Holy Spirit, through the process of inscripturation and without the suppression of their diverse capabilities and styles, to produce the Bible (1 Cor 2:13; Acts 4:25; 1 Pet 1:10–12). As a result of this, the autographs are God breathed or inspired, a quality that refers to the end product and not the process or the authors (2 Tim 3:16). Having been inspired verbally, this inspiration extends

30. Millard J. Erickson, *Introducing Christian Doctrine*, 52.

31. Millard J. Erickson, *Introducing Christian Doctrine*, 53–55.

32. Millard J. Erickson, *Introducing Christian Doctrine*, 58–59.

33. Bill T. Arnold and Bryan E. Beyer, *Encountering the Old Testament: A Christian Survey*, 2nd ed. (Grand Rapids: Baker Academic, 1999, 2008), 24–26.

to the very words of Scripture (1 Cor 2:13), and is also plenary, extending equally to every part of Scripture and all Scripture as originally given (2 Tim 3:16; 2 Pet 1:20–21). The implications of this theory are that the Bible can be considered to be trustworthy, reliable, and authoritative.

2.3 The Process of Canonization

The canon is not something the early medieval church leaders "imposed on their constituency."[34] The formation of the canon happened over several centuries. Throughout the second century and into the fourth centuries, several church councils met to determine which books should be included in the canon.

2.3.1 Canonization of the Old Testament

The recognition of which books belonged in the Old Testament was determined by the Hebrew people. However, among the general population, there was still a certain amount of confusion as to which books belonged and which didn't. For instance, the authority and inspiration of Esther was still questioned until the first century AD. Nevertheless, the Hebrew canon was somewhat fixed by the time the Greek translation (the Septuagint or LXX) was written. The question of canonicity was addressed by Jewish leaders on several occasions. The council of Jamnia met around AD 90 to discuss this issue. What they decided was that those books which had been recognized for generations were the ones which belonged in the Old Testament. In other words, the process was not one in which they determined which books belonged but rather, one of confirming which books were already recognized. In the Hebrew version, the books are divided into three main divisions: The Law (Torah), the prophets, and the writings. The English version of the Old Testament has five divisions: Law, historical books, poetical books, Major Prophets, and Minor Prophets.

There were three main criteria for recognition of a book as canonical.[35] First, a book had to have been written by a prophet or other spirit-led person. It was only God's Spirit that enabled the human authors to know God's will. Second, it had to be written to all generations. Although God's message was written to a particular audience, it had to be relevant to all generations. Third, it had to be written in accord with previous revelation. While a book could

34. Ben Witherington, *The New Testament Story* (Grand Rapids: Eerdmans, 2004), 96.

35. Arnold and Beyer, *Encountering the Old Testament*, 22.

add new revelation, it could not contradict earlier writings deemed to be part of God's message to humanity.[36]

2.3.2 Canonization of the New Testament

The canonization of the New Testament took a different path. There were several key factors leading to the canonization of the New Testament texts. The first is the Old Testament precedent for a canon. Already, the Jewish people were using the Old Testament canon as the basis for their personal lives and corporate existence. The early Christian communities also recognized these Jewish Scriptures and used the Greek translation (the Septuagint or LXX) as a precedent and analogy for the New Testament canon.[37] The second factor is the divine authorship of the New Testament which is provided through internal evidence. Several biblical texts note that the writings of the New Testament are inspired, or God-breathed (2 Tim 3:16), are communicated via the agency of the Holy Spirit (John 14:26) and have the witness of the Holy Spirit to affirm their scriptural status (John 16:13).

At first, the sayings of Jesus and the writings of the apostles were often quoted alongside the Old Testament Scripture as having a similar authority but not as themselves constituting Scripture. Given that Paul commanded that his epistles be read publicly in the congregation (1 Thess 5:27; see also Col 4:16), it is likely that he regarded his epistles as having scriptural status. The same goes for the author of Revelation (Rev 1:3; 22:18–19). In 2 Peter 3:16, Paul's epistles are actually called "Scriptures," and a gospel is identified as "the Scripture" in 1 Timothy 5:18. The use of the term "Scripture(s)" to denote New Testament writings became increasingly common through the second century and by the end of it was normal.

As in the canonization of the Old Testament, books had to meet certain criteria. The first was usage in the church. Those books that enjoyed a special status and were utilized both frequently and universally by the church were included. The second was quotation in ancient authorities.[38] This lent authority to a given writing. The third was the authority of Jesus. The authority of his words was primary, while that of the books was secondary and derivative. The fourth was apostolicity. A book had to have been written by an apostle

---

36. John Tullock and Mark McEntire, *The Old Testament Story* (London: Pearson Education, 2012), 22.

37. Walter A. Elwell and Robert W. Yarbrough, *Encountering the New Testament: A Historical and Theological Survey*, 2nd ed. (Grand Rapids: Baker Academic, 1998, 2005), 25–26.

38. Carson and Moo, *An Introduction to the New Testament*, 605.

or someone connected to an apostle. The fifth was orthodoxy (i.e., rule of faith/*regula fidei*). This was the determining criteria and was based primarily on content, as opposed to authorship. With the exception of prophetic and apocalyptic documents, inspiration was attributed to a book only after it was recognized as canonical.

Not all books were originally accepted. There was a widespread agreement to accept the four Gospels, Acts, thirteen epistles of Paul, 1 Peter and 1 John. The remaining seven, the so-called "Antilegomena" were only finally included at the end of the fourth century. Their earlier rejection was on several grounds. Hebrews was anonymous and stylistically different from the acknowledged Pauline epistles. However, this is because it was probably penned by an associate of Paul such as Apollos (see Heb 13:23). 2 Peter was stylistically different from 1 Peter. However, this could be due to Peter's use of different scribes. Revelation was different from the other letters of John and the Montanists claimed its support. However, the differences may be due to John having no help with his Greek when in exile on Patmos and the genre is totally different. Moreover, it does not really give support to Montanism. In 2 and 3 John, the author called himself "the elder." However, this does not mean he was not an apostle (see 1 Pet 5:1). Jude quoted the book of 1 Enoch. Nevertheless, it does not really recognize 1 Enoch as Scripture. The rejection of James was probably the teaching on justification given in chapter 2. However, James does not really agree with the Pharisees or disagree with Paul on justification. These are some responses to the challenges posed to canonization of specific books in the New Testament.

3. Transmission and Translation of the Bible

Apart from canonization, transmission and translation of the text is another major issue when it comes to the reliability and integrity of the Bible. Can we be certain that the text was faithfully transmitted? Can we be certain that our English translations reflect what the authors originally wrote in Hebrew, Aramaic and Greek?

3.1 Transmission

To answer the question of transmission, it is important to understand the role that scribes played in ancient societies. The Hebrew word means "counter." Scribes were used at various levels of society, for instance, by kings to record royal edicts, and by administrative officials to record various transactions.

Accuracy was a crucial factor in their trade. This was even more so for biblical scribes who "believed they were copying the very words of God."[39] The scribes that worked on the copying of the Old Testament text they had received were known as Masoretes (AD 500–1000). Their name is derived from the *masora*, which was "a complex system of markings they developed to achieve their purpose."[40] To ensure textual accuracy, the Masoretes developed the vowel system, accents and notes. The vowel system was intended to go with the already existing consonantal system of Hebrew writing and to preserve the oral tradition. The system of accents helped in pronunciation and to indicate the relationship between certain words and phrases in a sentence. The detailed notes on the text were a means of checking the accuracy of copied texts.

Most of the Old Testament was originally written in Hebrew but a few portions were written in Aramaic (Gen 31:47b; Exod 4:8–6:18; 7:12–26; Jer 10:11b; Dan 2:4b–7:28). This was the language of the Babylonians, under whom the Jewish people had lived in captivity for many years. The most important copies of the Hebrew Bible that have come down to us include the Masoretic text (which is the most reliable Hebrew text that we have), the Samaritan Pentateuch (which originated with the Samaritans and contains only Genesis to Deuteronomy) and the Dead Sea Scrolls (which date to around 200–100 BC and contain at least parts of every Old Testament book).

What about the New Testament? Some claim that some sort of whole-scale alteration of earlier manuscripts was undertaken in the fourth century which produced a New Testament quite different from what the original New Testament writers had in mind for their own works. It is a given that certain inevitable errors must result in the manual transmission of documents (e.g. the four different endings of Mark; John 7:53–8:11; Acts 6:8; 1 Thess 2:7; 1 John 5:7–8 [the Johannine comma]). There are two main causes of error in the transmission of the New Testament. The first is unintentional changes. These could be due to faulty eyesight (parablesis, dittography), faulty hearing, errors of the mind, and errors of judgement. Errors of judgement included incorporation of marginal notes by the scribes. The second major cause of error was intentional changes introduced by scribes offended by real or imagined errors of spelling, grammar and historical fact, or changes made because of doctrinal considerations.

However, these variants do not affect the reliability of the New Testament. In fact, 94 percent of its content is exactly the same in virtually all the existing

39. Tullock and McEntire, *The Old Testament Story*, 26.

40. Tullock and McEntire, *The Old Testament Story*, 26.

manuscripts. Of the remaining 6 percent, 3 percent constitute nonsensical readings that are transparently not original but the result of various scribal errors. Thus, only about 3 percent of the text are properly the subject of investigation.[41]

3.2 Translation

As for translation, there are many issues related to the nature of language and communication. The Old Testament was also translated and transmitted in other languages. The best-known Greek version of the Jewish Scriptures is the Septuagint (300–200 BC). It is not the earliest Greek version but the dominant one. According to tradition (Epistle of Aristeas; Philo; Life of Moses, 2.26–42), the Old Testament was translated into Greek under Ptolemy II, Philadelphus (285–246 BC). Legend has it that Philadelphus commissioned seventy or seventy-two scholars to translate the Hebrew Scriptures. Hence it was called the "Septuagint" (Greek for seventy; abbreviated by the Roman numeral LXX). The translation was prepared in Egypt and designed for Jews who understood Greek better than Hebrew, a testimony to the success of Alexander's program of Hellenization. It contains many works not included in the Hebrew canon. Some parts, such as the Pentateuch, are more carefully translated than others.[42] Other translations are the Targums. These are Aramaic translations and paraphrases of the Old Testament that date mainly from the early Christian era with some earlier parts.[43] The Targums came about during the time when the Jewish people understood Aramaic better than Hebrew. Because they provide both translation as well as commentary, they do not generally provide a reliable witness to the Old Testament text.

Early in its history, the New Testament was also translated into several languages and widely distributed. These include Syriac, Latin, and Coptic. At least eight thousand manuscripts exist in Latin alone.[44] These translations engender confidence in the text for at least four main reasons. The first is that we have a wealth of evidence. The New Testament is by far the best-attested writing of classical antiquity.[45] Over five thousand manuscripts containing at

41. Andreas J. Köstenberger, L. Scott Kellum and Charles L. Quarles, *The Cradle, the Cross and the Crown: An Introduction to the New Testament* (Nashville: B&H Publishing Group, 2009), 35.

42. Tullock and McEntire, *The Old Testament Story*, 28.

43. Tullock and McEntire, *The Old Testament Story*, 28.

44. Elwell and Yarbrough, *Encountering the New Testament*, 29.

45. Elwell and Yarbrough, *Encountering the New Testament*, 28.

least a fragment of the New Testament have been catalogued. The state of the manuscripts is very good. Compared with any and all other ancient documents, the New Testament stands up as ten times surer. For instance, we have five hundred different copies earlier than AD 500. The next most reliable ancient text we have is the Iliad, for which we have only fifty copies that date from five hundred years or less after its origin. We have only one very late manuscript of Tacitus's Annals, but no one is reluctant to treat that as authentic history.[46] There is simply no other ancient text in nearly as good a shape.

The second is the brief time lapse. There is a brief time span between the date when the documents were written and the date of the earliest copies we possess.[47] For instance John 18:31–33; 37–38, the John Rylands Papyrus (P 52) is dated AD 125. P 90 is also dated to within thirty to fifty years after the original manuscript was written. Codex Sinaiticus, an uncial[48] written in approximately 350, is the earliest extant copy of the entire New Testament. Other uncials, such as Codices Vaticanus, Alexandrinus, Ephraemi, and Bezae constitute significant witnesses as well.[49] The minuscules compose the largest group of Greek manuscripts and they are dated considerably later.

The third reason is related to the existence of different early versions and how they were quoted by the church fathers. There was a widespread distribution of the New Testament from a very early date. These versions reveal that the New Testament was faithfully rendered as it passed from scribe to scribe and from language to language such as Greek, Latin, Syriac, Ethiopic.[50] The early church fathers quoted from the New Testament, providing us with a valuable tool of comparison regarding the original texts from which they quoted.

The fourth is related to historiographical conventions of the day, particularly when one considers the narrative sections of the New Testament. Rather than doubt the credibility of the Gospels and Acts, the judicious interpreter will evaluate these documents with an understanding of the conventions of their day. Readers ought not to force modern conventions on the Gospels but must understand that the use of paraphrase and the telescoping of events were legitimate devices in ancient historiography. In addition, given that there were four different writers involved, one cannot expect to have identical translations

---

46. Köstenberger et al., *The Cradle, the Cross and the Crown*, 34.
47. Elwell and Yarbrough, *Encountering the New Testament*, 29.
48. Uncial and miniscule refers to the script in which the manuscripts are written.
49. Köstenberger et al., *The Cradle, the Cross and the Crown*, 33.
50. Elwell and Yarbrough, *Encountering the New Testament*, 29.

from the original Greek and Aramaic, nor should one expect a given event recounted in an identical fashion.[51] Moreover, there is sufficient agreement in the relating of accounts and the placement of events to engender confidence in the evangelists' credibility. Consequently, any approach to the interpretation of these texts must begin with the presumption that they are historically accurate and reliable.

Today, we have many different English language translations such as NIV, RSV, NASB, CEB, NLT, KJV, NKJV and so forth. This is because there are many translation theories and the versions we have today are all based on particular theories and approaches, and are intended for different purposes. These translations can be categorized alongside a linear scale between dynamic equivalence (i.e., those that focus on readability or meaning), and functional equivalence (i.e., those that focus on original rendering). Dynamic equivalence translations (e.g. NIV, NLT) focus on a sense-for-sense translation, with an aim for readability. Functional equivalence translations (e.g. NASB, KJV, ESV) focus on a word-for-word translation, with an aim for literal fidelity. However, we can be certain that what we have today is reliable.

4. Hermeneutical Questions

Having considered the classical questions, the second approach will be from a hermeneutical perspective. Given the reliability of the Bible, the question then is, how do we read it in such a way that we understand its message and apply it faithfully in our different contexts? Several prominent pan-Africanists have claimed that the Bible has been used as a tool of oppression in Africa. The various African hermeneutical approaches to the Bible will help the African ministry leader to develop confidence to engage with the Bible for the transformation of individual lives and communities in Africa.

The theory and practice of interpretation is known as hermeneutics. It comes from the Greek word *hermeneuein* which means "to understand." Friedrich Schleiermacher (1768–1834), a German, Protestant philosopher and theologian, is generally regarded as the father of modern hermeneutics. Prior to Schleiermacher, hermeneutics was often defined as the formulation of "rules" of interpretation. Hermeneutics has often faced the challenge of a lack of objective criteria as is expected of the natural sciences. Consequently, its status as a science has often been questioned. Nevertheless, as it involves

51. Craig L. Blomberg, *The Historical Reliability of the Gospels*, 2nd ed. (Downers Grove: InterVarsity Press, 1987, 2007), 113–89.

critical reflection on the processes of interpretation and understanding, it is both an art and a science.

4.1 The Value of Africentric Hermeneutics

From the onset of modern hermeneutics in the nineteenth and early twentieth centuries with figures such as Schleiermacher and Dilthey, many scholars argued that Bible interpretation was neutral. People generally tended to focus either on the world behind the text or the world of the text itself. However, more theories in hermeneutics now acknowledge that the world in front of the text is just as significant. All interpretation carries with it a certain ideology or ideologies that are brought in by the reader. There is the recognition of the two-sided nature of historical conditioning.[52] As Thiselton points out, the interpreter also stands in a given historical context and tradition; and the text and the interpreter are in constant engagement.[53] Since readers are contextually situated within their cultural settings and cannot realistically remove themselves totally from this situation, it is clear that there is a "mutually reinforcing relationship between our culture's worldview (with its underlying assumptions) and our interpretation."[54]

Most biblical interpretation in Africa is done using Eurocentric methods of hermeneutics. While these methods have been successful in Western contexts, they are problematic in African contexts for several reasons. The first is that such methods have often not been effective in facilitating dialogue between biblical cultures and assumptions and African cultures and assumptions. The second is the hermeneutical issue of language which leads to a lack of precision in translating concepts and words from the biblical language to many of the African languages. The third is ideological and has to do with the oft misunderstood race of Jesus Christ.[55] These three challenges have contributed to a deficient understanding of biblical texts.

Although the following statement applies to theology, one of the motivating factors behind Africentric approaches can be gleaned from Bediako's comment where he cites Hastings and Balz:

---

52. Elizabeth Mburu, *African Hermeneutics* (Carlisle: HippoBooks, 2019), 67–68.

53. Anthony C. Thiselton, *The Two Horizons: New Testament Hermeneutics and Philosophical Description with Special Reference to Heidegger, Bultmann Gadamer and Wittgenstein* (Carlisle: Paternoster Press, 2005), 11.

54. Mburu, *African Hermeneutics*, 24.

55. N. Onwu, "The Hermeneutical Model: The Dilemma of the African Theologian," *Africa Theological Journal*, 14 no. 3 (1985): 145–60.

> The question is whether an African theology that is "controlled in language and methodology by its European medium" can give adequate account of the apprehension of Christ at the "living roots of the churches," "where faith has to live."[56]

A corollary issue, which is also felt in theological studies, has to do with African identity. What does it mean to be Christian and African? As Bediako points out, "the African theologian's concern with the pre-Christian religious heritage becomes an endeavour to clarify the nature and meaning of African Christian identity."[57] African readers of the Bible bring their own questions to the text, a text that they believe embodies power in that it is both "a tactile object of power and a text of power."[58] These two issues affirm that Eurocentric approaches are deficient in interpreting texts in African contexts such that a consistent African Christian identity emerges. The implications of Africentric approaches to hermeneutics cannot be ignored.

In general, modern African hermeneutics have been driven by sociological and historical interests.[59] The aim of Africentric hermeneutics is to recover the message of the Bible and to separate it from Western assumptions. These approaches are based on a few common assumptions: Faith in God, the Holy Spirit is actively involved in the process of interpretation, the Bible is a significant sacred text, the Bible is powerful, the socio-cultural and religious contexts of the African reader are important, and interpretation is not just an academic exercise but should result in transformation of believers and society as a whole.[60] While Western assumptions and methods are by no means monolithic, either amongst communities or individuals given that there are confessional, historical, theological and ecclesiological distinctives,[61] there are

56. Kwame Bediako, "The Roots of African Theology," *International Bulletin of Missionary Research* (April 1989): 64.

57. Bediako, "The Roots of African Theology," 59.

58. Gerald O. West, "Indigenous Biblical Hermeneutics: Voicing Continuity and Distinctiveness," in *Postcolonial Perspectives in African Biblical Interpretations*, ed. Musa W. Dube, Andrew Mbuvi and D. R. Mbuwayesango (Atlanta: Society of Biblical Literature, 2012), 87.

59. Gerald O. West, "African Biblical Hermeneutics and Bible translation," in *Interacting with Scriptures in Africa*, ed. Jean-Claude Loba-Mkole and Ernst R. Wendland (Nairobi: Acton Publishers, 2005), 7.

60. Benno Van den Toren, Elizabeth Mburu and Samuel K. Bussey, "Biblical Hermeneutics," in *Bibliographical Encyclopaedia of African Theology*, 2021, https://african.theologyworldwide.com/encyclopaedia-bible-in-africa/biblical-hermeneutics.

61. Elizabeth Mburu, "The Importance of African Hermeneutics in African Theological Education, in *A Critical Engagement with Theological Education in Africa: A South African Perspective*, ed. Johannes Knoetze and Alfred Brunson (Cape Town, South Africa: AOSIS, 2021), 86–87, https://doi.org/10.4102/aosis.2021.BK273.

some commonalities which justify grouping them together.[62] Some Western assumptions might include "linear reasoning, a greater dependence on scientific methods and therefore more emphasis on neutrality, a more individualistic approach in understanding and representing texts, an antispiritualist approach, and a more fragmented view of reality (as opposed to African holism)."[63] As with Western assumptions, African assumptions are also not monolithic. Nevertheless, the commonalities (particularly south of the Sahara) justify the label "Africans," as in this chapter.

4.2 Hermeneutics in Africa

History records that interpretation of the Bible was being done by Africans almost two thousand years ago. In more recent times, missionaries re-introduced biblical hermeneutics into Africa. They inevitably brought with them cultural baggage from their Western context. Unfortunately, at around the same time, colonization was also taking place. Because of this, some Africans have objected to Western approaches, preferring instead to "decolonize" hermeneutics and make it applicable to the African context.[64] Consequently, African hermeneutics generally tends to be liberational and against the colonial missionary enterprise; done by ordinary Christians or church leaders at the "grassroots" level, for example, in worship, prayer and preaching; is not limited to academic study or even written forms of interpretation, but also includes oral hermeneutical reflection; and is functional. Biblical hermeneutics in Africa includes both the theories of interpretation as well as general principles and methods implicit in practices of interpretation.[65] In Africa, hermeneutics is functional. African hermeneutics recognizes that the Bible speaks powerfully into the present. This is the general impetus or motivation behind the development of the approaches below.[66]

62. "Western" is a general category that comprises the United States, Canada, and the countries of Western, Northern, and Southern Europe. Identifying all the distinctives represented in Western confessional, historical, theological and ecclesiological thought is beyond the scope of this study.

63. Elizabeth Mburu, "The Importance of African Hermeneutics," 87.

64. Mburu, *African Hermeneutics*, 4–5.

65. Van den Toren et al., "Biblical Hermeneutics," *Bibliographical Encyclopedia of African Theology*, 2021. https://african.theologyworldwide.com/encyclopaedia-bible-in-africa/biblical-hermeneutics.

66. A more thorough treatment of these approaches can be accessed in Van den Toren et al., "Biblical Hermeneutics," 2021.

4.3 Current Trends

How we read/interpret the Bible matters because it shapes our doctrine and practice. There is a general consensus now that Africans need to move away from the Western approaches that have been imposed on us because they promote a "foreign" way of reading the Bible that introduces a "double hermeneutical gap." A double hermeneutical gap occurs when a reader is forced to confront at least two cultures in the process of interpretation. For African readers, this is the Western culture, since most hermeneutical methods currently in use in Africa are developed in Western contexts. Readers face the challenge of first understanding the assumptions inherent in these methods before dealing with those in the biblical texts.

4.3.1 Ethiopian Hermeneutics

Over the centuries a distinctive form of interpretation developed known as andemta, which includes translation and commentary in Amharic on the Bible and related literature written in Ge'ez. This tradition existed in oral form until it was written down in the seventeenth century. Andemta commentary analyses the biblical text and gives thorough, often highly contextual, explanation, illuminating stories and key quotations from various authorities to establish its meaning. Typological explanation is common. As Van den Toren et al. note, "The importance of the andemta tradition for biblical hermeneutics is that it has developed independently in an African setting and is free from modern Western philosophical baggage."[67]

4.3.2 African Independent Hermeneutics

The motivation to start African Independent Churches (AICs), also called African Indigenous Churches or African Initiated Churches, was a response to Western missionary churches. These tended to be seen as too closely allied to colonial interests. In addition, they did not understand or consider the needs of African Christians. No systematic overview has been developed yet but there are some common aspects to note. The Bible is central in AIC worship and has a high authority, but this may be combined with the authority accorded to African traditions. Furthermore, the authority of Scripture does not exclude other authorities, such as the ancestors, healers and, most importantly, the spiritual leader, whose readings of Scripture are the final word in all matters of faith and practice. In AICs the Bible is interpreted quite literally. Biblical texts are used to support the continuation of traditional practices, such as polygamy

67. Van den Toren et al., "Biblical Hermeneutics," 2021.

or food laws.[68] The Scripture is understood as directly related to the challenges facing African Christians. Furthermore, the Bible is both an object and a text of power in that the very words are believed to have power which can be used for good or for evil.[69] This reverence is a spillover from the African traditional religious worldviews regarding the Supreme Being and his interaction with the world through his intermediaries.[70] Its presence or the repetition of certain texts can provide protection in situations of need, healing and/or success. Depending on one's theological position, this can be interpreted magically, sacramentally or therapeutically.

4.3.3 Liberation and Black Hermeneutics

The context of oppression and inequality in Latin America and amongst African Americans in North America in the 1960s and 70s gave rise to black liberation hermeneutics. They address the realities of injustice, oppression and colonization. In this approach, there are two ways of reading: hermeneutics of trust and hermeneutics of suspicion.

Liberation hermeneutics are characterized by the sequence of see-judge-act in which the understanding of the meaning of the Scriptures begins with an understanding of the context, particularly the realities of oppression and injustice. Exodus is the key text behind this method. This seeing is always involved in that it is engaged in the struggle for liberation. The main tools used are social analysis. This enables the interpreter to begin to judge the situation with the help of the text. Seeing and judging is not merely a theoretical exercise but must always be accompanied by action. This is the first hermeneutical principle. The second is that the poor are accorded epistemological preference or privilege on the basis of God's preferential option for the poor. This is because it is only from the "perspective of the poor from which one can understand both the nature of their struggles to which the Scriptures speak and to understand the revolutionary message of the Scriptures itself, which may well escape the powerful or may be suppressed by them."[71]

South African "Black hermeneutics" is the dominant form of liberation hermeneutics in English-speaking Africa. It shares its name and many of its themes with North American Black hermeneutics. However, the difference is

68. Allan H. Anderson, "The Hermeneutical Processes of Pentecostal-Type African Initiated Churches in South Africa," *Missionalia* 24.2 (1996): 173–75.

69. West, "Indigenous Biblical Hermeneutics: Voicing Continuity and Distinctiveness," 87.

70. Mburu, *African Hermeneutics*, 2019, 25–28.

71. Van den Toren et al., "Biblical Hermeneutics," 16.

that rather than a context of an oppressed racial minority, South African black hermeneutics originated in the apartheid context of an oppressed majority.

4.3.4 Feminist/Womanist Hermeneutics

African feminist hermeneutics falls in the general category of liberation hermeneutics. As in the West, African feminist hermeneutics focuses on the struggle against the subordination of women in contemporary society, and ecclesial and familial roles. African women are the subjects of interpretation. The term "feminist" to refer to a black feminist of colour is currently under debate because while African women share the common aspect of oppression on the basis of gender with Western and other women, their experiences are different. Consequently, some proponents prefer to use "womanist," African indigenous terms for example, *bosadi,* or the general "African women's" hermeneutics. Major proponents include Dube, Masenya, Mbuy-Beya, Nasimiyu Wasike, Oduyoye and Okure. There are common elements between feminist hermeneutics and inculturation and liberation hermeneutics. This is because feminist hermeneutics "has a strong religio-cultural emphasis and also seeks to critique and 're-read' Scripture in order to uncover its liberative message for women under the oppression of sex, race and class."[72] The goal is transformation that permeates all aspects of life. While it does not reject the Bible or Christianity it is nevertheless a hermeneutic of suspicion. It uses the conventional resources of hermeneutical critical tools and is interdisciplinary in approach. Assumptions that undergird feminist hermeneutics include the full humanity of women, the mutuality and equality of men and women, the value of the experience of black African women, and the participation of the ordinary reader.

4.3.5 Contextual Bible Study

While all African hermeneutics is context, the label "contextual Bible study" is a specific form of hermeneutics developed out of the Institute for the Study of the Bible in South Africa. The major proponent is Gerald O. West.[73] The ordinary, non-academically trained Bible reader, and particularly marginalized communities (the poor, women, HIV/AIDS groups) are foregrounded. It therefore has affinities with the various expressions of liberation theologies.

72. Van den Toren et al., "Biblical Hermeneutics," 18.

73. Gerald O. West, "Locating 'Contextual Bible Study' within Biblical Liberation Hermeneutics and Intercultural Biblical Hermeneutics," *HTS Teologiese Studies / Theological Studies* 70 no. 1 (2014): 1–10.

Epistemological privilege is given to the poor and the oppressed. Their situation enables them to understand and apply the text in their own context better. It tends to focus more on the significance of the text for the reader today than on the original meaning of the text in its historical context.

4.3.6 Pentecostal Hermeneutics

Pentecostal hermeneutics strives to actualize the meaning of Scripture "by the presence of the Holy Spirit in the believer and in the believing community."[74] The interpretation of the text is literal because of the understanding that the Holy Spirit is still active in the world today. There is therefore interpretive freedom. It does not merely provide a different interpretation of texts. It moves beyond the classic methods of interpretation and provides a new approach that is based on the role of the Holy Spirit and the church in the process of interpretation. Although it is focused on the world in front of the text (that is, the reader), the understanding is that the text is part of a larger metanarrative that is centered in Christ. Neo-Pentecostal hermeneutics is more like AIC hermeneutics in that it incorporates elements of the African traditional worldview.

4.3.7 Reconstruction Hermeneutics

The theology of reconstruction originated in Africa at the All Africa Conference of Churches meeting in Nairobi in 1990. This hermeneutic has similarities to liberation hermeneutics in that interpretation is done in the light of political, social and economic realities. However, it differs from liberation hermeneutics in that it has moved beyond the Exodus story and the fight against oppressors and tries instead to encourage the collaborative and inclusive task of reconstruction.[75] This reconstruction is holistic and includes spiritual and cultural renewal. Because of this, it integrates insights from inculturation theology. The texts that undergird this hermeneutic are the book of Deuteronomy guiding the reformation under king Josiah, the reconstruction of the land after the Exile under Nehemiah, and the Sermon on the Mount as a reinterpretation of the Old Testament law for the new people of God.

74. Van den Toren et al., "Biblical Hermeneutics."

75. Jesse N. K. Mugambi, "The Future of the Church and the Church of the Future," in *The Church of Africa: Towards a Theology of Reconstruction*, ed. All Africa Conference of Churches (Nairobi: All Africa Conference of Churches, 1991), 29–50.

4.3.8 Post-colonial Hermeneutics

Post-colonial hermeneutics "is a mode of reading inspired by postcolonial literary criticism that analyses how literary texts themselves are shaped by 'imperialism.'"[76] Texts are not neutral, but they reflect power struggles and the interests of the powerful. In this way, they support the imperialist agenda of the powerful and silence the voice of the "other."[77] At the same time, these subjugated voices need to be retrieved from the text. It has affinities with some expressions of liberation theology, such as Mosala and Mofokeng, "that see the Bible itself as a site of struggle between the interests of the oppressors and the voices of the oppressed."[78] This hermeneutic strives to highlight this struggle and to show how the voices of the oppressed are still present in subversive ways. Power differences and oppression are the dominant interpretative perspectives.

4.3.9 Mother Tongue Hermeneutics

Mother tongue hermeneutics uses indigenous language translations of the Bible as resources for interpretation. This rationale behind this method is that the mother tongue is the "heart language" of many Africans. It is the best medium for expressing their innermost feelings and thoughts and it also poses the least opportunity for misunderstanding the meaning of the biblical text. This method focuses on the world in front of the text and is a collaborative, communal task. It is an eclectic methodology that borrows from other methods including biblical studies, bible translation, linguistics, and anthropology.[79] It thus necessarily involves at least two kinds of dialogue: between the Christian and the African worldviews (intercultural), and between the translated texts and their originals (intertextual).

4.3.10 Inculturation and Intercultural Hermeneutics

There are several similarities between inculturation and intercultural hermeneutics. Both are Africentric, as opposed to Eurocentric; emphasize a two-way dialogue between the world of the biblical text and the world of traditional and contemporary African realities; include exegesis of the text as well as analysis of contextual African realities; focus on the religio-cultural

76. Van den Toren et al., "Biblical Hermeneutics," 26.

77. Van den Toren et al., "Biblical Hermeneutics," 26.

78. Van den Toren et al., "Biblical Hermeneutics," 26.

79. J. E. T. Kuwornu-Adjaottor, "Mother-Tongue Biblical Hermeneutics: A Current Trend in Biblical Studies in Ghana," *Journal of Emerging Trends in Educational Research and Policy Studies* 3 no. 4 (2012): 575–79.

dimensions of the text and the contemporary contexts; legitimize cultural diversity; are hermeneutics of trust rather than suspicion.

Inculturation hermeneutics is a contextual, interdisciplinary hermeneutic that acknowledges that there is no neutral or acultural exegesis and that explicitly makes the African context the subject of biblical interpretation. It therefore focuses on the world in front of the text. It was introduced by Justin Ukpong.[80] The goal is socio-cultural transformation, and its ethos is cultural diversity and identity in reading practices. Intercultural hermeneutics evolved from inculturation hermeneutics. The major development is that while inculturation hermeneutics focuses on the incarnation of the gospel in a culture as well as the evangelization of that culture, intercultural hermeneutics consolidates a constructive dialogue between the biblical and the African cultures.

4.4 Weaknesses and Strengths of African Approaches

As with all other hermeneutical approaches, African approaches have their strengths and weaknesses.

Weaknesses

1. Some of these approaches encourage syncretism.
2. Some of these approaches make the reader more important than the author or the text.
3. Some impose meaning on the text because of an overemphasis on what the reader needs to hear.
4. Some collapse the two horizons of meaning and significance by moving directly from text to application without actually engaging in interpretation.
5. Risk of a canon within a canon.

Strengths

While one must take note of the weaknesses, it is the strengths that provide a rationale for promoting African hermeneutics.

1. The biblical text finds a home in the African heart because it speaks to the contextual realities that believers face daily.

---

80. Justin S. Ukpong, "Rereading the Bible with African Eyes: Inculturation and Hermeneutics," *Journal of Theology for Southern Africa*, 91 (1995): 3–14.

2. Some approaches confront dichotomy and syncretism.
3. They acknowledge the multidimensionality/global character of the Christian faith.
4. They include ordinary readers.
5. They encourage transformation of society.
6. They promote understanding and interrogation of African contexts and awareness of our religious spaces.
7. They are holistic and give room for interdisciplinary approaches.
8. They help redefine African Christian identity.

5. Conclusion

This chapter has examined the question of the reliability of the Bible from two perspectives. The first included the classical questions within the discipline of apologetics such as the canonicity of the Bible, its transmission and translation, and its uniqueness among other sacred texts. It began with a brief Enlightenment and post-Enlightenment overview of approaches to the Bible. While sceptical readings are not common in Africa, it is important that Africans understand their root so as to avoid the pitfall of such approaches to interpretation. The second approach was from a hermeneutical perspective. The various African hermeneutical approaches to the Bible were intended to help the African ministry leader develop confidence to engage with the Bible for the transformation of individual lives and communities in Africa. This century has seen a radical shift in the growth of the church in the southern hemisphere. Reverse missions are increasing. Some of the biggest churches in Europe have been founded by Africans and they have begun to send missionaries back to Africa. This is just the tip of the iceberg. Without a doubt, the founders transplant their hermeneutics as well. Technology has also contributed to exposure of African hermeneutical approaches to a wider audience. African hermeneutics cannot be ignored either on a continental or a global level. It is a valuable tool in the task of apologetics.

Bibliography

Anderson, Allan H. "The Hermeneutical Processes of Pentecostal-Type African Initiated Churches in South Africa." *Missionalia* 24, no. 2 (1996): 171–85.

Arnold, Bill T., and Bryan E. Beyer. *Encountering the Old Testament: A Christian Survey.* 2nd edition. Grand Rapids: Baker Academic, 1999, 2008.

Barton, John. *The Nature of Biblical Criticism.* Louisville: Westminster John Knox Press, 2007.

Bediako, Kwame. "The Roots of African Theology." *International Bulletin of Missionary Research* 13, no. 2 (April 1989): 58–65.

Berkeley, George, and Colin Murray Turbayne. *A Treatise Concerning the Principles of Human Knowledge.* N.p.: Forgotten Books, (1710) 1957.

Blomberg, Craig L. *The Historical Reliability of the Gospels.* 2nd edition. Downers Grove: InterVarsity Press, 2007.

Bultmann, Rudolf K. *History of the Synoptic Tradition.* San Francisco: Harper San Francisco, 1976.

———. *The New Testament and Mythology and Other Basic Writings.* Minneapolis: Fortress Press, 1984.

Carson, D. A., and Douglas J. Moo. *An Introduction to the New Testament.* Grand Rapids: Zondervan, 2005.

Elwell, Walter A., and Robert W. Yarbrough *Encountering the New Testament: A Historical and Theological Survey.* 2nd edition. Grand Rapids: Baker Academic, 2005.

Erickson, Millard J. *Introducing Christian Doctrine.* 2nd edition. Grand Rapids: Baker Academic, 2001.

Fosdick, Harry Emerson. *The Living of These Days.* New York.: Harper Chapel Books: 1967.

———. "Shall the Fundamentalists Win? Defending Liberal Protestantism in the 1920's." *History Matters*, http://historymatters.gmu.edu/d/5070/.

Guicciardini, Niccolò. *Isaac Newton and Natural Philosophy.* London: Reaktion Books, 2018.

Gunkel, Hermann. *Genesis: Translated and Explained.* Translated by Mark E. Biddle 3rd edition. Macon: Mercer University Press, 1997.

Hastings, Rashdall. *The Idea of Atonement in Christian Theology.* London: Macmillan, 1919.

Hegel, Georg Wilhelm Friedrich. *The Science of Logic.* Translated by George Di Giovanni. Cambridge: Cambridge University Press, 2010.

Hume, David. *Enquiries Concerning Human Understanding and Concerning the Principles of Morals.* Reprinted from 1777 edition. 3rd edition. Edited by L. A. Selby-Bigge. Oxford: Clarendon Press, 2014.

Kant, Immanuel. *An Answer to the Question: 'What is Enlightenment?'* Translated by Hugh Barr Nisbet. London: Penguin Books, 2010.

Köstenberger, Andreas J., K., Scott Kellum, and Charles L. Quarles. *The Cradle, the Cross and the Crown: An Introduction to the New Testament.* Nashville: B&H Publishing, 2009.

Kuwornu-Adjaottor, J. E. T. "Mother-Tongue Biblical Hermeneutics: A Current Trend in Biblical Studies in Ghana." *Journal of Emerging Trends in Educational Research and Policy Studies* 3, no. 4 (2012): 575–79.

Locke, John. *The Reasonableness of Christianity, as Delivered in the Scriptures*. Edited by John C. Higgins-Biddle. Oxford: Clarendon Press, 1999.

Mburu, Elizabeth. *African Hermeneutics*. Carlisle: HippoBooks, 2019.

———. "The Importance of African Hermeneutics in African Theological Education." In *A Critical Engagement with Theological Education in Africa: A South African Perspective*, edited by Johannes Knoetze and Alfred Brunson, 85–102. Cape Town: AOSIS, 2021. https://doi.org/10.4102/aosis.2021.BK273.

McGrath, Alister E. *Historical Theology: An Introduction to the History of Christian Thought*. Oxford: Blackwell 1998.

Mugambi, Jesse N. K. "The Future of the Church and the Church of the Future." In *The Church of Africa: Towards a Theology of Reconstruction*, edited by All Africa Conference of Churches, 29–50. Nairobi: All Africa Conference of Churches, 1991.

Olson, Roger E. *The Story of Christian Theology: Twenty Centuries of Tradition and Reform*. Downers Grove: InterVarsity Press, 1999.

Onwu, N. "The Hermeneutical Model: The Dilemma of the African Theologian." *Africa Theological Journal* 14, no. 3 (1985): 145–60.

Thiselton, Anthony C. *The Two Horizons: New Testament Hermeneutics and Philosophical Description with Special Reference to Heidegger, Bultmann Gadamer and Wittgenstein*. Carlisle: Paternoster, 2005.

Tillich, Paul. *The Courage to Be*. New Haven: Yale University Press, 2008.

Tullock, John, and Mark McEntire. *The Old Testament Story*. London: Pearson Education, 2012.

Ukpong, Justin S. "Rereading the Bible with African Eyes: Inculturation and Hermeneutics." *Journal of Theology for Southern Africa* 91 (1995): 3–14.

Van den Toren, Benno, Elizabeth Mburu, and Samuel K. Bussey. "Biblical Hermeneutics." In *Bibliographical Encyclopaedia of African Theology*, 2021, https://african.theologyworldwide.com/encyclopaedia-bible-in-africa/biblical-hermeneutics.

West, Gerald O. "Locating 'Contextual Bible Study' within Biblical Liberation Hermeneutics and Intercultural Biblical Hermeneutics." *HTS Teologiese Studies / Theological Studies* 70, no. 1 (2014): 1–10.

———. "African Biblical Hermeneutics and Bible translation." In *Interacting with Scriptures in Africa*, edited by Jean-Claude Loba-Mkole and Ernst R. Wendland, 3–29. Nairobi: Acton Publishers, 2005.

———. "Indigenous Biblical Hermeneutics: Voicing Continuity and Distinctiveness." In *Postcolonial Perspectives in African Biblical Interpretations*, edited by Musa W. Dube, Andrew Mbuvi, and D. R. Mbuwayesango, 85–96. Atlanta: Society of Biblical Literature, 2012.

Witherington, Ben. *The New Testament Story*. Grand Rapids: Eerdmans, 2004.

2

An African Apologetic for the Resurrection

Robert Falconer, PhD

SATS Coordinator of MTh and PhD Programmes

Abstract

This chapter provides a biblical sketch of the doctrine of the resurrection, explores seven significant proofs for Jesus's resurrection, after which the author draws attention to contributions from African theologians. This chapter also engages with the doctrine of resurrection in African theology and then discusses resurrection hope for Africa in our present day.

Keywords: Apologetics, Resurrection

1. Introduction

Many people have seen Mel Gibson's movie, *The Passion of the Christ*, but few have watched the brilliant 2016 movie, *Risen*, an epic retelling of the story of the resurrection through the eyes of the non-believing Clavius (played by Joseph Fiennes), a Roman tribune, as he encounters the risen Christ Jesus played by the New Zealander, Cliff Curtis. The movie *The Case for Christ* came out the following year, which told the true story of Lee Strobel, who at the time was an atheist journalist and investigative reporter for the Chicago Tribune (nothing to do with the Roman Tribune). He set out to find evidence to disprove the resurrection of Jesus. Like the apostle Paul, and countless others, his life was changed when the evidence for the resurrection became irrefutable. Strobel is now a formidable Christian apologist and has defended the resurrection of Christ.

These films demonstrate how Jesus's resurrection is quite simply the apex of Christian hope and theology. The apostle Paul proclaimed in his first letter to the Corinthians that if Christ Jesus had not been raised, then their preaching was in vain and Christian faith was worthless (1 Cor 15:14). Paul continued, "And if Christ has not been raised, your faith is futile, and you are still in your sins. Then those also who have fallen asleep in Christ have perished. If in Christ we have hope in this life only, we are of all people most to be pitied" (1 Cor 15:17–19 ESV).

Yet, within a naturalistic worldview, the resurrection seems logically impossible and cannot in any way be proved by natural and scientific laws, but neither can such laws disprove such a miraculous event. Don't expect scientific explanations for any miracle because such miracles involve the direct intervention of God which transcends our natural laws and thus defy common sense. Therefore, just because certain events cannot be reasonably explained by science, does not mean they don't occur . . . they sometimes do.

Wolfhart Pannenberg, one of the most prominent and creative theologians of the twentieth century, used historical and philosophical arguments to defend the miracle of Jesus's bodily resurrection in his book, *Jesus – God and Man.*[1] Some decades later, the prolific New Testament Scholar N. T. Wright wrote his significant work *The Resurrection of the Son of God,*[2] which also argued for Jesus's resurrection. He did this by investigating ancient beliefs on life after death in the ancient Greco-Roman and Jewish worlds, the New Testament, and early Christian beliefs. His book has influenced my theological formation and framework quite profoundly. I have already mentioned Lee Strobel; his book *The Case for Easter: A Journalist Investigates Evidence for the Resurrection*[3] is also an important work that argues for the resurrection at a popular level. Another more recent work is Michael R. Licona's book *The Resurrection of Jesus,*[4] similar in some ways to the work of Pannenberg and Wright but still rather unique. Andrew Loke likewise argues for the resurrection of Christ. He takes a fascinating approach in his book *Investigating the Resurrection of*

1. Wolfhart Pannenberg, *Jesus, God and Man* (London: SCM, 1973).

2. N. T. Wright, *The Resurrection of the Son of God* (Minneapolis: Augsburg Fortress, 2003).

3. Lee Strobel, *The Case for Easter: A Journalist Investigates Evidence for the Resurrection* (Grand Rapids: Zondervan, 2009).

4. Michael R. Licona, *The Resurrection of Jesus: A New Historiographical Approach* (Downers Grove: IVP Academic, 2011).

Jesus Christ.[5] Loke considers an exhaustive list of hypotheses regarding the post-mortem appearances of Jesus. He tackles these and responds to each in detail. These hypotheses include combinations of hallucination with cognitive dissonance, memory distortion, and confirmation bias. More recent is another historical investigation by Gary Habermas,[6] titled *Risen Indeed.* These are some of the major works published in defence of the resurrection of Jesus Christ, no doubt there are many others. Lastly, and most importantly for this chapter, is the father of African theology, John Mbiti, and his important work, *New Testament Eschatology in an African Background.*[7]

I will begin this discussion by proving a biblical sketch of the resurrection. We will then explore seven significant proofs for Jesus's resurrection. Lastly, I will draw your attention to contributions on the resurrection from African theologians. After looking at resurrection in African theology, we will conclude with implications of the resurrection hope for Africa in our present day.

2. A Biblical Sketch of the Resurrection

The Old and New Testaments tell us of people who were raised from the dead, for example, the widow of Zarephath's son (1 Kgs 17:17–24), a Shunammite woman's son (2 Kgs 4:18–37) and an Israelite man (2 Kgs 13:20–21). In the New Testament we have the widow of Nain's son (Luke 7:11–17), Jairus's daughter (Luke 8:49–56), Lazarus (John 11:1–44), Tabitha, also called Dorcas (Acts 9:36–42) and Eutychus (Acts 20:7–12). But these are not the same as resurrection. Jesus's body was raised in glory at his resurrection, and so too will be the bodies of believers, that is, in glory and immortality. Those who were raised from the dead in Scripture were brought to life again, but they eventually died.[8] Nevertheless, the Old Testament does talk of a resurrection, but it is mostly an underdeveloped concept. The New Testament on the other hand develops its theology from Jesus Christ's resurrection and applies it to our future hope.

---

5. Andrew Loke, *Investigating the Resurrection of Jesus Christ: A New Transdisciplinary Approach* (Abingdon: Taylor and Francis, 2020).

6. Gary Habermas, *Risen Indeed: A Historical Investigation into the Resurrection of Jesus* (Bellingham: Lexham Press, 2021).

7. John S. Mbiti, *New Testament Eschatology in an African Background: A Study of the Encounter between New Testament Theology and African Traditional Concepts* (London: Oxford University Press, 1971).

8. Hans S. A. Engdahl, *African Church Fathers – Ancient and Modern: A Reading of Origen and John S. Mbiti* (Bellville, South Africa: UWC Press, 2020), 360.

Isaiah alludes to the resurrection of the saints when he wrote that the Lord of hosts "will swallow up death forever; and the Lord God will wipe away tears from all faces, and the reproach of his people he will take away from all the earth, for the Lord has spoken" (Isa 25:8 ESV). Again, in the next chapter, he proclaimed that "Your dead shall live; their bodies shall rise. You who dwell in the dust, awake and sing for joy! For your dew is a dew of light, and the earth will give birth to the dead" (Isa 26:19 ESV). Granted, there is some debate as to whether these passages are apocalyptic. Anyanwu points out that some scholars believe the prophecy to be pre-exilic and others argue that it is post-exilic.[9] It is hard to know with any degree of certainty whether these verses are metaphorical envisioning national political revival or the rebirth of the Jewish community. But be that as it may, a surface-level reading does seem to offer a hope for the bodily resurrection of the dead.[10]

Similarly, Ezekiel's vision of the valley of dry bones seems to promote the idea of national political revivalism, but it too has powerful imagery of the resurrection.[11] Ezekiel 37:7–10 reads,

> So I prophesied as I was commanded. And as I prophesied, there was a sound, and behold, a rattling, and the bones came together, bone to its bone. And I looked, and behold, there were sinews on them, and flesh had come upon them, and skin had covered them. But there was no breath in them. Then he said to me, "Prophecy to the breath; prophesy, son of man, and say to the breath, thus says the Lord God: Come from the four winds, O breath, and breathe on these slain, that they may live." So I prophesied as he commanded me, *and the breath came into them, and they lived and stood on their feet, an exceedingly great army.* (ESV; emphasis mine)

Perhaps Daniel 12:2–3 offers us the most explicit and developed resurrection theology of the Old Testament, "And many of those who sleep in the dust of the earth shall awake, some to everlasting life, and some to shame and everlasting contempt. And those who are wise shall shine like the brightness of the sky above; and those who turn many to righteousness, like the stars forever and ever" (ESV). As Anyanwu points out, Daniel seems to have articulated the general resurrection, a reward for the righteous, and "shame and

9. Matthew Maduabuchi Nsomma Anyanwu, *The Doctrine of Resurrection and the Challenge of Traditional Igbo (African) Eschatology* (Bamberg, Germany: University of Bambert, 2012), 123.

10. Anyanwu, *The Doctrine of Resurrection*, 125.

11. N. T. Wright, *Surprised by Hope: Rethinking Heaven, the Resurrection, and the Mission of the Church* (New York: HarperOne, 2008), 150.

everlasting contempt" for the wicked.[12] Hosea 6:1–3 also offers an expression of belief in resurrection, although this may reasonably be interpreted as "national restoration."[13]

This brings us to the New Testament in which the general resurrection is dependent on the bodily resurrection of our Lord Jesus Christ. The resurrection of Jesus was evidenced by his empty tomb and his appearances after his death and resurrection.[14] As one might expect, the theology of resurrection develops and matures in the New Testament because of Jesus having risen from the dead in glory (Mark 16:1–8; Matt 28; Luke 24; John 20). The most articulate teaching of the resurrection of Christ and the future general resurrection of the saints is found in 1 Corinthians 15 – although N. T. Wright believes that "the hope of the resurrection underlies" the entirety of Paul's letter to the Corinthian church.[15] Bako reminds us that the Old Testament predicted the resurrection at the end of the age, which was initiated in Jesus's resurrection, and is very much a part of the coming new creation. God will recreate our bodies through resurrection thus redeeming humanity for the new creation. This will happen at Jesus's second coming together with the consummation of the new creation which was inaugurated by his resurrection.[16] We read this in verse 21 when Paul wrote, "For as by a man came death, by a man has come also the resurrection of the dead" (ESV). In other words, Adam in the garden of Eden brought about death through his sin and disobedience, but Jesus Christ has conquered death and has overcome it by bringing life and resurrection from the dead![17] Engdahl said it well when he wrote,

> Men who are dead in sin do not need the picture of a dead Christ. They need one of the Christ who died-and-rose again. Only such a Saviour can inspire faith in this life and hope in the life to come. Only such a *Christus Victor* can uphold and sustain life in the resurrection mode of existence. This is the true portrait of Jesus Christ in the New Testament.[18]

---

12. Anyanwu, *The Doctrine of Resurrection*, 134.

13. Anyanwu, *The Doctrine of Resurrection*, 121.

14. Anyanwu, *The Doctrine of Resurrection*, 141.

15. Wright, *Surprised by Hope*, 155.

16. Ngarndeye Bako, "Eschatology in Folk Religion," University of South Africa (UNISA), 2009, 60.

17. Amevenku and Boaheng, *Introducing Eschatology*, 1:102; Venter, "Trends in Contemporary Christian Eschatological Reflection," 113.

18. Engdahl, *African Church Fathers – Ancient and Modern*, 360–61.

Anyanwu explains that the implications of Jesus's resurrection were profound. At Jesus's resurrection, the disciples lost hope and became timid as they struggled to grapple with their teacher's death. But witnessing the resurrected Christ for themselves changed everything for the disciples and the early Christian community. It transformed their faith evident also in their boldness and willingness to suffer for their newfound faith.[19] This resurrection as we will see continues to bring about hope for Africa, even today.

3. Arguments for the Resurrection

There has been continued debate about whether Jesus Christ truly rose from the dead.[20] However, with all the exhaustive and diverse scholarly research arguing for resurrection, it seems unreasonable to discount it as anything but true. The following are seven simple yet compelling pieces of evidence of the resurrection; there are many more sophisticated ones in the books already mentioned.

3.1 The Empty Tomb of Jesus

A major proof of Jesus's resurrection was that the stone that closed the tomb was rolled away, and the tomb was found empty. The tomb was sealed in two ways, it was sealed closed and sealed with the imperial stamp, as if to warn, "Don't touch this tomb, or else!" However, there has always been a "stolen-body hypothesis" that states that Jesus's disciples, his family, graverobbers, or even the Jewish leadership had his body removed.[21] This however seems very unlikely because, the next day after Jesus's crucifixion, the chief priests and the Pharisees came before Pilate stating that Jesus had said that he would rise after three days and feared that his disciples would come and steal away his body so they requested from Pilate that they would make the tomb secure. Pilate consented and had the tomb made as secure as he could and in addition set soldiers to guard it (Matt 27:63–66). With this in place, it's difficult to think anyone had access to Jesus's corpse.

---

19. Anyanwu, *The Doctrine of Resurrection*, 158.

20. See for example Gary R. Habermas, Anthony Flew and Terry L. Miethe, *Did Jesus Rise From the Dead? The Resurrection Debate* (Eugene: Wipf & Stock Publishers, 2003).

21. For detailed discussions on the "stolen body hypothesis" see Loke, *Investigating the Resurrection of Jesus Christ* §6.6 and §6.8; Josh and Sean McDowell, *Evidence for the Resurrection: What It Means for Your Relationship with God* (Grand Rapids: Baker Books, 2009), 222–27.

> Bewildered, some of the soldiers who guarded the tomb ran into the city and told the chief priests what had happened. The priests gave the soldiers a large sum of money and instructed them to lie and tell people that Jesus's disciples came during the night and stole his body while they were sleeping – never mind the struggle and commotion it would have taken to roll away the stone thus waking the soldiers! The soldiers took the money and did as they were told, and so this story was spread among the Jews and is still believed by some in our day. (Matt 28:11–15 ESV)

One might argue that the Bible and Jesus's disciples are biased, of course, they would record such a testimony, can we trust them? However, the next six pieces of evidence authenticate these testimonies and the truthfulness of Scripture.

3.2 The Women Eyewitnesses

Women were the first eyewitnesses of Jesus's resurrection. Any Jewish person in Jesus's time knew that if they wanted to provide a credible story, women were a poor choice to give public witness. The first-century Roman-Jewish historian, Flavius Josephus, knew this well when he wrote in his *Antiquities of the Jews*, "But let not the testimony of women be admitted, on account of the levity and boldness of their sex."[22] But as we have it, women gave the account of Jesus's resurrection to the apostles, namely, Mary Magdalene, Joanna, Salome, Mary the mother of James and Jose, and the other women (Mark 16:1–5; Luke 24:10). Presumably, Jesus's mother, Mary, also witnessed his resurrection. These unexpected eyewitnesses provide historical authenticity to the resurrection of Jesus Christ because surely if the disciples wanted to make their story believable, they would have given that function of first witnesses of the resurrection to men. Instead, the Gospel writers tell us the story of how it happened from their perspective, that several women saw the resurrected Christ first and proclaimed the good news to the disciples.

3.3 The Apostles' New-found Courage

Jesus's disciples were timid and afraid during Jesus's crucifixion. But the resurrection changed everything. They received newfound courage. Something

---

22. Josephus, *Antiquities*, Book 4, chap. 8, sec. 15.

remarkable happened in the lives of the disciples; these stories are told in the Acts of the Apostles recorded by Luke. This courage was evident in all the disciples, no doubt, but Acts highlights Peter and John specifically. Luke tells how at Pentecost, Peter stood there with the eleven apostles and "lifted up his voice to the crowds and addressed them: 'Men of Judea and all who dwell in Jerusalem, let this be known to you, and give ear to my words'" (Acts 2:14 ESV). Rulers of the people and elders also witnessed "the boldness of Peter and John, and perceived that they were uneducated, common men, they were astonished. And they recognized that they had been with Jesus" (Acts 4:5–13; esp. v. 13; ESV). Had Jesus not been resurrected and had the apostles not seen the resurrected Christ, it is doubtful whether any of them would have had this courage at all.

3.4 The Life of Jesus's Brother, James, Was Changed

The lives of many people were changed having seen the resurrected Jesus. It appears that Jesus's brother, James, was unbelieving and sceptical during Jesus's ministry (Mark 3:21, 31; 6:3–4; John 7:5). Yet, something profound happened when the resurrected Jesus appeared to James and changed his life (1 Cor 15:7). The New Testament suggests that James became a significant leader in the Jerusalem church (Acts 15:13; Gal 2:9). James was considered authoritative enough for his letter to "the twelve tribes in the dispersion" (James 1:1 ESV) to be included as Scripture. The resurrection changed James from a sceptic to a believer. He quickly became an influential leader of the early church.

3.5 Large Crowd of Eyewitnesses

I have mentioned some of whom Jesus appeared to after his resurrection, yet there were others,[23] for example, the two men with whom Jesus walked on the Emmaus Road. They did not recognize Jesus until they dined with him (Luke 24:13–35). The apostle Paul, who, by the way also saw the resurrected Jesus, wrote, "that he (Jesus) was buried, that he was raised on the third day in accordance with the Scriptures, and that he appeared to Cephas, then to the twelve. Then he appeared to *more than five hundred brothers at one time, most of whom are still alive*, though some have fallen asleep. Then he appeared to James, then to all the apostles" (1 Cor 15:4–7; emphasis mine). More than five hundred is a lot of people. Further, Paul makes a point of saying that most of

23. Loke, *Investigating the Resurrection of Jesus Christ*, ch. 1.

them are still alive so that his readers could go and ask them to confirm their testimony of the resurrection. If the resurrection were not true, it would have been best not to ask witnesses to confirm the event.

3.6 Paul's Conversion

Paul was confident of the resurrection account and the witness testimonies because he had seen the risen Christ himself. More than that, Paul's life was utterly changed. He is first mentioned in Acts as a ruthless persecutor of the early Christians (Acts 9:1–2; 1 Cor 15:9; Phil 3:5–6). On his way to Damascus Paul had a powerful encounter with the resurrected Christ. He fell to the ground and a light from heaven shone around Paul. A voice interrogated him, "why are you persecuting me?" to which he responded, "Who are you, Lord?" He proclaimed that he is Jesus, the one whom Paul was persecuting. Arise he told Paul, go into the city and you will be told what to do (Acts 9:3–19; 1 Cor 15:8). This was the start of Paul's conversion to Christianity, and as a result, he became a faithful servant of Christ and his church. He became an apostle writing numerous New Testament letters. For Paul to have changed from being a zealous persecutor of the church to an apostle of Jesus Christ, it seems reasonable to conclude that Paul truly had an encounter with the resurrected Christ.

3.7 The Apostles Died for Jesus

Lastly, history and Christian tradition say that Paul, along with the apostles, were all martyred for their faith, except for the apostle John who was thought to be tortured but died a natural death. The apostles were so convinced by Jesus's teachings and having witnessed his resurrection that they were willing to suffer and give up their lives for what they believed.[24] The obvious question is whether anyone would willingly suffer and die for something they had fabricated. It is very unlikely. Or as Andrew Loke says, "If the disciples lied about Jesus's resurrection, it is hard to believe that during times of severe persecution they would have evidenced genuine conviction that Jesus was resurrected in the presence of other Christians and of their persecutors, without letting out the hoax."[25]

---

24. Loke, *Investigating the Resurrection of Jesus Christ*, ch. 3.
25. Loke, *Investigating the Resurrection of Jesus Christ*, ch. 3.

Theories that seek to discount the resurrection such as (1) the wrong tomb theory, (2) the resuscitation (swoon) theory, (3) the stolen body theory, (4) the hallucination theory, (5) the impersonation theory, don't seem to add up logically considering the above that prove Jesus's resurrection.[26] The next discussion will move beyond arguments for Jesus's resurrection to exploring general resurrection in African Christian theology.

4. Resurrection in African Theology

The Kenyan Anglican priest and theologian, James Henry Owino Kombo, explains that a resurrected body in Christian theology has a physical nature, and is immortal and imperishable (1 Cor 15:42–43).[27] Amevenku and Boaheng, however, highlight the difference between traditional African belief and Christian belief. Traditional Africans, they say, hold that the immortality of the soul or the spirit means that it moves from one state of being to another, as an ancestor, and continues its life into the "abode of spirits." Christianity on the other hand understands that the soul or the spirit departs from the body at death and is maintained by God until the day of physical resurrection.[28] African Traditional Religion does not explicitly articulate a bodily resurrection. Some African cultures, nevertheless, understand resurrection as a kind of rebirth or reincarnation.[29] Resurrection in Christianity is very different from reincarnation or resuscitation. Resurrection is understood to be an eschatological event imbuing the body with "transphysical properties."[30]

Much of Christian theology was developed in the most northern parts of Africa in Christianity's infancy. These ancient African Christians had something important to say about the resurrection. Tertullian of Carthage in the Roman province of Africa (AD 155–220) wrote in his work *On the Resurrection of the Flesh* that as Christ rose after death, so too we will rise.

---

26. For more discussion on these theories see William Lane Craig, *The Son Rises: The Historical Evidence for the Resurrection for the Resurrection of Jesus* (Eugene: Wipf & Stock, 1981); McDowell and McDowell, *Evidence for the Resurrection*; Loke, *Investigating the Resurrection of Jesus Christ*.

27. James Henry Owino Kombo, "The Past, the Present, and the Future of African Christianity: An Eschatological Vision for African Christianity," in *All Things New: Eschatology in the Majority World*, edited by Gene L. Green, Stephen T. Pardue and K. K. Yeo. Majority World Theology Series (Carlisle: Langham Global Library, 2019), ch. 2.

28. Amevenku and Boaheng, *Introducing Eschatology*, 1:10.

29. Chukwuedo, "A Comparative Study of the Resurrection of the Body in Christianity and African Traditional Religion," 79–81.

30. An expression used by N. T. Wright, *The Resurrection of the Son of God*, 477.

Even as Jesus has manifested in our bodies an abundance of holiness, patience, righteousness and wisdom, so too his life will be made manifest in our mortal bodies. So as Jesus has already been resurrected from the dead, so too will we rise with him and be like him in the flesh, maintaining our own identity.[31] In his *Apology* Tertullian also taught that at the end, the faithful will be resurrected to everlasting life and the wicked will rise "to the doom of fire."[32] Writing on Tertullian's resurrection theology, N. T. Wright highlights how he "brought together 'an extravagantly materialistic notion of the resurrection body' and an equivalent emphasis, too, on 'radical change.'"[33]

Origen of Alexandria (AD 184–253) wrote on the resurrection against the Gnostics and Celsus and seems to argue for an entirely new body, rather than one that is raised from the grave, as was taught by most church fathers.[34] Origen picked up on the apostle Paul's concept of a "spiritual body"[35] and develops the idea of the resurrection body being a spiritual one that is suited for perfected souls and all of creation freed from corruption. These bodies, he envisions are heavenly, and great in splendor and brightness.[36] N. T. Wright explains that while Origen speaks of the resurrection body as being a real body, he sees this as both a continuation and discontinuation of the individual's previous body.[37] Like Origen, St. Cyprian of Carthage (AD 210–258) also spoke of bodily resurrection as "bright and eternal honour." He wrote that the Lord would transform our bodies into the likeness and brightness of Jesus's body.[38] St. Augustine (AD 354–430) too affirmed the resurrection and said that educated and uneducated Christians alike believed that the body of Jesus Christ was resurrected in the flesh and that this body ascended into the heavenly places.[39]

31. Tertullian, *On the Resurrection of the Flesh*, The Complete Ante-Nicene & Nicene and Post-Nicene Church Fathers Collection ANF03 (Grand Rapids: Eerdmans, 2014), 44; Kindle edition, Loc. 59530–59537, 63; Loc. 60073.

32. Tertullian, *Apology*, 18; Loc. 43756.

33. Wright, *The Resurrection of the Son of God*, 513.

34. Chukwuedo, "A Comparative Study of the Resurrection of the Body in Christianity and African Traditional Religion," 71.

35. See 1 Cor 15:44.

36. Origen, *On First Principles* (Notre Dame: Ave Maria Press, 2013), 325–26; Bk 3, ch. 6, Sec. 4; Wright, *The Resurrection of the Son of God*, 520.

37. Wright, *The Resurrection of the Son of God*, 527.

38. Cyprian, *The Complete Works of Saint Cyprian of Carthage*, edited by Phillip Campbell (Merchantville: Evolution Publishing, 2013), 10:525; Letter 76.2.

39. Augustine, *The City of God*, Translated by Marcus Dods (Peabody: Hendrickson Publishers, 2009), 735; Book 22, Sec. 5.

Amevenku and Boaheng explain that the belief in bodily resurrection in early Christianity was grounded upon the resurrection of Jesus Christ. They see his resurrection as the "prototype" and evidence that Christians would one day be resurrected too. This collective resurrection was expected upon the glorious second coming of Christ, often called the Parousia.[40]

As I mentioned earlier, while traditional Africans may expect reincarnation, or ancestorhood, to join at some point the "abode of spirits" where the spirits eventually lose their identity and personhood, they don't have any meaningful belief in a future collective bodily resurrection.[41] Matthew Ojo explains that "Africans generally conceive the world and life as cyclic – being born, living, dying, and being re-born" and so Christian eschatology is largely foreign to a traditional African worldview. At times this has created tension between an African cyclic cosmology and biblical eschatology for some Africans who become Christian.[42]

Elias Kifon Bongmba describes how the Africa Inland Mission (AIM) imported a futuristic eschatology and employed local terms to emphasize a "personal, visible and premillennial return of the Lord Jesus Christ; the literal resurrection of the body; the eternal blessedness of the saved, and the eternal punishment of the lost."[43] This kind of "rigid eschatological orientation," Bongmba explains, was promoted by AIM's hymns and curriculum for the catechumen.[44] The futurist approach was criticized by John Mbiti because he felt it was an escapist approach.[45] Thankfully, many African theologians like Matthew Michael affirm "the resurrection of the believers in Christ is a culmination of the divine program for the world."[46] Similarly, Bongmba argues that,

40. Amevenku and Boaheng, *Introducing Eschatology*, 1:44.

41. Amevenku and Boaheng, 1:11, 14; Bako, "Eschatology in Folk Religion," 89; Chukwuedo, "A Comparative Study of the Resurrection of the Body in Christianity and African Traditional Religion," 79–81; Matthew Michael, *Christian Theology and African Traditions* (Eugene: Resource Publications, 2013), 392, 394.

42. Matthew A. Ojo, "Eschatology and the African Society: The Critical Point of Disjunction," *Ogbomoso Journal of Theology*, 11 (2006): 93–100, 97–98.

43. Elias Kifon Bongmba, "Eschatology in Africa: Anticipation and Critical Engagement," in *The Routledge Handbook of African Theology*, edited by Elias Kifon Bongmba (New York: Routledge, 2020), 249.

44. Elias Kifon Bongmba, "Eschatology in Africa," 249.

45. Elias Kifon Bongmba, "Eschatology in Africa: Anticipation and Critical Engagement," in *The Routledge Handbook of African Theology*, edited by Elias Kifon Bongmba (New York: Routledge, 2020), 503–20.

46. Michael, *Christian Theology and African Traditions*, 401.

> It is important for the ecclesial community to move beyond the speculative approach to eschatology because those approaches tend to miss the eschatological orientation, which in my view calls for a broad and transformative social praxis and ecological responsibility. From that perspective, regardless of the apocalyptic images of the biblical texts, eschatology describes the orientation of the cosmos toward a telos, which we cannot map out with specificity. More importantly . . . the doctrine of the last things ought to serve as an invitation for the ecclesial community to renew its discourse and practice to befit persons who anticipate renewal and regeneration of the created order.[47]

No doubt resurrection is a significant part of eschatology, even in African Christian eschatology. John D. K. Ekem wrote a chapter where he examined Revelation 21:1–4, a passage which he says has a variety of interpretations among Ghanaian Christians. He argued that the eschatological issues emerging from this biblical passage have "a strong bearing on current African socio-political, economic, and religious realities, including ecological conservation." This is contrary to a "pie-in-the-sky" understanding of salvation and eschatology, he says, which has traditionally ignored the current concerns of this world. Ekem explains that the author of Revelation draws our "attention to a radical renewal of creation by a sovereign God who is not limited by time and space and whose rescue package embraces the entire ecology, including human beings."[48]

Likewise, Amevenku and Boaheng pick up on the famous German theologian Jürgen Moltmann's[49] theology of resurrection and eschatology, and argue for one that looks and moves forward and so revolutionizes and transforms the present. They proclaim that eschatology is more than Christian doctrine, it "is characteristic of all Christian proclamation, and of every Christian existence and of the whole church."[50] For them and Moltmann, eschatology affects and directs praxis. Creation ultimately "finds its consummation in the future of God's kingdom."[51]

47. Bongmba, "Eschatology in Africa," 503.

48. John D. K. Ekem, "Revelation 21:1–4 from an African Perspective," In *All Things New: Eschatology in the Majority World*, edited by Gene L. Green, Stephen T. Pardue and K. K. Yeo (Carlisle: Langham Global Library, 2019), 66.

49. Jürgen Moltmann, *Theology of Hope: On the Ground and the Implications of a Christian Eschatology* (Minneapolis: Fortress Press, 1993).

50. Amevenku and Boaheng, *Introducing Eschatology*, 1:66.

51. Amevenku and Boaheng, 1:69; see also Moltmann, *Theology of Hope*, 172.

5. Resurrection Hope for Africa Today

Jürgen Moltmann says that any Christian faith that fails to proclaim the resurrection of Jesus and resurrection faith is not Christianity at all.[52] As unimaginable as it is at present, Jesus's glorious, resurrected body is the model for our own resurrected bodies one day, says N. T. Wright.[53] As we will discover, resurrection offers tremendous hope for Africans and the continent of Africa. Resurrection is not some distant doctrine, but it has relevance for us even today.

Bako highlights the evidence of Jesus's bodily resurrection, as we have already seen earlier in this chapter, but it deserves repeating and summarization from an African theologian. (1) The recorded accounts in the Gospels of the resurrection appearances and the many named eyewitnesses. There are seventeen accounts of Jesus's resurrection appearances recorded in the New Testament. (2) The sealed stone that closed off the tomb where Jesus was laid to rest was rolled away. And most importantly, the tomb was empty. (3) The lives of Jesus's disciples were dramatically changed after they had encountered the resurrected Christ. They changed from being timid to being bold. (4) Jesus's resurrection is the very foundation of the church and Christianity. Without it, our faith is futile, as Paul announced in 1 Corinthians 15:17. The very day on which we worship is a testament to the resurrection. There is therefore no lack of evidence of the resurrection for the modern African.[54]

Despite the overwhelming evidence of the resurrection, Kombo explains that African eschatology exists within an African worldview, namely cultural traditions as we see in dying, death, ancestorhood, spirits, and the experience of time and seasons; not to mention Africa's long struggle with HIV-AIDS, military conflicts, and genocide. Although African Christian theology needs to promote an orthodox understanding of the resurrection and eschatology, it also needs "to bring unique African questions and responses to the global theological conversation," says Kombo.[55]

Oyetade says it beautifully when he reminds us that in the resurrection life that is to come, sickness, death and the evils of our world will be swallowed up. Resurrection is of the body to be sure, but it includes "the restoration of communion between God and humanity that had been broken by sin."[56]

---

52. Moltmann, *Theology of Hope*, 166.
53. Wright, *Surprised by Hope*, 149.
54. Bako, "Eschatology in Folk Religion," 111.
55. Kombo, "The Past, the Present, and the Future of African Christianity: An Eschatological Vision for African Christianity," 34.
56. M. O. Oyetade, "Eschatological Salvation in Hebrews 1:5–2:5," *Ilorin Journal of Religious Studies* 3 no. 1 (2013): 69–82, 73.

Similarly, Chammah Kaunda and Mutale Kaunda understand the narrative of Jesus's resurrection as the greatest source of life for our world. For them, Jesus embodies "relational eschatology," a reality that finds expression in the present. In other words, it promotes relationships that will ultimately "be fully realized in future relational harmony." They explain that resurrection is symbolic "resistance against anti-life forces," like social, political, economic, ecological injustices, and so on.[57]

Elias Kifon Bongmba also sees the resurrection as initiating an "eschatological community," one that is open to others without discrimination and inverts "relationships and power that is deployed for unconditional service and love." This no doubt demonstrates the reign of God in the new creation yet to be consummated. But even now, we can begin to express some of this future reality. In part, this is what a praxis for an eschatology of resurrection might look like in Africa today.[58]

The concept of Jesus's resurrection and our future bodily resurrection, as important as it is, also challenges the Christian community to address "problems caused by deforestation, desertification, and the erosion of soil and water resources through human activities that have not included a sustainable focus to maintain the fragile ecosystem," says Bongmba. If God is going to restore our bodies and environments through the resurrection of Christ, surely those are important to him and so it is our responsibility to actively seek the restoration of the balance to the ecosystem and "all life forms because all life is sacred and the ecosystem itself is filled with the presence of God."[59] This kind of engagement is one of several ways in which African Christianity, and indeed global Christianity can develop and promote an eschatological praxis ground in the resurrection.

The resurrection has implications in many parts of African life. Yes, we have the future hope that we too will enjoy bodily resurrected life as in Jesus's resurrection, but it also calls African Christians to participate together in the eschatological community, a community that actively seeks restoration, reconciliation, and harmony in the ecclesiastical, social, cultural, political, economic and ecological realms.

57. Kaunda and Kaunda, "In Search of Decolonial Eschatology," 480.

58. Bongmba, "Eschatology in Africa," 511.

59. Bongmba, "Eschatology in Africa," 514.

6. Conclusion

This chapter began by highlighting recent movies about Jesus's resurrection as well as significant scholarly contributions. Although apologetics for the truth and reality of the resurrection were offered, the discussions sought to push beyond that and show how the resurrection is significant not only for African Christianity but for African hope.

A biblical sketch of the resurrection demonstrated that the Old Testament has an underdeveloped concept of a general resurrection. The New Testament, however, takes Jesus's resurrection as the catalyst, or to put it biblically, "the firstfruits" (1 Cor 15:20–23) of our hope of a future resurrection. Resurrection theology undergoes considerable development in the New Testament. Apologetic arguments for Jesus's resurrection also offer a biblical focus. Without exploring some of the more sophisticated apologetics for the resurrection, the following are significant evidence: (1) the empty tomb of Jesus, (2) the women eyewitnesses, (3) the apostle's new-found courage, (4) the life of Jesus's brother, James, was changed, (5) the large crowd of eyewitnesses, (6) Paul's conversion, and (7) the apostles died for Jesus. These give very strong evidence for the truth of Jesus's resurrection. When we explored the resurrection in African theology, we discovered that traditional African belief provides important background. This offers a powerful opportunity to highlight the differences between the Christian expectation of a physical resurrection and the somewhat ethereal expectation in the African worldview. African Christian theologians, however, promote an eschatology and theology of the resurrection that revolutionizes and transforms the present. This became even more evident in our discussion on resurrection hope for Africa where sickness, death, and the evils of the world are swallowed up, and where communities ultimately come into harmony through restoration and reconciliation, and the social, cultural, political, economic, and ecological orders flourish.

This chapter explored an African apologetic for the resurrection. You and I are called to be a part of this diverse and dynamic community of the resurrection. One simply needs to ask oneself what kind of hope we have for Africa if there is no resurrection?! May we participate in Africa, and in the world as agents of that glorious hope by proclaiming and demonstrating the power of the risen Christ.

Bibliography

Amevenku, Frederick Mawusi, and Isaac Boaheng. *Introducing Eschatology in the African Context*. Volume 1. Accra: Noyam, 2021.

Anyanwu, Matthew Maduabuchi Nsomma. *The Doctrine of Resurrection and the Challenge of Traditional Igbo (African) Eschatology*. Bamberg: University of Bambert, 2012.

Augustine. *The City of God*. Translated by Marcus Dods. Peabody: Hendrickson Publishers, 2009.

Bako, Ngarndeye. "Eschatology in Folk Religion." University of South Africa (UNISA), 2009.

Bongmba, Elias Kifon. "Eschatology in Africa: Anticipation and Critical Engagement." In *The Routledge Handbook of African Theology*, edited by Elias Kifon Bongmba, 503–20. New York: Routledge, 2020.

Chukwuedo, Mercy Uwaezuoke. "A Comparative Study of the Resurrection of the Body in Christianity and African Traditional Religion." *Journal of Religion and Human Relations* 11, no. 1 (2019): 70–82.

Craig, William Lane. *The Son Rises: The Historical Evidence for the Resurrection of Jesus*. Eugene: Wipf & Stock Publishers, 1981.

Cyprian. *The Complete Works of Saint Cyprian of Carthage*. Edited by Phillip Campbell. Volume 10. Christian Roman Empire Series. Merchantville: Evolution Publishing, 2013.

Ekem, John D. K. "Revelation 21:1–4 from an African Perspective." In *All Things New: Eschatology in the Majority World*, edited by Gene L. Green, Stephen T. Pardue, and K. K. Yeo, 51–59. Majority World Theology Series. Carlisle: Langham Global Library, 2019.

Engdahl, Hans S. A. *African Church Fathers – Ancient and Modern: A Reading of Origen and John S. Mbiti*. Bellville: UWC Press, 2020.

Habermas, Gary. *Risen Indeed: A Historical Investigation into the Resurrection of Jesus*. Bellingham: Lexham Press, 2021.

Habermas, Gary R., Anthony Flew, and Terry L. Miethe. *Did Jesus Rise from the Dead? The Resurrection Debate*. Eugene: Wipf & Stock, 2003.

Josephus, Flavius. "Antiquities of the Jews." Translated by William Whiston. John E. Beardsley, 1895. Perseus Digital Library. http://www.perseus.tufts.edu/hopper/text?doc=Perseus%3Atext%3A1999.01.0146%3Abook%3D4%3Awhiston+chapter%3D8%3Awhiston+section%3D15.

Kaunda, Chammah J., and Mutale M. Kaunda. "In Search of Decolonial Eschatology: Engaging Christian Eschatology with Bemba Futurism." *Theology Today* 75, no. 4 (2019): 469–81.

Kombo, James Henry Owino. "The Past, the Present, and the Future of African Christianity: An Eschatological Vision for African Christianity." In *All Things New: Eschatology in the Majority World*, edited by Gene L. Green, Stephen T. Pardue, and K. K. Yeo, 33–50. Majority World Theology Series. Carlisle: Langham Global Library, 2019.

Licona, Michael R. *The Resurrection of Jesus: A New Historiographical Approach*. Downers Grove: IVP Academic, 2011.

Loke, Andrew. *Investigating the Resurrection of Jesus Christ: A New Transdisciplinary Approach*. Routlege New Critical Thinking in Religion, Theology and Biblical Studies. Abingdon: Taylor & Francis, 2020.

Mbiti, John S. *New Testament Eschatology in an African Background: A Study of the Encounter between New Testament Theology and African Traditional Concepts*. Oxford: Oxford University Press, 1971.

McDowell, Josh, and Sean McDowell. *Evidence for the Resurrection: What It Means for Your Relationship with God*. Grand Rapids: Baker Books, 2009.

Michael, Matthew. *Christian Theology and African Traditions*. Eugene: Resource Publications, 2013.

Moltmann, Jürgen. *Theology of Hope: On the Ground and the Implications of a Christian Eschatology*. Minneapolis: Fortress Press, 1993.

Ojo, Matthew A. "Eschatology and the African Society: The Critical Point of Disjunction." *Ogbomoso Journal of Theology* 11 (2006): 93–100.

Origen. *On First Principles*. Notre Dame: Ave Maria Press, 2013.

Oyetade, M. O. "Eschatological Salvation in Hebrews 1:5–2:5." *Ilorin Journal of Religious Studies* 3, no. 1 (2013): 69–82.

Pannenberg, Wolfhart. *Jesus, God, and Man*. London: SCM, 1973.

Strobel, Lee. *The Case for Easter: A Journalist Investigates Evidence for the Resurrection*. Grand Rapids: Zondervan, 2009.

Tertullian. *Apology*. The Complete Ante-Nicene & Nicene and Post-Nicene Church Fathers Collection ANF03. Grand Rapids: Eerdmans, 2014.

———. *On the Resurrection of the Flesh*. The Complete Ante-Nicene & Nicene and Post-Nicene Church Fathers Collection ANF03. Grand Rapids: Eerdmans, 2014.

Venter, Rian. "Trends in Contemporary Christian Eschatological Reflection." *Missionalia* 43, no. 1 (2015): 105–23.

Wright, N. T. *Surprised by Hope: Rethinking Heaven, the Resurrection, and the Mission of the Church*. New York: HarperOne, 2008.

———. *The Resurrection of the Son of God*. Christian Origins and the Question of God. Minneapolis: Augsburg Fortress, 2003.

3

Apologetics in the New Testament and Church History

Kevin Muriithi Ndereba, PhD

Lecturer at St. Paul's University, Kenya and Research Fellow, Department of Practical Theology and Missiology, Stellenbosch University, South Africa

Abstract

Although apologetics has found contemporary retrieval, it is a discipline and Christian calling that is grounded in the Scriptures and the church's history. The growth of Christianity is seen in its engagement with other philosophical and cultural constructs. Thus, apologetics developed as a tool of making a case for the Christian faith or defending it against ideological attacks from sceptics. The Bible in both the Old and New Testaments contains imperatives for apologetics as a valid ministry of the Christian community. As the early church moved into the apostolic, medieval, reformation and post-reformation eras, key people and movements have shaped the thinking and practice of apologetics in the church. This chapter will trace the apologetic engagement of the global church as it has faced different cultural, philosophical, and theological issues in its history, and explore the implications for the African church today.

Keywords: History of Apologetics, New Testament Apologetics, Post-New Testament Apologetics

1. Apologetics in the Gospels

The Gospels are the genre of literature that contain the life, ministry, death and resurrection of Jesus Christ. Their writings centre on the person and work of Jesus Christ in a narrative form. While each Gospel author approaches the story of Jesus from a different perspective – with Matthew writing for a Jewish audience, John writing with an evangelistic bent, and Luke writing apologetically – each of these stories is like a different facet of a diamond, with each side illuminating the others.[1] The thrust of the Gospels is therefore to paint a broad picture of Jesus Christ. While the New Testament history and epistles take the task of the exposition of the person and work of Jesus forward, even defending its significance for the Christian life, the Gospels set a precedent for what the apologetic task involves. Though subtle, the primary way the Gospels achieve this is in the interaction of Jesus with various groups. In his engagement and *apologia*, Jesus uses various methods to respond to some of the questions asked of him:

1. In a number of places, Jesus uses the Old Testament Scriptures to interpret particular claims of his audiences: for example, Luke 20:37–38 on the I AM self-definition of God, referring back to Exodus 3:6.
2. He sometimes uses silence, as a way of answering questions: for example, with Pilate in Matthew 27:11–14, Mark 15:2–5, Luke 23:2–3, and John 18:28–38.
3. Other times, he asks questions that seek to clarify assumptions or to reveal hidden motives: for example, in responding to the Pharisees' question about imperial tax in Mark 12:16.

The point is that the Gospels present the message of the gospel while the other New Testament writings expound on it. Particularly, it is the book of Acts that lays the foundation for apologetics as a critical ministry in the church's mission of taking the whole gospel to the whole world.

1. There are many critical and scholarly opinions on the sources of the Gospel writers and the compilations of their narratives. Chapter 1 explores some of these biblical issues. For further engagement, see Peter J. Williams, *Can We Trust the Gospels?* (Wheaton: Crossway, 2018).

2. Apologetics in Luke-Acts

In no other place is apologetics explicated as a handmaid to the evangelistic witness and mission of the church as in Luke-Acts.[2] Acts, as the historical literature of the New Testament, sets the tone for the apologetic engagement of the earliest Christian communities. In his preface to his two books, Luke intends to offer an *apologia* for Theophilus (Luke 1:1–3; Acts 1:1) and provides a prototype for the place of apologetics in the Christian life. Loveday Alexander, considering the different roles and ways in which apologetics functions in Luke-Acts, offers various typologies of apologetics in light of the different audiences in the books:[3]

Type	Audience	Purpose of Apologetic	Examples
Internal apologetics (or polemics)	Christian community	To deal with divisive issues within diverse Christian communities for example circumcision, Gnosticism[4] etc. (e.g. Acts 11:1–4)	Acts 11:1–4
External apologetics	Judaism	Reasoning with Judaizers to show Christ as the fulfilment of the Old Testament types and shadows.	Acts 6, 7, 15 Acts 17:2–4 1 Thessalonians
Evangelistic apologetics	Gentiles	Apostolic writing or ministry that engages pagan, Greek or other philosophical thinking with the claims of the Christian worldview[5]	Acts 14:11–18 Acts 17:16–34
Public or political apologetics	Political class / authorities	Christian engagement with the political powers to prove the innocence, orderliness, truthfulness or beauty of the gospel message	Acts 16

Figure 1: Author's summary of different types of apologetics from Alexander (1999)

2. The two books written by Luke are usually taken to be a unit Luke-Acts. While the book of Luke is primarily a narrative Gospel, the book of Acts is a historical narrative.

3. Loveday Alexander, "The Acts of the Apostles as an Apologetic Text," in *Apologetics in the Roman Empire: Pagans, Jews and Christians*, ed. Mark Edwards, Martin Goodman and Simon Price (Oxford: Oxford University Press, 1999), 15–44, 16.

4. Scholars have varying perspectives on when Gnosticism began, but many would agree that it is at least possible to see the seeds of Gnosticism in the various false teachings that the NT opposes. See for instance Mark Allan Powell, *Introducing the New Testament: A Historical, Literary, and Theological Survey* (Grand Rapids: Baker Books, 2018) and Pheme Perkins, *Gnosticism and the New Testament* (Minneapolis: Fortress Press, 1993), 32.

5. Loveday Alexander, "The Acts of the Apostles as an Apologetic Text," 17.

Thus, apologetics arises as a central tool in the spread of the Christian mission. In early Christian communities, it was used in a variety of ways depending on the audiences involved. In its internal function, apologetics takes the stance of polemics where it seeks to clarify doctrinal issues within Christian communities. In its external function, it engages with competing religious worldviews including Abrahamic faiths. More publicly, in its evangelistic function, it is developed for the purpose of engaging non-Christian thought. Finally, as a public discourse, apologetics is geared towards the political powers or authorities, for the purpose of commending the truth, beauty and ethical integrity of the Christian life.

3. Apologetics in the wider New Testament corpus

In the broader New Testament corpus, the word *apologia* is used in a variety of ways:

1. Defence
    1. before political authorities: for example Acts 25:16 – Paul answering Agrippa.
    2. against internal "church" attacks, that is, *polemics*: for example 1 Corinthians 9:3, 2 Corinthians 12:19 Paul and the super-apostles.
    3. of the gospel: for example Philippians 1:7, 1 Peter 3:15.
    4. against attacks towards the gospel: for example 2 Timothy 4:16 – Paul against Alexander the coppersmith, who did not stand by him when he was declaring the gospel.
2. Contending
    5. In Jude 1:3, the author writes and says that though he wanted to write about salvation, he saw a need to remind them to contend for the faith. Contend, ἐπαγωνίζομαι [*epagōnizomai*], refers to the positive offence and explanation of the gospel.

4. Post-New Testament Apologetics

4.1 Apologetics in the Early Church Period: AD 0–500

Post-New Testament apologetics is based on the pattern of New Testament apologetics. The task of this section is to explore how apologetics developed in the context of the early church. It covers the patristic period, just before the medieval age, which is to be covered in later sections. The earliest known work of apologetics in the post-New Testament era is Josephus' apology *Against Apion.* It consists of Jewish sentiments against Roman dominion in order to rebuild the Jerusalem temple. What was Josephus' contribution? It was to set the standard for the church apologists as they engaged with the cultural and philosophical backgrounds from which they came from and in which they existed.[6]

A similar trajectory can be traced in the apologetic engagement of the Christian communities beyond the first century. In the second century, Justin the Martyr (AD 100–165) wrote three works of apologetics. Justin Martyr wrote in the mid-second century, and Rajak says that "Justin's writings mark a major step forward in the history of Christian Apologetic literature."[7] A convert to Christianity and martyred in Rome, his three works, *First Apology*, *Second Apology*, and *Trypho* were written to respond to the political, cultural and religious forces that were in opposition to the faith of his contemporaries.

In his work *First Apology*, Justin ostensibly defends the Christian teachings and life in view of the emperors and the senate. In *Trypho*, Justyn writes a defence against Judaism, exemplifying how an external apologetic methodology can function as a sustained and intense critique.[8] He follows the apostle John's apologetic in the sense that he was equally exclusionary and equally damning. The characteristic feature of second-century apologists is a response to the ancestral customs and literary canons of their time.[9] Justin and his contemporaries reveal the tension of pursuing the new life in Christ in the context of the Greco-Roman culture that had nurtured them. Justin the Martyr was offering a philosophy of Christian life to those who wanted to pursue a philosophical life from Judaism.[10]

The Epistle to Diognetus (author unknown) is often placed in the second century but the form of the manuscript known today dates from the thirteenth or fourteenth centuries copied late in the sixteenth century.

> Since I see you, most excellent Diognetus, exceedingly desirous to learn the mode of worshipping God prevalent among the

6. Martin Goodman, "Josephus Treatise Against Apion," in Edwards, Goodman and Price, *Apologetics in the Roman Empire*, 58.

7. Tessa Rajak, "Talking at Trypho: Christian Apologetic as Anti-Judaism in Justin's Dialogue with Trypho the Jew," in Edwards, Goodman and Price, *Apologetics in the Roman Empire*, 60.

8. Rajak, "Talking at Trypho," 61.

9. Frances Young, "Greek Apologists in the 2nd Century," Edwards, Goodman and Price, *Apologetics in the Roman Empire*, 92.

10. Frances Young, "Greek Apologists in the 2nd Century," 84.

> Christians, and inquiring very carefully and earnestly concerning them, what God they trust in, and what form of religion they observe, so as all to look down upon the world itself, and despise death, while they neither esteem those to be gods that are reckoned such by the Greeks, nor hold to the superstition of the Jews; and what is the affection which they cherish among themselves; and finally, why this new kind or practice [of piety] has only now entered into the world, and not long ago; I cordially welcome this your desire, and I implore God, who enables us both to speak and to hear, to grant to me so to speak, that, above all, I may hear you have been edified, and to you so to hear, that I who speak may have no cause of regret for having done so.[11]

From the letter, Diognetus was concerned about how Christians should now relate with the Greek deities of their time, how they should respond to the Jewish superstition towards them, and how Christian (brotherly) love was countercultural. The Epistle is an apologetic work that therefore serves as an exhortation to the joyful acceptance and living out of the Christian truths.

Theophilus to Autolycus, written by Theophilus (bishop of Antioch between AD 169 to 182), shows the importance that this apologetic proved to the antiquity of Christianity in a set of three books. Literature in the ancient world was closely tied to the spoken word, and this is clearly evident from Theophilus' work to Autolycus which reads as a speech. Tatian (AD 120–180), a pupil of Justin, is another key figure of post-New Testament apologetics. Like Justin Martyr, he was converted to Christianity from a Hellenistic background. The differences are that while Justin in his *Dialogue* calls for a discontinuity between Christianity and Judaism, Tatian calls for the same break between Christianity in relation to Hellenism.[12] In *Homer or Moses*, Tatian suggests that Greeks got their culture from barbarians, thus critiquing Greco-Roman culture in favour of the philosophy and life of the Hebrews. In conclusion, second-century apologists utilized classical and biblical sources to formulate an apologetic against the literary and religious canons of the Greeks and Jews.[13]

Tertullian, Minucius Felix and Cyprian looked outward in their apologetics, yet had a genuine concern to strengthen believers in their day-to-day

11. *Epistle to Diognetus*, trans. Alexander Roberts and James Donaldson (Moscow, Idaho: Romans Road Media, 2015), 3.

12. Frances Young, "Greek Apologists in the 2nd Century," 83.

13. *Epistle to Diognetus*, 104.

engagements with non-believers.[14] Some of Tertullian's (AD 155–220) works included *To the Gentiles*, *Apology* and *On the Philosopher's Cloak*. He wrote in Carthage at the turn of the second and third centuries.[15] Born in Carthage, he did not have the advantage of a Christian heritage in his family.[16] Eastman, in his history of patristics in North Africa, observes that the conversion of Tertullian can be traced to around AD 197, and based on his early thinking and writing, that his previous education was likely in law.[17] As a theologian, he utilized this legal language to explicate the doctrine of the Trinity in his work *Against Praxeas*. In describing the Father, the Son and the Spirit each as having a *persona*, he makes the theological case that they own divinity, to use his language. As such, Tertullian is way ahead of his time as an African theologian as he explicates the doctrine of the Trinity about a century before the global church during the Nicene Creed (AD 325).[18] Thus, Tertullian appears as a creative and contextual theologian and apologist of his time.

Celsus "was a platonic philosopher who wrote an attack on Christianity called *The True Account*" (or *Word* or *Doctrine* or *Discourse*).[19] Some of his arguments against Christianity are still posed by sceptics of the Christian faith today.[20] First, Celsus wrestles with the co-existence of God and the Devil. Second, he challenges the reliability of the New Testament stories as "myths" that borrow from the Greco-Roman world. Third, he rejects the Christian faith on the account of the problem of evil and suffering. He was answered by Origen (AD 184–254), who was a prolific writer, and noted biblical interpreter who wrote a great deal – with the ancient writer Epiphanius claiming that Origen wrote 6,000 books.[21] Eusebius is less dramatic in his claim that 2,000 books can be attributed to Origen, but here the point is that Origen was a prolific author.[22] His apologetic *Against Celsus* is considered a very important work

---

14. Simon Price, "Latin Christian Apologists: Minucius Felix, Tertullian and Cyprian," in Edwards, Goodman and Price, *Apologetics in the Roman Empire*, 106.

15. Price, "Latin Christian Apologists."

16. David Eastman, *Early North African Christianity: Turning Points in the Development of the Church* (Grand Rapids: Baker Academic), 39.

17. David Eastman, *Early North African Christianity*, 40.

18. David Eastman, *Early North African Christianity*, 60–62.

19. Michael Frede "Origen's Treatise Against Celsus," in Edwards, Goodman and Price, *Apologetics in the Roman Empire*, 132.

20. Celsus, *The True Doctrine*. http://www.earlychristianwritings.com/text/celsus3.html.

21. Michael Freede, "Origen's Treatise Against Celsus," in Edwards, Goodman and Price, *Apologetics in the Roman Empire*, 131.

22. Michael Freede, "Origen's Treatise Against Celsus," 131.

of Christian apologetics. The purpose was to offer a critical response to the attacks levelled against Christianity, particularly written for young Christians to enable them to respond to critics.

Hence, polemics within Greek culture were less prominent compared to other literature. However, the socio-cultural makeup changed as many Greeks converted to Christianity. In the chapter "The Flowering of Latin Apologetic," Edwards observes that this apologetic produced the first displays of Christian rhetoric.[23]

Writing in the fourth century, the Bishop of Caesarea, Eusebius (AD 260/265–339/40), wrote to Christians who had converted from Greek Platonism, and who still cherished their Greek heritage.[24] Swain argues that Eusebius had written to Christians who still believed "in the fundamental correctness of Platonism, but is also ready to be persuaded that this Platonism is already to be found in the Bible long before Plato."[25] Constantine the Great is credited with the institutionalization of Christianity as a common citizen's faith hence uniting church and state. *Oration to the Saints*, which is attributed to him, was written to defend Christian ethics and to explain the significance of the incarnation for Christian life.[26] After Constantine, apologetic writings were characteristically not written to offer relief from distress but to offer an intellectual support for Christianity.[27]

Elsewhere, a few years prior, in the Egyptian and Libyan Christian communities, an elder called Arius (AD 256–336) was teaching errant views concerning the relationship of what would come to be known as the Trinity.[28] In effect, he was teaching that the Trinity was like a ladder of stairs, with the Father superior to the Son and the Son superior to the Spirit. It took the conciliar decision by the church leaders in the Council of Nicaea in AD 325 to develop a creed that captured the essence of the Christian doctrine on Jesus Christ (i.e., Christology). Athanasius, an Egyptian Bishop (AD 296–373) was influential in clarifying the deity of Christ by asserting that the "Father is true God, and the Son is true God." He would defend the doctrine as handed

23. Mark Edwards, "The Flowering of Latin Apologetic," in Edwards, Goodman and Price, *Apologetics in the Roman Empire*, 220.

24. Simon Swain, "Defending Hellenism: Philostratus, *In Honour of Apollonius*," in Edwards, Goodman and Price, *Apologetics in the Roman Empire*, 250.

25. Simon Swain, "Defending Hellenism," 250.

26. Simon Swain, "Defending Hellenism," 251.

27. Simon Swain, "Defending Hellenism," 251.

28. Michael Haykin, *Defending the Truth: Contending for the Faith Yesterday and Today* (Darlington: Evangelical Press, 2004), 75.

down from the saints by standing firm despite political pressure, leading to the slogan *Athanasius contra mundum*, "Athanasius against the world."[29] It is clear that as time progressed, the church needed to make confessional statements in creeds to protect the church from errant teaching both from within it and from without. These summative teachings have been seen to be of theological and apologetic value in ensuring that the church maintains doctrinal purity through the ages.

St. Augustine of Hippo (AD 354–430), the notable African theologian and church leader, wrote much about God's providence and human free will. His writings became the bedrock of the reformation apologists and theologians. According to Brown, Augustine's thought and apologetics is summed up in the phrase "faith seeking understanding" which was later developed by St. Anselm of Canterbury.[30] Augustine seemed to wrestle with the problem of evil, which the sceptics of his time launched as an argument against the existence of God,

> . . . that reputed nation of darkness [evil], which the Manichæans are in the habit of setting up as a mass opposed to Thee, have done unto Thee hadst Thou objected to fight with it?[31] (my italics).

Simply put,

> If we do not have free choice, we are not to be blamed or praised for our actions; rather, it is all God's doing. God becomes responsible for moral evil, either by causing it Himself or by punishing us who are not responsible for it.[32]

Augustine sees free will as part of the cause of evil,

> And I directed my attention to discern what I now heard, that free will was the cause of our doing evil, and Thy righteous judgment of our suffering it. . . . But what I did against my will I saw that I suffered rather than did, and that judged I not to be my fault, but my punishment.[33]

29. Michael Haykin, *Defending the Truth*, 79.

30. Montague Brown, "Augustine on Freedom and God," *The Saint Anselm Journal* 2.2 (Spring 2005), 60.

31. Augustine, *The Confessions of Saint Augustine* 7.2.3 (NPNF 1:103).

32. Brown, "Augustine on Freedom and God," 50.

33. Augustine, *Confessions* 7.3.5 (NPNF 1:104).

Hence God's justice is seen when we suffer as a result of his punishing of evil. However, he cannot fully reconcile the problem of evil because if God was good, where did evil come from, where was its first origin?

> Who made me? Was it not my God, who is not only good, but goodness itself? Whence came I then to will to do evil, and to be unwilling to do good, that there might be cause for my just punishment? Who was it that put this in me, and implanted in me the root of bitterness, seeing I was altogether made by my most sweet God? If the devil were the author, whence is that devil? And if he also, by his own perverse will, of a good angel became a devil, whence also was the evil will in him whereby he became a devil . . .[34]

As a converted philosopher from Manicheanism, Augustine's intellectual struggle shows that theodicy cannot be reconciled by philosophy, but that it rests in a God-ward and trusting theology. Augustine realizes that his former Manichean debauchery veils him from beholding the truth of God. He says,

> And I sought "whence is evil?" And sought in an evil way; nor saw I the evil in my very search. . . . but yet He, who is good, hath created them good, and behold how He encircleth and filleth them.[35]

In acknowledging his frailty, he is better able to appreciate God's providence in sustaining all things, confessing elsewhere

> and in all its greatest parts as well as smallest penetrable to receive Thy presence, by a secret inspiration, both inwardly and outwardly governing all things which Thou hast created.[36]

Augustine begins realizing that he would rather remain humble in seeking the answer to the question of evil and suffering by submitting himself to God. Through reading the books by Platonists of his time, Augustine found the seeds to the doctrine of the Word, in which he would be able to reconcile this problem of evil. He realizes that those who in their vanity oppose God through the problem of evil are farthest away from God, citing Romans 1:21–22:

---

34. Augustine, *Confessions* 7.3.5 (NPNF 1:104).
35. Augustine, *Confessions* 7.7.7 (NPNF 1:104–5).
36. Augustine, *Confessions* 7.1.2 (NPNF 1:103).

> For although they knew God, they did not honor him as God or give thanks to him, but they became futile in their thinking, and their foolish hearts were darkened. Claiming to be wise, they became fools. (ESV)

Augustine realizes that his own efforts are insufficient in coming to the knowledge of God, and only through Jesus Christ, could he be provided an outward help to know God:

> And I sought a way of acquiring strength sufficient to enjoy Thee; but I found it not until I embraced that "Mediator between God and man, the man Christ Jesus," "who is over all, God blessed for ever," calling unto me, and saying, "I am the way, the truth, and the life."[37]

Here I concur with Brown when he says that,

> however, natural reason cannot tell us how the two, *that is free choice and grace,* can be made one without denying one or the other. But theology can. Christ is God and man. Hence, every act of Christ is divine and human, including his free choices. This is the only adequate model for understanding the relation between human freedom and grace (my italics).[38]

Here we see Augustine's solution to his problem of evil. Brown says, "the only way for us to understand such things is for us to receive divine help: we understand, but only because we are helped."[39] Free-will defences to the problem of evil and suffering, while noting that moral evil comes from wrong human choices, cannot adequately account for moral evil. Joseph Okello in his chapter on suffering in this book makes the case for a more holistic perspective on the problem of evil and suffering.

While the *Confessions* portrays Augustine's existential quest for the answer to the problem of evil, moving from Manichean thought to an initial half-answer in human free will, Augustine will later see that the solution lies in communion with God by faith – which is only made possible by Christ's incarnational humility, he descends so that we can ascend.[40] This is the solution to the problem of evil, the greatest problem of evil, that is, sin. Thus,

---

37. Augustine, *Confessions* 7.18.24 (NPNF 1:112).

38. Brown, "Augustine on Freedom and God," 59.

39. Brown, "Augustine on Freedom and God," 60.

40. Matthew Levering, *The Theology of Augustine: An Introductory Guide to his most Important Works* (Grand Rapids: Baker Publishing Group, 2013). Loc: 11 of 19, Perlego

Augustine reveals how the church has wrestled with the problem of pain, evil and suffering, against the sceptical attacks of the same.

4.2 Apologetics in Early Medieval Era: AD 500–1000

The early medieval era also provided the Church with various approaches to apologetics. Thomas Oden has contributed much to the thesis of Africa being a critical contributor to the intellectual soil of global Christianity.[41] In his book *How Africa Shaped the Christian Mind*, he traces the history of Christianity in Africa through a brief chronology from AD 0–1000, whereby he mentions key dates, figures and events that shaped the Christian story in the continent.[42] Important dates and key issues from this history include:

- Bishopric transitions in the Coptic Church Patriarch of Alexandria.
- 519 End of Acacian Schism and acceptance of Chalcedon in the East, excepting "Monophysites" . . . The official shunning of Coptic language and intellectual tradition by Byzantines.
- 527–565 Era of Justinian the Great, Byzantine emperor.
- 533 Reestablishment of Byzantian empire from Mauretania to Armenia, with basilicas sprouting through Byzantine forms of Christian architecture.
- 553 Fifth ecumenical council, Second Council of Constantinople.
- 590–604 Pope Gregory the great (540–604) brings Augustinian theology to normative status in the West.
- 619–629 Persian occupation of Egypt ends Byzantine rule.
- 622 The Hejira, Muhammad's flight from Mecca to Medina, begins the Islamic era. The first year in Muslim calendar, 1 A.H. = Anno Hegirae.
- 622–624 Muhammad attempts to convert ten thousand Jews of Medina to no avail. He changes the direction of the *qibla* from Jerusalem to Mecca and deports or executes the Jewish tribes of Arabia.

---

e-edition. https://www.perlego.com/book/2050984/the-theology-of-augustine-an-introductory-guide-to-his-most-important-works-pdf.

41. Other historians of African Christianity are Elizabeth Isichei, *A History of Christianity in Africa: From Antiquity to the Present* (Grand Rapids: Eerdmans, 1995); and Mark Shaw and Wanjiru M. Gitau, *The Kingdom of God in Africa: A History of African Christianity* (Carlisle: Langham Global Library, 2020).

42. Thomas Oden, *How Africa Shaped the Christian Mind: Rediscovering the African Seedbed of Western Christianity* (Downers Grove: InterVarsity Press, 2007), 157–97.

- 622–680 Monothelite controversy.
- 625 Muhammad begins dictating Qur'an to a scribe.
- 632 Death of Muhammad at Medina.
- 634–642 Expansion of Islam in Palestine, Syria and Egypt.
- 642 Fall of Alexandria.
- 661–750 Muslims divide into Sunni and Shia, followers of caliph Ali.
- 680–681 Sixth ecumenical council, Third Council of Constantinople, began under Constantine IV and condemns monothelism and monoenergism. Confirms Christ's two inseparable wills and energies, thus affirming Chalcedonian Christology.
- 731 Bede writes his *Ecclesiastical History of the English People*, exploring from medieval European texts, the voices of the earlier African theologians Origen, Pachomius, Augustine and Cyril.
- 743 John of Damascus (c. 645–c. 749) writes his systematic theology, used mostly in the Orthodox churches.
- 787 Seventh ecumenical council, Second Council of Nicaea confirms veneration of icons.
- 800s Christianity in Ethiopia continues after the decline of Aksum.
- 900s Sawirus (Severus) Ibn al-Muqaffa, bishop of al-Ashmuayn, writes twenty-six books of history and theology in Arabic.

Thus, at the dawn of the second millennium, there were a number of theological controversies that the church faced, such as monothelism, monoenergism and iconoclasm; political tensions in the form of Roman empire and the patriarchates of Constantinople; as well as the challenge of the growing religion of Islam. Keith Wessel summarizes it this way:

> [N]ew theological problems surfaced in the forms of the 7th century Monotheletic Controversy ("one-will") and the Iconoclast Controversy (725–842), the latter over what role religious symbols (especially icons) ought to play in the life of the orthodox Christian. Between the Iconoclast Controversy and the separation from the West in 1054, the Photian Schism (mid-800's), essentially a struggle for supremacy between the popes of Rome and patriarchs of Constantinople, left the empire even further divided, a precarious situation in view of the continually rising tide of Islam in the Mediterranean world. Looking south of Byzantium, the rise of Islam literally forced three of the five ancient episcopal sees of prominence – Antioch, Jerusalem, and Alexandria – into relative obscurity. Yet throughout periods of

> persecution and peace, Christianity would retain a foothold in the heart of Moslem lands. The Coptic Church, believed to have been established by St. Mark himself, survived, as did her sister church further south in Ethiopia. In Syria, the Jacobite Church flourished and spread to Persia, but throughout the period up to 900 did little theologically. The Armenian Church, which did not participate in Chalcedon, found itself at odds with Western concepts of christology and the decisions of the council, and soon was isolated. It too had little theological activity, except for an occasional attempt at reconciliation with the Byzantine Church. All these churches were not only isolated from the mainstream of Christianity by locale and language; they each had adopted a Monophysite brand of theology condemned by Chalcedon.[43]

Apologetics took more of a polemic form as different Christian communities tried to grapple for dominance in the turn of the millennium. It would take the coming of the catholic philosopher and theologian Thomas Aquinas to appropriate the cosmological argument to make a philosophical case for the existence of God. Islamic philosophy had developed two arguments in the lines of Ibn Sina (980–1037), arguing from contingency, and al-Ghāzāli (1058–1111) arguing from causality.[44] These two lines of thought were taken up by Aquinas and developed in his *Summa Theologica* (1.2.3) and in his *Summa Contra Gentiles* (1.5, 13).[45]

4.3 Apologetics in the Late Medieval Era: AD 1000–1500

Following the turn of the first millennium, after Constantine's (274–337) merging of church and state so that Christianity was a "state religion," Thomas Aquinas (1225–1274) is among those who developed a more rigorous apologetic based on the combination of natural reason and divine revelation. This can be seen for instance in his *Summa Contra Gentiles* "no one strives with any

43. Keith C. Wessel, n.d., "Forward in Christ: At the Dawn of the Second Millennium," An Essay in Celebration of God's Grace upon the 150th Anniversary of the Wisconsin Evangelical Lutheran Synod. http://essays.wisluthsem.org:8080/bitstream/handle/123456789/900/WesselForward.pdf?sequence=1&isAllowed=y.

44. William L. Craig, *The Kalam Cosmological Argument* (Eugene: Wipf & Stock, 2000), 4–7.

45. Bruce Reichenbach, "Cosmological Argument," *The Stanford Encyclopaedia of Philosophy* (Winter 2021 Edition), ed. Edward N. Zalta, https://plato.stanford.edu/archives/win2021/entries/cosmological-argument/.

earnestness of desire after anything unless it be known to him beforehand."[46] Utilizing Aristotelian metaphysics, he builds up on the cosmology of St. Anselm of Canterbury (1033–1109) in Anselm's work *Monologium* to prove the existence of God as the first cause, that is, the prime mover.

Before him, St. Anselm (1033–1109) was one of the most remarkable men and most attractive characters not only of the Middle Ages, but the whole of Christianity. "He was much more than a monk. A great teacher, a great thinker, a great kindler of thought in others."[47] Anselm wrote the *Proslogion* (or *Proslogium*) as a discourse on the existence of God, concerning his contemplation of God as a means of "faith seeking understanding." In his own words: "I have written the following treatise, in the person of one who strives to lift his mind to the contemplation of God and seeks to understand what he believes."[48] In his pursuit of God, Anselm realizes that unless enabled by God's grace – God's special revelation – we cannot find him, and all we do is stumble upon ourselves. "Be it mine to look up to thy light, even from afar, even from the depths. Teach me to seek thee, and reveal thyself to me, when I seek thee, for I cannot seek thee, except thou teach me, nor find thee, except thou reveal thyself."[49]

Renowned for his "ontological" argument, Anselm's apology for God's existence can be summarized as follows:

1. It is one thing to understand an object and another to understand the existence of it. Here he uses the example of a painter who has a certain illustration in mind; as much as she understands it, the existence of the painting occurs only after she performs it. Speaking of God as the being whom "Nothing greater that can be convinced" his second proposition is:
2. "And whatever is understood, exists in the understanding"[50]

46. Thomas Aquinas, *Summa Contra Gentiles* 1.5.1 trans. Joseph Rickaby, S.J. (Grand Rapids: Christian Classics Ethereal Library), 13.

47. R. W. Church, *St. Anselm* (London: Macmillan, 1888), 7.

48. Anselm, Preface to *Proslogium*, in *Proslogium; Monologium; An Appendix in Behalf of the Fool by Gaunilon; And Cur Deus Homo*, trans. Sidney Norton Deane (Chicago: Open Court, 1903; Grand Rapids: Christian Classics Ethereal Library), 27.

49. Anselm, *Proslogium* 1, in *Proslogium . . . Cur Deus Homo*, 30.

50. Anselm, *Proslogium* 2, in *Proslogium . . . Cur Deus Homo*, 32.

3. "Hence, there is no doubt that there exists a being, than which nothing greater can be conceived, and it exists both in the understanding and in reality."[51]

And because God is the greatest being, then it is impossible for God not to exist because if a being greater than can be conceived "does not exist" then it would rise above conception, more like the creature rising above its creator – an impossible task. For the fool in Psalm 14:1 who denies God's existence, Anselm says:

> In the former sense, then, God can be conceived not to exist; but in the latter, not at all. For no one who understands what fire and water are, can conceive fire to be water, in accordance with the nature of the facts themselves, although this is possible according to the words. So, then, no one who understands what God is, can conceive that God does not exist; although he says these words in his heart, either without any or with some foreign, signification.[52]

Hence God is self-sustaining because he is being itself. Anselm acknowledges God's attributes as being compassionate, righteous, and good and just – his goodness is seen in his justifying of the wicked and pitying the sinners, because this is not normal of other beings:

> For, in sparing the wicked, thou art as just, according to thy nature, but not according to ours, as thou art compassionate, according to our nature, and not according to thine; seeing that, as in saving us, whom it would be just for thee to destroy, thou art compassionate, not because thou feelest an affection (*affectum*), but because we feel the effect (*effectum*); so thou art just, not because thou requitest us as we deserve, but because thou dost that which becomes thee as the supremely good Being. In this way, therefore, without contradiction thou dost justly punish and justly spare.[53]

St. Anselm's *Monologium* is a meditation that relies on natural revelation and reason alone to justify the being of God. Geisler summarizes the arguments in *Monologium* as cosmological arguments as below:[54]

---

51. Anselm, *Proslogium* 2, in *Proslogium . . . Cur Deus Homo*, 32.

52. Anselm, *Proslogium* 4, in *Proslogium . . . Cur Deus Homo*, 34.

53. Anselm, *Proslogium* 10, in *Proslogium . . . Cur Deus Homo*, 41.

54. Norman L. Geisler, *Baker Encyclopaedia of Christian Apologetics* (Grand Rapids: Baker Books, 1999), 47.

Anselm argued from goodness to God:

1. Good things exist.
2. The cause of this goodness is either one or many.
3. But it can't be many, for then there would be no way to compare their goodness, for all things would be equally good. But some things are better than others.
4. Therefore, one Supreme Good (God) causes the goodness in all good things.

Anselm argued from perfection to God, an argument C. S. Lewis emulated in *Mere Christianity*:[55:]

1. Some beings are more nearly perfect than are others.
2. But things cannot be more or less perfect unless there is a wholly perfect to which they can be compared.
3. Therefore, there must be a Most Perfect Being (God).

Anselm argued from being to God:

1. Something exists.
2. Whatever exists exists either through nothing or through something.
3. But nothing cannot cause something; only something can cause something.
4. And this something is either one or many.

St. Anselm divided *Cur Deus Homo* into two books, whose purpose he outlines as follows:

> The first contains the objections of infidels, who despise the Christian faith because they deem it contrary to reason; and also, the reply of believers; and, in fine, leaving Christ out of view (as if nothing had ever been known of him), it proves, by absolute reasons, the impossibility that any man should be saved without

---

55. C. S. Lewis contrasts the common concept of "Life force" as the cause of the evolution from the lowest life forms to man, with the materialist and religious views – which was not due to chance, as in the materialist view, but due to a "striving" or "purposiveness." If one argues this way, then they default to the religious view, and if the purposiveness is rooted in mind, then consequentially, one ends up with God. C. S. Lewis, *Mere Christianity* (New York: Harper Collins, 2001), 26.

> him. Again, in the second book, likewise, as if nothing were known of Christ, it is moreover shown by plain reasoning and fact that human nature was ordained for this purpose, viz., that every man should enjoy a happy immortality, both in body and in soul; and that it was necessary that this design for which man was made should be fulfilled; but that it could not be fulfilled unless God became man, and unless all things were to take place which we hold with regard to Christ.[56]

The necessity of God coming down to redeem humanity, a fact that unbelievers mock Christians about, is because of the fallenness of creation and Anselm asks in rhetoric: "who else would be befitting this ordeal save for the Creator himself?"[57] He goes on to explain Christ's dual natures in the following manner:[58]

> They who speak thus do not understand our belief. For we affirm that the Divine nature is beyond doubt impassible, and that God cannot at all be brought down from his exaltation, nor toil in anything which he wishes to effect. But we say that the Lord Jesus Christ is very God and very man, one person in two natures, and two natures in one person. When, therefore, we speak of God as enduring any humiliation or infirmity, we do not refer to the majesty of that nature, which cannot suffer; but to the feebleness of the human constitution which he assumed. And so there remains no ground of objection against our faith. For in this way we intend no debasement of the Divine nature, but we teach that one person is both Divine and human. In the incarnation of God there is no lowering of the Deity; but the nature of man we believe to be exalted.[59]

As we can observe, Anselm's apology was for both unbelievers and believers: in the former sense, to defend the faith and in the latter sense, to equip believers so that they could be able to offer the hope that they profess in.

Thomas Aquinas is renowned for focusing on reason in the pursuit of the knowledge of God. He says, "The discovery of truth is the fruit of studious

56. Anselm, *Cur Deus Homo* I.1, in *Proslogium . . . Cur Deus Homo*, 183.

57. Anselm, *Cur Deus Homo* I.5, in *Proslogium . . . Cur Deus Homo*, 189.

58. The two natures of Christ have been thoroughly engaged in Christian theology through the development of the doctrine called the *hypostatic union*.

59. Anselm, *Cur Deus Homo* I.6, in *Proslogium . . . Cur Deus Homo*, 190.

enquiry."[60] However, not many attain to this truth by way of this enquiry, that is based on reason alone, because human knowledge is insufficient to attain the knowledge of God which is the highest knowledge. Secondly, people's business and sloth, as two extremes, would hinder human beings from accessing God. Third, it takes a long time to discover this truth by reason, thus serving as an inadequate way to the knowledge of God. Fourth, Aquinas attributes the insufficiency of reason to wrong judgement and error, which clouds human investigation. This therefore necessitates the need for revelation. In his own words, "And therefore it was necessary for the real truth concerning divine things to be presented to men with fixed certainty by way of Faith."[61]

Some may here object that it is wrong to expect humanity to believe these articles of faith when they cannot be proved by logical reasoning. Aquinas sees this bridge between reason and revelation as an advantage, and his proofs for this are: 1) It enables us to strive for God, "No one strives with any earnestness of desire after anything unless it be known to him beforehand."[62] 2) The error of presumption that comes from the arrogance of humanity is leveled by the inability to attain to the knowledge of divinity by reason alone, and 3) that knowledge, however little, confers some perfection to the soul, and hence revelation of God is the highest knowledge.

Aquinas also argues that the truth of reason is not contrary to the truth of the Christian faith. "Since therefore falsehood alone is contrary to truth, it is impossible for the truth of faith to be contrary to the principles known by natural reason."[63] He proposes that since God is the creator of our nature and also our ultimate teacher, he has put some knowledge of the divine in us and whatever is contrary to this first principle of nature is not of God, for God cannot lie. He quotes Romans 10:8 to make his point. Jesus talking of the little children in Matthew 18:1–6 also preempts this point, showing that children have an "undefiled" nature (seeds of goodness) but through the process of life experiences, some of these first principles are lost. This then leads to his argument of self-evident truth, here borrowing from Anselm's ontological argument: "Things naturally known are self-evident: for the knowledge of them is not attained by enquiry and study."[64] Since humanity naturally tends to God

60. Thomas Aquinas, *Summa Contra Gentiles* 1.4, trans. Joseph Rickaby (Grand Rapids: Christian Classics Ethereal Library), 11.

61. Thomas Aquinas, *Summa Contra Gentiles* 1.4, 12.

62. Thomas Aquinas, *Summa Contra Gentiles* 1.5.1, 13.

63. Thomas Aquinas, *Summa Contra Gentiles* 1.7.1, 15.

64. Thomas Aquinas, *Summa Contra Gentiles* 1.10.4, 18.

as his highest and last end, then the existence of God is natural to humanity. Aquinas says that the existence of God can further be proved by demonstration, *a posteriori*, from the deducing of effects to cause. In his words, "The existence of God in so far as it is not self-evident to us, can be demonstrated from those of His effects which are known to us."[65]

Aquinas also uses Aristotelian metaphysics to prove the notion of God as the first cause, the prime mover: "Everything which is in motion is put and kept in motion by something else."[66] He quotes St. John Damascene's (*De Fid. Orthod.* I, 3) teleological argument that anything that has harmonious order is kept under some guidance by a power whose providence the world is governed with, that is, God.[67] Finally, through "negative differentiation" Aquinas suggests that we can be able to have a clearer and concise view of God. By defining the attributes of God, those who refute the attributes through negative statements only serve to explicate the very attributes.[68] He speaks briefly about the problem of evil by quoting Augustine, "Since God is the highest good, He would not allow any evil to exist in His works, unless His omnipotence and goodness were such to bring good even out of evil."[69]

4.4 Apologetics in the Reformation Era (1500–1700)

Rediscovering the sufficiency and authority of Scripture, apologetics in the Reformation era (AD 1517–1648) would be grounded on the presuppositions of Scripture and not so much on natural reason, which was central to the apologetic methodology of the previous era. This stems from the fact that the reformers held to the noetic effects of sin whereby the whole of a person is affected by sin, and therefore without the Holy Spirit, no one can respond positively to the claims of Jesus Christ, nor can reason unaided to God. This centrality towards the foundational teachings of the Scriptures in their apologetics was pertinent especially in a time when the cultural situation was influenced by humanism, and where the state religion (Roman Catholicism) had turned away from the core tenets of the faith. Thus, the apologetics of the reformation period took a polemic stance, where it was aimed at defending

65. Thomas Aquinas, *Summa Theologica* 1.2.2, trans. Fathers of the English Dominican Province (Grand Rapids: Christian Classics Ethereal Library), 25.

66. Thomas Aquinas, *Summa Contra Gentiles* 1.8.1, 22.

67. Thomas Aquinas, *Summa Contra Gentiles* 1.8.1, 23.

68. Thomas Aquinas, *Summa Contra Gentiles* 1.9.1, 25.

69. Thomas Aquinas, *Summa Theologica* 1.2.3, 29.

either the reformed or catholic teachings, during the subsequent phases of the reformations.[70] The contemporary theologians William Edgar and K. Scott Oliphint looking back to this period refer to the rebuttal of Martin Luther when he was asked to recant his views in the Diet of Worms in 1521:

> Unless I am convicted by Scripture and plain reason – I do not accept the authority of popes and councils, for they have contradicted each other – my conscience is captive to the word of God. I cannot and will not recant anything for to go against conscience is neither right nor safe.[71]

John Calvin (1509–1564), one of the leading theologians of the Reformation period addresses his systematic theology, *Institutes of Christian Religion*, to King Francis I where he sets out his main motive as a defence of the faith from an extreme emphasis on human traditions rather than on the light of the gospel which restores true piety and ultimately aims at God's glory.[72] Calvin took a stance against Roman Catholic practices that in his view were contrary to the apostolic teaching in the biblical canon as well as in opposition to patristic practice.[73] On the other hand, the Roman Catholic Church also intervened in a way to create a distinct identity against the protestant reformers. The Yale Historian Carlos M. Eire observes,

---

70. William Edgar and K. Scott Oliphint eds., *Christian Apologetics: Past and Present* (Wheaton: Crossway, 2011), 13.

71. Edgar and Oliphint, *Christian Apologetics*, 13. It is important to briefly outline here the doctrine of *sola scriptura*. According to the Reformers, Scripture was the final authority for Christian life and doctrine and interpretation of Scripture should be based on the apostolic tradition in their reception and transmission of the gospel message throughout the church's history. This view on interpretation was contrary to both contemporary methods of interpreting Scripture from a subjective view, and the Roman Catholic *Magisterium* as the sole, traditional authority in the church's biblical interpretation, the reformers saw the importance of tradition, a tradition that was important and subservient to the authority of the Scripture. See R. C. Sproul Jr., ed., *After Darkness Light: Essays in Honor of R. C. Sproul* (Phillipsburg: P&R Publishing, 2003). The same approach can be located in the Confessions and Catechisms of the Reformation.

72. Preface to John Calvin, trans. Robert White, *Institutes of the Christian Religion* (Edinburgh: Banner of Truth Trust, 2014), xvii, xix, xxii.

73. Calvin indicates that the Roman Catholic teaching caused Christians to ignore scriptural teaching and that their motive was to secure institutional authority and power. Some of the issues he raises include: delighting in the use of costly materials (gold and silver) during the Lord's Supper; their excommunication of those who had taken meat during lent; the papal vows not to work yet quoting Paul, "no one who works should eat"; their view on iconoclasm (putting up physical images in the church); their view on the physical presence of Christ in the Lord's Supper; their vows of celibacy; the legalizing of fasting and their high view of philosophy that was prone to "polluting God's Holy Word with the Sophists' clever tricks" (Calvin, *Institutes*, xxv–xxviii).

> But just as there is a seamlessness to the continuity of reform within the Catholic Church, so is there also a noticeable difference in its tone and vigor after the emergence of Protestantism. Polarization always sets in motion a certain dialectic between opposing sides, as they sharpen their identities in contradiction to one another.[74]

Hence, this polemical strain in apologetics would cast a long shadow even into the twenty-first century. Eire gives examples of the reforms of the Bishop of Milan, Carlo Borremeo, the Bishop in Catalonia Francesch Robuster and the monk St. John of the Cross, to show how their reforms within the Catholic church were met with opposition and the consequent suffering they would endure for their causes. Other Catholic apologists would respond to reformed apologetics by showing the fundamental flaw of the reformers: "novelty, inconsistency and plurality."[75] From these factional breaks within the church, polemics would be a definitive form of apologetics going forward.

4.5 Apologetics in the Enlightenment Era (1700–1900)

The modern era (ca. 1500–1945), which can be further divided into the early modern era and the late modern era, included the renaissance, the reformation and the enlightenment era. This age was undergirded by a philosophy of humanism, leading to the outcomes of the epistemological tenets of the late modern period. The respected theologian and apologist John S. Feinberg defining the modern period as "belief in reason and progress," outlines the central tenets of this period as human consciousness, certainty in knowledge, the importance of foundationalism, metanarratives and the objectivity of truth.[76] With such a heavy emphasis on rationality, the central task for apologists in this era was to refute the authority of reason alone. Blaise Pascal (1623–1662) and William Paley (1743–1805) are two examples in the early and late modern period who are exemplary in the area of apologetics.

Pascal, a famous mathematician, in his *Pensées* draws an analogy to show that while rational arguments may be worthwhile, they may be detached from the pragmatic experiences of life: "If the greatest philosopher in the world find himself upon a plank wider than actually necessary, but hanging over a

74. Carlos M. N. Eire, *Reformations: The Early Modern World, 1450–1650* (Yale: Yale University Press, 2016): Loc. 371 of 893.

75. Carlos M. N. Eire, *Reformations*, Loc. 373 of 893.

76. John S. Feinberg, *Can You Believe Its True: Christian Apologetics in a Modern and Postmodern Era* (Wheaton: Crossway, 2013), 38–50.

precipice, his imagination will prevail, though his reason convince him of his safety."[77] Perhaps his better-known argument is "*Pascal's Wager*." Here Pascal says in effect that it is better to believe that God exists and find out he does in heaven, rather than to believe that he doesn't exist and find out that he does in hell. In the first case, the worst that could happen would be that the Christian would have lived a morally upright life. In the second case, one would face the torment of hell. In such examples, Pascal wages a middle ground between an extreme reliance on the certainty of reason and on the other hand, an attachment to anti-reason. To summarize his method, Pascal "was not a traditional apologist, for he denied that the traditional theistic proofs would persuade nonbelievers. He was not a fideist, for he defended the faith. And he was not a pure presuppositionalist, for he used psychological and historical evidence to prove the truth of Christianity."[78] William Paley, on the other hand, viewed the recovery of the classical arguments of God's existence from nature as crucial in his apologetics, as can be seen in his works *Natural Theology* and *A View of the Evidences of Christianity.*

4.6 Apologetics in the Modern Era (1900–Today)

In the twentieth century, one of the most well known apologists was C. S. Lewis, the British novelist, essayist and academic. What has been characteristic of his work is the compatibility of rationality and imagination in his apologetics, as can be seen in the wide variety of his writing: best known are the narratives of the *Narnia Series* and the essays *Mere Christianity*, *Miracles* and *The Problem of Pain*. This has given him wide acclaim in the Christian and non-Christian world, probably due to his ability to reach out to people in a culture of the postmodern period defined by scepticism about objectivity and institutional authority as well as the absence of metanarratives.[79]

---

77. Blaise Pascal (Tr. W. F. Trotter), *Pensees* (Mineola: Dover Publications, 2003), Section 2: Paragraph 82 (Loc: 7 of 22) www.perlego.comss.

78. Phill Fernandes, "The Apologetic Methodology of Blaise Pascal," *Christian Apologetics Journal* 6.2 (2007), 110.

79. In my own analysis and readings, Lewis was more celebrated as an apologist posthumously – the comment on the postmodern retrieval seems to be supported by the number of organizations, ministries and books about him in the recent past. While he was feted as an acclaimed English writer of fiction before his death, there was a decline in his popularity after his death in 1963 based on western cultural changes (pg. 1–2). McGrath later observes "One of the most important outcomes of Lewis's apologetic method has been to secure cultural traction for Christianity after the slow death of modernity, in that its richer concept of reason allows it to resonate with some core themes of postmodern culture." See Alister E. McGrath, *The Intellectual World of C. S. Lewis* (Malden: John Wiley & Sons Incorporated, 2013), 134–35.

Given the historical development in the field of apologetics, in the contemporary setting it has now become an academic discipline that espouses different methodological approaches to the practice of apologetics. These are listed as classical, cumulative-case, Reformed epistemology, presuppositional and evidential approaches.[80] Contemporary apologists in the West utilizing some or a combination of these methods include John M. Frame, William Lane Craig, J. P. Moreland, Gary Habermas, John Lennox, and Alister McGrath. Amongst others, these methods explore the integration of:[81]

- Faith and theology: for example in the Westminsterian tradition of apologetics with figures such as Greg Bahnsen, Van Til, John Frame, William Edgar, among others.
- Faith and science: for example in the works of J. P. Moreland, Stephen Meyer and William Dembski.
- Faith and philosophy: for example, Alvin Plantinga, Dallas Willard and William Lane Craig; and,
- Faith and history (and archaeology): for example Gary Habermas's *Minimal Facts Approach.*

80. Stephen B. Cowan, ed., *Five Views on Apologetics* (Grand Rapids: Zondervan, 2000).

81. The Westminster theologian and apologist John Frame is a representative figure of the Van Til school of apologetics, or the presuppositional approach. See John M. Frame, *Apologetics to the Glory of God* (Phillipsburg: P&R Publishing, 1994). William Lane Craig is a philosopher and theologian, commonly known for his classical and philosophical approach to apologetics. See William Lane Craig, *No Easy Answers* (Chicago: Moody Press, 1990); "The Existence of God and the Beginning of the Universe," *Truth: A Journal of Modern Thought* 3 (1991): 85–96; *Reasonable Faith: Christian Truth and Apologetics* (Wheaton: Crossway, 2008); *The Atonement* (Cambridge University Press, 2018). His more recent work on Genesis, *In Quest of the Historical Adam: A Biblical and Scientific Exploration* (Grand Rapids: Eerdmans, 2021), has received several rebuttals in light of his construal of the creation account, the historical Adam and the genre of Genesis as mytho-history. See for example Peter J. Leithart, "Doubts about William Lane Craig's Creation Account," *First Things* (1 Oct 2021) and Thomas A. Howe, *A Critique of William Lane Craig's In Quest of the Historical Adam* (Eugene: Wipf & Stock Publishers, 2022). Cornelius Van Til wrote *Christian Apologetics* (Phillipsburg: P&R Publishing, 2003). J. P. Moreland has written on the interface of faith and science. See for example: J. P. Moreland, *Christianity and the Nature of Science* (Grand Rapids: Baker Book House, 1989). His more recent work is a rebuttal of atheists' rejection of Christianity on the grounds of scientific materialism, rather than on "science" being incompatible with faith. See for example: J. P. Moreland, *Scientism and Secularism: Learning to Respond to a Dangerous Ideology* (Wheaton: Crossway, 2018); Stephen Meyer, and the Discovery Institute, are proponents of Intelligent Design (ID) Theory which, consequentially, rejects Darwinian evolution. This theory is a scientific explanation that makes the case for design in the natural world. It has been used by theologians and apologists to make a case for the existence of God. See Stephen Meyer, *Darwin's Doubt: The Explosive Origin of Animal Life and the Case for Intelligent Design* (New York: Harper One: 2014); *Signature in the Cell: DNA and the Evidence for Intelligent Design* (New York: Harper One: 2009).

Conclusion

This chapter has offered a historical survey of the role of apologetics in the life of the church in dealing both with internal and external challenges towards the Christian faith. In the New Testament and in its earliest years, the role of apologetics largely deals with Greco-Roman culture, Hellenistic philosophy and the Jewish tradition. Within the medieval period, because church tradition had precipitated numerous power struggles between Eastern Orthodoxy and Roman Catholicism, and with the rise of Islam, apologetics took a more inward face in the form of polemics. The Reformers would reclaim the place of the Scriptures in the task of Christian theology and apologetics and mount a revival in the church. Based on this ultimate foundation and criterion of truth, the church was then able to face the contemporary challenges of rationalism in the Enlightenment period. Later apologists of the church, facing the modern and postmodern turns of culture, as well as the rise of scientism through global industrialization and new media, have had to appropriate various methodologies and approaches to the task of Christian justification of the content of its faith, or on the other hand, a defence against contemporary challenges to the Christian faith.

With the exception of Reuben Kigame's recent (2018) book *Christian Apologetics through African Eyes*, it is rather evident that not much apologetics has been written in view of or about the African continent, and this is a central concern of this book. Three reasons underlie this purpose: first, most scholars note that the center of Christianity is moving to the global South; second, while Christianity in the South is growing numerically, much is lacking in terms of the theological robustness of the African church. Third, the cultural transitions as earlier discussed present a challenge for the Christian witness in Africa. These are both from the outside, due to globalization, and also from within, with the perennial question of the relationship between African culture and the gospel still lingering.[82] In order to surmount these challenges, there is a serious need for apologetics in the African content, an apologetics enterprise that is firmly rooted in the historical contribution of the clouds of witnesses as well as one that is culturally aware in light of the complexities of this continent. What

---

82. African theologians in the postcolonial period of the continent have contributed several responses to the relationship between gospel and culture. Here is a representative list: E. Bolaji Idowu, *Olodumare: God in Yoruba Belief* (London: Longman, 1970); Byang H. Kato, *Theological Pitfalls in Africa* (Nairobi: Evangel Publishing House, 1975); John S. Mbiti, *African Religions and Philosophy* (Oxford: Heinemann, 1990); Kwame Bediako, *Theology and Identity: The Impact of Culture upon Christian Thought in the Second Century and in Modern Africa* (Carlisle: Regnum, 1992).

this chapter has aimed to do is to situate apologetics as a normative calling and undertaking for the Christian church, one that is central in advancing the gospel of Jesus Christ in the face of intellectual attacks. The other sections and chapters of this book serve to explore how faith intersects with African philosophy (section two), African culture (section three), and practical issues or approaches in light of various apologetic challenges (section four).

Bibliography

Alexander, Loveday. "The Acts of the Apostles as an Apologetic Text." In *Apologetics in the Roman Empire: Pagans, Jews and Christians*, edited by Mark Edwards, Martin Goodman and Simon Price, 15–44. Oxford: Oxford University Press, 1999.

Anselm, Saint. *Proslogium; Monologium: An Appendix in Behalf of the Fool, by Gaunilon; and Cur Deus Homo*. No. 54. McLean: Opencourt Publishing Company, 1903.

Aquinas, Saint Thomas. *The Summa Contra Gentiles*. London: Aeterna Press, 1975.

———. *The Summa Theologica: Complete Edition*. London: Catholic Way Publishing, 2014.

Augustine. *Confessions*. In vol. 1 of The Nicene and Post-Nicene Fathers, Series 1. Edited by Philip Schaff 1866–1889. Christian Classics Etheral Library. https://ccel.org/ccel/schaff/npnf101/npnf101.

Brown, Montague. "Augustine on Freedom and God." *The Saint Anselm Journal* 2, no. 2 (Spring 2005): 50–65.

Calvin, John. *Institutes of the Christian Religion*. Translated by Robert White. Edinburgh: Banner of Truth Trust, 2014.

Celsus, *The True Doctrine*. http://www.earlychristianwritings.com/text/celsus3.html.

Church, Richard William. *Saint Anselm*. Macmillan, 1890.

Cowan, Stephen B., and Stanley Gundry, eds. *Five Views on Apologetics*. Grand Rapids: Zondervan, 2000.

Craig, William Lane. *The Atonement*. Cambridge: Cambridge University Press, 2018.

———. *No Easy Answers*. Chicago: Moody Press, 1990.

———. "The Existence of God and the Beginning of the Universe." *Truth: A Journal of Modern Thought* 3 (1991): 85–96.

———. *Reasonable Faith: Christian Truth and Apologetics*. Wheaton: Crossway, 2008.

———. *The Kalam Cosmological Argument*. Eugene: Wipf & Stock Publishers, 2000.

Dulles, Avery. *A History of Apologetics*. San Francisco: Ignatius Press, 2005.

Eastman, David L. *Early North African Christianity: Turning Points in the Development of the Church*. Grand Rapids: Baker Academic, 2021.

Edgar, William, and K. Scott Oliphint, eds. *Christian Apologetics Past and Present*. Wheaton: Crossway, 2011.

Edwards, Mark, Martin Goodman, and Simon Price, eds. *Apologetics in the Roman Empire: Pagans, Jews and Christians*. Oxford: Oxford University Press, 1999.

Eire, Carlos M. N. *Reformations: The Early Modern World, 1450–1650*. New Haven: Yale University Press, 2016.

Epistle to Diognetus. Translated by Alexander Roberts and James Donaldson. Moscow, ID: Romans Road Media, 2015.

Feinberg, John S. *Can you Believe it's True? Christian Apologetics in a Modern and Postmodern Era*. Wheaton: Crossway, 2013.

Fernandes, Phill. "The Apologetic Methodology of Blaise Pascal." *Christian Apologetics Journal* 6, no. 2 (2007): 97–111.

Frame, John M. *Apologetics to the Glory of God*. Phillipsburg: P&R Publishing, 1994.

Freede, Michael. "Origen's Treatise Against Celsus." In *Apologetics in the Roman Empire: Pagans, Jews and Christians*, edited by Mark Edwards, Martin Goodman, and Simon Price, 131–56. Oxford: Oxford University Press, 1999.

Geisler, Norman L. *Baker Encyclopaedia of Christian Apologetics*. Grand Rapids: Baker Books, 1999.

Goodman, Martin. "Josephus Treatise Against Apion." In *Apologetics in the Roman Empire: Pagans, Jews and Christians*, edited by Mark Edwards, Martin Goodman, and Simon Price, 45–58. Oxford: Oxford University Press, 1999.

Haykin, Michael. *Defending the Truth: Contending for the Faith Yesterday and Today*. Darlington: Evangelical Press, 2004.

Howe, Thomas A. *A Critique of William Lane Craig's In Quest of the Historical Adam*. Eugene: Wipf & Stock, 2022.

Isichei, Elizabeth. *A History of Christianity in Africa: From Antiquity to the Present*. Grand Rapids: Eerdmans, 1995.

Kigame, Reuben. *Christian Apologetics Through African Eyes*. Eldoret: Posterity Publishers Limited, 2018.

Levering, Matthew. *The Theology of Augustine: An Introductory Guide to his most Important Works*. Grand Rapids: Baker Publishing Group, 2013. Perlego e-edition, https://www.perlego.com/book/2050984/the-theology-of-augustine-an-introductory-guide-to-his-most-important-works-pdf.

Lewis, C. S. *Mere Christianity*. New York: Harper Collins, 2001.

McGrath, Alister E. *The Intellectual World of C. S. Lewis*. Malden: John Wiley & Sons, 2013.

Moreland, J. P. *Christianity and the Nature of Science*. Grand Rapids: Baker Book House, 1989.

———. ed. *The Creation Hypothesis*. Downers Grove: InterVarsity Press, 1994.

Oden, Thomas. *How Africa Shaped the Christian Mind: Rediscovering the African Seedbed of Western Christianity*. Downers Grove: InterVarsity Press, 2007.

Pascal, Blaise. *Pensees*. Translated by W. F. Trotter. Mineola: Dover Publications, 2003. Perlego e-edition, https://www.perlego.com/book/4195836/penses-pdf.

Perkins, Pheme. *Gnosticism and the New Testament*. Minneapolis: Fortress Press, 1993.

Powell, Mark Allan. *Introducing the New Testament: A Historical, Literary, and Theological Survey*. Grand Rapids: Baker Books, 2018.

Price, Simon. "Latin Christian Apologists: Minucius Felix, Tertullian and Cyprian." In *Apologetics in the Roman Empire: Pagans, Jews and Christians*, edited by Mark Edwards, Martin Goodman and Simon Price, 105–30. Oxford: Oxford University Press, 1999.

Rajak, Tessa. "Talking at Trypho: Christian Apologetic as Anti-Judaism in Justyn's Dialogue with Trypho the Jew." In *Apologetics in the Roman Empire: Pagans, Jews and Christians,* edited by Mark Edwards, Martin Goodman and Simon Price, 59–80. Oxford: Oxford University Press, 1999.

Reichenbach, Bruce. "Cosmological Argument." In *The Stanford Encyclopaedia of Philosophy* (Winter 2021 edition). Edited by Edward N. Zalta. https://plato.stanford.edu/archives/win2021/entries/cosmological-argument/.

Shaw, Mark, and Wanjiru M. Gitau. *The Kingdom of God in Africa: A History of African Christianity*. Carlisle: Langham Global Library, 2020.

Sproul, Robert C. *After Darkness, Light: Distinctives of Reformed Theology: Essays in Honor of RC Sproul*. Phillipsburg: P&R Publishing, 2003.

Swain, Simon. "Defending Hellenism: Philostratus, In Honour of Apollonius." In *Apologetics in the Roman Empire: Pagans, Jews and Christians*, edited by Mark Edwards, Martin Goodman and Simon Price, 157–96. Oxford: Oxford University Press, 1999.

Tomlin, Graham. "Profiles in Faith: Blaise Pascal (1623–1662)." *Knowing and Doing* (2006): 1–4.

Young, Frances. "Greek Apologists in the 2nd Century." In *Apologetics in the Roman Empire: Pagans, Jews and Christians*, edited by Mark Edwards, Martin Goodman and Simon Price. Oxford: Oxford University Press, 1999.

Part II

Philosophical Issues

4

Why Natural Evil is Really Moral Evil in African Thought

Joseph Okello, PhD

Professor at Asbury Theological Seminary, Florida, USA

Abstract

Specific ascriptions of natural evil to the work of non-human free-willed agents highlights a view already held by African Christian philosophers and theologians, which, if re-incorporated into the discussion, will not only succeed in reducing natural evil to moral evil, but also render natural evil so reduced rather innocuous as evidence against belief in the existence of God. This ascription renders the dichotomy between natural evil and moral evil invisible in the African theological and philosophical mindset. This dichotomy between natural and moral evil never truly existed in pre-colonial African thought specifically because the distinction between the larger antecedent categories of good and evil, along with whatever caused them or brought them about, remained largely and, for that matter, fundamentally metaphysical.

Keywords: God, Good, Evil, Suffering, Pain

1. Introduction

The problem of evil is routinely presented as the problem of attempting to square the facts and the reality of evil with belief in the existence of God. In other words, theists have no right to believe in the existence of an all-good and an all-powerful God unless they reconcile this belief, in some way, with the facts and the reality of evil. Recent discussions on the problem of evil among Christian philosophers in Western academia seem to run counter to a motif long sustained by African Christian theology. I speak, here, of the ascription of the so-called natural evil to the actions of non-human free-willed agents. Quite unsurprisingly, not much of the Western writings acknowledge or give credit to the African contribution to this debate made by the likes of John S. Mbiti in the eastern part of Africa or by Kwame Gyekye in the western part of Africa. Rather, Christian philosophers in the West seem to present these formulations as if they were breaking new ground in the debate or as if they were reawakening a previously shelved vantage point by the West[1] – one to be revisited when the dust had settled on the more traditional discussions such as the logical, evidential, gratuitous or, for that matter, existential problems of evil.

I argue, in this work, however, that specific ascriptions of natural evil to the work of non-human free-willed agents highlights a view long held by African Christian philosophers and theologians, which, if re-incorporated into the discussion, will not only succeed in reducing natural evil to moral evil, but also render natural evil so-reduced rather innocuous as evidence against belief in the existence of God. By non-human free-willed agents, I refer to supernatural entities commonly identified as spirit beings in both scholarly and non-scholarly circles. This ascription renders the dichotomy between natural evil and moral evil invisible in the African theological and philosophical mindset. By way of review, moral evil is the kind of evil resulting from free human activity, whereas natural evil is any other kind of evil, the kind resulting, not from human sources, but from processes of nature un-initiated by human will.[2] This dichotomy between natural and moral evil never truly existed in pre-colonial African thought specifically because the distinction

1. African philosophers of religion have actually broached the topic of the problem of evil in two divergent ways. The "African theistic view" provides a theodicy based on a transcendent conceptualization of God while the African "limited God view" presents an atheistic opposition given a limited view of God's attributes in light of the problem of evil whereby this view "regards God as good and better than other beings, but not a morally perfect entity" (p. 8). See Luís Cordeiro-Rodrigues, and Ada Agada, "African Philosophy of Religion: Concepts of God, Ancestors, and the Problem of Evil," *Philosophy Compass* 17.8 (2022): 1–11. DOI: 10.1111/phc3.12864. However, other philosophers of religion note that there are scant literature addressing the problem of evil from an African perspective – Chimakonan and Chimakonan argues that this might be because the problem of evil, particularly in its logical form is based on a faulty dichotomous view of good and evil (p. 327). See Jonathan O. Chimakonam and Amara Esther Chimakonam, "Examining the Logical Argument of the Problem of Evil from an African Perspective," *Religious Studies* 59 no. 2 (2023): 326–39.

2. Alvin Plantinga, "The Free Will Defense," in *The Problem of Evil: Selected Readings*, ed. Michael L. Peterson, 2nd ed. (Notre Dame: University of Notre Dame Press, 2017), 112.

between the larger antecedent categories of good and evil, along with whatever caused them or brought them about, remained largely and, for that matter, fundamentally metaphysical. A cursory glance at African Traditional Religion (ATR for short) across the African continent will show how those committed to its (ATR) postulates routinely view both human and supernatural free-willed agents as sources of good and evil. The good originates from good spirits and good humans, and evil originates from evil spirits and, of course, evil humans.

2. The Westernized Approach

In order to trace a rough contour of the debate in the west, let me begin with Alvin Plantinga. Plantinga, a leading Christian philosopher in the west, finds it logically possible, in his highly influential work, "The Free Will Defense," that non-human free-willed agents cause natural evil.[3] For anyone familiar with angelology and demonology, Plantinga seems to appeal to supernatural entities as the source of natural evil. In his anthology, *Philosophy of Religion*, Louis Pojman seems to think that this, indeed, is what Plantinga seems to be saying.[4] In other words, despite whatever else one may think about Plantinga's postulations, at the very least, he seems to appeal to supernatural entities, such as demons, as the source of natural evil. However, a certain number of philosophers suggest a weaker interpretation of Plantinga. More specifically, they contend that Plantinga only proposes the logical possibility of this outcome rather than the actualization of it.[5] A logical possibility need not be seen as an actualized description of an obtained state of affairs. Hence, they would argue, if one confines oneself only to this work, one will perhaps not find enough evidence to think Plantinga attributes natural evil to the work of these agents.

However, Plantinga's "Felix Culpa Theodicy" seems to make the bolder claim already accepted by African philosophers, namely, that demons cause natural evil. Even though the appeal to demons as the source of natural evil is not the central thrust of his Felix Culpa Theodicy, it is certainly there. In his development of this very idea, Plantinga thinks the term "natural evil" is, perhaps, a misnomer in the sense that "natural evil" is really an instance of "moral evil." Quite possibly, Plantinga says, deeper layers to the sin and evil the

---

3. Plantinga, *God Freedom and Evil* (Grand Rapids: Eerdmans, 1974), 58.

4. Louis Pojman, ed., *Philosophy of Religion: An Anthology*, 2nd ed. (Belmont: Wadsworth Publishing, 1993), 164.

5. See, for example, Michael L. Peterson et al., *Reason and Religious Belief*, 1st ed. (New York: Oxford University Press, 1990), 107.

world displays exist, far deeper than those exhibited by human beings. More specifically, Plantinga says the suffering and evil of this sort, traditionally, gets attributed to the action of the devil and his cohorts. He notes, correctly, that the devil is a mighty non-human free creature who rebelled against God long before humans arrived on the scene. Much of the natural evil we see in the world results from the actions of the devil and his angels.[6]

Immediately after making this observation, Plantinga admits that this suggestion does not seem widely popular among thinkers in the West. It is not widely endorsed by the contemporary intellectual elite. However, Plantinga comes to its defence by observing that whatever Western academia might say by way of evidence against this view remains less than clear. In other words, Western academia does not have a forceful argument against the view that non-human free-willed agents do cause the so-called natural evil. Moreover, the view that beings of this sort get involved in the history of our world seems very likely with respect to traditional Christian theistic belief.[7]

Plantinga is not the only Western thinker subscribing, or possibly beginning to subscribe to this view, or perhaps revealing a secretly long-held conviction on his part, already long held by African thinkers and philosophers. Consider the fact that, in two of his works, Gregory Boyd demonstrates how God remains in conflict with supernatural free-willed creatures attempting to destroy his purpose and goals. Boyd seems to hold that these supernatural demonic forces are responsible for much, though not all, human suffering, such as disease, birth defects, floods and most of what we call natural evil.[8]

What should strike the reader as particularly interesting is the fact that Plantinga is a Calvinist and also a person committed to the view that God knows the future free actions of his creatures, while Boyd is an Arminian and also an open theist, committed to the view that God has limited himself with respect to knowing the future free actions of his creatures, hence he does not know the choices humans will make until they make them. Both Plantinga and Boyd agree, however, that demonic forces are indeed responsible for what we would call natural evil today. The point I press here is this: where a Calvinist such as Plantinga and an Arminian such as Boyd seem to agree, we need to take them seriously.

---

6. Plantinga, "Felix Culpa Theodicy," in *The Problem of Evil: Selected Readings*, 2nd ed., ed. Michael L. Peterson (Notre Dame: University of Notre Dame Press, 2017), 377.

7. Plantinga, "Felix Culpa Theodicy."

8. See, for example, Gregory Boyd, *God at War: The Bible and Spiritual Conflict* (Downers Grove: InterVarsity Press, 1997); and *Satan and the Problem of Evil: Constructing a Trinitarian Warfare Theodicy* (Downers Grove, IL; InterVarsity Press, 2001).

3. The African Perspective

Though this appeal to supernatural entities as the source or cause of natural evil seems to be gaining currency among Western philosophers and theologians, it is not new in both academic and non-academic circles among African philosophers and theologians. In an earlier work,[9] I outlined the former view, drawing from John S. Mbiti's work, *African Religions and Philosophies*. For example, Mbiti writes: "In nearly all African societies, it is thought that the spirits are either the origin of evil, or agents of evil."[10] Mbiti had been arguing that African societies hold that beings exercising free will do cause evil. Mbiti observes how people suspected of working maliciously against their relatives and neighbours exist in every community. How do they accomplish these acts of evil? They do so through the use of magic, sorcery and witchcraft. According to Mbiti, mystical power is neither good nor evil in itself. Rather, one experiences it as evil. This view, then, makes evil an independent and external object that must be intended by human or spiritual agents.[11] As one might suspect, this possibility leaves little to no room for natural evil. One can ultimately trace what we call natural evil all the way back to a free-willed agent, whether human or non-human.

This view finds acceptance among Africans in both the academic and the non-academic walks of life. The commonly accepted view among both camps reveals the conviction that supernatural entities do cause natural evil. A variety of African Christian philosophers seem even more specific. They subscribe to the view that demonic and satanic forces cause natural evil. The African academic circle also has its contribution to make toward this debate. Kwame Gyekye, for example, has done extensive research among the Akan people of Ghana on the problem of evil. Gyekye's research among the Akan people revealed the conviction that evil is not a creation of God. Rather, evil is a creation of the lesser spirits and humanity's free will. These two entities provide the sources for evil.[12] Suppose, then, that a person's path is strewn with failures, whether by his or her own actions, desires, decisions and intentions, or by the

---

9. See Joseph Okello, "An Analysis of An African Reflections on Evil," *African Journal of Evangelical Theology* 22 no. 2 (2003): 63–84.

10. John S. Mbiti, *African Religions and Philosophy* (Nairobi: East African Educational Publishers, 1994), 204.

11. Mbiti, *African Religions*, 204.

12. Kwame Gyekye, *An Essay on African Philosophical Thought* (New York: Cambridge University Press, 1987), 124.

activities of some supposed evil forces. Such a person, Gyekye notes, may try to do something about the situation by say, consulting priests and diviners.[13]

Notice, therefore, how, in this thinking, both human free will and supernatural entities seem widely regarded as the cause of evil. According to the Akan people, the capacity of these entities to do evil comes from the operations of the independent wills of those very beings, whether spiritual or human. Moreover, if God were to stop evil by intervening every time these creatures performed their evil acts, humans would act in a wholly determined way without the exercise of their free choice at all, which would then contradict the general nature of the idea of free will as understood by the Akan thinker.[14]

4. The Biblical Contrast

What I have outlined above concerning the African view, however, differs from the biblical understanding on an important front. Whereas the African view does attribute or appeal to non-human free-willed agents as the source of evil, African angelology and demonology remains different from the biblical view. For a majority of traditional non-Christian Africans committed to the tenets of ATR, good humans become good spirits when they die, and bad humans become bad spirits when they die. Hence, even though the African view seems to attribute the occurrence of natural evil to non-human free-willed agents, those agents were originally humans, and only became spirits after their deaths.

The biblical view, of course, is different. Humans remain in that category when they die. More importantly, they do not change to become demons or angels. Stated differently, demons were originally good angels, and merely became demons after their rebellion in heaven. The Christian believer, therefore, finds these demons as the cause of natural evil. Thus, even though both the traditional African view seems to agree with the orthodox Christian view concerning the source of natural evil, they differ in their understanding of how those demons became demons in the first place. In the Christian view, bad angels, or demons for that matter, were originally good angels before their rebellion in heaven and were never humans, while in the African traditional view, demons were originally bad humans and were never understood or classified as angels.

Therefore, what the African Christian does with this understanding is to accept the view that seems to have more explanatory power in its explication of

13. Gyekye, *An Essay*, 116.

14. Gyekye, *An Essay*, 124.

the facts. This requirement would take us too far afield and is certainly beyond the scope of this paper. Needless to say, the African Christian committed to the fidelity of Scripture will accept the biblical view as more adequate, not only from a rational perspective, but also from an empirical perspective. The former is the task of Christian apologetics, where the African view gets tested for explanatory power, factual adequacy and logical consistency. The latter remains the purview of religious experience where the power of the gospel literally comes to life in the area of deliverance from both demonic possessions and oppressions. This area of religious experience seems foreign to a majority of adherents to Western Christianity, hence the reluctance to engage the topic of demonology in their interlocutions about natural evil.

5. The Biblical Evidence

I have noted above how the African view seems to agree with the biblical view that natural evil can be traced back to the actions of non-human free-willed supernatural agents. I have noted the difference between the biblical view and the African view. While I note that the African view deviates from the Christian Bible in its demonology, it does find a common ground with the biblical view by supposing that natural evil is really the work of supernatural demonic forces. Given this observation, a reminder of how the Bible articulates this view remains in order. In what follows, I highlight this reminder to demonstrate the biblical evidence for this claim.

The first place the African theologian would turn to is the book of Job. The story begins with Job as an upright and blameless man who feared God and shunned evil. He was prosperous, he had seven sons and three daughters, and was quite wealthy, owning seven thousand sheep, three thousand camels, five hundred yoke of oxen and five hundred donkeys. He also had a large number of servants. He was the greatest man that ever lived among all the people of the East (Job 1:1–4).

However, the angels presented themselves before the Lord on a certain day and the devil came alongside them. After asking the devil where he came from, the Lord asked the devil whether he had considered his servant Job, a blameless man who feared God and shunned evil, and that he was unique in this way because no one else was like him. The devil, however, complained that God had put a hedge of protection around Job, around Job's household and around everything Job had. However, if God were to stretch out his hand against Job, the devil offered, Job would curse God to God's face. The Lord God gave the devil the permission to attack Job's wealth, and to attack his family, but he denied the devil any permission to touch Job himself (Job 1:8–12).

Scripture gives a graphic portrayal of how the devil went about the business of attacking Job's wealth. He begins by attacking Job's donkeys as they grazed. He used the Sabaeans to accomplish this task and allowed one of Job's servants to escape and tell Job the sad news. The Sabaeans put Job's servants to the sword as they attacked the five hundred donkeys and carried them off. As the servants relayed the news to Job, another messenger appeared and shared more sad news with Job. He said, "The fire of God fell from the sky and burned up the sheep and the servants, and I am the only one who has escaped to tell you!" (Job 1:13–16).

While he was still speaking, Scripture says, another messenger appeared and reported that the Chaldeans raided Job's camels and carried them off. They put the servants to the sword, and he alone escaped to report the news to Job. As he spoke, another messenger appeared and shares more painful news with Job, namely, that his children were feasting and drinking wine at the eldest brother's house. For some unexplainable reason to him, a mighty wind came in from the desert and struck the four corners of the elder brother's house and the walls of the house collapsed on the children and they all died, leaving the servant as the only escapee to relay the story (Job 1:17–19).

Job responds by mourning the loss, not only of his property, but his children. He tears his robe, shaves his head and falls to the ground in worship by acknowledging that he came to this world a naked man and that he will depart this world a naked man. He acknowledges that the Lord gives, and the Lord takes away, and for that reason, the name of the Lord is worthy to be praised (Job 1:20–22).

This story does not end here, as we all know. The devil presents himself before the Lord a second time, and the Lord points out to the devil that Job was an upright, blameless, Godfearing man who shunned evil, and despite the devil's intention to get Job to curse God, Job maintained his integrity. The devil, not satisfied with his attack on Job's wealth and family, suggests that if God were to attack Job's health, then Job would curse God to his face. Confidently enough, God gives the devil permission to attack Job's health but warns the devil to spare Job's life. The devil afflicts Job with painful sores from the soles of his feet to the top of his head. Job takes a piece of broken pottery and scraps himself with the pottery as he sits among the ashes (Job 2:3–10).

Notice what is going on here. From a human perspective, except for the Sabaean attack on Job's donkeys and the Chaldean attack on Job's camels (which easily fits the pattern of moral evil), the fire from the sky burning up the sheep and the collapse of the wall (caused by the mighty wind) upon Job's children fits the pattern of what philosophers call natural evil. This fire could easily pass for lightning. The gust of wind causing the walls to collapse on the children could have been a storm, or a tornado, or a hurricane, or any of those forces of nature combined – all of which serve as examples of natural evil. The explanations of these phenomena, as natural evil, are the sorts of explanations we would offer.

However, the *how* explanations fail to satisfy human curiosity because they answer the *how* aspect of the question and not the *why* aspect of the question. Job got to hear the how aspect, namely, the exact ways in which the devastation occurred, as reported by his servants. The why aspect of the question remained unanswered, and valiant attempts by his three friends remained a colossal failure. Anyone unfamiliar with the spiritual dimension of this story would readily reach this conclusion, leaving the question "why do bad things happen to good people?" without a formidable answer. The best shot the interlocutors in the debate could give by way of an answer is the claim that these events were instances of natural evil. Hence, in the absence of specific appeals to supernatural forces working behind the scenes, we have no answer.

However, a person familiar with the spiritual dimension of this story would appeal to the very context we find in the book of Job, namely: the devil is in the details! He is working behind the scenes to bring the devastation of the sort we see explained in that book. The devil is a non-human free-willed agent who causes much mischief in the lives of God's sentient creatures, and the story of Job is an instance of this outworking. The African traditional religionist would, quite possibly, be prepared to accept this explanation even if he or she would have a different understanding of the origin of the spiritual agent behind the catastrophes. The African Christian believer would embrace this very idea specifically because it is included in a book to which he or she remains committed as a rule of faith.

Therefore, from the orthodox traditional Christian perspective, natural evil can be traced back to the work of non-human free-willed agents. The book of Job clearly states that this agent is already working behind the scenes to cause the kind of evil we see in the world today. Notice, also, that the book of Job does not attribute the cause of natural evil to God, even though a character in the book of Job does attribute it to God when he says, "The fire of God fell from the sky and burned up the sheep." Not even the African traditional religionist would be willing to trace the cause of natural evil all the way back to God. As already noted from Mbiti, many African societies hesitate to attribute to God any occurrences of evil, whether moral or natural.[15] Also, Gyekye reports in his research that the Akan people locate the source of the problem of evil elsewhere than in the relationship between God's attributes and the fact of the existence of evil specifically because Akan thinkers do not hold that evil is a creation of God. The lesser spirits and human free will do provide the sources for evil.[16]

6. Implications for the Free Will Defence

This finding notwithstanding, the curious outcome of what we have, hitherto, observed, is not only the claim that non-human free-willed agents do, in fact cause evil. It brings out an even more important point we have alluded to several times throughout this paper, namely: Since all instances of natural evil can be traced to supernatural free-willed creatures such as the devil and his angels, we are led to conclude that all instances of natural evil are reducible to moral evil. Stated differently, every natural evil is moral evil. If all natural evil is moral evil, then no such thing as natural evil exists in the sense routinely construed, as compelling as that might be to the naked eye. Rather, all instances of natural evil must be reduced to moral evil. They only appear to happen naturally, but in reality, they are moral in the sense that all of them happen due to the exercise of free will, whether by humans, or by non-human choice-making agents.

Therefore, this consideration brings us to an interesting point in the debate concerning the problem of evil via the free will defence: if Alvin Plantinga's free will defence is successful, then the problem of moral evil has been solved. Alvin Plantinga's free will defence is, indeed, successful. Therefore, by *modus ponens*, the problem of moral evil has been solved. If all natural evil is moral evil, then the problem of natural evil has been solved as well. All natural evil is indeed moral evil. Therefore, by *modus ponens*, the problem of natural evil has been solved. The African contribution to the debate, then, is the observation that it positions natural evil in a way that allows it to be solved successfully by the free will defence presented by Alvin Plantinga.

How is Plantinga's free will defence successful? A recap of the argument Alvin Plantinga presented is in order. The free will defence is successful because it notes how a world with significantly free creatures is a better world than a world with no free creatures at all. God can create significantly free creatures, but he cannot create such creatures and, at the same time, determine them

15. Mbiti, *African Religions*, 204.

16. Gyekye, *An Essay*, 124.

to do only what is right. To be capable of moral good, a significantly free creature must also be capable of moral evil. Plantinga says God cannot give these creatures the freedom to perform evil and at the same time prevent them from doing so. However, some of the free creatures God created misused their freedom by doing wrong, and this is the source of moral evil. The fact that such creatures sometimes go wrong does not count against God's omnipresence or against God's goodness.[17] This fact enables the Christian believer to see how belief in the existence of God remains logically compatible with the facts and the reality of evil.

Plantinga formulated this defence against the logical problem of evil raised by J. L. Mackie who argued, roughly, that belief in God remains logically incompatible with the facts and reality of evil.[18] Mackie paraded three specific claims that the Christian theologian accepts, namely: God is all-good, God is omnipotent, and evil exists. The Christian cannot adhere to all three claims consistently, Mackie argued. If he or she accepts any two of these claims, the third claim would contradict the other two.[19] Plantinga's free will defence shows that Mackie fails to locate the exact nature of the inconsistency if Mackie accepts the logical possibility that an omnipotent being, namely, God, remains capable of creating free creatures such as us. In this sense, then, the free will defence is successful.

The complaint has been raised, in the past, that the free will defence fails to solve the problem of natural evil, even though it does solve the problem of moral evil. I argue, however, that if we accept the belief that natural evil is really moral evil because it can be traced back to the work of non-human free-willed agents, then the free will defence does apply to natural evil as well specifically because natural evil is really moral evil in disguise. This gives the Christian believer, African or otherwise, the apologetic tool for defending the Christian faith against the objection that it fails to account for the existence of natural evil, or the objection that belief in God is logically inconsistent with the facts and reality of natural evil.

To be sure, a majority of the alert African thinkers would find the view surprising, namely, that such a thing as natural evil exists or, to state it differently, that a natural catastrophe without a personalistic cause really does exist. As the African theologian Deusdedit Nkurunziza notes,

---

17. Plantinga, "The Free Will Defense," 112–13.

18. J. L. Mackie, "Evil and Omnipotence," in *The Problem of Evil: Selected Readings* (Notre Dame: University of Notre Dame Press, 2017), 81.

19. Mackie, "Evil and Omnipotence," 82.

> Every tragic event is believed to have a reason and a personal cause. The traditional Bantu are not satisfied with secondary explanations and have no appreciation for the concept of coincidence. The question why is fundamental for them. When illness occurs, merely listing the cause of the disease . . . is only of relative interest. They want to know why that particular person contracted the disease in question.[20]

The explanation, then, for so-called natural evil finds its basis in a personalistic origin. A personalistic explanation is more satisfactory and more complete for the African thinker wrestling with the problem of evil than the explanation that his or her tragedy is the result of an impersonal force.

To be sure, appealing to an impersonal force as an explanation for why an instance of tragedy occurred remains profoundly unsatisfactory. This kind of explanation is of the sort we find among methodological naturalists. As already noted, the spiritual background behind the story of Job not only helps to explain why Job suffered the way he did, it lends credence to the view hitherto adumbrated. I suggest all Christians, whether global North Christians or those from the global South, be bold in seeing the devil in the details, and surrendering those details to their Blessed Redeemer as the source of their redemption from evil. Indeed, we find this very redemption already provided not only by the cross of Christ, but also by his empty tomb.

Bibliography

Boyd, Greg. *God at War: The Bible and Spiritual Conflict.* Downers Grove: InterVarsity Press, 1997.

———. *Satan and the Problem of Evil: Constructing a Trinitarian Warfare Theodicy.* Downers Grove: InterVarsity Press, 2001.

Chimakonam, Jonathan O., and Amara Esther Chimakonam. "Examining the Logical Argument of the Problem of Evil from an African Perspective." *Religious Studies* 59, no. 2 (2023): 326–39. DOI: 10.1017/S0034412522000300.

Cordeiro-Rodrigues, Luís, and Ada Agada. "African Philosophy of Religion: Concepts of God, Ancestors, and the Problem of Evil." *Philosophy Compass* 17, no. 8 (2022): 1–11. DOI: 10.1111/phc3.12864.

Gyekye, Kwame. *An Essay on African Philosophical Thought.* New York: Cambridge University Press, 1987.

---

20. Deusdedit Nkurunziza, *Bantu Philosophy of Life in the Light of the Christian Message: A Basis for African Vitalistic Theology* (Frankfurt Main: Peter Lang, 1989), 118.

Mackie, J. L. "Evil and Omnipotence." In *The Problem of Evil: Selected Readings*, 2nd ed, edited by Michael L. Peterson, 81–94. Notre Dame: University of Notre Dame Press, 2017.

Mbiti, John S. *African Religions and Philosophy*. Nairobi: East African Educational Publishers, 1994.

Nkurunziza, Deusdedit. *Bantu Philosophy of Life in the Light of the Christian Message: A Basis for African Vitalistic Theology*. Frankfurt Main: Peter Lang, 1989.

Okello, Joseph. "An Analysis of African Reflections on Evil." *African Journal of Evangelical Theology* 22, no. 2 (2003): 63–84.

Peterson, Michael L., William Hasker, Bruce Reichenbach, and David Basinger.. *Reason and Religious Belief.* 1st edition. Oxford: Oxford University Press, 1990.

Plantinga, Alvin. "Felix Culpa Theodicy." In *The Problem of Evil: Selected Readings*, 2nd ed, edited by Michael L. Peterson, 363–89. Notre Dame: University of Notre Dame Press, 2017.

———. "The Free Will Defense." In *The Problem of Evil: Selected Readings*, 2nd ed, edited by Michael L. Peterson, 95–129. Notre Dame: University of Notre-Dame Press, 2017.

———. *God Freedom and Evil*. Grand Rapids: Eerdmans, 1974.

Pojman, Louis, ed. *Philosophy of Religion: An Anthology*, 2nd ed. Belmont: Wadsworth Publishing, 1993.

5

Do all Religions Lead to the Same God?

Mihretu P. Guta, PhD

Lecturer at Biola University, California, USA and Adjunct Professor at Azusa Pacific University, California, USA

Abstract

The question of whether or not all religions lead to the same God continues to stir controversies among philosophers of religion and theologians. Let us call this question, the Destination Question. Contemporary controversies over the Destination Question are advanced against the backdrop of three main views of salvation, namely pluralism, inclusivism, and particularism/exclusivism. A pluralist believes that all major world religions are capable of independently giving access to salvific encounters with the same divine reality. An inclusivist believes that a genuine salvific encounter with divine reality can be facilitated via multiple religious traditions. A particularist believes that a genuine salvific encounter with divine reality can only be had via one true religion. Discussions advanced in defence of these positions, although informative and interesting in their own ways, tend to do very little in terms of unpacking some of the complex philosophical/theological issues that underlie the Destination Question. In this chapter, I will try to show why a successful answer to the Destination Question is contingent on two things. In this case, an affirmative answer to the Destination Question succeeds only if its proponents satisfy what I call the Referent Identity Requirement. On the other hand, a negative answer to the Destination Question succeeds only if its proponents satisfy what I call the Elimination Principle Requirement. Either way tackling the Destination Question proves to be more complicated than many of us would like to admit. To see why this is the case, we need to engage in a second-order examination of the Destination Question. Finally, I will conclude this chapter by claiming why a lasting solution for the Destination Question continues to be contentious.

Keywords: Inclusivism, Logic, Particularism, Pluralism

1. Introduction

What is religion? There is no universally accepted definition of "religion."[1] But we can come up with a working definition. Michael Peterson et al. suggest such a definition. I describe it as follows:

A. Religion is constituted by a set of beliefs, actions, and experiences, both personal and collective, organized around a concept of an ultimate reality that inspires or requires devotion, worship, or a focused life orientation.[2]

B. This [ultimate] reality may be understood as a unity or a plurality, personal or nonpersonal, divine or not, differing from religion to religion.[3]

Both (A) and (B) tell us about the core features of religion. In the case of (A), the features consist of (i) doctrine or teachings (e.g. beliefs); (ii) praxis (e.g. actions and experiences); (iii) a concept of ultimate reality (e.g. God

1. Giving a watertight definition of the notion of religion requires satisfying a set of necessary and sufficient conditions. But meeting such a stringent expectation is extremely difficult, if not impossible. Unfortunately, coming up with such a definition of religion continues to be elusive (see Mihretu Guta, "Conceptual Analysis: What is Religion?," unpublished paper). For helpful discussion on some of these issues, see Stephen Prothero, *Religion Matters: An Introduction to the World's Religions* (London: Norton, 2020), 14–17; Jeffrey Brodd et al., *Invitation to World Religions* (Oxford: Oxford University Press, 2019), 8–10; Michael Peterson et al., eds., *Reason and Religious Belief: An Introduction to the Philosophy of Religion*, 5th ed. (New York: Oxford University Press, 2012), 6–8; R. D. Geivett, "Religious Diversity and the Futility of Neutrality," in Robert B. Stewart, ed., *Can Only One Religion Be True?: Paul Knitter and Harold Netland in Dialogue* (Minneapolis: Augsburg Fortress Press, 2013), 181–202, 181–83; A. S. Nigosian, *World Faiths* (New York: St. Martin's Press, 1994), ch. 1.

2. Peterson et al., *Reason and* Religious *Belief*, 7.

3. According to Peterson et al., *Reason and Religious Belief*, "every cultural phenomenon that we call a religion fits this definition" (7).

and Brahman); and (iv) devotion/worship (e.g. rituals). Let's call the features described in (i)–(iv) collectively, the *UR-centric features.*[4]

In the case of (B), the features in question concern diverse conceptions of ultimate reality, namely: (a) unity or a plurality; (b) personal or nonpersonal; and (c) divine or not. Let's call the features in (a)–(c), the *non-monolithic conceptions of UR*. These features can be analyzed in two stages, namely the first order and the second-order levels respectively.

The first-order level discussions concerning the UR-centric features and the non-monolithic conceptions of UR are primarily descriptive in nature. That is, such discussions focus on descriptive accounts of the history, the teaching(s), and the ritual(s) of religions like Hinduism, Buddhism, Christianity, Islam, Daoism and Sikhism. At this level, the focus is not on evaluating whether or not, say, the teachings of a particular religion are correct. Rather a descriptive analysis in question focuses on stating what religions such as Buddhism teach, which also includes what their adherents practice. This is what we read in any standard textbooks on world religions.[5] At the first-order level, we encounter no direct philosophical examination of the contents of the teachings of religions.[6] The latter task belongs to a second-order level inquiry. In this case, our analysis shifts to a systematic philosophical examination of the first-order teachings of religions. The second-order level approach takes a centre stage in the philosophy of religion (one of the branches of philosophy). As Peterson et al., point out, the philosophy of religion attempts to analyze as well as critically examine religious beliefs for their consistency, coherence, and reasonableness.[7]

In this chapter, my goal is to critically examine the following question: do all religions lead to the same God? Let's call this question the Destination Question. I will examine this question against the backdrop of the foregoing distinction between the first order and the second-order levels. However, my aim is not to engage in a descriptive (first-order level) analysis of the Destination Question. So my focus will be on advancing the second-order

---

4. Here and throughout this paper, I use UR as a short form for Ultimate Reality. For excellent discussion on religious doctrines, see Paul J. Griffiths, "The Universality and Uniqueness of Religious Doctrines," in Peterson et al., *Reason and Religious Belief*, 599–605.

5. See for example, Brodd et al., *Invitation to World Religions*; Prothero *Religion Matters* and Nigosian, *World Faiths.*

6. See for example, Brodd et al., *Invitation to World Religions*; Prothero *Religion Matters* and Nigosian, *World Faiths.*

7. Peterson et al., *Reason and Religious Belief*, 10; also see 1–9, and Chad Meister and Paul Copan, *The Routledge Companion to Philosophy of Religion*, 2nd ed. (New York: Routledge, 2007/2013), esp. parts I–III.

level discussion of the Destination Question. As I see it, an adequate answer to the Destination Question must satisfy, at least, two conditions.

First, an affirmative answer to the Destination Question must satisfy what I call the *Referent Identity Requirement* (the Referent Identity-R). Second, a negative answer to the Destination Question must satisfy what I call the *Elimination Principle Requirement* (the Elimination Principle-R). The former deals with reference whereas the latter deals with establishing one true religion. Whichever answer one happens to embrace, as we shall see, establishing a conclusive answer to the Destination Question proves to be harder than many of us would like to admit.

For the present discussion, I do not explicitly attempt to discuss my own position on the issue at hand. I do this for purely pedagogical reasons thereby inviting readers in general, and seminary students in particular, to establish the answers to the Destination Question that they think are defensible and plausible. Contemporary discussions over this issue often gloss over some of the complex philosophical issues that underlie the Destination Question. The discussion to follow will make some contribution toward addressing this deficiency. The discussion will proceed as follows:

In section 2, I will clarify and discuss the inner logical structure of the Destination Question. In section 3, I will discuss what it would take to satisfy both the Referent Identity-R and the Elimination Principle-R. In section 4, I will discuss how the three views of salvation, namely pluralism, inclusivism, and particularism fair in terms of satisfying the Referent Identity-R and the Elimination Principle-R. Pluralists argue that the major religions of the world are capable of independently giving people access to salvific encounters with the same divine reality. Inclusivists argue that genuine salvific encounters with divine reality can be facilitated via multiple religious traditions. Particularists argue that genuine salvific encounters with divine reality are possible only via one true religion.[8] In section 5, I will consider one objection and reply. Finally, in section 6, I will conclude this chapter by claiming why solutions to the Destination Question continue to be contentious.

2. The Destination Question Clarified and Analyzed

It could be said that the Destination Question requires no more than a "yes" or a "no" answer. But that is not the case. The Destination Question has an inner

8. See for example, Gundry, Okholm and Phillips, eds., *Four Views on Salvation in a Pluralistic World* (Grand Rapids: Zondervan, 1995).

logical structure. Understanding this logical structure is important to properly analyze it. But how can we show the inner logical structure in question? We can do this by introducing some modifications to the Destination Question. Here we need some strategy. In this case, we should convert the Destination Question into truth-evaluable categorical statements or propositions. We can carry out this task by deploying classical (Aristotelian) logic and first-order predicate logic.

2.1 Classical Logic

At the heart of classical logic lie categorical propositions. But what is a proposition?[9] A proposition is said to relate two classes denoted by a subject term, *S*, and a predicate term, *P*. Taken this way, a proposition denies or affirms that one class, say, *S*, is included in some other class, say, *P*, either in whole or in part. In light of this, classical logic identifies four kinds of categorical propositions. These propositions are represented by four special letters, namely A, E, I and O.[10]

A represents universal affirmative propositions; **E** represents universal negative propositions; **I** represents particular affirmative propositions, and **O** represents particular negative propositions. The standard form of these propositions or statements is stated as follows:[11]

A All *S* is *P*.

E No *S* is *P*.

I Some *S* is *P*.

O Some *S* is not *P*.

We can use the foregoing four kinds of propositions as tools to establish the conversion of the Destination Question into a statement. The conversion takes the following form:

---

9. Philosophers distinguish between, sentences and statements/propositions, see for example, Trenton Merricks, *Propositions* (Oxford: Oxford University Press, 2015). For present purposes, I use the words "statements" and "propositions" interchangeably.

10. Readers with no logic background may find my discussion in this section and in the next a bit abstract and technical. However, the details are being kept to a minimum.

11. For details see Copi, Cohen and McMahon, *Introduction to Logic* (New York: Routledge, 2011), chs. 5–7. The letters A, E, I, O are standard notations for each statement. See also Hurley, *A Concise Introduction to Logic*, 5th ed. (Belmont: Wadsworth, 1994), ch. 4.

1. All religions are paths to the same God.
2. No religions are paths to the same God.
3. Some religions are paths to the same God.
4. Some religions are not paths to the same God.

Using Rs to represent religions and Ps to represent paths, we can formalize the propositions in (1)–(4) as follows:

1. All Rs are Ps.
2. No Rs are Ps.
3. Some Rs are Ps.
4. Some Rs are not Ps.

Logical Relations

Notice that (1) is a universal affirmative proposition of an **A**-type; (2) is a universal negative proposition of an **E**-type; (3) is a particular affirmative proposition of an **I**-type, and (4) is a particular negative proposition of an **O**-type. These four statements are logically related. This can be shown by using the *square of opposition.*[12]

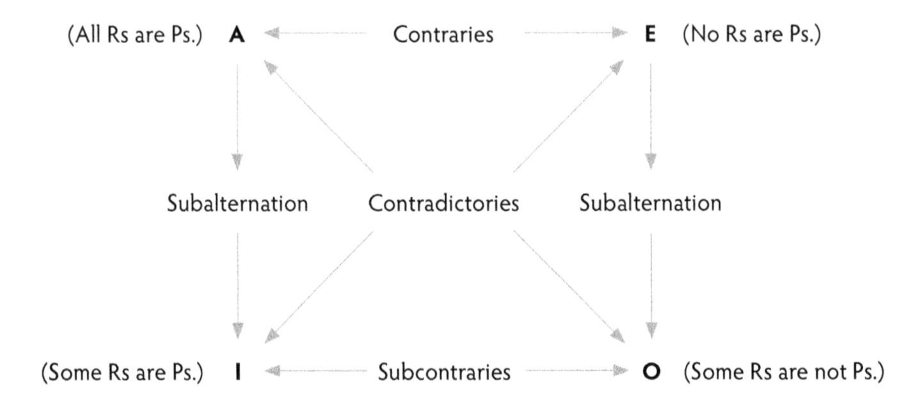

Figure 2: Square of Opposition

12. This is often described as a square diagram, see example, Copi, Cohen and McMahon, *Introduction to Logic*, 178.

In the above square of opposition, (1) "All Rs are Ps" and (2) "No Rs are Ps" are *contraries*, or they cannot both be true. That is, if the proposition, "All religions are paths to the same God" is true, then its opposite proposition, "No religions are paths to the same God" must be ruled out and vice versa. However, both of these statements can be false. (3) "Some Rs are Ps" and (4) "Some Rs are not Ps" are subcontraries. These propositions cannot both be false. But they may both be true. In the case of subalternation, a universal affirmative proposition **A** implies its corresponding particular affirmative proposition **I**. In this case, the proposition, "All religions are paths to the same God" implies its corresponding proposition, "Some religions are paths to the same God." But the converse does not hold. Similarly, a universal negative proposition **E** implies its corresponding particular negative proposition **O**. That is, the proposition, "No religions are paths to the same God" implies its corresponding proposition, "Some religions are not paths to the same God." But the converse does not hold.

Finally, a universal affirmative proposition **A** and a particular negative proposition **O** are *contradictories*. That is, the proposition, "All religions are paths to the same God" and the proposition, "Some religions are not paths to the same God" are contradictories. Similarly, a universal negative proposition **E** and a particular affirmative proposition **I** are contradictories. That is, the proposition, "No religions are paths to the same God" and the proposition, "Some religions are paths to the same God" are contradictories. In a nutshell, any given two propositions are said to be contradictory if one is the negation of the other. Contradictories cannot both be true. They cannot also both be false.

Notice that here our goal is to show the internal structure of the Destination Question. To this effect, we have already taken the crucial step of stating the four categorical propositions as explained above. The question remains: which one of the categorical statements should be adopted to establish the conversion of the Destination Question into a statement? We can answer this question based on determining the scope of the Destination Question. In this case, the scope in question extends to all religions. In light of this, of the four categorical propositions, (1) captures the statement form of the Destination Question. As we recall, (1) is a universal affirmative proposition that takes the form, "All Rs are Ps" (i.e. all religions are paths to the same God). Although our main focus is on (1), the other remaining propositions, namely (2), (3), and (4) also play their own distinctive roles in our analysis of the Destination Question. But my main focus remains to be on (1).

Competing Interpretations

There are two competing interpretations of (1) which must be raised. These are the Aristotelian and the Boolean interpretations respectively.[13] The interpretations in question revolve around the idea of existential import. As Copi, Cohen and McMahon state, "a proposition is said to have existential import if it typically is uttered to assert the existence of objects of some kind."[14] Details aside, for Aristotle, all the four kinds of categorical propositions briefly discussed above do have existential import. As we recall, a universal affirmative proposition **A** implies a particular affirmative proposition **I**. Similarly, a universal negative proposition **E** implies a particular negative proposition **O**. Aristotle fully embraced and endorsed such inferences. For Aristotle, all these four kinds of propositions have existential import.

But George Boole partly agreed and partly disagreed with Aristotle. Like Aristotle, Boole also endorsed that particular propositions **I** and **O** do have existential import. However, unlike Aristotle, Boole rejected that such particular propositions can be inferred from their corresponding **A** and **E** propositions. That is, for Boole, we cannot infer the truth of "Some religions are paths to God" from its corresponding proposition, "All religions are paths to the same God." By the same token, we cannot infer the truth of "Some religions are not paths to the same God" from its corresponding proposition, "No religions are paths to the same God." In commenting on Boole's rejection of the inference in question, Copi, Cohen and McMahon claim that if the **I** and **O** propositions have existential import then they validly follow from their corresponding **A** and **E** propositions. This means that **A** and **E** propositions must also have existential import. But this is said to create a serious problem.[15]

So Boole argued that the best way to handle the **A** and the **E** propositions is to interpret them *conditionally*.[16] For example, "All religions are paths to the

13. A Boolean interpretation refers to the nineteenth-century British mathematician George Boole who modified Aristotle's interpretation of a universal affirmative statement and a universal negative statement. For details, see Copi, Cohen and McMahon, *Introduction to Logic*, ch. 5.

14. Copi, Cohen and McMahon, *Introduction to Logic*, 190.

15. Copi, Cohen and McMahon describe this problem as follows "We know that **A** and **O** propositions, on the traditional square of opposition, are contradictories . . . contradictories cannot both be true, because one of the pair must be false; nor can they both be false, because one of the pair must be true. But *if* corresponding **A** and **O** propositions do have existential import . . . then both contradictories *could* be false . . . if they are both false, they *cannot be contradictories!*" (*Introduction to Logic*, 191–92).

16. Boole is also worried that if we take the **A** and the **E** propositions in the Aristotelian sense (i.e. taking them to have existential import), then non-existent things could be said to exist. For example, "All Unicorns are kind" implies its corresponding particular proposition, "Some

same God" becomes, "If there are such things as religions, they are paths to the same God." Similarly, "No religions are paths to the same God" becomes, "If there are such things as religions, they are not paths to the same God." Notice that understood conditionally, the **A** and the **E** propositions do not have existential import at all. Conditionally stated, such universal propositions neither categorically assert nor deny the existence of anything. This, Boole argues, is one of the key advantages of the modification he made in Aristotle's classical logic. Aristotle's interpretation of the **A** and the **E** propositions can be said to be *strong*. By contrast, the Boolean interpretation of the **A** and the **E** propositions can be said to be *weak*. We shall see in section 4 why each of these interpretations plays a significant role in our analysis of the Destination Question as it pertains to the three views of salvation, namely pluralism, inclusivism, and particularism.

Limitations

Having analyzed and converted the Destination Question into a statement form (i.e. "All religions are paths to the same God") we can now construct an example of a formal deductive argument as follows:

- All religions are paths to the same God.
- Christianity is a religion.
- Therefore, Christianity is a path to the same God.

The above argument is valid. However, there is one problem with it. That is, by using the resources of classical logic alone, we cannot show adequately the inner logical structure of (1).[17] For example, if we symbolize the foregoing argument, it would look like this:

- A
- R
- Therefore, P

But as it stands, the symbolized argument here does not seem to be valid. This is because the argument form does not allow us to capture the inner structure of the premises of the argument. To show the inner logical structure, we need more advanced logical machinery or technique. In this case,

unicorns are kind." But unicorns do not exist! Such issues raise puzzles; see for example, William Lycan, *Philosophy of Language: A Contemporary Introduction* (New York: Routledge, 2000); S. A. Kripke, *Naming and Necessity* (Cambridge, Mass.: Harvard University Press, 1972/1980).

17. Propositional logic also suffers from the sort of inadequacy attributed to classical logic.

a quantification theory provides us with the technique we need to undertake the task at hand.[18]

2.2 Predicate Logic

Quantification allows us to interpret noncompound premises (such as the ones displayed above) as compound statements without any loss of meaning. By using predicate logic, we can show the inner structure of propositions that concern the relations between subjects and predicates. In this case, we rely on quantifiers, namely, "all," "no," and "some." These quantifiers range over a certain domain. For general propositions, we use what is known as the *universal quantifier*. This is symbolized as (x) or (∀x) and it is read as: "Given any x" or "for all x." For particular propositions, we use what is known as the *existential quantifier*. This is symbolized as: (∃x). We read this symbol as: "There is at least one x such that . . ." We also use the horseshoe symbol, "⊃," or an arrow sign "→." This is read as: "if – then." We use a dot symbol, "•" to indicate conjunction, *and*. We use the tilde symbol "~" to indicate a negation, *not*. By deploying these technical tools of the predicate logic, we can symbolize the four kinds of, **A**, **E**, **I**, and **O** propositions as follows:

1. All religions are paths to the same God: (x) (Rx ⊃ Px). This is read as: Given any x, if x is a religion, then x is a path to the same God.
2. No religions are paths to the same God: (x) (Rx ⊃ ~ Px). This is read as: Given any x, if x is a religion, then x is not a path to the same God.
3. Some religions are paths to the same God: (∃x) (Rx • Px). This is read as: There is at least one x such that x is a religion and x is a path to the same God.
4. Some religions are not paths to the same God: (∃x) (Rx • ~ Px). This is read as: There is at least one x such that x is a religion and x is not the same path to the same God.

When (1) is quantificationally symbolized as (x) (Rx ⊃ Px), it is easy to see its inner logical structure. In this case, the quantifier (x) governs the

18. For excellent detailed discussion on this and other related issues, see Copi, Cohen and McMahon, *Introduction to Logic*, ch. 10. In what follows I will present a brief application of predicate logic to analyse the structure of the Destination Question. My discussion draws upon Copi, Cohen and McMahon, ch. 10.

entire statement function[19] in parentheses, namely, $(Rx \supset Px)$.[20] That means that the variables that occur in the statement function $Rx \supset Px$ are bound variables since they fall within the scope of the quantifier (x). The substitution instance of the statement function $Rx \supset Px$ can take truth evaluable form. For example, if we put an input value for the variable x, say, Christianity, we get a substitution instance of the conditional statement: $Rc \supset Pc$. We read this conditional statement as: if Christianity is a religion, then Christianity is a path to the same God. Put this way, such a conditional statement can be evaluated for its truth value. But any adequate assessment of the truth value of the substitution instance of (1) as shown above must consider the following three interrelated but distinct aspects of the Destination Question.

First, the scope of the quantifier in (1) must be determined. Here, the focus should be on whether the universe of discourse associated with the universal quantifier (x) is restricted. If it is restricted, what determines the domain of the quantifier? Second, the nature of the paths to the same God must be specified. By what means does a person get access to the same God? Third, the sense of "the same God" must be specified. Is the notion of "sameness" invoked here numerical or qualitative? Collectively these three aspects make up the Destination Question. We can illustrate the tripartite aspect of the *Destination Question* (DQ) as follows:[21]

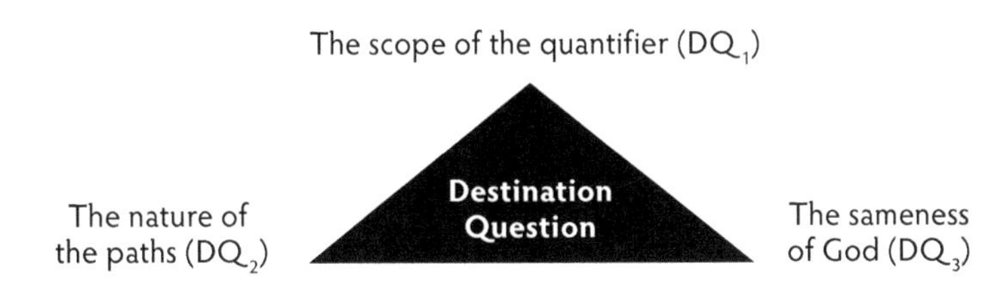

Figure 3: Illustration of the Tripartite Aspect of the Destination Question (DQ)

Now that we have a good grasp of the inner logical structure of the Destination Question as well as its three core aspects, it is time to look at what

19. The concept of a statement function refers to a pattern of the statement. Such a statement does not make definite assertions about anything in the universe. Since it has no truth value, a statement function is not considered as a statement, see Hurley, *Concise Introduction to Logic*, 404.

20. The same thing is true of existential quantifier. That is, both 3 and 4 fall within the scope of the existential quantifier.

21. The subscripts in (DQ_1–DQ_3) are meant to represent the three aspects of the Destination Question.

it would take to tackle it. In this regard, some conditions must be satisfied, namely the Referent-Identity-R and the Elimination Principle-R respectively. In section 3, I will briefly discuss these two requirements.

3. The Referent Identity-R and the Elimination Principle-R

Suppose that Mary and John engage in a serious disagreement as to what constitutes the right answer to the Destination Question. Mary claims that the Destination Question must be answered affirmatively. That is, defending (1), "All religions are paths to the same God." But John disagrees with Mary. He claims that the Destination Question must be answered negatively. That is, arguing against (1). Of course, there could be a third option that neither supports nor rejects (1). The third position is non-committal or agnostic as to what constitutes the right answer to the Destination Question. For present purposes, we won't discuss the third option. That said, to make progress in establishing their respective answers to the Destination Question, Mary and John will have to satisfy certain requirements (conditions).

3.1 The Referent Identity-R

Mary's Challenge

When Mary claims that the Destination Question should be answered affirmatively, she is implying that all religions are capable of being paths to the same God. Put this way, Mary's approach covers all three aspects of the Destination Question, namely, DQ_1 (the scope of the quantifier, *all*), DQ_2 (the nature of the paths), and DQ_3 (the sameness of God). But the biggest challenge that Mary faces in establishing her affirmative answer to the Destination Question boils down to DQ_3. This is because the success of Mary's argument(s) in defence of DQ_3 rests squarely on whether or not a good case can be made to satisfy what I call the *Referent Identity-R*.

Without getting into the current complicated controversies surrounding reference and identity,[22] we can capture the notion of *referent identity* via

22. See for example, Lycan, *Philosophy of Language*, esp. chs. 1–4; E. J. Lowe, *Forms of Thought: A Study in Philosophical Logic* (Cambridge: Cambridge University Press, 2013), Part I; and Kripke, *Naming and Necessity*. On issues related to identity, see E. J. Lowe, *More Kinds of Being: A Further Study of Individuation, Identity, and the Logic of Sortal Terms* (Malden, MA and Oxford: Wiley-Blackwell, 2009); E. J. Lowe, *An Introduction to the Philosophy of Mind* (Cambridge: Cambridge University Press, 2000), Part I and E. J. Lowe, *The Possibility of Metaphysics* (Oxford: Oxford University Press, 1998), chs. 1–2.

familiar examples. In a natural language such as English, we use linguistic expressions to refer to various sorts of items in the world. In this case, singular terms such as proper names, singular personal pronouns, demonstrative pronouns, and definite descriptions are used to refer to individual objects, people, and places.[23] For example, consider the following sentence, "Barack Obama was the 44th first African American President of the United States." This is a typical subject-predicate sentence. The proper name "Barack Obama" is a subject term whereas "was the 44th first African American President of the United States" is a predicate term. The referent is captured via the proper name "Barack Obama," which picks out the person who was the 44th first African American President of the United States. Here the referent is the *person* who is identified as Barack Obama. We can also refer to Mr. Obama without even mentioning his given name. In this case, we can simply refer to him via definite description such as, "the 44th first African-American President of the United States." In a nutshell, a referent is a thing a word stands for or picks out.

In metaphysics (philosophy), the concept of the *referent* is also related to the concept of *identity*. By "metaphysics" I mean a branch of philosophy that concerns itself with the study of the features of reality taken in the broadest possible sense.[24] In talking about metaphysical identity, we are not talking about identity as it is broadly understood, say, ethnic, racial, social, cultural and political. Here we are interested in the most basic metaphysical notion of identity. This sort of identity is a relation that is said to hold between a thing and itself. It is a necessary relation, that is, that nothing fails to be identical to itself. This is an instance of self-identity. It is symbolized as follows: $(\forall x) \Box (x = x)$.[25] This is to be read as: for all x, necessarily x is identical to x.

A concrete example of this sort of identity would be: Necessarily, Barack Obama is identical to Barack Obama. This sort of identity is also known as Leibniz's Law of the Indiscernibility of Identical. This law states that for all x

23. Singular terms are contrasted with general terms such as "blue" which can be applied to many things. Examples of proper names include ("Billy Graham," "Barack Obama," "Nairobi"), singular personal pronouns ("he," "she"), demonstrative pronouns ("this," "that") and definite descriptions ("the current president of the USA," "the most famous south African apartheid fighter"). For details see Lycan, *Philosophy of Language*, esp. chs. 1–4.

24. For an excellent introduction to analytic metaphysics, see S. J. Crumley II, *An Introduction to Metaphysics* (Ontario: Broadview Press, 2022); Michael J. Loux, and Thomas M. Crisp, *Metaphysics: A Contemporary Introduction* (New York: Routledge, 2017); R. Koons and T. Pickavance, *Metaphysics: The Fundamentals* (Malden: Wiley Blackwell, 2015); E. Conee and T. Sider, *Riddles of Existence: A Guided Tour of Metaphysics* (Oxford: Oxford University Press, 2014); and E. J. Lowe, *A Survey of Metaphysics* (Oxford: Oxford University Press, 2002).

25. "X" is a variable or a place holder for any appropriate value. The equals sign = means identical. The box sign □ is a modal operator which is read as: necessarily.

and for all y, if x is identical to y, then, for any property, P, x has P if and only if y has P.[26] Schematically expressed: $(\forall x)\ (\forall y)\ [(x = y) \rightarrow (P)\ (P\,x \leftrightarrow P\,y)]$. The notion of identity discussed here is called strict numerical identity. Given this law, if x has a property that y lacks or y has a property that x lacks, then the two objects are different. That is, they are not numerically identical. Whenever we invoke numerical identity, we have in mind a single object.

This kind of identity should not be confused with another kind of identity known as qualitative identity, which is said to hold between two or more objects that share their properties in common.[27] Consider, for example, two exactly similar or identical china cups. These cups have the same colour, size, and shape. Yet the two cups are numerically distinct. So in saying that the two china cups are identical, we should only mean that they exactly resemble each other in their qualities. We can also say that an object has a different qualitative identity when an apple changes, say, its colour from being green at one time to being red at another time. In this case, the apple in question is qualitatively different but numerically identical.

Numerical identity is what we need in talking about the *Referent Identity-R*. In light of the foregoing discussion we can define it as follows:

> Referent Identity $=_{df}$ x is an entity and y is an entity such that x is strictly identical to y, if and only if, x is numerically identical to y.[28]

Two Questions

Now John is in a better position to see what it would take for Mary to satisfy the *Referent Identity-R* in defending DQ_3. It would take Mary nothing less than showing that all religions in one way or another refer to the *same* God – that is, *sameness* understood in the strict numerical identity sense. At this point, at least two questions come to John's mind:

---

26. This sort of identity must be distinguished from another very controversial kind known as *Identity of indiscernible*. In a nutshell, this law of identity states that if any given two things share identical properties, then they are numerically identical. Symbolically put: $(\forall x)\ (\forall y)\ [(P)\ (P\,x \leftrightarrow P\,y) \rightarrow (x = y)]$. The problem with this law of identity is that sharing similar properties would not necessarily make the objects in question to be numerically identical. As Moreland remarks, "we could have two red and round discs that . . . could share all and only the same properties but still be two discs and not one because an individual thing like a disc is not exhausted by its properties." J. P. Moreland, *Universals* (Montreal & Kingston: McGill-Queen's University Press, 2001), 21; see also ch. 7.

27. See Lowe, *A Survey of Metaphysics*, chs. 2–4.

28. A lot can be said in defence of the definition proposed here. I also anticipate that not everyone would embrace this definition. But for now, I won't engage in that discussion.

First, how can Mary reconcile the non-monolithic conceptions of UR with the Referent Identity-R? John thinks that tackling this question may entangle Mary's efforts to establish an affirmative answer to the Destination Question in logical contradictions. This is because different religions despite displaying some broad similarities (in some situations) often make wildly conflicting claims regarding ultimate reality or God.

For example, Hinduism offers different senses in which ultimate reality could be conceived, namely monotheistic, polytheistic, pantheistic, atheistic, agnostics, dualistic, monistic, or pluralistic.[29] As Dalai Lama points out, "for Buddhists, the universe has no first cause and hence no creator, nor can there be such a thing as a permanent, primordially pure being."[30] For Christianity, the ultimate reality is a Trinitarian God who is said to be one in essence but three in personhood, namely Father, Son, and Holy Spirit.[31] For Islam (also true of Judaism), the ultimate reality is strictly monotheistic, that is, an absolute oneness of God.[32] These are just a handful of examples of diverse conceptions of ultimate reality across religions.

Second, how can Mary reconcile the non-monolithic conceptions of UR with the problem of reference? As some of the examples used earlier presuppose, linguistic expressions are used to refer to individual objects or people, or places. However, John thinks that such referring linguistic devices do not always pick out or stand for the things in question. Matters are less straightforward than they might seem to be when taken at the most basic intuitive level. Some influential philosophers, most notably Bertrand Russell, raised serious doubts against the referential role of singular terms in general and definite descriptions in particular. The details of Russell's argument are too complicated to discuss here.[33] Russell's doubts were motivated by certain kinds of puzzles that do seem to seriously undermine the referential role of singular terms. These puzzles are: (i) the problem of apparent reference to non-existents, (ii) the problem of negative existentials, (iii) Frege's puzzle of identity, and (iv) the problem of substitutivity.[34]

---

29. Nigosian, *World Faiths*, 75.

30. Dalai Lama, "Buddhism and Other Religions," in Peterson et al., *Reason and Religious Belief*, 595–98, 596.

31. Brodd et al., *Invitation to World Religions*, 473.

32. Nigosian, *World Faiths*, 442. See also N. Geisler and A. Saleeb, *Answering Islam* (Grand Rapids: Baker House, 1993/2002), ch. 1.

33. See for example, Lycan (*Philosophy of Language*, ch. 2): Loc 11 of 29. Accessed on 3rd November 2023 from www.perlego.com.

34. Lycan. ch. 2.

Here are some examples. In the case of (i), "The present king of France is bald." In the case of (ii), "The present king of France does not exist." Notice that as they stand, (i) and (ii) are instances of subject-predicate statements. Wait a minute! What is going on with these statements? Currently France has no king. But (i) is denoting France's present king. If so, what does "the present king of France" stand for or pick out? In short, what is its referent? Similarly, when it comes to (ii) how can something, that does not exist in this case, the present king of France, be said to have a referent? The point here is that the intuitive view that every time referring linguistic expressions or devices are used, they pick out something is not always true.[35]

In the case of (iii), "Barack Obama = the 44th first African American President of the United States." This sentence contains two singular terms. What it says is trivial because whichever singular term we use, we know exactly who is being referred to. So one could ask: what is so special about the above sentence? Yet there is something special about the statement. That is, the name "Barack Obama" is not informative. But the definite description, "the 44th first African American President of the United States" is informative. This is because it gives us more information about Mr. Obama.

Finally, in the case of (iv), it has been said that any given two singular terms insofar as they denote the same thing, they also turn out to be semantically equivalent. That is, in any sentence where the singular terms in question occur, they can be swapped without changing the truth value of the sentence. But consider the sentence: "Smith believes that the author of the *Philosophiæ Naturalis Principia Mathematica* is the smartest physicist who ever lived." Furthermore, suppose that unknown to Smith that the author of *Philosophiæ Naturalis Principia Mathematica* also published the book entitled *The Reality of God's Existence*. Smith believes that the author of *The Reality of God's Existence* is scientifically illiterate. In this case, we cannot swap "the author of *Philosophiæ Naturalis Principia Mathematica*" for "the author of *The Reality of God's Existence*" without changing the meaning of the original sentence. If we do, we get a false sentence.

The foregoing John's two questions and all the issues that accompany them have profound implications for Mary's attempt to establish an affirmative answer for the Destination Question. The road ahead for Mary seems quite daunting and success may or may not be guaranteed, to say the least.

35. See Lycan. ch. 2.

3.2 The Elimination Principle-R

John's Challenge

Unlike Mary, John thinks that the Destination Question should be answered negatively. This involves arguing against (1) which states that "All religions are paths to the same God." In arguing against (1), John is presupposing that only one religion can be a path to the same God. Here John fully embraces DQ_3. However, he has to reject DQ_1 since in arguing against (1), John is denying that the universal quantifier (∀x) ranges over the entire domain of religion. So in place of the universal quantifier (∀x), John can deploy an existential quantifier (∃x). In doing so, John can argue that there is at least one thing (in this case, one religion) such that the thing in question is true and it is a path to the same God. Schematically: (∃x) (Tx • Px). In light of this, John can modify (1) as follows:

> (1') Only one true religion is a path to a divine being.

But how can one go about figuring out which religion satisfies (1')? Answering this question is where, as it were, the rubber meets the road. Every religion operates on the assumption that it is the only true religion. Yet portraying one's own religion as the only true religion could be said to be a "question begging" move to take. This sort of mistake happens when one already assumes the truth of, say, a certain premise that one wants to establish or prove. But this does not mean that one cannot have good (independent) reasons for thinking that (1') is true. One can make an informed judgement as to which religion is true and which one is not. To this effect, some philosophers of religion argue that a positive answer can be given to (1'). For example, Keith E. Yandell remarks:

> The answer as to whether just one religion can be true is "Yes." A religion proposes a diagnosis of a deep, crippling spiritual disease universal to non-divine sentience and offers a cure. A particular religion is true if its diagnosis is correct, and its cure is efficacious. The diagnosis and cure occur in the setting of an account of what there is – an account whose truth is assumed by the content of the diagnosis and cure. Some religions at least do not assert logically incompatible propositions. So it is possible that at least one religion be true – that its account of what exists is correct.[36]

36. Keith Yandell, "How to Sink in Cognitive Quicksand: Nuancing Religious Pluralism," in M. L.. Peterson and M.L. VanArragon, eds., *Contemporary Debates in Philosophy of Religion* (Oxford: Blackwell, 2004), 191–201, 191–92. See also Stewart, *Can Only One Religion Be True.*

Yandell's point is that a rubric, as it were, for true religion consists in its efficacy in providing an appropriate solution(s) for the human spiritual predicament. Furthermore, the solution in question needs to be situated within the right kind of ontology (i.e. the study of being or what there is). What is being presupposed by such claims is particularism (exclusivism). Yandell's remarks stand in stark contrast to that of Mary's approach. On the other hand, Yandell's remarks mesh well with John's particularist approach, which is essentially what (1') presupposes. That being said, the major burden of proof that awaits John in defending (1') concerns satisfying the Elimination Principle-R. According to the Elimination Principle, of any given two or more religions, only one of them can be a path to the same divine being. This means that other religions must be eliminated. But satisfying the Elimination Principle-R is exceedingly difficult and extremely controversial. But it is not impossible.

It seems that the challenge John faces is no less demanding than that of Mary's. As I already pointed out at the start of this chapter, it is not my aim to adjudicate the controversies between Mary and John. I leave that task for my readers.[37] Here, my aim is only to point out the complexities that underlie the Destination Question. In section 4, we will briefly look at the three views of salvation, namely particularism, inclusivism, and pluralism, and illustrate how they each cope with the challenges discussed above.

4. The Mary-John Challenges and the Contemporary Views of Salvation

4.1 Particularism

Defending (1') is one of the hallmarks of particularism (also known as exclusivism/restrictivism). But what exactly is particularism? Peterson et al. describe it as follows:

> For the *exclusivist*, all humans face the same serious predicament that needs to be addressed. Salvation, liberation, human fulfilment, whatever else one considers as resolving that predicament is found

37. For excellent contemporary discussions over this matter, see for example, Peterson et al., *Reason and Religious Belief*, Part 13 and ch. 14; Peter Byrne, "It is Not Reasonable to Believe That Only One Religion is True," in Peterson and VanArragon, eds., *Contemporary Debates in Philosophy of Religion* (Oxford: Blackwell, 2004), (Part 3): Loc. 20 of 28; Stewart, *Can Only One Religion Be True*; "A Defense of Religious Exclusivism," in F. J. Sennett, ed. *The Analytic Theist: An Alvin Plantinga Reader* (Grand Rapids: Eerdmans, 1998), 187–210; and J. P. Moreland, Khaldoun A. Sweis and Chad V. Meister, *Debating Christian Theism* (Oxford: Oxford University Press, 2013).

> solely in or through one particular religion. Although all religions contain truths, one religion, in its central beliefs, exclusively and accurately describes both the predicament and what we need to address it.[38]

Central to the remarks in the above quote is the assumption that a solution to the human predicament is found in only one particular religion. But particularism is not just only a positive thesis about making a case for where and how a solution can be found for the human predicament. It is also a negative thesis that takes upon itself declaring that the other religions are not qualified to resolve the human predicament. In light of this, we can say that particularism engages in what apologists describe as constructing a preferred view while deconstructing the opposing viewpoint.[39] Alvin Plantinga captures this aspect of particularism nicely in his paper entitled: "A Defence of Religious Exclusivism." As Plantinga remarks:

> The exclusivist holds that the tenets or some of the tenets of *one* religion – Christianity, let's say – are in fact true; he adds, naturally enough, that any propositions, including other religious beliefs, that are incompatible with those tenets are false.[40]

Plantinga's own defence of exclusivism is rooted in two propositions:[41]

(A). The world was created by God, an almighty, all-knowing, and perfectly good personal being.

(B). Human beings require salvation, and God has provided a unique way of salvation through the incarnation, life, sacrificial death, and resurrection of his divine son.

Christian exclusivists like Plantinga wholeheartedly embrace (A) and (B). However, they do have differences on how best to understand the application of (B). In this case, they differ over DQ_2. For example, Plantinga defends (A) and (B) within the framework of his "reformed epistemology," according to which, belief in God is "properly basic." That is, belief in God can be said to be true and rational without providing a piece of evidence or argument in support

38. Peterson et al., *Reason and Religious Belief*, 322.
39. An example of this sort of approach is nicely illustrated in Craig, *Reasonable Faith*.
40. Plantinga, "A Defence of Religious Exclusivism," in Sennett, *The Analytic Theist*, 189.
41. Plantinga, "A Defence of Religious Exclusivism," 188.

of it.[42] Other particularists take an evidentialist approach to particularism. In this regard, R. Douglas Geivett and W. Gary Phillips argue that individual salvation must depend on explicit personal faith in Jesus Christ.[43] There are also particularists who despite embracing (B) opt to remain agnostic when it comes to the fate of the unevangelized or those who never have heard the gospel. They argue that since we are epistemically limited to say anything definitive regarding the destiny of the unevangelized, the best we can do is defer to God himself. This view is defended by Alister E. McGrath.[44]

How do the particularists be it a Christian variety or otherwise cope with the Mary-John challenges? Here particularists can effectively dodge Mary's first challenge. Recall that this is the challenge that concerns reconciling the non-monolithic conceptions of UR with the Referent Identity-R. We saw how handling this issue could entangle one in logical contradictions. But given that the particularists are committed to defending (1'), the problem of logical contradiction does not arise. This is because, by embracing (1'), particularists are automatically rejecting DQ_1. That means that particularists are not in the business of establishing an affirmative answer to the Destination Question, which is what, as we indicated, leads to a logical contradiction. In short, for particularists, incompatible truth claims are false.

Particularists can also dodge Mary's second challenge which concerns reconciling the non-monolithic conceptions of UR with the problem of reference. Since particularists are committed to (1') they face no incompatible referents. In the case of Christian exclusivists, as shown by Plantinga's (A) and (B) above, there is one true religion whose object of worship is one true God. In light of this, broadly speaking, particularism could handle well the four puzzles of reference we saw earlier, namely (i) the problem of apparent reference to non-existents, (ii) the problem of negative existentials, (iii) Frege's puzzle of identity, and (iv) the problem of substitutivity. Just like particularists consider that incompatible claims are false, they can also argue that the above four puzzles do not pose a threat to their defence of (1'). Here particularists

42. For an extended discussion see Plantinga's *Warranted Christian Belief* (Oxford: Oxford University Press, 2000), esp. part 3. For an abridged version of Plantinga's view, see W. L. Craig, ed., *Philosophy of Religion: A Reader and Guide* (New Brunswick: Rutgers University Press, 2002), 40–65.

43. See R. D. Geivett and G. W. Phillips, "A Particularist View: An Evidentialist Approach," in Stanley N. Gundry, Dennis L. Okholm and Timothy R. Phillips, eds., *Four Views on Salvation in a Pluralistic World* (Grand Rapids: Zondervan, 1995), 213–45.

44. See A. E. McGrath, "A Particularist View: A Post-Enlightenment Approach," in Gundry, Okholm and Phillips, *Four Views*, 151–80.

can adopt the Boolean as opposed to the Aristotelian methodology in dealing with universal categorical statements.

In this case, for example, they can interpret (i) and (ii) as conditional statements. In doing so, they can avoid the attribution of direct existential import, say, to statements like "the present king of France." Such statements can only be said to have some positive truth value if the individuals in question actually exist. For lack of space, I can't belabour this point.

Overall, for particularists, the prospects of avoiding Mary's challenges seem very promising. But the same is not true of John's challenges. Here particularists can't escape the burden of proof to satisfy the Elimination Principle-R. Recall that this principle states that of any given two or more religions, only one of them can be a path to a divine being. So other religions should be eliminated in the sense of considering them being false. However, we should keep in mind that exclusivism is not a uniquely Christian phenomenon. Other religions such as Islam and Buddhism do also embrace exclusivism.[45] That means that the real issue within the particularists' camp boils down to what I call "in-house fighting" in dealing with the Elimination Principle-R. Particularists would find themselves being forced to engage in construction-deconstruction apologetics to demonstrate which particular religion is in a better position to be identified with the one true religion stated in (1').[46]

4.2 Inclusivism

We can capture the central tenets of inclusivism via Karl Rahner's four theses.

> Thesis # (a): "Christianity understands itself as the absolute religion, intended for all men, which cannot recognize any other religion beside itself as of equal right."[47]
>
> Thesis # (b): "a non-Christian religion . . . does not merely contain elements of a natural knowledge of God, elements, moreover, mixed up with human depravity . . . [it also] contains

45. See for example, Peterson et al., *Reason and Religious Belief*, 321–24.

46. For particularists who make a compelling case for why Christianity has everything it takes to be the one true religion to solve the human predicament, see P. Copan, "Why the World Is Not Religiously Ambiguous: A Critique of Religious Pluralism" and R. D. Geivett, "Religious Diversity and the Futility of Neutrality," both in Stewart, 181–202 and 139–62; H. Netland, "Jesus Is the Only Way to God," in Moreland et al., *Debating Christian Theism*, ch. 37; Geivett and Phillips, "A Particularist View"; and Plantinga, "A Defence of Religious Exclusivism," 189.

47. K. Rahner, "Religious Inclusivism," in Peterson et al., *Philosophy of Religion*, 606–13, 607.

> supernatural elements arising out of the grace which is given to men as a gratuitous gift on account of Christ. For this reason, a non-Christian religion can be recognized as a *lawful* religion."[48]
>
> Thesis # (c): "Christianity does not simply confront the members of an extra-Christian religion as a mere non-Christian but as someone who can and must be regarded in this or that respect as an anonymous Christian."[49]
>
> Thesis # (d): "It is possibly too much to hope, on the one hand, that the religious pluralism which exists in the concrete situation of Christians will disappear in the foreseeable future . . . it is absolutely permissible for the Christian himself to interpret this non-Christianity as Christianity of an anonymous kind."[50]

Rahner's four theses situate inclusivism somewhere in-between exclusivism and pluralism. In this case, Thesis # (a) echoes exclusivism in describing Christianity as an absolute religion. Whereas Theses # (b)–(d) echo pluralism in the sense of fully embracing other religions, in addition to Christianity, as having a crucial role to play in channelling out divine grace for salvation. Rahner encourages us to consider members of other faiths as anonymous Christians. Other inclusivists such as Clark Pinnock also argue that God's grace is at work among all people (regardless of their religion). That means that, as Pinnock argues, other religions play a role in that they prepare people for the Gospel of Christ whose work alone makes salvation possible.[51]

Even though Christ remains to be an anchor of salvation in inclusivism, it takes the Mary-John challenges to a new level. This is partly because inclusivism as a view of salvation seems to be a mixture of exclusivism and pluralism. Taken this way, answering the Destination Question against the backdrop of inclusivism becomes muddier and messier. The difficulty begins with reversing the modification introduced to DQ_1, that is, the universal quantifier in (1). Recall that the modification made to (1) gave us (1'). This modification restricts salvation to one true religion. But inclusivism reverses that move by endorsing the possibility of many religions as being facilitators of

48. Rahner, "Religious Inclusivism," 609.

49. Rahner, "Religious Inclusivism," 612.

50. Rahner, "Religious Inclusivism," 613.

51. See H. C. Pinnock, "An Inclusivist View," in Gundry, Okholm and Phillips, *Four Views*, 95–123.

genuine salvific experiences. In this way, inclusivism broadens and multiplies the paths stated in DQ_2. But the problem with inclusivism begins here.

For example, as Peterson et al. ask: "if many religions believe that they are the one true religion, how does one decide which religion makes the correct claims?"[52] Answering this question exposes inclusivism to John's challenge, that is, satisfying the Elimination Principle-R. But then given inclusivism's endorsement of pluralism, it should be in a position to dodge John's challenge. However, how inclusivism successfully can carry out such a task remains entirely unclear. This is because inclusivism also embraces some key exclusivist claims, one of which is the centrality of Christ in salvation. The situation gets even worse for inclusivism. The reversal of (1') back to (1) means that Mary's challenges stand in the way of inclusivism with full force. In this case, inclusivism faces the challenge of demonstrating how the non-monolithic conceptions of UR can be reconciled with the Referent Identity-R. It also faces the challenge of reconciling the non-monolithic conceptions of UR with the problem of reference. What this means is that inclusivism brings upon itself problems from both Mary's and John's camps. Yet, it ends up lacking a promising strategy to solve the problems of either camp. It is a bad place to be in.

4.3 Religious Pluralism

John Hick defines pluralism as the view according to which, "the transformation of human existence from self-centeredness to Reality centeredness is taking place in different ways within the contexts of all the great religious traditions. There is not merely one way but a plurality of salvation or liberation."[53]

Notice that Hick's characterization of pluralism is entirely compatible with all three aspects of the Destination Question, that is, (DQ1)–(DQ3). This means that pluralists would entirely reject (1') since it goes against the key tenet of pluralism. That is, multiple ways are available in different religions for genuine salvific experiences. In light of this, pluralists like Hick fully embrace the idea that great religious traditions have equal status as being the paths to the same God or divine reality. Thus, as Hick argues, a genuine salvific experience

52. Peterson et al., *Reason and Religious Belief*, 337.

53. John. Hick "Religious Pluralism," in Peterson et al., *Reason and Religious Belief*, 614–21, 616. Also see Hick, "Is Christianity the Only True Religion, or One among Others?," in Stewart, *Can Only One Religion Be True?*, 105–15; and "A Pluralist View," in Gundry, Okholm and Phillips, *Four Views*, 29–59.

is not confined to one particular religion, say, Christianity. Hick believes that there is a plurality of saving human responses to the same divine reality.[54]

But pluralists make clear that one's allegiance to a certain particular religion would not impede one from recognizing that people in other religions are also equally in a position to experience divine reality.[55] Hick claims that Christians (like himself) can see Jesus as the one who has revealed God to them, showed them how to live as citizens of the kingdom, and respected spiritual leader. They can also see Jesus as their inspiration and role model. Similarly, people in other religions can look up to their own spiritual leaders and sacred texts to experience similar spiritual experiences that the followers of Jesus are said to have.[56]

As it stands, pluralism can easily put aside John's challenge that is, satisfying the Elimination Principle-R. If all the great religious traditions have equal status and no particular religion has any special privilege in leading someone to the same divine reality, then it follows that no particular religion should assume the burden of proof to eliminate other religions. Every major religion stands on its own feet and access as Hick puts it, "Ultimate Reality" or "the Real." Hick following Immanuel Kant's well-known bifurcation of reality *as it is in itself* and *as it appears to us*, argues that our knowledge of "the Real" is partial and never complete or concrete.[57]

Of course, as finite beings, we can readily concede that our knowledge of God is incomplete. But does it follow from such limited knowledge of God that we have no knowledge of God in and of himself? Given pluralism, the answer to this question should be "yes." If so, pluralism faces Mary's challenges in full force. Given that "the Real" or God is inaccessible in and of himself, how can pluralism reconcile the non-monolithic conceptions of UR with the Referent Identity-R? Moreover, how can pluralism handle the non-monolithic conceptions of UR and the problem of reference? For example, as Yandell nicely remarks, "having reference is . . . a matter of having referential success or having a referential failure."[58] But given Hick's inaccessible God, there does

54. Hick "Religious Pluralism," 616.

55. For example, Knitter claims, "to believe in the Christian God is to believe in a God of many ways." P. F. Knitter, "There Are Many Ways to God," in Moreland, Sweis and Meister, *Debating Christian Theism*, 509.

56. Hick, "A Pluralist View," 59.

57. Peterson et al., *Reason and Religious Belief*, 614–21. For Kant's distinctions, see for example, *Critique of Pure Reason*, trans. Norman Kemp Smith (London: Macmillan, 1929), 266–75.

58. Yandell, "How to Sink in Cognitive Quicksand," 197.

not seem to be any way to tell referential success from referential failure. This is a very bad place to be in for any believer in God, to say the least. It remains entirely unclear how given pluralism, Mary's challenges can successfully be settled. The situation gets even worse for pluralism. Earlier we assumed that pluralism can easily brush aside the Elimination Principle-R. Not so fast.

Details aside, both Yandell and Copan in their own way, independently argue that religious pluralism itself is exclusivist. For example, Yandell remarks, "RP [religious pluralism] is in fact exclusivist regarding religious explanation (in a way that is inconsistent with the truth of various religious traditions) and regarding the correct diagnosis and cure. RP offers its own brand of exclusivism while often criticizing others for being exclusivist."[59] If Yandell and Copan are right in saying that pluralism has its own brand of exclusivism, John's central challenge (i.e., Elimination Principle-R) for pluralism snaps right back in place. In this case, pluralism not only comes face to face with Mary's challenges but also with John's as well.

5. Objection and reply

Before I end this chapter, I want to consider one objection against the Destination Question. However, the objection I consider here is not focused specifically on the Destination Question per se; rather, it is an objection that applies against religion taken in general. I construct the objection I have in mind from Daniel Dennett's highly praised book, *Breaking the Spell: Religion as a Natural Phenomenon.*[60]

The Destination Question does imply that religion is a phenomenon that has a non-human and non-cultural origin. This does not, of course, mean that religion lacks socio-cultural components. I already pointed out this aspect of religion in the introduction of this chapter by what I called the UR-centric features. However, the non-human, as well as the non-socio-cultural origin of religion, is something that Dennett seems to be dismissive of.

5.1 Objection: Religion is purely natural/cultural invention

For Dennett, religion is not a product of human intellectual activity. Dennett claims that religions are transmitted culturally via language and symbolism.

59. Yandell, "How to Sink in Cognitive Quicksand," 214.

60. D. Dennett, *Breaking the Spell: Religion as a Natural Phenomenon* (New York: Penguin Books, 2006), 24–25.

People get their religion from their parents in a similar way that they get their language, through upbringing. Dennett claims that religion is thoroughly natural as opposed to having any genuine aspects of supernatural. That means that religion is entirely a human phenomenon. Dennett argues that religion is composed of events, organisms, objects, structures, patterns and the like. Such phenomena, as Dennett claims, obey the laws of physics or biology. Dennett argues that the phenomena in question do not involve miracles. Dennett claims that it could be true that God exists. Such a being may even be an intelligent, conscious, loving creator of us all. However, for Dennett, religion itself is a complex set of phenomena. It is a perfectly natural phenomenon.[61]

5.2 Reply

Dennett is right in saying that in some indisputable sense religion is a natural phenomenon with all its socio-cultural elements. However, Dennett's dismissal of the possibility of the supernatural origin of religion is entirely question-begging. This is because Dennett simply seems to be assuming that if the origin of religion is not understood in a way he already framed it, then no account that grants a supernatural origin for religion is justified.

For one thing, there could well be religions that trace their origin to entirely socio-cultural sources. However, there are also religions, say, Christianity, Judaism, and Islam that unequivocally attribute their origin to a supernatural source. For Dennett's objection to work, he would have to deal not just with religion taken in general, he also has to take up specific religious traditions and show why he thinks their accounts of the supernatural origin of their religions do not hold up. But that is not what Dennett does in his discussion of the origin of religion. Dennett also demands that religions should be exposed to scientific scrutiny to see if indeed what they say is true. Here Dennett's claim is highly questionable and misguided. This is because, among other things, religious/theological truth claims do have their own independent source of justification. Science cannot set the tone for an entire gamut of theological truths.[62] Dennett's objection against the supernatural origin of religion is deeply ill-conceived.

---

61. We should note that in saying that God exists, Dennett is not implying that he genuinely believes it to be the case. This is simply a philosopher's way of granting a hypothetical possibility.

62. Elsewhere I discussed in detail why appealing to science to challenge non-scientific theological/religious truths should be carefully handled. See for example, P. M. Guta "Metaphysics, Natural Science and Theological Claims: E. J. Lowe's Approach," *An International Journal for Philosophy of Religion and Philosophical Theology*, 5 no. 2 (2021): 129–60. See also R. Swinburne, *The Existence of God*, 2nd ed. (Oxford: Oxford University Press, 2004); Plantinga,

6. Conclusion

In this chapter, I attempted to show the complexities that underlie the Destination Question. We looked at why giving an affirmative answer invites the problem of reconciling the non-monolithic conceptions of UR with the Referent Identity-R. It also invites the non-monolithic conceptions of UR and the problem of reference. On the other hand, giving a negative answer to the Destination Question invites the Elimination Principle-R. Finally, we looked at the three views of salvation and briefly discussed what challenges they each face in answering the Destination Question. In light of all this, a lasting solution for the Destination Question continues to be contentious.

Bibliography

Brodd, J., L. Little, B. Nystro, R. Platzner, R. Shek, and E. Stiles.. *Invitation to World Religions*. Oxford: Oxford University Press, 2019.

Byrne, P. "It Is Not Reasonable to Believe that Only One Religion Is True." In *Contemporary Debates in Philosophy of Religion*, edited by Michael L. Peterson and Raymond J. VanArragon, 201–11. Oxford: Blackwell, 2004.

Conee, E., and T. Sider *Riddles of Existence: A Guided Tour of Metaphysics*. Oxford: Oxford University Press, 2014.

Copan, P. "Why the World Is Not Religiously Ambiguous: A Critique of Religious Pluralism." In *Can Only One Religion Be True?: Paul Knitter and Harold Netland in Dialogue*, edited by Robert B. Stewart, 139–62. Minneapolis: Augsburg Fortress Press, 2013.

Copi, I. M., C. Cohen, and K. McMahon. *Introduction to Logic*. New York: Routledge, 2011.

Craig, W. L., ed. *Philosophy of Religion: A Reader and Guide*. New Brunswick: Rutgers University Press, 2002.

———. *Reasonable Faith*. 3rd edition. Wheaton: Crossway, 2008. Perlego e-edition,. https://www.perlego.com/book/1414192/reasonable-faith-3rd-edition-christian-truth-and-apologetics-pdf.

Crumley, J. S., II. *An Introduction to Metaphysics*. Ontario: Broadview Press, 2022.

Dennett, D. C. *Breaking the Spell: Religion as a Natural Phenomenon*. New York: Penguin Books, 2006.

Warranted Christian Belief; J. M. Erickson, "General Revelation, Inclusivism, Pluralism, and Postmodernism," in Stewart, *Can Only One Religion Be True?*, 91–103; Geivett, "Religious Diversity," 181–83; P. J. Moreland, *Christianity and the Nature of Science* (Grand Rapids: Baker Book House, 1989), chs. 1–3.

Erickson, M. J. "General Revelation, Inclusivism, Pluralism, and Postmodernism." In *Can Only One Religion Be True?: Paul Knitter and Harold Netland in Dialogue*, edited by Robert B. Stewart, 91–103. Minneapolis: Augsburg Fortress Press, 2013.

Geisler, N., and A. Saleeb. *Answering Islam*. Grand Rapids: Baker House, 1993/2002.

Geivett, D. R. "Religious Diversity and the Futility of Neutrality." In *Can Only One Religion Be True?: Paul Knitter and Harold Netland in Dialogue*, edited by Robert B. Stewart, 181–202. Minneapolis: Augsburg Fortress Press, 2013.

Geivett, D. R., and G. W. Phillips. "A Particularist View: An Evidentialist Approach." In *Four Views on Salvation in a Pluralistic World*, edited by Stanley N. Gundry, Dennis L. Okholm, and Timothy R. Phillips, 213–45. Grand Rapids: Zondervan, 1995.

Griffiths, P. J. "The Universality and Uniqueness of Religious Doctrines." In *Philosophy of Religion*, edited by Michael Peterson, William Hasker, Bruce Reichenbach, and David Basinger, 599–605. Oxford: Oxford University Press, 2014.

Gundry, N. S. N., D. L. Okholm, and T. R. Phillips, eds. *Four Views on Salvation in a Pluralistic World*. Grand Rapids: Zondervan, 1995.

Guta, M. P. "Metaphysics, Natural Science and Theological Claims: E. J. Lowe's Approach." *An International Journal for Philosophy of Religion and Philosophical Theology* 5, no. 2 (2021): 129–60.

Guta, P. M. "Conceptual Analysis: What is Religion?" Unpublished paper.

Hick, J. "A Pluralist View." In *Four Views on Salvation in a Pluralistic World*, edited by Stanley N. Gundry, Dennis L. Okholm, and Timothy R. Phillips, 29–59. Grand Rapids: Zondervan, 1995.

Hick, J. "Is Christianity the Only True Religion, or One among Others?" In *Can Only One Religion Be True?: Paul Knitter and Harold Netland in Dialogue*, edited by Robert B. Stewart, 105–15. Minneapolis: Augsburg Fortress Press, 2013.

Hick, J. "Religious Pluralism." In *Philosophy of Religion*, edited by Michael Peterson, William Hasker, Bruce Reichenbach, and David Basinger, 614–21. Oxford: Oxford University Press, 2014.

Hurley, P. J. *A Concise Introduction to Logic*. 5th ed. Belmont: Wadsworth, 1994.

Kant, I. *Critique of Pure Reason*. Translated by Norman Kemp Smith. London: Macmillan, 1929.

Knitter, F. P. "There Are Many Ways to God." In *Debating Christian Theism*, edited by J. P. Moreland, Khaldoun A. Sweis and Chad V. Meister, 509–19. Oxford: Oxford University Press, 2013.

Knitter, F. P., and H. A. Netland. "Can Only One Religion Be True?: A Dialogue." In *Can Only One Religion Be True?: Paul Knitter and Harold Netland in Dialogue*, edited by Robert B. Stewart, 17–54. Minneapolis: Augsburg Fortress Press, 2013.

Koons, R. C., and T. Pickavance. *Metaphysics: The Fundamentals*. Malden: Wiley Blackwell, 2015.

Kripke, S. A. *Naming and Necessity*. Cambridge: Harvard University Press, 1980.

Lama, D. "Buddhism and Other Religions." In *Philosophy of Religion*, edited by Michael Peterson, William Hasker, Bruce Reichenbach, and David Basinger, 595–98.. Oxford: Oxford University Press, 2014.
Loux, M. J., and T. M. Crisp *Metaphysics: A Contemporary Introduction*. New York: Routledge, 2017.
Lowe, E. J. *Forms of Thought: A Study in Philosophical Logic*. Cambridge: Cambridge University Press, 2013.
———. *An Introduction to the Philosophy of Mind*. Cambridge: Cambridge University Press, 2000.
———. *More Kinds of Being: A Further Study of Individuation, Identity, and the Logic of Sortal Terms*. Malden,: Wiley-Blackwell, 2009
———. *The Possibility of Metaphysics*. Oxford: Oxford University Press, 1998.
———. *A Survey of Metaphysics*. Oxford: Oxford University Press, 2002.
Lycan, W. *Philosophy of Language: A Contemporary Introduction*. New York: Routledge, 2000. Perlego e-edition, https://www.perlego.com/book/1617260/philosophy-of-language-a-contemporary-introduction-pdf.
McGrath, A. E. "A Particularist View: A Post-Enlightenment Approach." In *Four Views on Salvation in a Pluralistic World*, edited by Stanley N. Gundry, Dennis L. Okholm and Timothy R. Phillips, 95–123. Grand Rapids: Zondervan, 1995.
Meister, C., and P. Copan. *The Routledge Companion to Philosophy of Religion*. Second Edition. New York: Routledge, 2013.
Merricks, T. *Propositions*. Oxford: Oxford University Press, 2015.
Moreland, J. P. *Universals*. Montreal & Kingston: McGill-Queen's University Press, 2001.
———. *Christianity and the Nature of Science*. Grand Rapids: Baker Book House, 1989.
Moreland, J. P., A. K. Sweis, and V. C. Meister. *Debating Christian Theism*. Oxford: Oxford University Press, 2013.
Netland, H. "Jesus Is the Only Way to God." In *Debating Christian Theism*, edited by J. P. Moreland, Khaldoun A. Sweis and Chad V. Meister, 497–508. Oxford: Oxford University Press, 2013.
Nigosian, S. A. *World Faiths*. 2nd ed. New York: St. Martin's Press, 1994.
Peterson, M., W. Haske, B. Reichenbach, and D. Basinger., eds. *Philosophy of Religion*. Oxford: Oxford University Press, 2014.
Peterson, M., W. Hasker, B. Reichenbach, and D. Basinger. *Reason & Religious Belief: An Introduction to the Philosophy of Religion*. 5th edition. Oxford: Oxford University Press, 2012.
Peterson, M. L., and R. J. VanArragon. *Contemporary Debates in Philosophy of Religion*. Oxford: Blackwell, 2004.
Pinnock, C. H. "An Inclusivist View." In *Four Views on Salvation in a Pluralistic World*, edited by Stanley N. Gundry, Dennis L. Okholm and Timothy R. Phillips, 95–123. Grand Rapids: Zondervan, 1995.
Plantinga, A. *Warranted Christian Belief*. Oxford: Oxford University Press, 2000.

Prothero, S. *Religion Matters: An Introduction to the World's Religions*. London: W. W. Norton, 2020.
Rahner, K. "Religious Inclusivism." In *Philosophy of Religion*, edited by Michael Peterson, William Hasker, Bruce Reichenbach, and David Basinger, 606–16. Oxford: Oxford University Press, 2014.
Sennett, J. F., ed. *The Analytic Theist: An Alvin Plantinga Reader*. Grand Rapids: Eerdmans, 1998.
Stewart, R. B., ed. *Can Only One Religion Be True?: Paul Knitter and Harold Netland in Dialogue*. Minneapolis: Augsburg Fortress Press, 2013.
———. "Can Only One Religion Be True? Considering This Question." In *Can Only One Religion Be True?: Paul Knitter and Harold Netland in Dialogue*, edited by Robert B. Stewart, 1–16. Minneapolis: Augsburg Fortress Press, 2013.
Swinburne, R. *The Existence of God*. 2nd ed. Oxford: Oxford University Press, 2004.
Yandell, K. A. "How to Sink in Cognitive Quicksand: Nuancing Religious Pluralism." In *Contemporary Debates in Philosophy of Religion*, edited by Peterson, M. L. and R. J. VanArragon, 191–201. Oxford: Blackwell, 2004.

6

God and Objective Moral Values

Samuel Waje Kunhiyop, PhD
ECWA Theological Seminary, Kagoro, Nigeria

Abstract

Defending the Christian faith, which involves refuting falsehood and heresy and articulating correct doctrine, is a biblical mandate according to 1 Peter 3:15–16. Christian apologetics is not done in a vacuum but is situated in a real context, and for the purposes of this chapter, an African context. African Christianity is confronted with many cultural, religious, and ideological truth claims which contradict its core beliefs and practices. Some of these false religious claims, such as African traditional religions, Islam and secularism, etc., also have foundational beliefs in God and moral laws. These systems and worldviews propagate certain non-biblical truth claims that must be refuted and substituted with explicitly biblical and Christian truth claims. Africans have strong beliefs in God whom they see as the supreme being with many other deities. This supreme being and other spirit beings are the basis of moral laws. There is no clear concept of the existence of a triune God who is the source of moral laws. The knowledge of Jesus Christ is also completely non-existent. Islam on the other hand has the concept of the one God but completely denies triunity which is critical for understanding biblical teaching and Christianity. Jihadism or militancy is a core belief of Islam from its historic origins to its current status, which also undermines the explicit teaching of a loving God who is compassionate to all his creation. Secularism seeks to undercut and uproot all religious foundations in God and morality. In secularism, God is dethroned and consequently, morality becomes personal and relative. In this chapter, it is observed that without a clear belief in the triune God, all religious beliefs and practices become idolatrous. God is triune and exists as God the Father, the Son, and Holy Spirit. This triune God has revealed himself through his Son, Jesus Christ who provides salvation for the world and is the redeemer of all those who believe in him. The word of God, inspired by the Holy Spirit is completely true and the ultimate source of ethics and morality (2 Pet 1:21–22; 2 Tim 3:16–17). This chapter argues that moral laws which have their source in God and reflect his holy nature are objective and universally binding.

Keywords: Apologetics, Truth Claims, African Traditional Religion, Jihadism, Secularism

1. Introduction

There are pertinent questions/issues that should be intentionally and purposely situated in Africa. To make headway, this chapter will discuss the kind of God the African Christian believes in, not whether or not this God exists. The question of whether or not God exists is not an African problem and there is no need to belabour the point. What is the nature of this God? What do African names of God reveal about who he is and his nature or character? What is the Christian concept of the Trinity in relationship to the African view of a plurality of gods? How does God make himself known and can he be known? What is the nature of morality and how does that relate to God? Is this morality subjective or objective? Is this God the only source of morality? How do human beings relate to the moral God and moral decision-making? What are the criteria for evaluating the concept of God and morality that are biblically and theologically valid? This chapter explores these, and more questions.

2. Worldview Challenges in Africa

Africa, with vibrant churches, is faced with many religions and philosophies that promote certain truth claims that are contrary to the truth biblical Christianity upholds. We will mention very briefly three major challenges that are confronting Christians in Africa that require a response or a rational defence and sometimes even a polemic. We will focus on traditional religious beliefs and practices, Islam and secularism.

2.1 African traditional religion

It is common knowledge that cultural beliefs, particularly religious beliefs still have a stronghold on Africans, even after they profess to be Christians. Clifford Geertz argues that religion perseveres, endures, and motivates and moulds behaviour.[1] Morality and justification of right and wrong are explained by religious beliefs and values. These are traditional ways of morality in African traditional religion. One clear implication and lesson from Geertz is that African traditional beliefs/values did not disappear when the people converted to Christianity. The fact is Christianity also comes as a religious worldview that meets an African mind that is informed by the traditional worldview and is in turn "recasted and transformed" into a different quality in terms of "religious meanings, realities, motivations and expectations."[2] A question that is often neglected, and which is answered in chapter 11, is whether the African knew God and whether or not the various gods worshipped in traditional African societies are the same as God revealed in the Scriptures?

2.2 Islam

We cannot speak about Islam mainly in terms of its belief in a strongly monotheistic belief in one God, but also that it is the obligation of a believer in Prophet Mohammed and his teachings that it is required to take up arms and impose the religion of Islam on other nonbelievers. This is basic in the Islamic version of religion.[3] One important and crucial aspect of jihad is not just to convert people to the religion of Allah, but it has a political dimension that must be established by the sharia. Its belief in one God as one (unitary) is radically opposed to the Christian teaching on the triunity of God. This has often generated a lot of passionate debate among adherents of the two faiths. One big question in contemporary debate is this: is Allah the same as the Christian God? While this question is not the central thrust of this chapter, Christian apologists have offered several responses.[4]

---

1. Clifford Geertz, *The Interpretation of Cultures* (New York: Basic Books, 1973), 96.

2. Yusuf Turaki, *Engaging Religions and Worldviews in Africa. A Christian Theological Method* (Bukuru, Nigeria: HippoBooks, 2020), xxxii.

3. Important studies in this regard are Robert Gleave, and István Kristó-Nagy (eds.), *Violence in Islamic Thought from the Qur'an to the Mongols* (Edinburgh: Edinburgh University Press, 2015); Mark Juergensmeyer, "Terror in the Mind of God: The Global Rise of Religious Violence," *Police Practice and Research* 6 no. 2 (2005): 201–208; John L. Esposito, *The Oxford History of Islam* (Oxford: Oxford University Press, 1999).

4. See for example Nabeel Qureshi, *No God but One: Allah or Jesus? A Former Muslim Investigates the Evidence for Islam and Christianity* (Grand Rapids: Zondervan, 2016).

Consequently, is it morally justifiable to seek to impose this religion of Allah upon other non-believers? An important and serious threat to the African Christian is the ideological teaching of a violent and militant Islam. Globally, continentally, nationally, and individually Islam and especially militant Islam occupies an important part of the narrative. From Mohammed, its founder to its contemporary sects all over the world, jihadism has been a main feature of Islam. Mohammed used it to spread it in its early stages. A jihad is "a holy war; a war which is fought in the name of Allah, by Allah's followers to spread the Islamic faith."[5] Relevant passages in the Koran are very explicit. "Fight in the cause of Allah those who fight you . . . and slay them wherever you catch them until there is no tumult or oppression, and there prevails justice and faith in Allah" (Sura 190–193). The command is to keep fighting, to keep slaying wherever you catch the enemies of God. In Sura 2:216, God says this to the Muslim community "fighting is prescribed upon you and ye dislike it. But it is possible to dislike a thing which is good for you, and that ye love a thing which is bad for you. But Allah knoweth it and ye know not."[6] Is moral policing appropriate, whereby morality is imposed, or should it be left to the individual?

2.3 Secularism

Secularism was originally referred to as "the removal of property from the control of the established ecclesiastical authorities."[7] In a word, secularism, and a materialistic mindset without God, dominates the human race. It is an orientation or outlook that seeks to have a perspective that neglects a belief in God and religious convictions. Secularization is "the process by which sectors of society and culture are removed from the domination of religious institutions and symbols."[8] Secularism underlies many aspects of life such as education, culture, lifestyle, etc. Cultural, political, scientific, economic developments are done without recognition of the role of God. Genetic engineering, with its many achievements, is threatening to downplay, disregard, or even to "play" God. "Secularism involves an affirmation of immanent, this-worldly realities, along with a denial or exclusion of transcendent, otherworldly realities. It is

5. Michael Omolewa, *Certificate History of Nigeria* (Lagos: Emaconprint Ltd, 1986), 111.

6. R. C. Sproul and Abdul Saleeb, *The Dark Side of Islam* (Wheaton: Crossway Books, 2003), 87.

7. Peter L. Berger, *The Sacred Canopy: Elements of a Sociological Theory of Religion* (New York: Doubleday Anchor Book, 1967), 107. Berger adds that "in Roman canon law the same term has come to denote the return to the 'world' of a person in orders," 106.

8. Berger, *The Sacred Canopy*, 107.

a worldview and lifestyle oriented to the profane rather than the sacred, the natural rather than the supernatural. Secularism is a non-religious approach to individual and social life."[9]

Even Africa, which has been described as incurably religious, can no longer lay that claim without feeling guilty.[10] A materialistic and hedonistic outlook on life has handcuffed people. Even the church is guilty of this irreligious perspective. "It affects the totality of cultural life and ideation, and may be observed in the decline of religious contents in the arts, in philosophy, in literature, and most important of all, in the rise of science as an autonomous, thoroughly secular perspective on the world."[11] The subjective side of secularization is that it is "an intentional, deliberate and focused secularization of consciousness."[12] Media which includes the movie industry such as Nollywood, Kennywood, etc, TV, and so on is a powerful means where secular ideas permeate society. BNaija is a version of Big Brother Africa which is an intentional cover for secular beliefs and values.[13] The impact and negative influence of secularism on the Christian has been accurately described as "a secular squeeze."[14]

All of the above systems of religion and philosophy are unique and pose a challenge to God and principles of behaviour and morality. It is the duty of Christianity therefore to articulate the truth as a response to these contrary voices which have an impact on the belief in God and morality.

3. Christian Worldview and Ethics

3.1 The Knowledge of God

It is almost ridiculous to ask whether or not Africans believe in God. God is everywhere present in African life and even death. Life and existence will simply cease to make sense if God is taken out of the equation. God can be seen

9. D. W. Gill, "Secularism, Secular Humanism," in *Evangelical Dictionary of Theology*, ed. Walter A. Elwell (Grand Rapids: Baker, 1984), 996. The insights of Dennis P. Hollinger on secularism are also relevant such as "in secularism, religion is viewed in an uncompromisingly negative light." *Choosing the Good: Christian Ethics in a Complex World* (Grand Rapids: Baker Academic, 2002), 100.

10. Turaki, *Engaging Religions and Worldviews*, 15.

11. Berger, *The Sacred Canopy*, 107.

12. Berger, *The Sacred Canopy*, 109.

13. Berger, *The Sacred Canopy*, 6.

14. John F. Alexander, *The Secular Squeeze: Reclaiming Christian Depth in a Shallow World* (Downers Grove: InterVarsity Press, 1993).

in the variety of names among all African peoples, as well as in religious beliefs and practices, prayers, songs, music and dance, rituals, and sacrifices. God is invoked in all life's major circles/cycles, such as marriage, birth, and death. God is viewed as supreme, all-powerful, all-knowing, loving, and caring. The strong presence of God in all aspects of life everywhere involving everybody and everything has led to the conclusion that Africans are "incurably religious." Wilbur O'Donovan's statement is valid:

> African life is rich with an awareness of the Supreme Being . . . God is known to be the creator and the sustainer of life. He is respected and honoured as the exalted One, high above all his creation, and high above all other divinities, all spirits, and all men. It is partly because God is known to be the highly exalted One that he seems to be removed and separated from the everyday lives of many people. He must be approached through intermediaries.[15]

Can we claim that Africans know the God of true nature as he has revealed himself in Scripture and his Son Jesus Christ?

The question is not whether or not God can be seen and acknowledged among Africans but whether or not they know and worship God who is the same as the God revealed in the Scriptures and his Son? How would one know if indeed Africans in their pre-Christian state knew and worshipped God who revealed himself in Scripture and his Son? Turaki probes the African concept of God when he asks: "Do Africans in their traditional religions derive knowledge of God through revelation or human intuition, perception, or self-understanding? What is the content of this knowledge of God? In what ways do Africans respond to this knowledge?"[16] If Africans do not know and worship God, who then do they believe in, worship, and offer sacrifices to? Put differently, is the supreme being whom Africans acknowledge the same as the God of the Bible? If the supreme God that Africans believe in is not the revealed God, who then is this supreme God? Is he just a figment of their imagination? These and many other questions have provoked a lot of discussions and debates. We will try to briefly discuss the major points.

There are two broad positions. On the one hand are those who will argue that Africans know and worship the same God as the one revealed in the Scriptures and worshipped by Christians. On the other hand, some will argue

15. Wilbur O'Donovan, *Biblical Christianity in African Perspective* (Oasis International, 1997), 41.

16. Turaki, *Engaging Religions and Worldviews*, 63.

that Africans did not know and worship the same God as the revealed God of the Scriptures. John Mbiti, probably the most prominent and influential African theologian on this subject, takes the former position and believes that Africans know and worship the same God revealed in the Scriptures. Idowu Bolaji, also argues based on general revelation that God has revealed himself to Africans and is worshipped by them. Similarly, the philosophy of *Orita* (which was the journal of the Department of Religious Studies of the University of Ibadan) is described as:

> The aim of the Department of Religious studies at the University of Ibadan is to promote the study and understanding of the phenomenon and the social implications of religion in general and religion in Africa in particular. This involves more specifically the fields of history and phenomenology of religions, theology, and philosophy, aiming at an interpretation and understanding of African Traditional Religions; Christianity and Islam, separately and in so far as there has been cross-fertilization between them.[17]

Orita, which suggests that "all ways lead to Rome," argues that just as Hebrews had their worship of Yahweh in their way, and the Western Christians through Christ, so Africans worshipped God through their means. It is probably the case that most religious studies departments in many African universities use the same phenomenological approach in studying religions.

Dr. Byang Kato is probably the strongest advocate of those who argue that Africans did not know God in their pre-Christian state. He along with other conservative evangelical theologians like Yusuf Turaki believe that the religion of the Africans and the God Christians believed in according to the revealed word of God are not on the same level. There are some key issues in the debate that need to be considered. First, the belief and assumption of those who place the revealed God of the Scripture and African traditional religion on the same epistemological level is a critical mistake that leads to a wrong conclusion. It is assumed by authors like Mbiti, Idowu and other liberal thinkers, and journals like *Orita*, that the God of the two religions is the same without making some clarifications. It has not been proven beyond a shadow of a doubt that the God of the Bible is the same as the God of traditional religion. To assume that they are the same will be a serious error that could and is often misleading.

---

17. Quoted in Byang H. Kato, *Theological Pitfalls in Africa* (Nairobi, Kenya: Evangel, 1975), 92–93.

Comparing the concept of God among African traditionalists and the concept of God among Christians may not yield much because the criterion of comparison is completely inadequate. Turaki points out the logical implications of such an approach:

> Although the traditional concepts and attributes of God as stated by the African pioneering theologians and scholars are comparable to those of Christianity and other religions, it is clear that in traditional religious thought, the meanings and import of these terms have to be measured by the traditional religious elements. They cannot be interpreted using Christian theological categories, for then they will lose their traditional meaning and authenticity.[18]

Second, methods and methodology in African traditional religion are also problematic. Proponents use religious traditions, symbols, philosophies and cultures to arrive at a concept of God in religions that may not be suitable or proper for the God of the Christian faith. Christianity, which is based on the revealed word of God, is on a different level from African traditional religion, Islam, and other religious systems. The method of trying to compare all religions as equivalent fails to deal with revelation; using only natural reason will distort an understanding of Christianity.

When one uses radically different methods of measuring anything, the results are going to be very dissimilar. In the study of African traditional religion, humans are the subject and they choose which materials to study this God. In contrast, the God of the Christian religion is the initiator of revelation, and this is recorded in the revealed word and his Son. Disregarding the inspired word of God and the incarnation is unacceptable. We conclude this aspect of knowing God by stating that knowing God is more than gathering some information from nature and traditional practices about him. Conjuring God in our minds, even with the best intentions, only can result in postulating a god (God with a small letter) in our image or kind. Our minds can only construct a god who is finite as we are. Gleanings from traditions, customs, beliefs, even using the best scientific method, can never result in God whom the almighty God revealed in Scripture.

A God constructed from our ethnic traditional worldview will be a God who resembles and has the qualities and traits of a cultural construct. Comparing the concepts of God in various religions such as Islam and traditional African religious beliefs and practices will not produce the almighty

18. Turaki, *Engaging Religions and Worldviews*, 63–64.

God who creates, redeems, and is sovereign. We must look elsewhere for an authoritative resource approved by God almighty himself if we are to know a God that is true. It is knowing him in his way and in the way he has revealed himself. J. I. Packer states what knowing God means:

> [W]e know God in the manner of a son knowing his father, a wife knowing her husband, a subject knowing his king, and a sheep knowing its shepherd (these are four main analogies employed). All four analogies point to a relationship in which the knower "looks up to the one known, and the latter takes up responsibility for the welfare of the former. This is part of the biblical concept of knowing God, that those who know Him – that is, those by whom he allows Himself to be known – are loved and cared for by Him."[19]

Who then is this God that has revealed himself in his word and his Son?

3.2 The Triune God

The beliefs and practices of African traditional religion convey only a faint and incomplete understanding of who God is. For example, even if we grant the concept of the supreme God who is the same as the God of the Bible, we must ask, "What about the concept of the triune God in the African concept of God?"[20] Again, the use and application of certain aspects of God are emphasized at the expense of other equally important aspects of God. For example, some argue for the idea of relationship as the most important aspect of God while others will argue that the ontological aspect or otherness of God is what is to be emphasized. Some important issues need to be raised. First, Ogbonnaya uses community theism from an African perspective to explore the Christian concept of the Trinity.[21] He proposes communitheism as a substitute for the word Trinity. An important question here is, can one say that Trinity as used in historic biblical Christianity is synonymous with the community of the gods that Ogbonnaya proposes? What is unclear and ambiguous is the identity of the community gods. Who these community gods are is not explained. Whereas historic Christianity explicitly argued that the Father, Son and Holy Spirit have the same ontological substance, African gods are never viewed as ontologically

19. J. I. Packer, *Knowing God* (Downers Grove: InterVarsity, 1973), 33.

20. See Kevin Muriithi Ndereba, "Analysing African Traditional Gods Through a Trinitarian Apologetic," *African Theological Journal for Church and Society* 3, no. 2 (2022): 72–89.

21. A. Okechukwu Ogbonnaya, *On Communitarian Divinity an African Interpretation of the Trinity* (St. Paul: Paragon House, St Paul, MN, 1994).

the same. In the African worldview, there is a hierarchy among the gods. The supreme being is the highest being followed by other lesser divinities. To equate the two concepts is therefore unacceptable and would duplicate the heresies that the early church vigorously sought to avoid. Second, Ogbonnaya proposes that communality is the essence of the gods and relationship is key to the idea of community. To his credit, there are great lessons that can be learned about the relational aspect of the Godhead in terms of relationships within the persons.

However, it must be pointed out that the image of the community of relationships within the gods in the African sense at best underscores the importance of relationships, but fails to deal with the equality and substance in the Godhead as biblical Christianity affirms. To posit relationship as the most important factor in the Trinity is to put the cart before the horse and can only spell danger. The point is that relational and communal aspects of the Trinity are not the same as metaphysical issues of the Trinity. For Ogbonnaya, the Trinity must be true because Africans so perceive it in their world. As we argued in *African Christian Theology*, seeking to justify and authenticate our theology from our own experience or from below has its inherent weaknesses.[22] The attempt to construct the concept of God from human experiences, from below, to God who is ontologically different, would emphasize what may not be essential. The possibility of missing out when we try to understand and construct God from below is just too high. If the concept of God is true, it must be derived first from above or as revealed in his word, otherwise, we end up with a doctrine that is our cultural contraption. The Bible, not our worldview, is the textbook for evaluating our doctrine. Though there is a community of gods, the supreme God is ontologically not equal to the other gods. The most severe criticism of communitheism or social theory is that of polytheism – the plurality of many gods. The plurality of gods (multiple gods) is closer to polytheism (many gods) and tritheism (three gods) which both biblical revelation and historic biblical Christianity see as heretical. Community among these many gods cannot be postulated as the best tool for understanding and stating Christian trinitarian theology.

Christians do not just believe in God, they affirm the real existence of three persons in the Godhead, namely God the Father, God the Son, and God the Holy Spirit. This is not a simple belief. This highly thought out and very complex concept has been in existence from the rise of Christianity to its present articulated position. The belief in the triune God is not only an abstract theological postulation by sophisticated theologians but has serious

22. Samuel Waje Kunhiyop, *African Christian Theology* (Nairobi: HippoBooks, 2012).

meaning and implications for Christian spirituality and practice. Why is a study on the Trinity important? Harold O. J. Brown stated it well: "Without a coherent doctrine of the Trinity, the New Testament witness to the activity of God in Christ and the work of the Holy Spirit will tend to force one either into modalism or a kind of tritheism."[23] In other words, one cannot ignore it and not fall into serious heresies of some sort. Though, as we will argue, biblical Christianity cannot exist without trinitarian theology, sadly we find out that Christianity as practiced in most contemporary African beliefs, either ignores, disregards or simply does not appreciate its meaning and significance. This development is especially worrisome as the Pentecostal movement is attracting millions of members who are untaught and ignorant of the key tenets of the Christian faith.

In some Christian circles, preachers make pronouncements such as "Don't expect to understand it, just believe or accept it." The problem is that the statement is half true and half false. Yes, indeed, we cannot fully understand the Trinity, but it does not mean that we are unable to understand anything about the Trinity as difficult and complex as it is. Yes, it is a mystery, but it does not mean that God has not revealed anything about this concept that we cannot say anything intellectually rational. It is not enough to believe in the existence of God, as Africans do. Simply put, "vague theism is futile. The cutting edge of faith is due to its definiteness . . . The Christian has decided for God who has spoken – in nature, in history, in the prophets, in Christ."[24] A general belief in the supernatural may be adequate for African traditional religions, but it is inconclusive when it comes to the understanding and grounding of Christian ethics, which is rooted in the Judeo-Christian revelation.

Essential elements of the teaching on the triune God are as follows. God is one, not several gods. Biblical Christianity teaches the unity of God. Three Gods (tritheism) is categorically condemned in Scripture. The unity of God is expressed in Deuteronomy 6:4: "Hear, O Israel: The Lord is our God, the Lord alone." The Christian upholds this essential truth. Each of the three persons is equally God. God the Father, Son, and the Holy Spirit are qualitatively one. Some relevant passages express the unity of the triune God: Matthew 28:19,

---

23. Harold O. J. Brown, *Heresies: The Image of Christ in the Mirror of Heresy and Orthodoxy from the Apostles to the Present* (Grand Rapids: Baker, 1988), 154 cited in Samuel Waje Kunhiyop, "The Trinity in Africa: Trends and Trajectories," pp. 55–68, Gene L. Green, Stephen T. Pardue and Khiok-Khng Yeo, eds. *The Trinity among the Nations: The Doctrine of God in the Majority World* (Carlisle: Langham Global Library, 2015), 56.

24. William Temple, *What Christians Stand for in the Secular World* (Philadelphia: Fortress Press, Philadelphia, 1965), 9.

"Go therefore and make disciples of all nations, baptizing them in the name of the Father and of the Son and the Holy Spirit"; 2 Corinthians 13:14, "The grace of the Lord Jesus Christ, the love of God, and the communion of the Holy Spirit be with all of you." The Son is equally God as the Holy Spirit is equally God with the Father and Son. Historic biblical Christianity holds this absolute truth. Each person of the Godhead, though ontologically the same, has different roles; there is an economy of function in God's nature. For example, the Father is not the Son, neither is the Holy Spirit the Son nor the Father. It was the Son who died on the Cross, and it is the Holy Spirit who indwells believers. All of the three persons in the Godhead (Trinity) are eternal. None is older or younger than the other. Moses referred to God as "the eternal God" (Deut 33:27). In John 8:58, Jesus refers to himself as "I AM," the name of the God of the Old Testament (Exod 3:14), and Isaiah the prophet testifies to his coming and states that he will be called "Eternal Father" among other titles (Isa 9:6; see also Gen 1:2; Heb 9:14).

4. God and Morality

What is the nature of morality and how does that relate to God? Is this morality subjective or objective? Is this God the only source of morality? What are other sources of African morality? How do human beings relate to the moral God and moral decision-making? What are the criteria for evaluating an apologetic that is biblically and theologically valid? The African sense of morality, of ethical reasoning and basis of morality, is profoundly impacted by traditional values and worldview. The influence of secularism and a post-Christian worldview is also influencing Christian morality. We have also mentioned that the rise of Islam and its militancy and jihadist ideology must receive appropriate and rational attention. The basic presupposition of a Christian apologetic stance is as follows.

4.1 The Triune God is the Source of Morality

What should be a source of morality? Africans traditionally held that the supreme being, who has many names in all African ethnic groups, is one of the major sources of morality. The many gods, the ancestors, and the community all play important roles in shaping and moulding morality. In Islam, the Koran and the Hadith are sources of moral conduct. Secularism rejects the supernatural as having any control or direction in morality. John S. Feinberg and Paul D. Feinberg discussed three main sources of ethics.

Reason-based systems hold that "ethical norms are generated from and discerned by reason."[25] There are both Christians and non-Christians who hold to reason-based systems. Christians in this category "hold that revelation plays a role, but even if revelation provides some norms, reason alone could have generated those norms." In secular ethics, Immanuel Kant is the most prominent proponent who held to reason-based ethics as the norm for ethics. In his famous categorical imperative, he states that "Act only according to that maxim by which you will that it should become a universal law."[26] Natural law is also reason-based ethics that has Thomas Aquinas as its prominent proponent. Natural law ethics has been adopted by the Roman Catholic Church for its ethical practice. Accordingly, natural law ethics postulates that "the end (the goal toward which it strives) of each thing in the natural order is built into the thing itself. Thus, by observing an object in nature, one can easily discern its intended purpose in the natural order. This end immediately indicates how the thing should act."[27]

Prescription-based systems argue that "ethical norms originate from an authority figure who mandates them . . . Command in reason-based systems is determined by reason alone, whereas prescriptions in prescriptive theories come from an authority figure . . . Prescriptive theories often appeal to God as the prescriber."[28] For the Christian though, the source of morality is God and in a clearly biblical and Christian sense, it is the triune God and the revealed word or Scriptures.

The famous Decalogue or Ten Commandments (Exod 20:1ff) was given by God which means the commandments have their source in God. In this commandment, the introduction is "I am God who brought you out of Egypt and redeemed you." He is the giver of these moral laws. The Israelites, the people of God, should always understand that the giver and source of their moral conduct is the almighty God. The ontological grounding of ethics is the triune God.[29]

Often this God is seen as only interested in the spiritual and not the secular. God's revelation and participation in the creation and his revelation in the incarnation of Jesus Christ demonstrate that God is not only a spiritual being

---

25. John S. Feinberg and Paul D. Feinberg, *Ethics For a Brave New World* (Wheaton: Crossway, 1993), 24.

26. Feinberg and Feinberg, *Ethics For a Brave New World*, 25.

27. John Stott, *Issues Facing Christians Today* (London: Marshall Pickering, 1990), 25.

28. Feinberg and Feinberg, *Ethics For a Brave New World*, 25.

29. Kunhiyop, *African Christian Ethics*, 51. I argued in the book that the source of Christian ethics is the triune God.

interested in spiritual matters only, but he is a God who has a personal and intimate relationship with his creation. The Holy Spirit's continuing work in creation and especially in the life of the believer also makes God very intimate in the life of his created order.

4.2 Morality is a Reflection of God's Nature and Character

Morality or principles of behaviour must reflect the nature and character of the triune God. Leviticus 20:26 states, "You shall be holy to me, for I the Lord am holy, and I have separated you from the other peoples to be mine." Matthew 5:48 states that "Be perfect, therefore, as your heavenly Father is perfect." Hollinger notes correctly that the "content of our moral responses are certainly known and shaped by the biblical norms in various forms, but ultimately, they are reflections of God's character, purposes, and actions in the world."[30] Moral laws are rooted in God's nature, character, and attributes. They are not rooted in a spoken word, but the moral character and attributes of God. These moral laws are universal and eternal because God is eternal, and his eternal nature is universal in scope. They are also binding upon all moral agents, human beings, and spirit beings. Moral agents are to emulate the eternal moral character of God. They function to define how moral agents are to relate and be responsible to God, creation, and humanity. There are consequences for not living a good moral life or breaking them. God's moral laws are binding upon all moral agents with no exception.

Universal moral laws are rooted in the knowledge of God and the Bible. They are quite distinct from the morality derived from human cultures, traditions, metaphysics, philosophies and sciences. Christians should understand this and make such a distinction. As Turaki argues:

> Moral laws are rooted in God's nature, character, and attributes. They are not rooted in a spoken word, but the moral character and attributes of God. These moral laws are universal and eternal because God is Eternal, and his eternal nature is universal in scope. They are also binding upon all moral agents, human beings, and spirit beings.[31]

---

30. Hollinger, *Choosing The Good*, 64–65.

31. Yusuf Turaki, *Universal Moral Laws: Theistic and Creational Foundations of Morality and Ethics* (Unpublished Manuscripts, Jos, Nigeria, 2022), 25–26.

Several observations are in order. First, morality, ethical behaviour and principles of ethical decision-making must be rooted in God. This God, who is triune, has revealed himself in the incarnation of his son, Jesus Christ, and the Holy Spirit. This triune God is the foundation of morality. Second, this triune God has revealed himself through the written word or Scriptures. 2 Timothy 3:16–17 states that "All Scripture is breathed out by God and profitable for teaching, for reproof, for correction, and training in righteousness, that the man of God may be completely equipped for every good work." This means that the Scriptures are indeed the word of God which should be the criterion of morality and reasoning. It is the final authority in belief and morality. Another passage is 2 Peter 1:21 "For no prophecy was ever produced by the will of man, but men spoke from God as they were carried along by the Holy Spirit." The producer of the word which is the Scripture was not a human agency, but it has a divine initiation. From all the Old Testament writers to the New Testament authors, their writings were inspired by God. Human agency was involved, but it was thoroughly and completely controlled and directed by God. Third, moral behaviour or conduct must be modelled after God's nature – righteousness. No more and no less is required when it comes to modelling our ethical behaviour.

4.3 Moral Laws are Universal and Binding

Morality which is rooted and directed in God is universally binding on his created beings. The moral laws of God are not selective or discriminatory, they are universal, and God requires his creatures to obey them. If God's moral laws are binding, should they be imposed on people as the Muslims have adopted moral policing in some instances? John Stott provides some insights by discussing three options.

Imposition

"Here are Christians with a commendable zeal for God. They believe in revelation, and they care deeply about God's revealed truth and will. They long to see society reflecting it. So the desire to achieve this end by force is an understandable temptation."[32] The historical examples of the Inquisition in Europe and the Prohibition in the United States, namely the legal ban on the manufacture and sale of alcoholic liquor, "is a foolish, nostalgic desire for a Christendom which has long since vanished."[33]

32. John Stott, *Issues Facing Christians Today*, 46–47.

33. Stott, *Issues Facing Christians Today*, 48.

Laissez-fare

This is the opposite of imposition. It means "a mood of apathy and indifference." Laissez-faire has even sometimes been an attitude adopted by Christian people in the name of tolerance."[34] In his criticism of laissez-fare, Stott rightly asked "But how can we Christians be intellectually tolerant of opinion we know to be false or actions we know to be evil. What kind of unprincipled indulgence is this?"[35] This kind of tolerance is tantamount to compromising our Christian faith.

Persuasion

This option stresses persuasion by an argument which is apologetics. John Stott argues that when the Bible states that "come now, let us reason together, says the Lord" is

> a basic ground for this is the human conscience which must be treated with the greatest respect . . . this principle, which arises out of the Christian doctrine of human beings, should affect our social behaviour and institutions. It is the reason why Christians oppose autocracy and favour democracy. Autocracy crushes conscience, democracy respects them.[36]

Stott, therefore, proposes "doctrinal apologetics in evangelism (arguing the truth of the gospel) and ethical apologetic in social action (arguing the goodness of the moral law). Apologetics of both kinds are wanted urgently in today's church and world."[37] In this book and chapter, we concur with John Stott in underscoring the urgency of apologetics in an African context.

Fifth and finally, our understanding of God and morality must be "Bible-based, Christ-centred and Spirit-based." This is the motto of the South African Theological Seminary which is a major criterion of evaluating all programs and research. Our idea of God and morality must be constantly checked against the biblical and theological affirmation of the inspiration, infallibility, authority of the Scripture, Christ-centred and directed and empowered by the Holy Spirit.

34.

35. Stott, *Issues Facing Christians Today*, 48.

36. Stott, *Issues Facing Christians Today*, 31, 32.

37. Stott, *Issues Facing Christians Today*, 52.

5. Conclusion

The triune God is the ontological grounding of the Christian faith and consequently of morality. Proper Christian faith must subscribe to an unambiguous assertion in God the Father, the Son, and the Holy Spirit. God is revealed in his Son and the Scriptures. The triune God revealed himself in his Son and his word. The revelation of God in his Son takes precedence over all other forms of revelation either through other persons such as prophets, priests, or even ancestors. Hebrews 1:1–2 says, "In the past God spoke to our ancestors through the prophets at many times and in various ways, but in these last days he has spoken to us by his Son, whom he appointed heir of all things, and through whom also he made the universe" (see also 2 Pet 1:21; 2 Tim 3:16–17). The finality of God's revelation is Jesus Christ and the right knowledge and understanding of this God are through the Scripture, the final word of God.

For the Christian faith, divine revelation is a fundamental belief without which Christianity has no basis for existence. It is the self-disclosure of God to his creation. Revelation, in the strictest sense, means God's initiative, disclosure, and unveiling. Divine revelation is therefore cardinal to the Christian religion. Indeed, Scripture insists that knowledge of a personal and sovereign God combined with the worship of him through other divinities boils down to idolatry (Rom 1:21, 25).

Morality must be based on the nature and character of God. Christian morality is not human-based or community-based but is fundamentally God-based. Leviticus 19:2 states "Be holy for I the Lord your God am holy." Holiness which means "separateness from other gods unto God" means in essence that morality should be God-based. In the New Testament, Christian behaviour is to follow the righteousness of God and in very practical terms means that Christians should be Christ-followers and follow in "his footsteps" (1 Pet 2:21).

Finally, morality is universally binding and objective for all God's creatures. Despite the many religious claims of God and morality which are propounded by traditional religions, Islam and secularism, the triune God who has revealed himself in his Son, Jesus Christ, and the Scriptures, requires everybody and everywhere to submit to his moral laws.

Bibliography

Alexander, John F. *The Secular Squeeze: Reclaiming Christian Depth in a Shallow World.* Downers Grove: InterVarsity Press, 1993.

Berger, Peter L. *The Sacred Canopy: Elements of a Sociological Theory of Religion*. New York: Doubleday, 1967.
Brown, Harold O. J. *Heresies: The Image of Christ in the Mirror of Heresy and Orthodoxy from the Apostles to the Present*. Grand Rapids: Baker, 1988.
Cowan, Steven B., and Stanley N. Gundry, eds. *Five Views on Apologetics*. Grand Rapids: Zondervan, 2000.
Edgard, William, and Scott Oliphint, eds. *Christian Apologetics. Past & Present. A Primary Reader* (Vol. 1. To 1500). Wheaton: Crossway Books, 2000.
Elwell, Walter A., ed. *Evangelical Dictionary of Theology*. Grand Rapids: Baker, 1984.
Feinberg, John S., and Paul D. Feinberg. *Ethics for A Brave New World*. Wheaton: Crossway, 1993.
Frame, John M. *Apologetics: A Justification of Christian Belief*. 2nd edition. Edited by Joseph E. Torres. Phillipsburg: P&R Publishing, 2015.
Geertz, Clifford. *The Interpretation of Cultures*. New York: Basic Books 1973.
Geisler, Norman L. *Christian Apologetics*. Grand Rapids: Baker Books, 1976.
Hiebert, Paul D. *Cultural Anthropolog*. 2nd edition. Grand Rapids: Baker Academic,1983.
———. *Transforming Worldview: An Anthropological Understanding of how People Change*. Grand Rapids: Baker Academic, 2008.
Hollinger, Dennis P. *Choosing the Good: Christian Ethics in a Complex World*. Grand Rapids: Baker Academic, 2002.
Kato, Byang H. *Theological Pitfalls in Africa*. Nairobi: Evangel, 1975.
Kunhiyop, Samuel Waje. *African Christian Ethics*. Carlisle: HippoBooks, 2008.
———. *African Christian Theology*. Carlisle: HippoBooks, 2012.
McDowell, J., and Sean McDowell. *Evidence that Demands a Verdict: Life Changing Truth for a Sceptical World*. London: Authentic Media Press, 2017.
McDowell, J. *Evidence that Demands a Verdict: Historical Evidence for the Christian Faith*. Nashville: Thomas Nelson, 1972.
Moreland, J.. *Scaling the Security City: A Defense of Christianity*. Grand Rapids: Baker Academic, 1987.
Ndereba, Kevin Muriithi. "Analysing African Traditional Gods Through a Trinitarian Apologetic." *African Theological Journal for Church and Society* 3, no. 2 (2022): 72–89.
O'Donovan, Wilbur. *Biblical Christianity in African Perspective*. Oasis International, 1997.
Ogbonnaya, A. Okechukwu. *On Communitarian Divinity an African Interpretation of the Trinity*. St Paul: Paragon House, 1994.
Omolewa, Michael. *Certificate History of Nigeria*. Lagos: Emaconprint Ltd, Lagos, 1986.
Packer, J. I. *Knowing God*. Grand Rapids: InterVarsity Press, 1973.
Pinnock, Clark. *Set Forth Your Case: Studies in Christian Apologetics*. Chicago: Moody Press, 1971.
Ramm, Bernard. *Protestant Christian Evidences*. Chicago: Moody Press, 1954.
Sproul, R. C. and Abdul Saleeb. *The Dark Side of Islam*. Wheaton: Crossway Books, 2003.
Stott, John. *Issues Facing Christians Today*. London: Marshall Pickering, 1990.

Temple, William. *What Christians Stand for in the Secular World*. Philadelphia: Fortress Press, 1965.
Turaki, Yusufu. *Engaging Religions and Worldviews in Africa. A Christian Theological Method*. Carlisle: HippoBooks, 2020.
———. *Universal Moral Laws: Theistic and Creational Foundations of Morality and Ethics*. Unpublished Manuscripts, n.d.
Van Til, Cornelius. *Christian Apologetics*. Phillipsburg: P&R Publishing, 1976.
———. *The Defense of the Faith*. Phillipsburg: P&R Publishing, 1955.

Part III

Cultural Issues

7

The Case for Christianity as an African Religion

Kyama Mugambi, PhD

Assistant Professor of World Christianity at Yale Divinity School, Connecticut, USA

Abstract

Dire social, political, and economic realities fuel a fierce public debate about Christian identity in relation to Africa. These realities along with historical issues form the basis of a sustained argument for the rejection of Christianity in the continent. This chapter argues that, despite the challenges, Christianity is, in fact, more rooted in Africa than is often admitted. This historical connection of the faith to the continent has implications for apologetics discourse, particularly as it engages three key objections. The first objection has to do with a clear response to Africa's colonial history. The second objection has to do with the attendant issues of the modern missionary enterprise. The third issue is the secularization trend within organized Christianity, particularly as the faith has engaged with Western postmodernity and atheism in the continent. In response to these, this chapter engages the biblical and historical connections of the Christian faith in the continent, the doctrinal contributions of the African church to global Christianity as well as the enduring African Christian traditions in the continent.

Keywords: African Christianity, African Traditional Religions, Colonialism in Africa, Missionary Christianity, Decolonization, Decolonizing Christianity

1. An Overview of African Objections to Christianity

Three objections surround conversations about the alienness of Christianity in Africa. The first involves Africa's colonial history. With the exception of southern Africa, much of the continent's colonial history is fairly recent. Colonies in this region came under foreign political rule for less than a century beginning in the late nineteenth century. That brief, difficult colonial episode often forms the basis for evaluating the identity of Christianity as an African religion. By contrast, missionary initiatives began earlier, from the late eighteenth century.[1]

The second objection challenging the authenticity of Christianity as African stems from the collective failures of the missionary enterprise. Missionaries often came with noble evangelism ideals, delivered with displays of remarkable ineptitude of ethnic sensitivities. They exchanged the vulnerability and humility Jesus taught in Luke 10 with an acute lack of cultural knowledge, unsophisticated anthropological approaches, attended by mixed imperialistic motives. The consequences of these failures inflicted festering cultural, social and emotional wounds still felt today. Bitter debates initiated by African intellectuals from the 1970s continue to rage, spurred on by ever present examples of missionaries' condescension of African culture.[2]

A third issue comes from the current secularization trends away from organized religion, particularly Christianity and Islam. In part, these shifts stem from the Western modernist reverence for science. Emanating from the Enlightenment, these ideas seek ways to explain away human questions from the perspective of science and empirical thought.[3] Subsequent postmodern culture has tried to diminish the function of religion in society. Popular currents within postmodernism promote relativism which challenges the notion of absolute truth, as presented by Christianity. Modern and post-modern ideologies also highlight the triumph of human supremacy over religious submission. Such

---

1. I argue more extensively using Kenya as a case study in my article. Kyama M. Mugambi, "Christianity and the Fate of Africa: A Critique of the Debate," *Missio Africanus Journal of African Missiology*, 5 no. 1 (September 2020); R. Elliott Kendall, *The End of an Era: Africa and the Missionary* (London: SPCK, 1978); Roland Anthony Oliver, *The Missionary Factor in East Africa* (London: Longmans, Green, 1965).

2. Examples of such literature about. See for example Okot p'Bitek, *Song of Lawino and Song of Ocol* (Nairobi: East African Publishers, 1995); Ngũgĩ wa Thiong'o, *A Grain of Wheat*, vol. 2 (New York: Penguin, 2012).

3. These are the products of post-Enlightenment thought. Andrew Walls examines this from a World Christianity point of view here: Andrew F. Walls, *Crossing Cultural Frontiers: Studies in the History of World Christianity*, ed. Mark R. Gornik (Maryknoll: Orbis Books, 2017), 41–43.

secularist and materialist views of culture envision a prosperous human society that does not depend on religious input.

Following these objections, pockets of activists, off and on the continent, attempt to shift societal focus away from religion even in highly Christianized societies. Fuelled by commercial mass media, public discourse in Kenya, for example, has often pitted the majority Christians against a small but highly vocal atheist society. The debates are most vibrant among educated and Westernized demographics of the continent. They often table questions about the value of Christianity and what it has done for the continent since its advent.[4]

A proper understanding of Christianity's rootedness in Africa, and Africa's contribution to Christianity is therefore an urgent apologetic task. I propose that Christianity is an African religion for several reasons. The first is the biblical connection to Africa which is well laid out in the New Testament. Second, Christianity is also an African religion also because of the imprint of early African contributions affirming and shaping the faith. Third, evidence of Christianity's African identity lies in its evangelistic resilience in the twentieth century against the colonial history along with the catastrophic failures of the missionary enterprise. Beyond this, it should not escape notice that there are at least two enduring Christian traditions in Africa established before the constitution of Europe as we know it today. Their identity cannot be anything else but African. Africa's stake in global Christianity has more recently been affirmed by prolific growth through local agency. The result is a wide variety of expressions which legitimately claim African provenance and expression.

An important question to ask before we delve into the discussion is: Who or what is Africa? The word "Africa" as used by Romans dates back to the second century BC. The noun referred, then as it does now, to the land and people south of the Mediterranean. Though the etymology of the word is unclear, Africa has for millennia been a well-accepted geographic, political, ethnic, and even racial category. Can Christianity therefore be African? Can it be considered an African religion? The answer to that question lies in the extent to which we see Africans own this faith as part of their identity. The way Africans affirm and express this faith in their own unique ways demonstrates how much Africa is Christian, and how much Christianity is African. This is our task in this chapter. My contention together with others is that Christianity's

---

4. Paul Gifford echoes these same questions in his own reflections about Christianity in Africa. See Paul Gifford, *Christianity, Development and Modernity in Africa* (London: C. Hurst & Co. Publishers Ltd, 2015).

ability to incarnate into human life and culture is its genius.[5] This genius is how much Christianity is African in ways that are different from other cultures into which it enters. The following section explores how this history can be traced in the biblical data, particularly the place of African people and places in the Old and New Testaments.

2. The Biblical Connection to Africa

The Old Testament contains numerous interactions with the continent of Africa. Abraham's connection with Egypt saw him spend years there as part of the redemptive plan. The narrative of Israel in Egypt and the Mosaic deliverance after a 400-year sojourn is a foundational feature of the salvation story. Africa features in prophetic literature as Cush, or Egypt. These mentions sometimes occur in a positive light and, at other times, in a negative light.

It is in the New Testament, however, that we find a much more elaborate link between the continent and the start of Christian faith. Jesus's own life began with an exile in Egypt during the Herodian infanticide. There is no explicit mention of African leaders until the end of the gospels. For instance, Simon of Cyrene, in modern day Libya, emerged as a key figure in the passion of Christ. Acts 2 contains references to people from Libya, Cyrene, and Egypt as participants in the Pentecost event. We learn from various Christian traditions that the faith eventually took root in these parts of the continent through local agency coming out of Pentecost.

Luke devotes a considerable amount of time to Philip's dramatic evangelistic encounter with the Ethiopian eunuch in Acts 8. Ethiopian Christian tradition considers this an important event establishing Christianity there. Subsequent missionary engagements in Ethiopia from the Middle East served to strengthen the church.

Acts chapter 13 is about the first formal commissioning of missionaries in early Christianity. Set in the port city of Antioch, this section outlines the calling of Paul and Barnabas from amongst the five key leaders and opinion shapers of that church. A fact often overlooked is that of these five leaders,

---

5. Translation is the term Andrew Walls, Lamin Sanneh, Mark Shaw and others give to describe this phenomenon. It is the entry of Christian message into the thought, life, and culture of the recipients. Andrew F. Walls, *The Missionary Movement in Christian History: Studies in the Transmission of Faith*, 1st ed. (Maryknoll, NY; Edinburgh: Orbis Books; T&T Clark, 1996); Lamin O. Sanneh, *Translating the Message: The Missionary Impact on Culture* (Maryknoll: Orbis Books, 1989); Mark Shaw, *Global Awakening: How 20th-Century Revivals Triggered a Christian Revolution* (Downers Grove, Ill.: IVP Academic, 2010).

two were Africans. Lucius came from Cyrene in modern day Libya. Simon the Niger literally means Simon the dark man or the black man. Since people from the Middle East had a darker skin tone, Simon the Niger would have been so named to distinguish him from his fellow Christians from the area. He may well have been from Ethiopia, or Nubia. Acts 18 records the work of Apollos, a highly respected Christian often referred to in Paul's letters to the Corinthians. Apollos was a well-educated Jew who skilfully taught the Scriptures. His ability to connect Hebrew Scriptures with Christianity had a profound impact on the church. That he was from Africa seems to have been taken for granted in commentaries and sermons about him.

Beyond these accounts in the New Testament, various traditions consider the apostles to have been very connected to the continent of Africa. Matthew for example is said to have preached and died in Ethiopia.[6] Others suggest that Philip evangelized in Carthage. Coptic tradition considers Mark the evangelist an African who took the gospel to the Egyptian city of Alexandria.[7] Copts credit him as the founder of the Alexandrian catechetical school from which some of Christianity's greatest theologians hailed. Such admissions of African contributions to Christian history were not problematic through the first fifteen centuries of Christianity. This is largely because of the absence of the vitriolic racial prejudice levied against Africa in more recent times. With regard to faith, racial origin did matter as much then as it does now. The point I make here is that Christianity has deep biblical and apostolic roots in the continent, despite recent omissions in the writing of Christian history.

3. Africans Shaping Christian Doctrine

We now look at the role of Africans in shaping Christian orthodoxy. Christian faith derived its *force majeure* from the dedication of its devotees combined with the refinement of its tenets. Together with others in the ancient world, early African Christians demonstrated their deep commitment to the faith through their martyrdom. Two notable early examples are Perpetua and Felicity in the second century. They were young women in their early 20s or late teens who emulated Christ by paying the ultimate price. Another dimension of this deep devotion came in the form of astute theological reflection.

6. Jacobus de Voragine, *The Golden Legend: Readings on the Saints* (Princeton: Princeton University Press, 2012).

7. Thomas C. Oden, *The African Memory of Mark: Reassessing Early Church Tradition* (Grand Rapids: InterVarsity Press, 2011).

A set of distinguished early African theologians made significant contributions to the refinement of Christian doctrine.[8] Tertullian, born Quintus Septimius Florence Tertulianas (AD 155–220) came from Carthage in modern day Tunisia. His wide-ranging writings employed his background as a lawyer to articulate pertinent issues on Christian faith. Among his many theological contributions was the important work he did to develop the doctrine of the holy Trinity.

Origen Adamantius of Alexandria (AD 184–253) produced highly detailed treatises which served as the precursor to the modern-day approaches to systematic theology. Origen wrote prolifically with many of his works becoming essential texts for successive generations of theologians. His sermons and commentaries provided crucial building blocks for the historic development of doctrine. The desert fathers and mothers were ascetic Christians from the Egyptian desert whose lives and teachings invigorated future monastic movements. Anthony (AD 251–356) and Pachomius (AD 292–348) are two from this community credited with the establishment of monasticism. The monastic movement eventually became crucial for the growth of Christianity especially in Europe through the Middle Ages.

Athanasius (AD 293–373), a bishop of Alexandria, argued significantly for the divinity of Jesus. He crafted elements that allowed a more fully orbed argument for the Trinity. He was also instrumental in the council of Nicaea in AD 325 from which the initial draft of the Nicene creed came. The creed became an essential statement of faith for many Christian expressions today. In addition to this, Athanasius established a system through which the dates for Easter are calculated today. Another key theologian responsible for the shaping of Christianity in the Western world was Augustine of Hippo from modern day Algeria. Augustine, a prolific writer, distinguished himself as one of the great apologists of the patristic era. His books the *City of God and the City of Man* and *The Confessions* are among the ancient Christian classics which laid the theological framework for protestant doctrine. Augustine was instrumental in the reformer Martin Luther's own understanding of concepts such as salvation by grace through faith. Interestingly, some recent research

8. Oden discusses African contributions extensively in Thomas C. Oden, *How Africa Shaped the Christian Mind: Rediscovering the African Seedbed of Western Christianity* (Downers Grove, Ill.: IVP Academic, 2010).

notes that Martin Luther also had tremendous respect for Ethiopian Orthodox Christianity, after an encounter with Michael the Deacon.[9]

Why then, one would ask, is this early African connection with Christianity hidden from current discourse? The answer to this baffling question lies in assessing the influence of recent scholars such as church historian Adolf Harnack (1851–1930). He advanced the idea that despite their identity, early African Christians were not really African but Greek or Latin intellectuals who used these European languages for their work.[10] This is as difficult to sustain as the notion that the writer of this chapter should be presumed to be (White and) British or American, because the chapter is in English and uses a Western polemic approach.[11] Identity is found in much more than a small section of writings for a particular audience. Furthermore, this argument did not consider the bilingualism of such early African theologians as Athanasius, who also spoke Copt.

This flawed thesis of the early African theologians' identity overlooks the self-description of Athanasius, Augustine and other leaders who self-identified as Africans. Patristic writings for among the bishops, for example, contain evidence of a well-developed self-perception of this early church as African.[12] Several themes reinforced African identity in this self-governing, self-perpetuating church. They, for instance, believed in a mutual transparency among themselves on the continent. It was a self-regulating community in terms of arising disciplinary issues. They saw themselves as an African community stretching from Egypt all over northern Africa into Mauritania, with an inclusive vision of mission for the continent of Africa.[13]

---

9. For insightful treatments of these themes see Thomas C. Oden, *The Rebirth of African Orthodoxy: Return to Foundations* (Nashville: Abingdon Press, 2016); David Daniels III and Lawrence Anglin, "Luther and the Ethiopian Deacon," *Lutheran Quarterly* 32 no. 4 (2018): 428–34; David L. Eastman, *Early North African Christianity: Turning Points in the Development of the Church* (Grand Rapids: Baker Academic, 2021).

10. This is evident in Harnack's body of work. See for example Adolf von Harnack, *History of Dogma*, trans. Neil Buchanan, vol. IV (Boston, Mass: Little, Brown and Company, 1907), 1–20.

11. I mean here in terms of race and identity. Political and geographic origins are obviously a part of the complex discourse about identity. A black British national who goes by the name Kyama could have written this chapter. The point however is made that Harnack's assumptions about ancient scholars who explicitly identified as African simply cannot be held to be true.

12. See Athanasius, "Ad Afros Epistola Synodica: To the Bishops of Africa" (AD 368); "Council of Carthage (A.D. 419): The Code of Canons of the African Church," (AD 419), 219. See https://www.newadvent.org/fathers.

13. Much more could be said about this. Anyone wishing to delve deeply into this can find useful material in the document "Council of Carthage (A.D. 419): The Code of Canons of the African Church."

4. An Alternative to the Colonial and Missionary Enterprise

Christianity's success in Africa in spite of the at times disastrous colonial and missionary enterprise is a testament to the faith's connection with the continent. To fully grasp this, we need a nuanced understanding of the missionary era. With the exception of Liberia and Sierra Leone, it is a fact that the majority of the initial missionaries to the continent in the 1800s were white Europeans.[14] Narratives abound of the low view missionaries had of Africans. Many could not find wholesome, virtuous things to say about the people and cultures they found in Africa.[15] Despite these shortcomings, the majority of the missionaries had noble motives for the expansion of the kingdom of God. Though they did not always agree with each other, or with colonial authorities, some missionaries inadvertently promoted the priorities of imperialists.

The colonial enterprise was at its core a white European initiative on the continent. It came decades after missionaries had already begun their work. Missionary letters, records, and studies provided fodder for the increasing appetite of Western European commerce.[16] Nested within this relational triangle of missionary-imperialist-African was a complex symbiotic relationship between the white colonial settlers, white civil servants, and the missionaries. After all, white non-missionaries also wanted to exercise their own religion.

Even with this connected background, the colonial project and the missionary enterprise were separate. While one had imperialistic, economic motives the other for the most part harboured evangelistic goals. To this end,

14. Missionary activity in Africa by Africans deserves more discussion than we can afford in this chapter. There was vibrant missionary activity in Liberia, Sierra Leone in the 1800s, and, since the Middle Ages, from Coptic Egypt. See for example Andrew F. Walls, "Sierra Leone, Afroamerican Remigration and the Beginnings of Protestantism in West Africa (8th-19th Centuries)," *Transkontinentale Beziehungen in Der Geschichte Des Außereuropäischen Christentums*, 2002, 45–56; Ugo Zanetti, "The Ethiopian Church, an Adult Daughter of the Coptic Church," *Journal of the Canadian Society for Coptic Studies* 8 no. 1 (2016): 11–31; Otto Meinardus, "A Brief History of the Abunate of Ethiopia," *Wiener Zeitschrift Für Die Kunde Des Morgenlandes* 58 (1962): 39–65.

15. Consider the variety of sentiments about "natives" in such early accounts as Harry Leakey, "Highlands of Kikuyu," *Church Missionary Gleaner*, May 2, 1910; David Livingstone, *Livingstone's Travels and Researches in South Africa: Including a Sketch of Sixteen Years' Residence in the Interior of Africa, and a Journey from the Cape of Good Hope to Loanda on the West Coast, Thence Across the Continent, Down the River Zambesi, to the Eastern Ocean* (J. W. Bradley, 1860).

16. On nineteenth-century mission and exploration, note the differences in publication dates of missionary accounts and the commercial colonial enterprise. See for example the difference between Krapf and Lugard's publications. Frederick D Lugard, *The Rise of Our East African Empire: Early Efforts in Nyasaland and Uganda*, vol. 1, 3 vols. (Edinburgh: William Blackwood and Sons, 1893); Johann Ludwig Krapf and E.G . Ravenstein, *Travels, Researches, and Missionary Labors during an Eighteen Years' Residence in Eastern Africa* (London: Ticknor and Fields, 1860).

missionaries invested much effort and money into the translation of Scriptures. The investment bore much fruit after the missionaries left in the 1940s. In responding to the gospel now heard in their own language, Africans received this faith and embraced it as their own.[17]

The relationships between the missionaries and African Christians was not always a smooth one. In some instances, as early as the 1500s African Christians in Congo challenged the integrity of missionaries sent from Europe. These African converts demanded better accountability and a Christianity more consistent with Scripture.[18] More recently, in the twentieth century for example, the East Africa revival grew as an indigenous movement among African Christians. It thrived from the 1940s–1970s within historic mission expressions such as Anglicans, Presbyterians, Methodists, and Lutherans. Like their Congolese counterparts, Revivalists challenged the depth of piety from their missionary pastors. Throughout the continent, Christians on the continent received the message of Christianity as their own. They operated within and nurtured this faith despite the colonial impulses and missionary failures. Drawing from their faith they were confident enough to challenge the piety of their missionary counterparts. They were Africans and proudly Christian.[19]

5. Enduring African Christian Traditions

We have so far considered the African Christian contributions to the patristic, medieval and modern periods, we now turn to Christianities that join these two eras. Coptic Christianity is an important community in this regard. Tradition has it that Mark the evangelist was the founding patriarch whose memory lives on in that community.[20] Based in Alexandria, the most important intellectual and Christian centre of the first century, Coptic Christianity is significant for several reasons.

A centre of Greek learning, Coptic Alexandria was home to the catechetical school. Gaining notoriety in the second century, the institution was home to a

17. Examples of this abound in missionary archives I have visited such as the CMS archive, the mission archives of the Pentecostal Assemblies of Canada.

18. See more about this in Mark Shaw and Wanjiru M. Gitau, *The Kingdom of God in Africa: A History of African Christianity* (Langham Global Library, 2020).

19. Consider this autobiographical account in John G. Gatũ, *Fan into Flame* (Nairobi: Moran Publishers and Worldreader, 2017); John G. Gatũ, *Joyfully Christian. Truly African* (Nairobi: Acton Publishers, 2006).

20. Oden, *The African Memory of Mark.*

long, distinguished list of theologians. The list includes Origen, Dionysius "the Great," and Didymus the Blind. We have already discussed the significance of Origen. In addition to providing leadership for the church, Dionysius opposed the Novatian rigorist position on apostates. In the middle of the third century, he taught that Christian deserters during the persecution should not be denied communion. This is an important theme which Augustine developed a century and a half later in his arguments against Donatism, a similar controversy. Didymus was somewhat of a genius theologian with an incredible memory. Blind from the age of four, he memorized Scriptures and great swathes of theological material. Devoted to his mentor Origen, Didymus' personal piety and writings contributed to the body of knowledge from which historical orthodoxy derives. We do not have the time here to expound on the prominent place the school had in the theological scene of the Middle East. For example, Jerome and Basil of Caesarea made trips to the school to interact with the intellectual environment there. What we can say here is that the catechetical school is an African contribution of the Coptic Church to global Christianity.

The Arabic Conquest for the sake of trade in the eighth and ninth centuries had a profound impact on the wellbeing of Christianity in Northern Africa. Arabs alternated between short periods of persecution of Christians and longer seasons of economic incentives for converts to their Islamic faith. North African Christianity struggled to thrive against this relentless onslaught. Against the odds, the Coptic church survived, keeping its indigenous language, writings, and traditions alive through hundreds of years of Islamic dominance in the region. Not only did the church survive, but it also supplied leadership for the Ethiopian church until the mid-twentieth century. From its language to its traditions, to its stubborn resilience in the face of obstacles, Coptic Christianity remains a shining example of an enduring African Christian tradition.[21]

We now turn briefly to Ethiopian Christianity. Like the Coptic Orthodox church, Ethiopian Orthodox churches relied on their own indigenous language and script. Ge'ez remains the language of liturgy and learning for a wide network of monasteries within the Ethiopian tradition. Unlike Egypt which had to contend with a heavy Muslim presence, Ethiopian Christianity had a free rein in most parts of modern-day Ethiopia. The result is an indigenous Christian culture so pervasive that it is inconceivable to isolate its non-Christian elements. In other words, much of Ethiopian culture is actually Christian by

21. For more about the Coptic church see Jill Kamil, *Christianity in the Land of the Pharaohs: The Coptic Orthodox Church* (New York: Routledge, 2002); Otto Friedrich August Meinardus, *Two Thousand Years of Coptic Christianity* (Cairo: American Univ. in Cairo Press, 2002).

nature and origin.[22] I posit that on account of these two important enduring traditions, Christianity does have an African root which is largely free of modern European influence.

6. Recent Indigenous African Christian Growth

Christianity is also African because of its very recent unprecedented, and unexpected growth on the continent. From under 10 million in 1910, the number of African Christians has grown to over 600 million in 100 years. Central and Eastern Africa shifted from being over 90 percent traditional religion to over 80 percent Christian in the twenty-first century.[23] These are some of the highest incidences of Christian demographic growth anywhere in the world.

Much of this growth came about between the 1960s and the 1980s, decades after the missionary era ended. Lamin Sanneh and Andrew Walls argue that this growth is the result of the translation of Christianity into the life and culture of recipient communities.[24] During the twentieth century, Africans from previously non-Christian areas took responsibility for their own evangelization. They found ways to articulate their own faith in languages, concepts, and metaphors that their fellow Africans understood. In doing this, Christianity attained its own indigenous expressions on the continent. Wherever it thrived, Christianity was vibrant exuding local manifestations of spiritual energy. Whether one looks at historic mission denominations, or at indigenous churches, one finds a church in Africa that is markedly different from missionary Christianity.[25]

---

22. See Philip F. Esler, *Ethiopian Christianity: History, Theology, Practice* (Waco: Baylor University Press, 2019), https://muse.jhu.edu/book/68151; Zanetti, "The Ethiopian Church, an Adult Daughter of the Coptic Church."

23. Gina A. Zurlo and Todd M. Johnson, *World Christian Encyclopaedia*, 3rd edition (Edinburgh: Edinburgh University Press, 2019), 8.

24. See Sanneh, *Translating the Message*; Andrew F. Walls, *The Cross-Cultural Process in Christian History: Studies in the Transmission and Appropriation of Faith* (Maryknoll: Orbis Books, 2002).

25. David Barrett and Allan Anderson discuss this at length for earlier African initiatives in Christianity. I also examine at length the uniqueness of African Christian expression in twenty-first century Africa. David B. Barrett, *Schism and Renewal in Africa: An Analysis of Six Thousand Contemporary Religious Movements* (Oxford: Oxford University Press, 1968); Allan H. Anderson, *African Reformation: African Initiated Christianity in the 21st Century* (Trenton, N.J.; London: Africa World; Turnaround, 2001); Kyama M. Mugambi, *A Spirit of Revitalization: Urban Pentecostalism in Kenya* (Waco: Baylor University Press, 2020).

African Christian spirituality envisages God acting in the world in ways that are different from those highlighted in post-Enlightenment European Christianity. For instance, African Christian spirituality withdraws from Euro-American dualism as it incorporates a holistic worldview similar to first-century Christianity. The music and aesthetic, especially in the more charismatic variants, reflects its African cultural context. Like the ancient Christianity described above, African Christianity is not without misunderstandings and misconceptions. Errors are present in theology and praxis, demanding careful attention. Nevertheless, this prolific indigenous Christianity finds itself at ease in Africa.

Demographically, self-confessing followers of Christ constitute the most dominant religion on the continent. Today, Christian Africa contributes more to global Christianity numerically than it ever did. There are more Christians in Africa than in Asia and North America combined. The continent contains 100 million more Christians than there are in Europe.[26] Phillip Jenkins wrote that if "we want to visualize a 'typical' contemporary Christian we should be thinking of a woman living in a village in Nigeria."[27] If not for anything else, the quantitative strength of Christian expressions on the continent signifies the grounding of Christianity in Africa's spiritual identity.

7. Conclusion

I have argued that Christianity is an African religion because it connects with the continent from biblical times. It finds its African roots in the Holy Scriptures as its African identity remains indelibly stamped through the names, identities, and places in the New Testament. Christianity also connects to the continent because of its role in the history of shaping the key tenets of the faith. The imprint of African theologians can be found in Eastern Orthodox, Roman Catholic and Protestant Christianity.

Christianity's *Africanness* reflects in its growth against the historical, colonial backdrop and the serious missionary failures of the nineteenth century. It is a resilient Christianity because of its infinite translatability into the cultures of the world. This faith enters the life of the people who receive and internalize it. The fact that Christianity has taken root in Africa, is evidence

26. Gina A. Zurlo, Todd M. Johnson and Peter F. Crossing, "World Christianity and Religions 2022," 76.

27. Philip Jenkins, *The Next Christendom: The Coming of Global Christianity* (Oxford; New York: Oxford University Press, 2011), 2.

of its incarnational nature affirmed in the gospels. We singled out Coptic and Ethiopian Orthodox Christianity as case studies of highly resilient traditions that have endured for centuries within the African context. Christianity is African through its widespread growth and rootedness on the continent after European missionaries left. Its demographic dominance makes it impossible to ignore as a major religion of the continent, and of the world.

These facts place present an apologetics opportunity to remedy the mis-telling of a Christian history that omits the place of Africa in the global story of Christianity. Conversations, research, writing, theologizing, and preaching need to recover the missing elements of African agency in the story of the Christian faith. Beyond these apologetic implications, it is important to, in solidarity with early African doctors of the church, focus on a well-grounded theology and discipleship. African Christians reading this can draw their inspiration from the excellence of patristic and medieval Christianity in Alexandria, Carthage and Cyrene. Such careful reflection coupled with a stronger sense of Christian self-identity might inspire viable solutions out of the social, political and economic challenges on the continent. Despite its difficulties, the African church equipped with the gospel message is well suited to engage in such a task of the "re-imagination" of Africa.[28]

Foremost in the agenda for reimagining Africa is the engagement of contextual issues with the gospel. Armed with this rich historical and contemporary witness, African Christians can now devote themselves to the incarnation of Christ into every facet of their individual and communal existence. The Coptic and Ethiopian churches serve as a living reminder that it is possible to have an enduring identity as both African and Christian. Like the aforementioned ancient communities, there is an urgent task to devote resources to strengthening the discipleship of Christ followers in ways that will build endurance of the faith on the continent. Such a task is the responsibility of the most Christian continent on the globe in the twenty-first century.

Bibliography

Anderson, Allan H. *African Reformation: African Initiated Christianity in the 21st Century*. Trenton; London: Africa World; Turnaround, 2001.

Athanasius. "Ad Afros Epistola Synodica: To the Bishops of Africa." 368 AD.

28. Emmanuel Katongole, *The Sacrifice of Africa: A Political Theology for Africa* (Grand Rapids: Eerdmans, 2010), 101.

Barrett, David B. *Schism and Renewal in Africa: An Analysis of Six Thousand Contemporary Religious Movements*. Oxford: Oxford University Press, 1968.
Bitek, Okot p'. *Song of Lawino and Song of Ocol*. Nairobi: East African Publishers, 1995.
"Council of Carthage (A.D. 419): The Code of Canons of the African Church." 419 AD.
Daniels III, David D., and Lawrence Anglin. "Luther and the Ethiopian Deacon." *Lutheran Quarterly* 32, no. 4 (2018): 428–34.
Eastman, David L. *Early North African Christianity: Turning Points in the Development of the Church*. Grand Rapids: Baker Academic, 2021.
Esler, Philip F. *Ethiopian Christianity: History, Theology, Practice*. Waco: Baylor University Press, 2019. https://muse.jhu.edu/book/68151.
Gatũ, John G. *Fan into Flame*. Nairobi: Moran Publishers and Worldreader, 2017.
———. *Joyfully Christian. Truly African*. Nairobi: Acton Publishers, 2006.
Gifford, Paul. *Christianity, Development and Modernity in Africa*. London: C. Hurst & Co., 2015.
Harnack, Adolf von. *History of Dogma*. Translated by Neil Buchanan. Vol. IV. Boston: Little, Brown and Company, 1907.
Jenkins, Philip. *The Next Christendom: The Coming of Global Christianity*. Oxford: Oxford University Press, 2011.
Kamil, Jill. *Christianity in the Land of the Pharaohs: The Coptic Orthodox Church*. New York: Psychology Press, 2002.
Katongole, Emmanuel. *The Sacrifice of Africa: A Political Theology for Africa*. Grand Rapids: Eerdmans, 2010.
Kendall, R. Elliott. *The End of an Era: Africa and the Missionary*. London: SPCK, 1978.
Krapf, Johann Ludwig, and E. G. Ravenstein. *Travels, Researches, and Missionary Labors during an Eighteen Years' Residence in Eastern Africa*. London: Ticknor and Fields, 1860.
Leakey, Harry. "Highlands of Kikuyu." *Church Missionary Gleaner*, May 2, 1910.
Livingstone, David. *Livingstone's Travels and Researches in South Africa: Including a Sketch of Sixteen Years' Residence in the Interior of Africa, and a Journey from the Cape of Good Hope to Loanda on the West Coast, Thence Across the Continent, Down the River Zambesi, to the Eastern Ocean*. J. W. Bradley, 1860.
Lugard, Frederick D. *The Rise of Our East African Empire: Early Efforts in Nyasaland and Uganda*. Vol. 1. Edinburgh: William Blackwood and Sons, 1893.
Meinardus, Otto. "A Brief History of the Abunate of Ethiopia." *Wiener Zeitschrift Für Die Kunde Des Morgenlandes* 58 (1962): 39–65.
———. *Two Thousand Years of Coptic Christianity*. Cairo: American University in Cairo Press, 2002.
Mugambi, Kyama M. *A Spirit of Revitalization: Urban Pentecostalism in Kenya*. Waco: Baylor University Press, 2020.
———. "Christianity and the Fate of Africa: A Critique of the Debate." *Missio Africanus Journal of African Missiology* 5, no. 1 (September 2020): 33–50.

Oden, Thomas C. *The African Memory of Mark: Reassessing Early Church Tradition.* Grand Rapids: InterVarsity Press, 2011.

———. *How Africa Shaped the Christian Mind: Rediscovering the African Seedbed of Western Christianity.* Downers Grove.: IVP Academic, 2010.

———. *The Rebirth of African Orthodoxy: Return to Foundations.* Nashville: Abingdon Press, 2016.

Oliver, Roland Anthony. *The Missionary Factor in East Africa.* London: Longmans, Green, 1965.

Sanneh, Lamin O. *Translating the Message: The Missionary Impact on Culture.* Maryknoll: Orbis Books, 1989.

Shaw, Mark. *Global Awakening: How 20th-Century Revivals Triggered a Christian Revolution.* Downers Grove, Ill.: IVP Academic, 2010.

Shaw, Mark, and Wanjiru M. Gitau. *The Kingdom of God in Africa: A History of African Christianity.* Carlisle: Langham Global Library, 2020.

Thiong'o, Ngũgĩ wa. *A Grain of Wheat.* Vol. 2. New York: Penguin, 2012.

Voragine, Jacobus de. *The Golden Legend: Readings on the Saints.* Princeton: Princeton University Press, 2012.

Walls, Andrew F. *Crossing Cultural Frontiers: Studies in the History of World Christianity.* Edited by Mark R. Gornik. Maryknoll: Orbis Books, 2017.

———. *The Cross-Cultural Process in Christian History: Studies in the Transmission and Appropriation of Faith.* Maryknoll: Orbis Books, 2002.

———. *The Missionary Movement in Christian History: Studies in the Transmission of Faith.* 1st edition. Maryknoll; Edinburgh: Orbis Books; T&T Clark, 1996.

———. "Sierra Leone, Afroamerican Remigration and the Beginnings of Protestantism in West Africa (8th–19th Centuries)." *Transkontinentale Beziehungen in Der Geschichte Des Außereuropäischen Christentums* (2002): 45–56.

Zanetti, Ugo. "The Ethiopian Church, an Adult Daughter of the Coptic Church." *Journal of the Canadian Society for Coptic Studies* 8, no. 1 (2016): 11–31.

Zurlo, Gina A., and Todd M. Johnson. *World Christian Encyclopaedia.* 3rd edition. Edinburgh: Edinburgh University Press, 2019.

Zurlo, Gina A., Todd M. Johnson, and Peter F. Crossing. "World Christianity and Religions 2022: A Complicated Relationship." *International Bulletin of Mission Research* 46, no. 1 (2022): 71–80.

8

The Doctrine of Christ and Traditional Eldership Rites[1]

mbũrĩ cia kiama

Kevin Muriithi Ndereba, PhD

Lecturer at St. Paul's University, Kenya and Research Fellow Department of Practical Theology and Missiology, Stellenbosch University, South Africa

Abstract

Among the *Agĩkũyũ* or *Kikuyu* (a Bantu ethnic community concentrated in Central Kenya, East Africa) Christians, the traditional council of elders have been pushing for a "return to our roots." Part of this return is the call to give away a goat or goats, called *mbũri cia kiama*, which is usually given to the council of elders as part of the progression of a man into the status of eldership. Some churches and church leaders have taken the position that this practice has no bearing on one's faith in Jesus Christ, and that *Gĩkũyũ* men should see no harm in doing this. Further, it would be a sign of celebrating the *Gĩkũyũ* or African identity of Christian men. Utilizing Bevan's contextualization methods, I make use of an integral approach to theological reflection by engaging christology in the book of Hebrews with the anthropological findings of the aforementioned practice. I argue that while there are some positive elements

1. Originally published as Kevin Muriithi Ndereba, "The Supremacy of Jesus Christ: A Theological Response to the Resurgence of Mbũri cia Kiama." *African Theological Journal for Church and Society* 2 no. 2 (2021): 40–57.

in such practices including the African values of communality, mentorship and respect for elders, the covenantal underpinning of the practice obfuscates the new covenant in Christ and should therefore be repudiated. I therefore show how the continuities and discontinuities of *Gĩkũyũ* culture and Christianity impacts African Christianity and African theology and suggest implications for Christian ministry.

Keywords: African Theology, African Traditional Religion (ATR), Atonement, Christology, Contextual Theology, *Gĩkũyũ* Culture and Religion, Rites of Passage, Systematic Theolog

1. Introduction: The Need for Contextualization

This chapter reflects on how the gospel intersects with African cultural practices, particularly the practice of *mbũri cia kiama* among *Agĩkũyũ* Christians. This chapter reveals that contextualization is necessary when it comes to such cultural practices as it seriously considers the underlying issues while utilizing the tools of theological reflection, including the Bible, communities of faith and church history. In the enterprise of contextualizing theological reflection, several options have been proposed. This chapter begins with the assumption that the gospel of Jesus Christ is unchanging and supra-cultural. Yet on the other hand, as the gospel interacts with different cultures, it must consider the contexts of the peoples that it comes across. Hesselgrave and Rommen consider the necessity of contextualization as arising from gospel communication across cultures.[2] Thus, models of contextualization arise from the reality of considering how theological reflection can carefully and biblically engage with different cultural contexts. I make use of Bevan's synthetic model of contextualization in this chapter.[3]

Bevans observes the necessity of contextualization through the poles of social change (culture) and gospel message (tradition). Different models seek to balance these two aspects as illustrated above. Translation models remain as close to the text as possible with little consideration of the culture. Anthropological models take the culture seriously while downplaying the universalities of Christian doctrine. Among the other three models, the synthetic model seeks the "difficult task" of balancing fidelity to scriptural

2. David J. Hesselgrave and Edward Rommen, *Contextualization: Meanings, Methods, and Models* (Pasadena: William Carey Library, 2000), 11.

3. Steven Bevans, *Models of Contextual Theology* (Maryknoll: Orbis Books, 1999).

revelation while deeply engaging traditional heritage in the past and present.[4] This is a helpful grid for considering African cultural practices, because they have both positive and negative elements. Arguably, an integral vision for missiological engagement is one that touches all the areas of the African's life, including their culture.[5] If the gospel message is to be embedded in African communities, it must engage cultural issues.

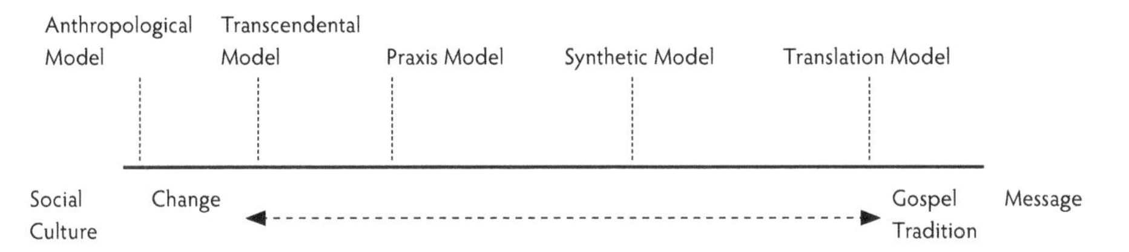

Figure 4: Bevan's Models of Contextualization

Integrating Christian theological reflection with cultural realities is premised on several reasons. First, Christianity does not belong to any particular culture. The late African historian and missiologist, Lamin Sanneh, powerfully observed that the Christian faith is an act of translation into culture.[6] Second, as Hesselgrave and Rommen show, the Bible exemplifies cross-cultural communication and engagement.[7] The Old Testament reveals that although the Israelites were the chosen people of God, they were also a means of blessing to all the nations (Gen 12:1–2; Ps 18:49–50; 57:11). In the New Testament, being justified by faith in Christ removes cultural barriers and unites Christians from diverse cultures (Gal 3:28–29; Col 3:11). The passage in Galatians speaks of justification while the passage in Colossians speaks of sanctification. In summary, being declared righteous in Christ and progressing in the new life are realities common to all Christians, regardless of culture. Third, the end goal of cultural diversity is to show the riches of God's grace. In the book of Revelation, all ethnicities and nationalities will worship God together and proclaim his glory which is seen in their redemption (Rev 5; 7:9–17).

4. Steven Bevans, *Essays in Contextual Theology* (Leiden; Boston: Brill, 2018), 7.

5. James Nkansah-Obrempong, "Africa's contextual realities: Foundation for the Church's Holistic Mission." *International Review of Mission* 106 no. 2 (2017): 292, https://doi.org/10.1111/irom.12186.

6. Lamin Sanneh, *Translating the Message: The Missionary Impact on Culture* (Maryknoll: Orbis Books, 2009).

7. Hesselgrave and Rommen, *Contextualization: Meanings, Methods, and Models*, 2.

Therefore, as Christians express their faith through the richness of their cultural diversities, the end goal is the glory of God in his redemption of his people. On the other hand, there are several ways in which our cultural expressions hinder God's will. One example is Peter who because of his Jewish cultural background was initially hesitant about God's inclusion of the gentiles (Acts 10:9–33). A second example is how we can entertain diverse cultural practices in order to accommodate everyone. This seems to have been the issue Paul had with Peter in Galatians 2:11–14 – especially seeking to accommodate cultural practices that were legalistic, that is, teaching that particular cultural practices are what makes one a Christian. An extension of this may be excluding Christians of other cultural backgrounds because of practices that one culture holds in high regard. This can be seen in the decision of the church elders in the Jerusalem Council in Acts 15:1–2. The last cultural issue is that of breaking away from old cultural practices that would either compromise or take away from the work of Christ (Acts 15:28–29), in this particular instance, the gentile or pagan practices of sacrificing foods to idols and sexual immorality.

I will proceed to unpack the specific cultural practice of *mbũri cia kiama* in *Gĩkũyũ* traditional culture. In this chapter, I utilize such a synthetic model of contextualization by making use of the doctrine of christology, particularly as it emerges in the book of Hebrews, and its relationship with the presuppositions in the practice of *mbũri cia kiama*. I argue that there are some beneficial African values that emanate from the practice, such as mentorship, communality as well as respect of elders. However, I also argue that since the practice is anchored in a covenantal understanding that is at odds with the new covenant in Christ, the practice hinders Christian formation and should be repudiated, even as we explore relevant ways to nurture boys and men within African Christianity.

2. Christological Reflections in African Theology

Stinton interacts with the written christologies of the Ghanian Bediako, the Tanzanian Nyamiti and the South African Mofokeng.[8] She also interviews lay Christians and also leading African theologians from different theological backgrounds as follows:

- Benezet Bujo: Congolese, francophone, Roman Catholic

8. Diane Stinton, "Africa's Contribution to Christology," in *African Theology Comes of Age: Revisiting Twenty Years of the Theology of the Ecumenical Symposium of Eastern Africa Theologians (ESEAT)*, edited by Laurenti Magesa (Nairobi: Paulines Publications Africa, 2010), 13–34.

- Jean-Marc Ela: Cameroonian, francophone, Roman Catholic
- J. N. K. Mugambi: Kenyan, Anglican
- Anne Nasimiyu Wasike: Kenyan, Roman Catholic
- Mercy Oduyoye: Ghanaian, Methodist
- John Poebee: Ghanaian, Anglican

Her work is broad in scale and looks at various conceptual, methodological, practical, and contextual issues surrounding christology. Bediako's call is to engage in theological reflection that is in touch with the grassroots, in his words "where faith lives."[9] This type of theological reflection is one that is in tune with the realities on the ground and removes the burden of academic theology as a disengaged activity. Part of what this means is that African theological reflection must consider the unique worldviews that are a part of African traditional religions. For the Akan for example, Bediako argues that a christology that touches them must explore the theme of *Christus Victor*, where Jesus Christ is seen as victorious over their spiritual world – including their supreme being (*Onyame*) and gods (*abosom*).[10] Thus, considering each cultural context is key if the gospel message is to permeate deeply into the cultural soul. Stinton acknowledges Mbiti's pillars of theological reflection as the Bible, African tradition, lived experiences as well as one's theological tradition.[11] I follow this similar concern by applying christological reflection to the contemporary resurgence of cultural practices within Christian expressions of faith – with particular reference to *mbũri cia kiama* among *Agĩkũyũ* Christians – from a reformed and broadly evangelical theological background.

In both the global North and South, there is a resurgence of African culture within the church. In America for example, there has been the rise of Christian groups such as the Black Hebrew Israelites. This group is largely made up of African Americans who trace their African lineage to the Israelites in the Old Testament. Their major conviction is the ignored black presence in the Bible and of peoples of African descent – although there have been commendable responses on this theme by several scholars.[12] This is to be

9. Kwame Bediako, *Jesus in Africa: The Christian Gospel in African History and Experience* (Akropong-Akuapeng, Ghana: Regnum Africa, 2013), 17.

10. Kwame Bediako, *Jesus in Africa*, 22.

11. Diane Stinton, "Africa's Contribution to Christology," 19.

12. See for instance Thomas Oden, *How Africa Shaped the Christian Mind: Rediscovering the African Seedbed of Western Christianity* (Grand Rapids: IVP Academic, 2010); Harold C. Felder, *The African American Guide to the Bible* (Meadville: Christian Faith Publishing, 2018); Eric Mason, *Urban Apologetics: Restoring Black Dignity with the Gospel* (Grand Rapids:Zondervan, 2018).

understood from their location within the United States of America that has a long history of racial tensions. This has been recently protracted through the Black Lives Matter (BLM) movement and Critical Race Theory (CRT) debates in contemporary global discourse.

In post-colonial Africa, scholars have noted the rise of African Initiated or Indigenous Churches (AICs). These churches were formed in order to contextualize African culture within the Christian faith inherited from the missionaries and missionary-instituted churches. Some of the positive outcomes were the use of local languages in worship liturgies and the use of African expressions in songs and prayers. By and large, this is to be commended. However, in the recent past, traditional elders in various ethnicities in Kenya have issued various calls to incorporate particular traditional practices in their Christian faith. Some of these practices are very syncretistic of the traditional religions and take away from the person and work of Christ. I will shortly pay attention to the specific practice of giving of the *mbũri cia kiama.*

3. *Mbũri Cia Kiama* in *Gĩkũyũ* Tradition and Culture

3.1 Continuity and Discontinuity between Gĩkũyũ *Culture and Christianity*

The Very Rev. Dr. John Gatũ, past moderator of the Presbyterian Church of East Africa observes that there were many similarities between *Gĩkũyũ* as well as the Old Testament worship. Gatũ mentions monotheism, deification of mountains and the sacrificial system as examples.[13] Similarly, some of the oral narratives in the *Gĩkũyũ* culture have parallels to the Hebraic narratives of the Old Testament – similar to the Ancient Near Eastern background narratives and the Old Testament. They worshipped God, *Ngai* or *Mwene Nyaga* and observed the fig tree *Mũgumo* and certain mountains as sacred – such as *Kirinyaga* or Mt. Kenya to the North, *Kiambiruiru* (Ngong' hills) to the south, *Kianjahi* (Ol Donyo Sabuk) to the east and the Aberdares or *Nyandarua* to the west.[14] However, there were many traditional practices that were against the faith which churches such as the Presbyterian Church of East Africa rejected –

13. John Gatũ, *Fan into Flame: An Autobiography* (Nairobi: Moran Publishers, 2016), 65.

14. John G. Gatu says that diviners pointed to these four mountains, imitating the sign of the cross, before meditation (65). My late grandfather, a Mau Mau secretary who was converted to Christ (Presbyterian faith) told me that in the past, before the nineteenth century missionary presence, there were discoveries of a cross in *Gĩkũyũ* land. This is an unsubstantiated anecdote. Kenyatta observes some few cultural practices that are, in my observation, similar to the Old Testament sacrificial system: they offered sacrifices on specific days and seasons, the elders entrusted with the sacrificial duties were to observe sexual purity, recitation of special prayers, the abhorrence of witchcraft and their death penalty if discovered.

this includes issues of Female Genital Mutilation (FGM) as well as the Mau Mau oathing.

On the other hand, several discontinuities emerge. The concepts of God in biblical theology in light of *Gĩkũyũ* culture denotes several distinctions. For one, the concept of the triune God is something unique to the biblical understanding. Secondly, the work of Christ in redemption is also something unique to the biblical worldview, even though there were foreshadows in the *Gĩkũyũ* sacrificial system just as in the Old Testament sacrificial system. In short, there are both continuities and discontinuities in the area of Christianity and *Gĩkũyũ* culture.

3.2 Mbũri Cia Kiama *as Part of Initiatory Rites into Adulthood*

With many African cultures being hierarchical, *Gĩkũyũ* culture respected elders. Some *Gĩkũyũ* (2017) anthropologists observe seven critical stages between birth and death for a *Gĩkũyũ* male:

1. *Gakenge* – A newborn baby for the first few months or so. After that he is referred to as *Kaana*, baby. Major ceremony – being born, *gũciarwo kwa mwana.*

2. *Kahĩĩ* – A young boy frolicking about like a young kid goat. Major ceremony – the second Birth, *gũcokia mwana ihu-iinĩ.*

3. *Kĩhĩĩ* – A big boy nearing circumcision which would be anything from 12 to 18 years. To be called a *Kĩhĩĩ* (*Kĩhĩĩ gĩkĩ*), is an insult as it is a reference to the fact that one is due or overdue for "straightening" or circumcision – *nĩ ũtigĩtie handũ.*

4. *Mumo* – *Kiumĩri* (singular), literally means "coming out," "emerging" like a butterfly from a cocoon into the full bloom of God's creation. Circumcision ceremonies – These were the most important of the *Gĩkũyũ* ceremonies of becoming. *Mambura ma irua.*

5. *Mwanake* – A young man until marriage. God's material creation in its full glory. God, Ngai, did not create a child but a fully grown man. A young man is literally God's fragment that was fashioned into a man by the creator, *Mũmbi. Mwanake nĩ kĩenyũ kĩa Ngai. Mwanake wa Njaama ya ita* is a member of the warrior coupes, military. *Mwanake wa Njaama ya kamatimũ* is a member of the policing and guard coupes, Police.

6. *Mũthuuri – Karabai.* Married man who can still be called upon to serve military duty in a major war.

7. *Mũthuri wa Kĩama* – An elder who serves in one or more of the many councils. Because the *Gĩkũyũ* system of government had no chiefs or kings, all government was through consensus in the various tribal councils.

After a boy was circumcised, he became a man but had to go through stages of preparation into eldership. Humphrey Waweru enumerates this preparation into five stages.[15] The first stage was the council of boys (*Ngutu*), who had trained responsibilities such as organizing games from the family level to the village level. The second level, which was the next stage, was called the council of commons (*Kamatimu*). It was the warrior stage and was accessed through the giving of one goat, usually given by the father, and a calabash of beer. As junior elders, they are assistants and messengers of peace, to the senior elders. The next stage was the council of peace (*Matathi*). The condition for joining this council meant the stopping of raiding and having one's child circumcised.[16] A person was required to give another goat to the elders and Waweru observes that it took about 15–20 years to move to this stage. A mark of maturity in this stage ended in the initiate being given a staff (*Muthigi*) and leaves from a tree (*Matathi*). These junior elders would be given minor cases to exercise judgement, which was part of their ongoing training into the next stage. The next stage was called the governing council (*Maturungaru*). Through the giving of two extra goats, the elder was officially initiated into the governing council and is referred to as *muthamaki* or full leader. Because of the age requirement, wisdom characterized most of these leaders. If a young man exhibited elevated levels of wisdom, he would be approached and assisted to join the council of governing elders. It was possible to see a young man in a council of elders. The last stage was the religious council of elders (*Kiama kia guthathaiya*). The requirements were to have their children's children circumcised and his wife to be sexually inactive and to have stopped childbearing. This was the most honored stage whose purpose was to offer national and communal sacrifices

15. Humphrey Waweru, *The Bible and African Culture: Mapping Transactional Inroads* (Limuru: Zapf Chancery, 2011), 52.

16. Godfrey Muriuki, "A History of the Kikuyus to 1904" (PhD Thesis, University of London, 1969), 162. http://erepository.uonbi.ac.ke/.

and prayers. Few got to this stage.[17] Waweru observes that women also had their own councils within their different clans (*mnari*).

3.3 The Concept of Sacrifice and Intermediaries within Eldership Initiation Rites

Sheep and goats were held in high regard in terms of their economic value. They were the currency of the day and it was said that "it is better to have sheep than to have a shilling because a shilling cannot give birth to another shilling."[18] Jomo Kenyatta, Kenya's first president and a noted anthropologist, observes that these animals were important for the religious and cultural life of the *Agĩkũyũ* – They were used for purification and sacrificial rites.[19] They were also a prominent part of initiation into the council of elders. The anthropologist Louis S. B. Leakey, who wrote the substantive three-volume work on the Kikuyu *The Southern Kikuyu before 1903*, concurs on the importance of goats and sheep in the social organization and religious rites of the *Agĩkũyũ.*[20]

Mbiti observes the importance of sacrifices in African religions as the interaction of the visible and invisible words – and Karangi notes the role of sacrifices (*mathĩnjĩro*) as a communication between *Ngai* (God) and his people.[21] Mbiti distinguishes between sacrifices and offerings in that sacrifices involve the shedding of blood whereas offerings include the giving of things such as foodstuffs, milk, or honey.[22] Mbiti also notes that prayers are also involved through the giving of offerings and sacrifices.[23] These are not always offered to God but can be offered to lesser spiritual beings – such as "divinities, spirits and the departed."[24] Since in *Gĩkũyũ* traditional religion, priests, kings, the living dead and ritual elders are seen as mediators between humans and God, then it would be fair to conclude that the eldership system in *Gĩkũyũ*

17. My late grandfather told me that before he became a Christian, he had started the initiatory rites to become part of the religious council. As a Christian, he served as a deacon in the Presbyterian Church for many years.

18. Jomo Kenyatta, *Facing Mount Kenya: The Traditional Life of the Kikuyu* (Nairobi: Kenway, 2011), 45.

19. Kenyatta, *Facing Mount Kenya*, 45.

20. Louis Seymour Bazett Leakey, *The Southern Kikuyu before 1903* (Nairobi: Richard Leakey, 2007), 207.

21. Matthew Muriuki Karangi, "The Gĩkũyũ Religion and Philosophy: A Tool for Understanding the Current Religio-Political Debates in Kenya," *Anthropos* 2 (2013): 612–22.

22. John S. Mbiti, *Introduction to African Religions* (Long Grove: Waveland Press, 1991), 63.

23. John S. Mbiti, *African Religions and Philosophy* (Oxford: Heinemann, 1999), 66.

24. Mbiti, *African Religions and Philosophy*, 66.

traditional religion is also seen as a mediatorial office. Mbiti actually observes that in traditional African religions:

> In order to reach God effectively, it may be useful to approach him by first approaching those who are lower than he is but higher than the ordinary person.[25]

As earlier cited, some of the intermediaries here include the ritual elders. Mbiti acknowledges that in using the intermediaries, Africans do not directly worship them but use them as "conveyer belts" in showing their reverence in approaching God. The point seems to be that eldership is seen as a mediatorial office within *Gĩkũyũ* culture. In fact, many religious functions in the *Gĩkũyũ* tradition had to be conducted by a priest – these priests comprised the head of the family or clan and was assisted by other junior elders.[26] Thus, the eldership system was also mediatorial in function. Since this cultural thinking is carried over into the church, it is evident that there is a sense of reverence that is given to church elders.

The literature on the actual process of initiation into eldership is scanty.[27] However, from my research, it involved a call and response type of oathing that is similar in many other African cultures – and also a part of other *Gĩkũyũ* customs. Kabetũ gives the oathing done during this process, after the meat was shared:

> *Atiririi kiama, tondu nitwaria ngoima cia ng'ania twamutonyia kiama-ini-ri, toigai kiama kiromwenda, magacokia: Kiromwenda. Toigai angikanatua cira urothira, magacokia: Urothira. Ugai angikanateithurana mbaara irothira, magacokia: Irothira. Ugai angikanahorohaniria kundu gutemanitwo, horohio io ironina uuru, magacokia: Ironina uuru. Ugai angikanaigwithania andu mahitanitie maroiguana, magacokia: Maroiguana.*[28]

[ENGLISH TRANSLATION follows][29]

25. Mbiti, *African Religions and Philosophy*, 68.

26. Leakey, *The Southern Kikuyu before 1903*, 1082.

27. I personally tried to contact *Mũkũyũ*, who keeps the website *Gĩkũyũ Center for Cultural Studies*, for this specific information. I was informed that this information is only given to the initiates of these rites.

28. Mathew Njoroge, *Kabetũ, Kĩrĩra kia ũgĩkũyu: Kuuma Mũndũ Amonyokio O Nginya Rĩria Akahinga Riitho Aarĩkia Kwĩgaya* (Nairobi: Kenya Literature Bureau, 2017), 103.

29. By one of the *wazees* (meaning, an elder – respectable old man), mzee Kimeria, whom I interviewed for this research.

> Now council members, since we have eaten the meat from this candidate's (name inserted) goats for his admission into the eldership of this council as one of us, say: May he now be admitted as a full member of the council.
>
> And they reply: May he be admitted as a full member of the council.
>
> Elder in charge says: Whenever he exercises judgement on whatever case that may be brought to him, may his judgement be final.
>
> And members repeat: May it be final.
>
> Elder in charge says: If he arbitrates where there are disputes or quarrels, may his word be final.
>
> And they repeat: May his word be final.
>
> Elder in charge says: Whenever he reconciles between fighting parties where injuries or blood has been shed, may his wise counsel end the bitterness thereof.
>
> And they repeat: May his wise counsel end the bitterness thereof.
>
> Elder in charge says: Whenever he arbitrates between two parties in dispute, may his counsel result in lasting peace.
>
> And they reply: May his counsel result in lasting peace.

Afterwards, the new elder is inducted into the council and advised on the proper conduct of an elder and his manner of speech. He spends the rest of the days walking closely with the elders to understand the responsibilities of the oaths that he took. These initiation rites that are crucial for the lifecycle of the *Gĩkũyũ* man are also observed in other cultures such as the *Akamba.*[30] Chege also observes similar rites of passage among the *Ameru*, another close "relative" of the *Agĩkũyũ.*[31] What is instructive is the place of offering sacrifices, usually a sheep or ram, during the rite of circumcision (*irua* in *Gĩkũyũ*) as well as the rite of *ntuiko* or *ituĩka* (in *Gĩkũyũ*) which refer to the handing over of judicial power to the next generation (or age set) of elders. Chege observes that these sacrifices were accompanied by the shedding of blood as a sign of thanksgiving

30. Mbiti, *African Religions and Philosophy*, 122.

31. Jane Chege, "The Meru Religious Beliefs and Practices with Particular Reference to their Sacrificial Rites: A Case Study of the Igembe Sub-Ethnic Group," Master's Thesis, University of Nairobi, Nairobi, 1985. Accessed on 12 January 2021 from http://erepository.uonbi.ac.ke/.

to God as well as a libation to the ancestors.[32] Among the *Ameru*, for the elders to serve in these sacrificial rites, they had to have the right pedigree – character, age, proper teeth formation, proper birth process, among others.[33]

In summary, when considering the question of *mbũri cia kiama* it is necessary to consider the relationship between *Gĩkũyũ* culture and Christianity. First, we need to appreciate the similarities between Old Testament Judaism and *Gĩkũyũ* culture – and the same could be stretched to other African cultures. Secondly, it seems that to a considerable extent, the practice of giving *mbũri cia kiama* reveals strong hints of animism as well as legalism. The animism can be seen in the shedding of blood as well as pouring of libation. Since these practices have ceased under the new covenant, there is no longer any need for them. The legalism can be seen in the entire conceptualization of the lifecycle as a hierarchical process of growing from one stage to the next – through certain do's and don'ts. It is commendable that there was a powerful sense of mentorship between the elders and younger men and that is something we have lost in contemporary and post-modern Africa, even within the urban African churches.[34] However, by and large, forcing *Gĩkũyũ* Christians to go back to this practice is similar to the Judaizing group of the early church who were forcing the rite of circumcision for both Hebraic and gentile believers. I will now offer a biblical and theological response to support my point.

4. A Consideration of Christology in the Bible

4.1 The Old Testament Similarities: The Priestly and Sacrificial Systems

From the foregoing research, it seems that many African traditional religious and societal practices are remarkably close to the Hebraic conceptualization of the same. Exodus records the laws about altars (20:22–25), laws about restitution (21:3–15) as well as laws about social justice (22:16–23:9). Consecration of the priests is recorded in Exodus 29 with Leviticus expounding on the offerings and sacrificial system at length (Leviticus 1–7). I was struck by the many similarities between *Gĩkũyũ* traditional religious worldview and the Jewish religion in the Old Testament. These include the wide variety of ceremonial purification laws rituals including *rũruto* (misfortune), *mũrimũ* (disease), *ũrogi* (witchcraft),

32. Chege, "The Meru Religious Beliefs and Practices," 166.

33. Chege, "The Meru Religious Beliefs and Practices," 123.

34. This is the reason the Presbyterian Church of East Africa began the Rites of Passages (ROPES) programmes for the early adolescents who are transitioning into high school and who have undergone circumcision in order to pass on important cultural and Christian values.

contact with the dead, contact with menstrual blood, natural events, among others.[35] There are also similarities in the nature of the priests in Old Testament and *Gĩkũyũ* traditional religion – who played a similar role to the *athuri a kiama*. These are just but a summarized version of the similarities between *Gĩkũyũ* religion and the Old Testament. However, the differences emerge in the New Testament interpretation of their significance.

4.2 The New Testament Relevance of Jesus Christ as Sacrifice, Priest and Mediator

Although God related in a unique way with Israel, his chosen nation, they were to be a channel of blessing to the nations. This is revealed not only in the adamic covenant but also in the other covenants – including the Noahic, Abrahamic as well as the Davidic covenants. In the Noahic covenant, God promises that he will never destroy the visible world as the time of Noah. In the Abrahamic covenant, Abraham is promised offspring as many as the stars in the sky and the sand in the sea. In the Davidic covenant, David is promised a king who will sit on his throne and bring blessing to the nations. Although the ministry of Jesus in the Gospel accounts is mainly geared towards Israel, the Acts of the Apostles begins in Jerusalem but spreads to Judea, Samaria and all the known world (Acts 1:8). The mission of Christ was not a privilege for only one culture but for the entire world.

The problem with some of the Jewish believers was that they struggled with cultural pride. Peter the apostle struggles with the vision he receives concerning the inclusion of the gentiles in the kingdom of God (Acts 10). The elders have to make several decisions concerning Jewish-Gentile relations in Acts 15. In the Pauline epistles, Paul also tackles the issues of Jewish-Gentile relations and specifically rejects the sectarian groups that tried to force their cultural practices on the rest. In fact, on the matter of Jewish circumcision, Paul teaches Christians that this outward practice had spiritual significance. To go back to that practice would be to take the shadow instead of the reality, to which circumcision pointed to – that is the spiritual birth through the new covenant promise (See Col 2:16–23; Heb 10). These issues are handled at length in the Pauline epistles.

35. Leakey, *The Southern Kikuyu Before 1903*, 1232–42.

The book of Hebrews is of particular significance in its exposition of christology which is foundational to New Testament christology.[36] Kvidahl and Lioy note that the book's emphasis on the high priestly ministry of Jesus makes it unique within the New Testament corpus.[37] The book of Hebrews looks back at the Old Testament figures and sacrificial system and finds its fulfilment and realization in Christ. So, for instance, Jesus Christ is seen as the great high priest in the order of Melchizedek, the Old Testament priest of Salem (Heb 7:15–17). This highlights the significance of Jesus Christ as the supreme priest-king (Ps 110:4). The high priesthood of Jesus Christ transcends that of the Mosaic Law – the eminent John Owen in his commentary to the Hebrews (8:1–6) observes that Jesus Christ's priestly ministry is distinguished for its dignity, excellence, and efficacy.[38] Jesus Christ is also contrasted with the Old Testament priests in Hebrews 10:11–13. Although the Old Testament priests "stand" daily, and offer sacrifices repeatedly, their sacrifices cannot take away sins. On the other hand, Jesus Christ is "seated" at the right-hand God, offers a "single sacrifice" for sins which "made perfect forever those who are being made holy" (Heb 10:14). Jesus Christ is truly the king-priest that the Old Testament predicts. Jesus Christ is also seen as the mediator of the new covenant, which takes effect through the shedding of Christ's blood (Heb 8; 9:11–28).[39] In doing this, he makes some of the older religious practices obsolete (Heb 8:6–8, 13). In other places, Jesus Christ is referred to as the only mediator between God and humans (1 Tim 2:5). The book of Hebrews sees Jesus Christ's death on the cross as the better sacrifice – that the sacrificial system of the Old Testament was merely a shadow of this great sacrifice on the cross (Heb 10:1–14). Jesus Christ is greater than the Old Testament religious system and through his various roles procures redemption, reconciliation, and victory for his people (Heb 2:14–15; 4:14–16; 9:12, 15, 21–22, 28; 10:14). To go back to the old system would be not only retrogressive but "shrinking

36. Mikeal C. Parsons, "Son and High Priest: A Study in the Christology of Hebrews," *Evangelical Quarterly* 60 no. 3 (1988): 195–215.

37. Clifford B. Kvidahl, and Dan Lioy, "'You are a Priest Forever': An Exegetical and Biblical Theology of High Priestly Christology," *Conspectus: The Journal of the South African Theological Seminary* 29 no. 1 (2020): 40–60.

38. John Owen, *An Exposition on the Epistle to the Hebrews*, Vol. 6 (Grand Rapids: Baker, 1980), 10.

39. One of the old *wazees*, mzee Kimeria, noted that the underlying issue in the understanding of the *mbũri cia kiama* is the concept of covenant. For the believer who is under the new covenant, the old covenant is made obsolete. He concluded that those who dub in both Christian faith and *mbũri cia kiama* practices are confused as they participate in two covenants which is impossible.

back" to slavery – even in the face of suffering for identifying and living for Christ (Heb 9:26–28; 10:39).

5. Conclusions and Implications for the African Church

Banda articulates the importance of christology for practical African Christian life.[40] For instance, he observes that the fear that undergirds the African traditional worldview and which leads to excesses in our understanding of the spiritual life – including deliverance ministries and witchcraft practices – can be better understood by considering the effectiveness of the atonement of Christ. Part of this doctrine includes the importance of reconciliation, redemption, and victory, which are the various interpretive foci of the various atonement theories in the history of the church.

This chapter has briefly explored the global resurgence of African cultural practices, and in particular, the practice of *mbũri cia kiama* in the African churches. By doing this, this chapter traced the continuities and discontinuities between *Gĩkũyũ* religion and Jewish religion in the Old Testament, as well as their interpretation in the New Testament. This interpretive key was offered through the doctrine of christology, including atonement theories, the offices of Christ, and the new covenant, concepts that are at the heart of a covenantal and redemptive-historical approach to biblical interpretation. This chapter offers the following conclusions:

1. African theologians should pay close attention to the African traditional religious (ATR) worldview and cultural practices. This is because they have a clear outworking in the practical life of Christians in Africa. Secondly, considering ATR is a helpful way of theological reflection that is contextual and relevant and honors the gains made by the forerunner African theologians including Augustine, Athanasius, Mbiti, Idowu, Bediako and Sanneh.
2. Theological reflection with African realities must robustly engage Scripture. I suggest that a redemptive-historical and covenantal hermeneutic as one that honours what the whole Bible says on particular issues and finds its centre in Christ. Even while we take our cultures as sources of theological reflection, biblical revelation

40. Collium Banda, "Complementing Christ? A Soteriological Evaluation of the Anointed Objects of the African Pentecostal Prophets," *Conspectus: The Journal of the South African Theological Seminary* 2 (2018): 61.

is the supreme authority – as per the reformed understanding of *sola scriptura* and *tota scriptura*.

3. African Christians can learn from their traditional culture. One positive lesson from the practice of *mbũri cia kiama* is the importance of mentorship with our African traditional cultures. Within contemporary African societies, many of the ills we are seeing including family breakdown, complexities in adolescent development and youth transitions, could be minimized through mentorship. For African Christians especially, mentorship must begin in the home through family discipleship and in the church through holistic discipleship of young people.
4. Although African culture is highly oral, we must not use that as an excuse to disengage in Scripture study – with many translations available in local languages, Bible study must take principal place in African Christian practices. Additionally, Africans still pay more allegiance to their cultural practices rather than their Christian convictions. Since we are a new body in Christ, our allegiance to Christ is what informs our core identity as Christians. Where there is a conflict between Christ and culture, it is clear that Christ is Lord of all – including culture.

Bibliography

Banda, Collium. "Complementing Christ? A Soteriological Evaluation of the Anointed Objects of the African Pentecostal Prophets." *Conspectus: The Journal of the South African Theological Seminary* 2 (2018): 55–69.

Bediako, Kwame. *Jesus in Africa: The Christian Gospel in African History and Experience*. Akropong-Akuapeng: Regnum Africa, 2013.

Bevans, Steven. *Models of Contextual Theology*. Maryknoll: Orbis Books, 1999.

———. *Essays in Contextual Theology*. Leiden: Brill, 2018.

Chege, Jane N. "The Meru Religious Beliefs and Practices with Particular Reference to their Sacrificial Rites: A Case Study of the Igembe Sub-Ethnic Group." Masters Thesis, University of Nairobi, Nairobi, 1985. Accessed on 12 January 2021 from http://erepository.uonbi.ac.ke/.

Gatu, John. *Fan into Flame: An Autobiography*. Nairobi: Moran Publishers, 2016.

Gĩkũyũ Center for Cultural Studies. 2017. "Stages of a Gĩkũyũ Man's Life." https://mukuyu.wordpress.com/tag/mburi-ya-kiama/.

Hesselgrave, David J., and Edward Rommen. *Contextualization: Meanings, Methods, and Models*. Pasadena: William Carey Library, 2000.

Kabetũ, Mathew Njoroge. *Kĩrĩra kia ũgĩkũyu: Kuuma Mũndũ Amonyokio O Nginya Rĩria Akahinga Riitho Aarĩkia Kwĩgaya*. Nairobi: Kenya Literature Bureau, 2017.

Karangi, Matthew Muriuki. "The Gĩkũyũ Religion and Philosophy: A Tool for Understanding the Current Religio-Political Debates in Kenya." *Anthropos* 2 (2013): 612–22.

Kenyatta, Jomo. *Facing Mount Kenya: The Traditional Life of the Kikuyu*. Nairobi: Kenway, 2011.

Kvidahl, Clifford B., and Dan Lioy. "'You are a Priest Forever': An Exegetical and Biblical Theology of High Priestly Christology." *Conspectus: The Journal of the South African Theological Seminary* 29, no. 1 (2020): 40–60.

Leakey, Louis Seymour Bazett. *The Southern Kikuyu before 1903*. Nairobi: Richard Leakey, 2007.

Mbiti, John S. *African Religions and Philosophy*. Oxford: Heinemann, 1999.

———. *Introduction to African Religions*. Long Grove: Waveland Press, 1991.

Muriuki, Godfrey. "A History of the Kikuyus to 1904." PhD Thesis, University of London, 1969. http://erepository.uonbi.ac.ke/.

Nkansah-Obrempong, James. "Africa's contextual realities: Foundation for the Church's Holistic Mission." *International Review of Mission* 106, no. 2 (2017): 280–94. https://doi.org/10.1111/irom.12186.

Owen, John. *An Exposition on the Epistle to the Hebrews*. Volume 6. Grand Rapids: Baker, 1980.

Parsons, Mikeal C. "Son and High Priest: A Study in the Christology of Hebrews." *Evangelical Quarterly* 60, no. 3(1988): 195–215.

Sanneh, Lamin. *Translating the Message: The Missionary Impact on Culture*. Maryknoll: Orbis Books, 2009.

Stinton, Diane B. "Africa's Contribution to Christology." In *African Theology Comes of Age: Revisiting Twenty Years of the Theology of the Ecumenical Symposium of Eastern Africa Theologians (ESEAT)*, edited by Laurenti Magesa, 13–35. Nairobi: Paulines Publications Africa, 2010.

Waweru, Humphrey. *The Bible and African Culture: Mapping Transactional Inroads*. Limuru: Zapf Chancery, 2011.

9

Christian Faith and Dowry Practices

Lobola

Primrose Muyambo
FOCUS Zimbabwe

Abstract

Lobola (bride-price) is a common practice among most African cultures in which a man makes a payment in the form of cattle, money, or other material form to his future in-laws. This is an age-long tradition. Initially, the purpose of *lobola* was to promote love and unity between the couple and the two families. However, the tradition has become a commercial activity for families to acquire wealth. As a result, the tradition has led to unhappy marriages, premarital sex, and abuse of women. Sadly, this kind of greed is also found among Christian families. The issue that needs further discussion is the legitimacy of *lobola* in consideration of the Christian faith. The aim of this chapter is to understand the original purpose of *lobola* and see how it can be done by Christians in a way that portrays a godly attitude towards money and material possessions. It will be argued that *lobola* is legitimate within Christian marriages if it is guided by Christian principles pertaining to the godly attitude towards money and material possessions. It is the responsibility of Christian families to provide a godly example to follow to the societies around them when practicing the tradition of *lobola*.

Keyterms: *Lobola*, Dowry Practices, Bride-price

1. Introduction

Lobola or dowry practices is one of the most common cultural practices in most parts of Africa including the Shona culture of Zimbabwe. This practice is done differently in various parts of Africa. Speaking of the Shona culture, *lobola* "has been defined as the payment, in cattle and money or in other material forms, by a son-in-law or a member of his family to the father-in-law or legal guardian of a woman for the purpose of entering into a marriage with a woman."[1] It is an important procedure that should happen between the groom's and the bride's families. This cultural practice is meant to bring two families together as the bride and the groom seek to get into a marriage relationship. However, this cultural practice has evolved so much from its original intention to commercialization or a way that the bride's family acquires wealth. It is now often characterized by greedy and selfish motives whereby the parents of the bride overcharge the groom's family as if they are selling their daughter. Even Christian families are not excluded from this.

This has led to so many people voicing against this cultural practice and consider it illegitimate. The argument of this chapter is that *lobola* is legitimate within Christian marriages if it is guided by Christian principles. If Christian families promote a *lobola* practice that is guided by Christian principles, there is hope that this tradition will slowly be transformed by the gospel. This chapter will first give a brief background to dowry practices, *lobola,* by using literature review within the African traditional cultural context. Second, it will discuss the way *lobola* is practiced in the contemporary context by using written literature and my personal experience as a married Shona woman. Third, the discussion will consider the dowry practices in view of the Christian faith. The key text for this section will be the Bible. Finally, the chapter will give suggestions and conclusion. As noted above, dowry practice is done differently in various African cultures. This chapter will focus on the Shona culture of Zimbabwe and a few that are like it.

---

1. O. Ngundu, *Mission Churches and African Customary Marriage: At what point should a Couple married by African Custom be Recognised as Married in the Sight of God?* (Saarbrucken, Germany: Lambert Academic Publishing, 2010), 20.

2. Understanding *Lobola*

2.1 Meaning of Lobola

As noted above, *lobola* refers to "the payment, in cattle and money or in other material forms, by a son-in-law or a member of his family to the father-in-law or legal guardian of a woman for the purpose of entering into a marriage with a woman."[2] *Lobola* payment shows the husband's acceptance of responsibility over his wife and a pledge to protect and look after her for the remainder of their lives together.[3] Using Shona culture as an example, *lobola* negotiations are done by the two heads of the two families. The groom's family would bring someone who can operate as a mediator between the two families during the negotiations. Ngundu calls this person, a "go-between" or "intermediary."[4] Cattle or other form of payment are transferred to the bride's family.[5] According to my experience of Shona culture, soon after the negotiations of *lobola*, a big meal was prepared, and the two families would eat together in celebration of the new relationship.

Referring to the Shona culture as an example, *lobola* payment has several stages, and these stages include payment for different things. An example of this is *gusvi*: payment to greet the in-laws; *kukumbira ndiro*: payment to ask for a plate from the in-laws where money would be placed during the negotiations; *rusambo*: the biggest part of *lobola*; and many others.[6]

Moreover, according to Mutua and Chichen, bride-price is the way an African man expresses how much he loves and values his wife.[7] Shope presents one response from his interview with an older Xhosa man of South Africa about the *lobola* in the past, he says:

> If you do pay *lobolo* for your wife, you respect her and then you don't easily say "go away." You understand where this person comes from and then how she is linked to you and then the meaning of

2. Ngundu, *Mission Churches*, 20.
3. Ngundu, *Mission Churches*, 20.
4. Ngundu, *Mission Churches*, 19.
5. M. K. Chiweshe, "Wives at the Market Place: Commercialisation of Lobola and Commodification of Women's Bodies in Zimbabwe," *The Oriental Anthropologist* 16 (2016): 229–43, 230.
6. Chiweshe, "Wives at the Market Place," 233.
7. K. Mutua and D. Chinchen, "Dowry in Africa: A Wife Purchased, or a Wife Cherished?" *Learning from other Stories* 42 (2006): 16–22, 22.

> her to be in your house with you. So that's why you start to respect the *lobolo*. You give your wife respect if you pay *lobolo*.[8]

According to my experience of the Shona culture, if a man fails to give his wife's parents at least a very small amount, the woman feels unloved and unvalued, resulting in an unhappy wife. This is so because in most African cultures, the payment of *lobola* is the accepted traditional way of marriage. Also, it is a way of showing "gratitude to the wife's parents . . . for bearing and rearing a wife for them."[9] Thus, if *lobola* is not paid, then there is no marriage.

Furthermore, Bourdillon argues that bride-price gives status to women in their husbands' family.[10] Also, it is only when *lobola* is paid that someone is recognised as an in-law.[11] This shows that the cultural practice of bride-price plays a significant societal role rather than just relating to wealth acquisition.[12]

2.2 Origin of Lobola

Originally, *lobola* could be paid through three or four cows and other material gifts that the groom's family could afford to give.[13] In this era, the primary purpose of *lobola* was not accumulation of wealth. According to Gelfand, the *lobola* paid for a daughter could be used to help a son pay his own *lobola*.[14] Also, if a man did not have means to pay his *lobola*, the bride's parents could invite him to come live with them for a period of time-offering service. This service could go up to ten years.[15] Shope says "In the past, *lobolo* forged a relational bond among families . . . it celebrated the addition of the woman into the husband's family . . . it is a way of making a relationship between two families."[16] In addition to this, bride-price was meant to "legitimatize" a

8. Janet Hinson Shope, "'Lobola is here to Stay': Rural Black Women and the Contradictory Meanings of Lobolo in Post-Apartheid South Africa," *Agenda* 20, no. 68 (2006), 66.

9. Chiweshe, "Wives at the Market Place," 233.

10. M. F. C. Bourdillon, *The Shona Peoples: An Ethnography of the Contemporary Shona, with Special Reference to their Religion* (Gweru: Mambo Press, 1976), 50.

11. Chiweshe, "Wives at the Market Place," 234.

12. Ngundu, *Mission Churches*, 20.

13. John S. Mbiti, *African Religions and Philosophy* (Garden City: Anchor Books Doubleday & Company, 1970), 180–81.

14. M. Gelfand, *The Genuine Shona: Survival Values of an African Culture* (Gweru: Mambo Press, 1973), 45.

15. Chiweshe, "Wives at the Market Place," 235.

16. Shope, *Lobola is Here to Stay*, 65.

marriage relationship between a husband and a wife.[17] This is so because in most African contexts, marriages were "not formalized in courts but traditionally in the community."[18] This answers the objections that most missionaries had that *lobola* was merely "commercial transactions, degrading women as mere chattels."[19]

Furthermore, looking at the history of bride-price, it was meant to bring two families together in a relationship.[20] The cattle paid represents the "relational value."[21] It is believed that this kind of bond between the two families makes it difficult for the two married people to divorce, making divorce less likely to happen.[22] Also, it has to be noted that in the past fathers could help their children to raise *lobola*. This means that the burden of *lobola* was not only upon the young man.[23]

2.3 Contemporary Practice of **Lobola**

According to Chiweshe, "In a cash economy, the gifts have changed from the traditional use of hoes, axes or cattle to mainly money."[24] Chiweshe points out that, nowadays fathers are demanding extremely high amounts of *lobola*, "some are even demanding satellite dishes, cars, furniture, and huge amounts of groceries. Modern lobola payments include cash, cattle, clothes, shoes, and groceries."[25] Referring to the Shona culture of Zimbabwe, a man can be asked to pay up to US$4,000 cash plus other material things.[26] This suggests that *lobola* has become more "materialistic."[27]

17. Ngundu, *Mission Churches*, 20.

18. M. Elijah Baloyi, "Paying *Lobola* when my Wife Dies: An African Pastoral Study about the Practice of forcing People to pay *Lobola* after their Wives passed Away," *Journal of Human Ecology* 48 (2014): 135–43, 136.

19. Nicola Ansell, "Because it's Our Culture! (Re)Negotiating the Meaning of 'Lobola' in Southern African Secondary Schools," *Journal of Southern African Studies* 27 (2001): 697–716, 699.

20. Mbiti, *African Religions and Philosophy*, 181.

21. Mutua and Chinchen, "Dowry in Africa," 19.

22. Mutua and Chinchen, "Dowry in Africa," 22.

23. C. Vijfhuizen, *The People you Live with: Gender Identities and Social Practices, Beliefs and Power in the Livelihoods of Ndau Women and Men in a Village with an Irrigation Scheme in Zimbabwe* (Harare: Weaver Press, 2002), 29.

24. Chiweshe, "Wives at the Market Place," 233.

25. Chiweshe, "Wives at the Market Place," 235.

26. Chiweshe, "Wives at the Market Place," 235.

27. Chiweshe, "Wives at the Market Place," 235.

The demand for large sums of money has led parents to refuse burying their daughter upon death if *lobola* had not been paid.[28] In cases like this, the groom's family are forced to pay *lobola* for the dead wife, showing that *lobola* payment cannot be escaped.[29] In most African contexts, "daughters have become a high priced commodity . . . where *lobola* has become a means of escaping poverty . . . *Lobola* nowadays has thus tended to become an epitome of the commodification of daughters wherein daughters are seen as a pension fund."[30]

In addition, the world is calling for high price *lobola* that does nothing but bring bitterness to the young couple or lead them to opt for premarital sexual relations because the groom could not afford the expected amount for *lobola* payment. It is interesting that not everyone is against this commodification of *lobola*. Chabata quoted by Chiweshe noted that:

> Married women also told me that lobola gives them status because "if a large sum of money is paid for you, it shows that you have value." Most women interviewed said that if the woman is loved and has value then "real" money has to be paid. They argued that the payment of a higher fee can denote true love.[31]

This is one of the reasons why commodification of *lobola* has persisted over time.

3. Christian Faith and Dowry Practices

3.1 Dowry Practices are not Inherently Wrong

As presented above, it can be said that *lobola* is not inherently wrong. What has gone wrong is the fact that *lobola* has become a commercial business; a way of acquiring wealth. This has led most people, especially those outside cultures that do dowry practices, to consider it as an illegitimate practice. Chiweshe refers to the *lobola* practice with reference to Zimbabwe as "commodification of women's bodies."[32] This comes from the greed that characterizes the whole practice. To support his argument, Chiweshe gives an illustration of a man who had to pay several cows for his bride, including a cow to thank the bride's

28. This is so because in some cultures such as Shona culture, if a wife dies, the in laws cannot bury her without the approval from her parents.

29. Chiweshe, "Wives at the Market Place," 236.

30. Chiweshe, "Wives at the Market Place," 238.

31. Chiweshe, "Wives at the Market Place," 237.

32. Chiweshe, "Wives at the Market Place," 229.

mother for carrying his bride, another one to thank the mother again for giving birth to the bride and several cows to the father of the bride for raising his daughter.[33] If calculated into the monetary values, the cows that a man had to pay for *lobola* cost a few thousand dollars. This has led several people to have negative connotations against *lobola*.

There are several negative connotations against *lobola*, especially high priced *lobola* presented by some authors. First, Kambarami quoted by Chireshe and Chireshe argues that *lobola* gives man the right to exercise power over women.[34] This leads to women being viewed as nothing but acquired property, especially in cases where *lobola* is set at a high price. Gelfand points out that when a Shona man pays *lobola*, he considers his wife as his property.[35] Mvududu also argued the same point when she said that "*Lobola* negotiations resemble a market where there is buying and selling of women because a price for the woman is usually negotiated."[36]

Second, Chiweshe viewed this as a promotion of patriarchal practices which places men as superior over women whereby a woman has no say against her husband's promiscuous activities.[37] Quoting Chakona, Chiweshe presents that "patriarchy ultimately is a gendered power system: a network of social, political and economic relationships through which men dominate and control female labour, reproduction and sexuality as well as define women's status, privileges and rights in a society."[38]

Third, Chakabva mentioned a story of a Shona man who expected his wife to do everything for him, including male jobs like fishing, because he paid the bride-price. When he bought meat, he would not share even with his children because of his attitude that, "I have wasted my riches . . . So I will do what I want without fear of interference from anyone."[39] This attitude inevitably has resulted in abuse of several women and in some cases divorce.

Fourth, incidences of conflicts within families have been recorded. Some people have fought for a share of the *lobola* money that the groom has paid. Other extreme examples are of family members who killed each other over

---

33. Chiweshe, "Wives at the Market Place," 233.

34. Chireshe and Chireshe, "Monogamous marriage," 212.

35. Gelfand, *The Genuine Shona*, 14.

36. S. C. Mvududu, *Lobola: Its Implications for Women's Reproductive Rights* (Harare: Weaver Press, 2002), 40.

37. Chiweshe, "Wives at the Market Place," 231.

38. Chiweshe, "Wives at the Market Place," 231.

39. D. Chakabva, "Gore was a Greedy Man," in *Shona Customs*, ed. Clive and Peggy Killeff (Gweru: Mambo Press, 1970), 81.

lobola money.[40] The question here is: How can *lobola* (dowry practices) be transformed by the gospel?

3.2 Biblical Reflections

A Biblical Example from Matthew 6:19–21

In the Bible, there is neither a prescription on how *lobola* should be done nor a condemnation of the culture. Exodus 22:16–17 comes in the context of laws about social justice. It spells out that a man who entices a virgin girl to have sexual intercourse with her should pay bride-price to the parents of the girl and marry her. Another instance is Genesis 24:52–54; Abraham gave gifts that he could afford to Rebekah's parents on behalf of his son Isaac as bride-price. In this case, it was the groom's family who decided what to give to the family of the bride. These examples show no prescription or condemnation of the practice as it was practiced by the Ancient Near Eastern people.

However, there are principles that we can draw from the Bible that can help the *lobola* payment practice to be shaped and guided by the gospel. In Matthew 6:19–21, Jesus warns his disciples not to store up their treasures on earth where moth and other insects destroy but rather to store up their treasure in heaven. This passage comes in the context of Jesus's Sermon on the Mount. According to Brown, the Lord's prayer in the previous verses (6:9–13) asks for the kingdom of God to arrive. This "leads naturally into a teaching on what one values in light of God's imminent reign."[41] Other sages during Jesus's time believed that Jesus here is against material possessions as evil. The issue here is on priority; valuing what our Lord Jesus Christ values as important to his kingdom.[42] The contrast to storing up one's treasure on earth is storing up one's treasure in heaven (6:20). Storing up one's treasure in heaven shows allegiance to the kingdom of heaven.[43] This allegiance can be shown through meeting the needs of other people who are in need instead of accumulating possessions more than we need to ourselves. By doing this, a disciple is storing up their treasure in a safe place (eternity) where no insect can destroy. Storing treasures for oneself in this world is temporary and unsatisfying as shown by

40. Chiweshe, "Wives at the Market Place," 236.

41. Jeannine K. Brown, *Matthew (Teach the Text Commentary Series)* (Grand Rapids: Baker Books, 2015), 70.

42. Craig S. Keener, *A Commentary on the Gospel of Matthew* (Grand Rapids: Eerdmans, 1999), 220–21.

43. Brown, *Matthew*, 70.

the reference to moth (and other insects), rust and thieves that can destroy the stored treasures.

The reason for this warning is given in 6:21, "For where your treasure is, there your heart will be also." The reference to the heart and treasure together shows what is of vital importance in someone.[44] If one's heart is on their treasures, then it is difficult for them to focus on God and what matters to his kingdom. Therefore, Jesus in 6:24 says that "No-one can serve two masters." This is a call for Jesus's disciples to focus on Jesus and his kingdom. Considering this, Keener says, "Jesus, warns his audience that one must choose which master one will serve: those who work for possessions will end up hating God; those who work for God will end up hating possessions."[45] This inevitably calls Christians to love God through loving their neighbours, their brothers, and sisters.

One principle that can be draw from this passage is that Jesus's disciples should treasure Jesus and what matters for him. Considering the highly-charged issue of *lobola* that has become normal in most African societies, if Christian parents understand that they should store their treasures in heaven, they will not over-charge *lobola*. If they understand that Jesus wants them to focus on what matters for his kingdom, they will not seek to acquire wealth through over-charging a man who wants to marry their daughter. If the mind of the Christian parents in Africa is shaped by the gospel and the love of Christ, they would know that overcharging a man who is interested in marrying their daughter is not loving one's neighbour.

Luke 12:15 – Right Attitude towards Money and Material Possessions

In Luke 12:15, Jesus is about to tell a parable of a rich man who decided to tear down his old barns to build the new one, because he had so much grain that needed to be stored. In this parable, the rich man thought that this is all that his soul required. He did not realize that his soul belongs to God and not to the things of this world, until his soul is taken away that same night. According to Bock, "the parable of the rich fool shows how selfish and self-satisfied one can become if one seeks riches; this displeases God. Jesus calls on disciples to trust in the Father's care, for people are more important than the birds and the grass that God cares for."[46] What the disciples should seek is the kingdom of God.

---

44. Brown, *Matthew*, 70–71.

45. Keener, *Matthew*, 233.

46. D. L. Bock, *A Theology of Luke's Gospel and Acts* (Grand Rapids: Zondervan, 2011), 73.

The two imperatives "beware" and "be on guard" or "keep yourselves from" in this passage show the command to isolate oneself from the love of material possessions. These imperatives call for immediate action without any kind of compromise. The principle that can be drawn here is that disciples of Jesus should seek heavenly treasures, not earthly ones. It is to be noted that, Jesus here is not condemning acquiring wealth, but he is condemning the wrong attitude towards worldly riches.

Considering *lobola* practice, high-priced *lobola* which is characterized by greed and a search for selfish gain has become normal. If Christian parents are guided by the gospel, they would realize that giving their daughters in marriage is not a way of acquiring wealth but rather getting two families in a long-lasting relationship. As argued above, *lobola* practice is not inherently wrong but rather it should be practiced in a way that displays the values of Christ's kingdom. *Lobola* is a legitimate practice if it is characterized by a right attitude towards money. Overcharging *lobola* for any reason is wrong, and a clear picture of a greedy and improper attitude towards material possessions.

1 Timothy 6:6–12 – Right Attitude towards Money

In 1 Timothy 6:6–12, Paul is giving instructions to Timothy about how the church should operate. Chapter 6 gives a specific attention to false teachers and true contentment. The previous verses describe the teaching of the false teachers who taught that "godliness is a means to financial gain" (6:5). However, Paul contrasts this teaching (seen by the word ["but"] at the beginning of verse 6) by saying that "godliness with contentment is great gain" (6:6).

According to Towner, the phrase "great gain" here in association with godliness "exceeds the limited material 'gain' sought by the opponents."[47] Godliness, according to Paul's teaching here, comes from one's contentment with what they already have and not from acquiring material wealth. The reason for this is stated in verse 7, "for we brought nothing into the world, and we cannot take anything out of the world." This verse repeats a powerful negation ("nothing") which emphasises the fact that we did not bring anything into this world, and we are not going to take anything with us when we die. Commenting on this, Towner says that Paul first:

> . . . places life on earth into eternal perspective. While he does not devalue human earthly life in any sense, he does force the reader to view it in temporary terms. Second, following from

47. P H. Towner, *The Letters to Timothy and Titus* (Grand Rapids: Eerdmans, 2006), 701.

> this, an eschatological understanding of human life as beginning in a temporal mode but destined for an eternal mode invites a rethinking of focus that will accord the appropriate value to each stage of life and a balanced approach to material living.[48]

Paul here is not condemning material possessions, but he is calling people to understand the temporality of earthly life and material possessions. Having this understanding and being content with basic things like food and clothes that we already have (v. 8) spell out godliness in this passage.

In verse 9, Paul points out the three dangers that come with the desire to get rich. First, is the danger "to fall into temptation," second, the danger to fall into a "trap" and third the danger to fall into "many foolish and harmful desires that plunge people into ruin and destruction" (verse 9). It is good to want to be rich, but it is wise to be aware of these dangers. The love of money or avarice mentioned in verse 10 refers to extreme greed for wealth, and it is this extreme greed for wealth that is the root of all evil, according to this verse. Extreme love of money can lead people to do whatever it takes to get money whether they keep their godliness or not. It is not bad to want to have money, but it is the extreme love of it that is wrong.

Thus, considering the practice of *lobola* in most African contexts, few practical principles can be drawn out from 1 Timothy 6:6–12:

1. Godliness is not defined by material gain.
2. Material gain is temporary; we came into this world with nothing, and we will leave it with nothing. Thus, we should live our lives with the eternal perspective.
3. The great gain is godliness with contentment of things that we already have. This helps us to focus on Jesus Christ who gives eternal life.

God gave African parents precious daughters who are already valuable in his sight. Daughters should not be turned into some form of money-making business. While many Africans go to extremes of claiming large sums of money to fulfil their desires to get rich, this is exactly what Paul is warning against in the passage studied above. The avarice displayed by most African parents has led them to compromise the godly life that they are supposed to live and has become the root of so much evil: some young people have opted for premarital sex only because they could not afford the *lobola* demands, while other women

48. Towner, *The Letters to Timothy and Titus*, 704.

have become victims of domestic and gender-based violence because their husbands are bitter from the *lobola* demands by their wives' parents, and some couples ended up divorcing each other because of the bitterness caused by high demands of *lobola*.

In addition to this, high *lobola* charges have led most women to be seen as inferior to men, in some cases resulting in the wife not having any say in decision-making because the husband paid his *lobola*. According to Shoko, "A woman is regarded as 'sold' at marriage because of the bride-price which is paid to the in-laws. A husband can ill-treat and abuse her without complaint. The woman is expected to be docile."[49]

Regardless of the positives mentioned above, bride-price has affected the understanding of headship and submission in Shona marriages a great deal. Most Shona men have used a bride-price payment as a tool to oppress their wives. Gelfand points out that when a Shona man pays *lobola*, he considers his wife as his property.[50] Mvududu also argued the same point when she said that "*Lobola* negotiations resemble a market where there is buying and selling of women because a price for the woman is usually negotiated."[51] Although the original meaning of bride-price was to cement relationship and love as Ngundu points out, most Shona men have twisted its original intention to ensure superiority over women.[52]

This is one of the evils that has been normalized in most African contexts, and which can be avoided if *lobola* is Christ-centred. Unless Christ is exalted over money, the ills brought by the greed for money shown by high *lobola* charges will continue. The challenge from 1 Timothy is to keep Christ at the centre of our lives. Yes, we need money but the extreme love of it, to the point where the young men asking for a hand in marriage are to pay thousands of dollars, inevitably pushes Christ to the peripheries of our lives.

Genesis 1:27 – The Imago Dei in Daughters and Women

Another important principle that we can learn from the Bible is that daughters are created in the image of God and are valuable in his eyes. No money can pay their worth. Most African parents charge *lobola* for their daughters depending

---

49. T. Shoko, *Indigenous Religion in Zimbabwe: Health and Well-Being* (Harare: University of Zimbabwe, 2007), 20.

50. M. Gelfand, *The Background: The Traditional Culture of the Shona-Speaking People* (Cape Town: Juta & Company Limited, 1965), 14.

51. Mvududu, *Lobola*, 40.

52. Ngundu, *Mission Churches*, 19.

on her level of education and background.[53] In most cases, if the bride has degrees or a respectable job, the bride price is extremely high. The reason is that the bride's parents expect the groom to compensate for the "worth" of their daughter by paying high-priced *lobola*. These parents view the marriage of their daughter as a loss for them, as she will no longer look after her parents as she did prior to marriage, therefore by paying high-priced *lobola* that "loss" is compensated.

Passages such as Genesis 1:27 clearly show that both men and women were created in the image of God.[54] The idea here is that human beings were created in a way that resembles God, and this resemblance is in both men and women. This shows that all human beings are equally valuable in the eyes of God. Other parents think that having the groom paying a high amount of *lobola* gives their daughter the value she is worth; however, this cannot be true if a daughter already has value in the eyes of God. There is nothing in this world that can add or give value to a daughter.

In 1 John 3:1, John calls the readers to see the great love that God has lavished on them through the death of Jesus Christ on the cross. It is because of this love that they are called "children of God." It is interesting that John adds an emphatic statement "And that is what we are!" This clearly shows that our value is found in the finished work of Christ. We know him and we are his children. This is the truth that can really affect the way most African parents think that *lobola* gives value to a daughter. A principle that can be drawn out from this verse is that the value of a daughter is not found in the bride-price attached to her. Her value is found in the finished work of Christ. As noted above, this chapter is not arguing against the culture of *lobola* payment, but it is against the greed that so often comes with the practice. For those who are Christians, every cultural practice must be Christ-centered.

4. Suggestions and Conclusion

In conclusion, the culture of *lobola* practiced in several African countries is an age-long tradition. Originally, it was meant to build a relationship between two families of the bride and the groom. The payment of *lobola* was a way

53. G. Heeren, John B. Jemmott III, Joanne C. Tyler, S. Tshabe and Z. Ngwane, "Cattle for Wives and Extramarital Trysts for Husbands? Lobola, Men, and HIV/STD Risk Behaviour in Southern Africa," *Journal of Human Behaviour in the Social Environment* 21 (2011): 73–81, 74.

54. The arguments pertaining to the meaning of the "image of God" in humans are beyond the scope of this chapter.

two people could be accepted as married in the African context. The groom could use hoes, beads, cattle, and other available resources to pay his lobola. The father of the groom could make every effort to help his son in raising the lobola requirements. Nowadays *lobola* is mostly paid using cash and the groom is expected to raise the money on his own. As noted above, in most parts of Africa including Zimbabwe, *lobola* has been commercialized. This means that, most parents have normalized the culture of demanding high-prized lobola.

This has led to most people arguing against the culture of *lobola* payment because of the negative effects that come with it. Some of these are: abuse of women, premarital sex, bitter marriages, divorce and so many others. This has somehow defeated the original meaning and purpose of *lobola* mentioned above.

This chapter has argued that *lobola* is legitimate within Christian marriages if it is guided by Christian principles. Thus, this chapter has drawn out a few biblical principles (from the passages discussed above) that can help lobola to be Christ-centered. These principles are:

(1) Christians should have a right attitude towards money and material possessions bearing in mind that material possessions are temporary.

(2) Godliness is not defined by material gain.

(3) Material gain is temporary because we came into this world with nothing, and we will leave it with nothing. Thus, we should live our lives with an eternal perspective.

(4) The great gain is godliness with contentment of things that we already have. This helps us to focus on Jesus Christ who gives eternal life.

(5) Human value is found in the finished work of Christ. Therefore, the value of a daughter is not found in high-priced *lobola*.

If Christian parents take these principles seriously, they will be able to display the right attitude towards money and material possessions whenever they practice *lobola*.

Bibliography

Ansell, Nicola. "Because it's Our Culture! (Re)Negotiating the Meaning of 'Lobola' in Southern African Secondary Schools." *Journal of Southern African Studies* 27 (2001): 697–716.

Baloyi, M. Elijah. "Paying *Lobola* when my Wife Dies: An African Pastoral Study about the Practice of forcing People to pay *Lobola* after their Wives passed Away." *Journal of Human Ecology* 48 (2014): 135–43.

Bock, D. L. *A Theology of Luke's Gospel and Acts*. Grand Rapids: Zondervan, 2011.

Bourdillon, M. F. C. *The Shona Peoples: An Ethnography of the Contemporary Shona, with Special Reference to their Religion*. Gweru: Mambo Press, 1976.

Brown, Jeannine K. *Matthew (Teach the Text Commentary Series)*. Grand Rapids: Baker Books, 2015.

Chakabva, D. "Gore was a Greedy Man." In *Shona Customs*, edited by Clive and Peggy Killeff, 81–83. Gweru: Mambo Press, 1970.

Chireshe, E., and R.Chireshe. "Monogamous Marriage in Zimbabwe: An Insurance against HIV and AIDS?" *Agenda: Empowering Women for Gender Equity* 25 (2011): 93–101.

Chiweshe, M. K. "Wives at the Market Place: Commercialisation of *Lobola* and Commodification of Women's Bodies in Zimbabwe." *The Oriental Anthropologist* 16 (2016): 229–43.

Gelfand, M. *The Background: The Traditional Culture of the Shona-Speaking People*. Cape Town: Juta & Company Limited, 1965.

———. *The Genuine Shona: Survival Values of an African Culture*. Gweru: Mambo Press, 1973.

Heeren, G., John B. Jemmott III, Joanne C. Tyler, S. Tshabe, and Z. Ngwane. "Cattle for Wives and Extramarital Trysts for Husbands? *Lobola*, Men, and HIV/STD Risk Behaviour in Southern Africa." *Journal of Human Behaviour in the Social Environment* 21 (2011): 73–81.

Keener, Craig S. *A Commentary on the Gospel of Matthew*. Grand Rapids: Eerdmans, 1999.

Mbiti, John S. *African Religions and Philosophy*. Garden City: Doubleday & Company, 1970.

Mutua, K., and D. Chinchen. "Dowry in Africa: A Wife Purchased, or a Wife Cherished?" *Learning from Other Stories* 42 (2006): 16–22.

Mvududu, S. C. *Lobola: Its Implications for Women's Reproductive Rights*. Harare: Weaver Press, 2002.

Ngundu, O. *Mission Churches and African Customary Marriage: At what point should a Couple married by African Custom be Recognised as Married in the Sight of God?* Saarbrucken: Lambert Academic, 2010.

Shoko, T. Karanga. *Indigenous Religion in Zimbabwe: Health and Well-Being*. Harare: University of Zimbabwe, 2007.

Shope, Janet Hinson. "'*Lobola* is here to Stay': Rural Black Women and the Contradictory Meanings of Lobolo in Post-Apartheid South Africa." *Agenda* 20, no. 68 (2006): 64–72.

Towner, P. H. *The Letters to Timothy and Titus*. Grand Rapids: Eerdmans, 2006.

Vijfhuizen, C. *The People you Live with: Gender Identities and Social Practices, Beliefs and Power in the Livelihoods of Ndau Women and Men in a Village with an Irrigation Scheme in Zimbabwe*. Harare: Weaver Press, 2002.

10

A Christian Response against Domestic Violence

Seyram B. Amenyedzi, PhD
University of Western Cape, South Africa

Abstract

Domestic violence is among the top global religious and socio-cultural vices that have lived with us over the years. Domestic violence/abuse is not always physical but also emotional, verbal, economical, religious and sexual. This may happen in a subtle form, which is often overlooked or in an acute manner even leading to injuries or death of victims. Although everyone is at risk of domestic abuse, in Africa, women and children are at higher risk given the patriarchal nature of our cultures and religions. While it is a criminal offence, most religions have justified some form of domestic abuse in the name of fulfilling religious norms and/or values. Christianity cannot be ignored in the conversations around domestic violence. Many Christians have used the Bible to reinforce different forms of violence against partners or children. Interpretations of biblical texts on submission of wives to their husbands, for instance, have been the main reference point and excuse for violence against women in Christian homes. Similarly, those texts on obedience for children have no doubt contributed to the exertion of various forms of violence against them in the home. It is in this light that it is imperative to apologetically make a case against domestic violence within the African Christian context. This chapter proposes a Christian response against domestic violence from biblical and socio-cultural perspectives.

Keywords: Domestic Violence/Abuse, Christian Response, Women, Children, African Culture

1. Introduction

Nearly half a million people experience lethal violence every year. Although anyone can experience violence, empirical evidence proves that women are more often the victims. 30 percent of women encounter some form of violence in their lifetime, usually from intimate partners.[1]

There are various forms of violence, but prevalent is the domesticated type. In Africa, our patriarchal cultures affirm the practice as normal so that women and children suffer in silence. As mentioned earlier, violence can lead to death, but what about the instances where it is not lethal? In such circumstances, victims just have to make do with this abuse as a norm or sign of submission and/or humility. Domestic violence is not limited to physical and/or sexual abuse but can be emotional, psychological, verbal, economic and religious.[2] Our religions, Islam, African Traditional Religion and Christianity – the primary religions in the African continent – have been used to foster patriarchal attitudes that negatively affect women and children and worsen the issue of gender-based violence. This chapter focuses on Christianity and socio-cultural dimensions of domestic violence while a case is made against gender-based violence.

2. Conceptualizing Domestic Violence

Domestic violence is any kind of violent behaviour against a relative within the home setting. Although domestic violence has been typically associated with intimate partner relationships, it is relevant to highlight the broader context in the household. Abuse in the home is not only towards partners but extends to children, house helps and other members of the family.[3] Domestic

---

1. Walby et al., "Different Forms of Violence," in *The Concept and Measurement of Violence*, 1st ed. (Bristol: Bristol University Press, 2017), 57–102; Jonathan Herring, "The Severity of Domestic Abuse," *National Law School of India Review* 30 no. 1 (2018): 37–50.

2. Herring, "The Severity of Domestic Abuse," 39; Isabel Apawo Phiri, "Domestic Violence in Christian Homes: A Durban Case Study," *Journal for the Study of Religion* 14 no. 2 (2001): 91–92; United Nations, *COVID-19 Response: What is Domestic Violence?* https://www.un.org/en/coronavirus/what-is-domestic-abuse.

3. Tabitha Naisiko, "The Paradox of Love and Violence against Women in Families: A Loophole in the Agents of Socialization?," *East African Journal of Traditions, Culture and Religion* 5 no. 2 (2022) 12–23, https://doi.org/10.37284/eajtcr.5.2.611.

violence/abuse is usually not isolated but may be triggered by economic, power, socio-cultural and religious factors. The United Nations in its response to domestic violence during the COVID-19 pandemic period has provided a list to help identify its traces.[4] Even though the list of abusive behaviours below is related mainly to intimate partner relationships, it can be applied to other household members.

Does your partner . . .

- Embarrass or make fun of you in front of your friends or family?
- Put down your accomplishments?
- Make you feel like you are unable to make decisions?
- Use intimidation or threats to gain compliance?
- Tell you that you are nothing without them?
- Treat you roughly – grab, push, pinch, shove or hit you?
- Call you several times a night or show up to make sure you are where you said you would be?
- Use drugs or alcohol as an excuse for saying hurtful things or abusing you?
- Blame you for how they feel or act?
- Pressure you sexually for things you aren't ready for?
- Make you feel like there is "no way out" of the relationship?
- Prevent you from doing things you want – like spending time with friends or family?
- Try to keep you from leaving after a fight or leave you somewhere after a fight to "teach you a lesson"?

Do you . . .

- Sometimes feel scared of how your partner may behave?
- Constantly make excuses to other people for your partner's behaviour?
- Believe that you can help your partner change if only you changed something about yourself?
- Try not to do anything that would cause conflict or make your partner angry?
- Always do what your partner wants you to do instead of what you want?

4. United Nations, "COVID-19 Response: What is Domestic Abuse?" (n.d.). https://www.un.org/en/coronavirus/what-is-domestic-abuse.

- Stay with your partner because you are afraid of what your partner would do if you broke up?

> If any of these things are happening in your relationship, talk to someone. Without help, the abuse will continue. Making that first call to seek help is a courageous step.[5]

The list identifies various traits of violence. It is evident that domestic violence is not only exerted physically but it can be emotional, psychological, sexual, and verbal among others. In fact, during the COVID-19 pandemic, a report records that 243 million women and girls aged 15–49 years old experienced sexual or physical violence perpetrated by an intimate partner.[6] Herring[7] in measuring the severity of domestic abuse asserts that it is not just a form of assault but also includes coercive control, abuse of trust and danger to children, and influences gender inequalities. What is interesting is that domestic violence disproportionately affects both women and children.

2.1 Domestic Violence as a Human Right (Legal) Issue

Domestic violence was late to be included on the human rights agenda due to conflicts between international and local orientations. Thankfully, it is now embraced as a human rights issue which is evident especially in international and national laws and conventions. This means that abuse of any victim is an abuse of his/her human rights.[8] Therefore, domestic violence is criminal, hence perpetrators must be dealt with legally. Usdin et al· assert that "South Africa's first democratic government passed the Domestic Violence Act (DVA) into law in 1998 as part of local and international commitments to protecting the human rights of women.[9] Although the Act was welcomed as ground-breaking legislation, delays in implementing it led to increasing frustration."

---

5. United Nations, "What is Domestic Abuse?" *COVID-19 Response* (n.d.). https://www.un.org/en/coronavirus/what-is-domestic-abuse.

6. United Nations, "Policy Brief: The Impact of COVID-19 on Women" (2020), 19. Accessed on 5th October 2023 from https://www.un.org/sites/un2.un.org/files/2020/04/policy_brief_on_covid_impact_on_women_9_apr_2020_updated.pdf.

7. Herring, "The Severity of Domestic Abuse," 39.

8. Jane Freedman, "Domestic Violence through a Human Rights Lens," in *The Routledge International Handbook of Domestic Violence and Abuse*, ed. John Devaney et al. (New York: Routledge, 2021), ch. 6.

9. Shereen Usdin et al, "The Value of Advocacy in Promoting Social Change: Implementing the New Domestic Violence Act in South Africa," *Reproductive Health Matters* 8 no. 16 (2000): 55, http://www.jstor.org/stable/3775271.

This is not the case only in South Africa but in other countries on the continent and beyond. In Ghana for instance, there is a whole police department dedicated to domestic violence with rapid response mechanisms in place. However, even though domestic violence is criminalized, whether the laws are effective, and perpetuators are brought to book, is a whole conversation on its own. The difficulty is that while some physical abusers evade the judiciary for religious, cultural or social factors, what happens to those instances when the abuse is not too obvious yet emotionally and psychologically torturing? This is not to say domestic violence legislation is not gender inclusive, for everyone is protected, yet it is evident that females are most affected.[10] Freedman[11] also identifies the backdrop in attempts to ensure family privacy resulting in the neglect of pursuing the human rights agenda.

2.2 Domestic Violence as a Cultural Issue

Culture, being the way of life of a people group in a specific context, implies that culture touches every aspect of their livelihood including what happens in the home setting. Kasturirangan, Krishnan and Riger argue that the focus on engendered domestic abuse presents a backdrop that may not consider intersectionality of social identities in the discourse.[12] Hence, all women may be grouped together, but it is notable that experiences within racial and ethnic lines will differ. It is worth highlighting the womanist theory and concept which assert that the experiences of the black woman are not the same as the white woman. Culture plays a major role in domestic violence. This paper focuses on the African cultures which are mostly patriarchal.[13]

---

10. Anne Carol Douglas, "Gender Violence in Africa: African Women's Response," *Off Our Backs: A Women's News Journal* 30 no. 3 (2000): 9–19, http://www.jstor.org/stable/pdf/20836570.pdf; Hilde Jakobsen, "What's Gendered about Gender-Based Violence? An Empirically Grounded Theoretical Exploration from Tanzania," *Gender and Society* 28 no. 4 (2014): 537–61, https://doi.org/10.1177/0891243214532311.

11. Freedman, "Domestic Violence through a Human Rights Lens," ch. 6.

12. Aarati Kasturirangan, Sandhya Krishnan and Stephanie Riger, "The Impact of Culture and Minority Status on Women's Experience of Domestic Violence," *Trauma, Violence, & Abuse* 5 no. 4 (2004): 318–32, https://doi.org/10.1177/1524838004269487.

13. Seyram B. Amenyedzi, "Leadership Roles for Indigenous Ghanaian Women: The Case of Prof. Jane Naana Opoku Agyemang as Vice-Presidential Candidate for the National Democratic Congress (NDC)," *African Thought: A Journal of Afro-Centric Knowledge* 1 no. 1 (2021): 169–91; Clenora Hudson-Weems, Africana Womanism: Reclaiming Ourselves (London: Routledge, 2019), https://doi.org/10.4324/9780429287374; Patricia Hill Collins, "What's in a Name? Womanism, Black Feminism, and Beyond," *Black Scholar*, 26 no. 1 (1996), published online in 2015, https://doi.org/10.1080/00064246.1996.11430765; Naisiko, "The Paradox of Love and Violence against Women in Families"; Esther E. Acolatse, "Christian Divorce Counselling

Patriarchal cultural orientations have defined roles for both the male and female. The woman is supposed to take care of the home, be a wife and a mother while the man assumes the role of power and control.[14] The section on domestic violence, gender and power control also flags this pattern. Religion is also a contributing factor. In certain African communities, the male even from birth has power over the female siblings in terms of inheritance and service in the home. Society demands that the man exhibits masculinity, and this is normally expressed by exerting power and control over women especially and children. [15] It is interesting to note that "many of the countries where wife-beating is rare are those where female genital mutilation is prevalent."[16] Also, cultural values and norms may compel women especially to suffer abuse in silence.[17]

2.3 Domestic Violence, Gender, and Power

Research in Ghana shows that domestic violence is engendered, explaining that male partners violate their wives as a way of portraying masculinity. The study proved that religious, cultural and social factors which are also rooted in patriarchy inform the construction of masculinity. Hence, violence is seen as a legitimate means of exerting authority and a sign of masculinity.[18] Jakobsen[19] poses the question: "What's Gendered about Gender-Based Violence?" as a title to an article which explores gender-based domestic violence in Tanzania. Such a quest is needful especially in instances where a case has been made those men also experience some form of violence.

Criminologists and sociologists have widely studied this subject and underline employment for any or both partners as a mechanism that can

---

in West Africa: Seeking Wholeness through Reformed Theology and Jungian Dreamwork," *Journal of Pastoral Theology* 21 no. 1 (2011): 2–18, https://doi.org/10.1179/jpt.2011.21.1.002.

14. Seyram B, Amenyedzi, *The Lady Pastor: Reflections on Women in Ministry in Ghana*. Paul's Theology on Men and Women Webinar, South African Theological Seminary (2019).

15. Amenyedzi, *The Lady Pastor*; Yandisa Sikweyiya, et al., "Patriarchy and Gender-Inequitable Attitudes as Drivers of Intimate Partner Violence against Women in the Central Region of Ghan." *BMC Public Health* 20 no. 1 (2020): 1–11, https://doi.org/10.1186/s12889-020-08825-z.

16. Douglas, *Gender Violence in Africa*, 9.

17. Kasturirangan, Krishnan and Riger, "The Impact of Culture and Minority," 321; Sikweyiya, et al., "Patriarchy and Gender-Inequitable Attitudes," 1, 5, 8.

18. Sikweyiya, et al., "Patriarchy and Gender-Inequitable Attitudes," 7.

19. Jakobsen, "What's Gendered about Gender-Based Violence?," 538–42.

reduce domestic abuse due to less time spent together. But Aizer[20] makes an important revelation that takes the employment discourse to another level. She posits that the wage gap between partners has a huge impact on reducing abuse as when the income of the female is high and offers her independence and/or outside options, she can walk out easily from an abusive relationship.

2.4 Domestic Violence and Children

Children who live in an abusive home are endangered physically, psychologically and/or emotionally. Even if the abuse is not directly towards them, it could be traumatic to see the mother for instance being abused. This also shapes behaviours, perceptions, and worldview.[21] While the parents have full responsibility to see to the total wellbeing of their children, an abusive environment poses a huge threat to both the child and mother in most cases. The negative effects of domestic violence on children are enormous and detrimental. Either the child experiences direct abuse or observes or overhears a parent being abused, in any case s/he is affected emotionally, psychologically and/or physically. Such situations impact negatively on mother-child relations especially if infants need to totally depend on the mother heavily at a tender age. The child can suffer right from the womb when the mother is tortured emotionally, psychologically, or physically; these may have implications on the development of the child possibly causing some injuries or disability.[22] Studies show that many children find themselves in such complex and challenging situations without fully grasping or understanding what actually is happening. It takes time for them to understand their experience is actually an abuse or violation. Even those children who somehow escape such abusive situations

---

20. Anna Aizer, "The Gender Wage Gap and Domestic Violence," *The American Economic Review* 100 no. 4 (2010): 1849–53, http://www.jstor.org/stable/27871277.

21. Herring, "The Severity of Domestic Abuse," 46–47; John W. Fantuzzo, and Wanda K. Mohr, "Prevalence and Effects of Child Exposure to Domestic Violence," *Future of Children* 9.3 (1999): 22, https://doi.org/10.2307/1602779; Betsy McAlister Groves, "Mental Health Services for Children Who Witness Domestic Violence," *Future of Children* 9 no. 3 (1999): 122–32, https://doi.org/10.2307/1602786.

22. Margaret Kertesz, Larissa Fogden and Cathy Humphreys, "Domestic Violence and the Impact on Children," in *The Routledge International Handbook of Domestic Violence and Abuse*, ed. John Devaney et al. (New York: Routledge, 2021), ch. 10.

also reported the effects of having to leave behind valuable friends, environment and possessions.[23]

It is worthy to note another variant of domestic abuse which is the adolescent-parent-abuse. In this instance, it is the adolescent who abuse parents physically or emotionally. Sometimes, they may vent their anger from outside with friends on parents or other relatives.[24] For this reason, Holt argues that engendering domestic violence may not paint a fair and equal picture of the kind of violence that occurs in the home.

2.5 Domestic Violence as a Health Issue

Domestic violence is a pandemic and a public health issue.[25] Health plays a vital role in humanity's livelihood; hence any health threat must not be underrated. Domestic violence as a health issue has different facets ranging from psychological, sexual, physical injuries and in severe cases leading to death. Hence, this is a public health problem that needs to be identified, with preventive and intervening measures.[26] Psychologically, this menace is flagged within the "risk" bracket highlighting the nature of risks associated with domestic abuse. While it is a risk factor for various forms of mental illnesses including depression, it could also pose a perpetual risky situation or an environment to an individual as victims of abuse are more likely to experience it again in the future. It is however relevant to note that such cases are normally individualized and approached subjectively.[27]

The sexual abuse aspect could be in a form of rape, sodomy and commonly in an intimate relationship where the male exerts power over the female as

23. Debbie Noble-Carr, Tim Moore and Morag McArthur, "Children's Experiences and Needs in Relation to Domestic and Family Violence: Findings from a Meta-Synthesis," *Child & Family Social Work* (2019), doi:10.1111/cfs.12645.

24. Amanda Holt, "Adolescent-to-Parent Abuse as a Form of 'Domestic Violence': A Conceptual Review," *Trauma, Violence, and Abuse* 17 no. 5 (2016): 491, https://doi.org/10.1177/1524838015584372.

25. Anuj Kapilashrami, "Tackling Domestic Violence and Abuse using a Rights-Oriented Public Health Lens," in *The Routledge International Handbook of Domestic Violence and Abuse*, ed. John Devaney et al. (New York: Routledge, 2021), ch. 7.

26. VAWnet, "Impact of Domestic Violence on Health," https://vawnet.org/sc/impact-domestic-violence-health.

27. Floretta Boonzaier and Taryn van Niekerk, "Psychology and Domestic Violence against Women," in *The Routledge International Handbook of Domestic Violence and Abuse*, ed. John Devaney et al. (New York: Routledge, 2021), ch. 3.

his property with no right in such matters, usually as a result of religious and patriarchal systems.[28]

2.6 Domestic Violence and Disability

Experiences of persons with disability are usually neglected in many conversations because they are mostly excluded from our societies. It is imperative to bring to light the ordeal of persons with disability. Their ordeal is in many forms which does not reflect the normal patterns in society; consequently, their plight could be forgotten. There are several empirical and non-empirical proofs that persons with disability are neglected, stigmatized and excluded from societal life.[29]

Socio-cultural constructions of disability in the African context are associated with curse, punishment, misfortune, demonology and exorcism. For these reasons, it is bad news when a child is born with disability. In some cultures, they are considered as river gods so are left by the river or left in the forest to perish.[30] A family with disability is perceived as cursed, and therefore many prefer to hide a child with disability. The stigma, exclusion, and stereotypes in themselves are violations of human rights which also have psychological effects on people's health. Most children with disability are most likely unable to access education and other rights and privileges as their other siblings. Most of them are victims of sexual abuse and maltreatment from relatives. Women with disability are perceived to be asexual, this prevents them accessing marriage. Even for those with children, there is the high possibility of refusing to allow them to experience real motherhood and bond with the child.[31] Just as adolescent-parent abuse has been highlighted, I propose that

---

28. Sikweyiya, et al., "Patriarchy and Gender," 7, 9; Kertesz, Fogden and Humphreys, "Domestic Violence and the Impact on Children," ch. 10.

29. Seyram B. Amenyedzi, "Equity and Access for Persons with Disability in Theological Education, Ghana," PhD Thesis, Stellenbosch University, 2016.

30. Enock Takyi, "Barriers to Mainstream Participation of Persons with Disabilities: A Qualitative Study of Persons with Physical Disabilities in Techiman, Ghana," Masters Thesis, Norwegian University of Science and Technology, 2013, 54–79.

31. For further reading on disability and various forms of abuse, see Seyram Amenyedzi, "'We are forgotten': The Plight of Persons with Disability in Youth Ministry," *Scriptura*, 120 no. 1 (2021): 1–17, https://dx.doi.org/10.7833/120-1-1459; Amenyedzi, "Equity and Access for Persons with Disability" (2016); Michael Baffoe, "Stigma, Discrimination & Marginalization: Gateways to Oppression of persons with Disabilities in Ghana, West Africa," *Journal of Educational and Social Research*, 3 no. 1 (2013): 187–98; Tsitsi Chataika, "Cultural and Religious Explanations of Disability and Promoting Inclusive Communities in South Africa in Theology and Disability: Changing the Conversations in Disability," in *Searching for Dignity: Conversations on Human*

abuse for persons with disability is taken seriously too as they suffer silently in most cases.

2.7 Domestic Violence and COVID-19

Bettinger-Lopez and Bro[32] in their article titled "A Double Pandemic: Domestic Violence in the Age of COVID-19" report that due to lockdowns to contain the COVID-19 pandemic, there was a rise in domestic abuse with children, women and LGBTQ+ individuals at the highest risk. The home is just not safe for victims of abuse. According to Marshall,[33] the following are some statistics from the African continent during the pandemic. South Africa was reported as having received 87,000 calls to the domestic abuse helpline in the first month of lockdown. The Women's Aid Organization in Malaysia also had a 44 percent rise in calls to its hotline. There was a report in Kenya on a 16-year-old female who was held captive and sexually abused by a man who just needed female company to survive the government-imposed lockdown. These are high indicators of how COVID-19 was not only a viral pandemic but also that of domestic violence. These data exclude unreported cases. Countries and institutions are trying their best to put support systems in place. These initiatives must be intensified while victims must also fearlessly make use of available interventions.[34]

Dignity, Theology and Disability, ed. Julie Claassens, Leslie Swartz and Len Hansen (Stellenbosch: Sun Media, 2013), 117–128; Reuben Kigame, "Cultural Barriers to the Disabled People's Participating in Church Life," in *Disability, Society and Theology: Voices from Africa*, ed. Samuel Kabue, Esther Mombo, Joseph Galgalo and C. B. Peter (Limuru: Zapf Chancery, 2011), 121–37.

Mina Lintvelt, "Disability and Gender: Twofold Discrimination," in *Living with Dignity: African Perspectives on Gender Equality*, ed. Elna Mouton, Gertrude Kapuma, Len Hansen and Thomas Togon (Stellenbosch: EFSA, 2015), 285–305; Joseph Shiriko, "Disability: Social Challenges and Family Responses," in *Disability, Society and Theology: Voices from Africa*, ed. Samuel Kabue, Esther Mombo, Joseph Galgalo and C.B . Peter (Limuru: Zapf Chancery, 2011), 168–96; Joseph Sinyo, "Gender and Disability Challenges within the Church," in *Disability, Society and Theology: Voices from Africa*, ed. Samuel Kabue, Esther Mombo, Joseph Galgalo and C.B . Peter (Limuru: Zapf Chancery, 2011), 209–19.

32. Caroline Bettinger-Lopez and Alexandra Bro, "A Double Pandemic: Domestic Violence in the Age of COVID-19," *Domestic Violence Report* 25 no. 5 (2020): 85–86.

33. Katherine Marshall, "Religious Responses to Domestic Abuse During the COVID-19 Pandemic" (June 2020), https://berkleycenter.georgetown.edu/posts/religious-responses-to-domestic-abuse-during-the-COVID-19-pandemic.

34. This paper was written during the COVID-19 pandemic hence, it was an ongoing conversation.

3. Domestic Violence in Christian Homes

Various religions have reinforced cultural values, societal norms, and structures to somehow legitimize domestic abuse. In Christianity, interpretations of scriptural verses on marriage and parenthood lay foundations for domestic abuse. A case study conducted by Isabel Phiri[35] at a Pentecostal church in Durban in South Africa proves the occurrences of domestic violence in Christian homes. Statistically, 16 percent of the female participants experienced all categories of domestic violence namely: physical, sexual, emotional, verbal, and psychological, economic, and spiritual. The most prevalent form was physical violence at 84 percent, followed by 76 percent experiencing spiritual violence, then 67 percent each for the following: economic, emotional, verbal, and psychological violence. The remaining 16 percent who did not admit to experiences of domestic violence may have done so to protect their husbands who were church leaders; some indicated that they could not share their domestic issues due to leadership roles they held. Similarly, it is worth noting that my personal experience as a minister for over two decades with first-hand information of domestic violence in Christian homes include those of pastors. Phiri's research found that women who were victims of violence were not willing to use non-church-based facilities.

Another significant finding in her study was how pastors have not been that helpful when help was sought from them. It is important to note also that it was mentioned that the majority of pastors are not professional marriage counsellors which impacted on their ability to offer appropriate assistance. The women who participated in the research found it hard to comprehend why Christian women must suffer abuse from their husbands. Acolatse[36] further expounds on how pastors interpret domestic violence, marriage, and divorce from supposedly biblical and theological views without offering much room for psychodynamic considerations which is a health threat to especially women.

Cassiday-Shaw in her book *Family Abuse and the Bible: The Scriptural Perspective*[37] sought to make sense of the situation in the Christian context broadly. This book reveals that aside from verbal and physical abuse, spiritual

---

35. Phiri, "Domestic Violence in Christian Homes," 92–98.

36. Acolatse, "Christian Divorce Counselling in West Africa," 2–18.

37. Aimee K. Cassiday-Shaw, *Family Abuse and the Bible: The Scriptural Perspective* (New York: Routledge, 2012). Biblical verses are direct quotes from Cassiday-Shaw (2012), unless otherwise noted, all Scripture is taken from the New International Version of the Bible. All references to the Greek and Hebrew original translations are from Strong's Concordance with Hebrew and Greek-Lexicon. Aimee is a survivor of domestic abuse, a founder of a family abuse ministry and a social worker. She holds a Bachelors in Psychology and a Masters in Criminology.

abuse must also be emphasized as one that happens in many Christian homes but is usually neglected. The author does not leave out satanic and demonic influence on domestic violence. Esther Acolatse[38] from a West African perspective and other scholars have highlighted how domestic violence is a pandemic in Christian homes and how unfortunately the Bible and Christianity have been used to foster such grievous acts. The following subsections present various forms of abuse that occur in Christian homes.

3.1 Marital Relationship

Cassiday-Shaw[39] identifies two main Scriptures, Ephesians 5:22 and Colossians 3:18, as a basis for abuse in marriage. She explains "The apostle Paul wrote in Ephesians 5:22: Wives, submit to your husbands as to the Lord. Likewise, in Colossians 3:18 he wrote: Wives, submit to your husbands, as is fitting in the Lord." The misunderstanding, misinterpretation and misapplication of these verses impact heavily on domestic violence in Christian homes. Paul emphasizes that the wife-husband relationship is viewed from a wife-God relationship perspective. It suggests the wife is already submitting to the Lord and must likewise do the same to the husband. To submit basically means to yield to one's authority.

> Strong's Greek Concordance defines "submit," or *hupotasso*, as it is translated in both referenced verses as "to arrange under," "to subordinate,"[40] and further clarifies it as "a Greek military term meaning 'to arrange [troop divisions] in a military fashion under the command of a leader.' In non-military use, it was "a voluntary attitude of giving in, cooperating, assuming responsibility, and carrying a burden." This is different from the usage of the word "slave" or *doulos*, which is also translated as "servant."[41]

It is important to note that the wife according to the Bible is not required to be a slave to the husband in order to be a subordinate in terms of leadership. However, the wife's relationship with the Lord Jesus Christ becomes a model. On the other hand, in Ephesians 5:23, "For the husband is the head of the wife,

38. Acolatse, "Christian Divorce Counselling in West Africa."

39. Cassiday-Shaw, *Family Abuse and the Bible*, ch. 1.

40. John R. Kohlenberger, *The NIV Exhaustive Bible Concordance* (Grand Rapids: Zondervan, 2015), 1572.

41. Aimee K. Cassiday-Shaw, *Family Abuse and the Bible*, 4.

as Christ is the head of the church, his body, of which he is the Saviour," the husband's role as the head is also modelled after Christ whose role as a head is coupled with humility and responsibility. Cassiday-Shaw opines that women are compelled to stay in abusive relationships in a supposed obedience to Scripture that demands that they submit to their husbands. Another contention for women, especially from a feminist perspective, is the use of "obey" as synonymous to "submit" at marriage ceremonies to be problematic. At this point, it is clear that marriage must be modelled after the church and our personal relationship with Christ, and not a slave-master relation as may be conceptualized in some Christian traditions, especially in most African cultures.

There are other concepts, theologies and doctrines that trigger gendered abuse, such as the inferiority of the woman discourse, image of God and image of man debate and headship of the man misconceptions. Acolatse[42] has reiterated that Christianity has compounded the problem of Christian women in West Africa as they are compelled to stay in abusive relationships for socio-cultural and spiritual reasons. She shares the stories of two women who were counselled by their pastors to remain in abusive relationships, submit to the husband and continue to pray. The most worrying part in the narratives is that even a mother encouraged her daughter to stay and endure such inhumane experiences. Acolatse traces this to reformed theologies of John Calvin and Karl Barth who stand for marriage as a lifelong commitment that cannot be broken.

3.2 Parent-Child Relationship

Domestic abuse is not limited to the husband and wife but also includes other household members such as children. Abuse in Christian homes is also rooted in misconceptions and misinterpretations of biblical verses as identified by Cassiday-Shaw[43] as follows.

> Folly is bound up in the heart of a child,
> but the rod of discipline will drive it far away. (Prov 22:15)
>
> Do not withhold discipline from a child;
> if you punish them with the rod, they will not die. (Prov 23:13)
>
> A rod and a reprimand impart wisdom,
> but a child left undisciplined disgraces its mother. (Prov 29:15)

42. Acolatse, "Christian Divorce Counselling in West Africa."
43. Cassiday-Shaw, *Family Abuse and the Bible*, ch. 4.

> Discipline your children, for in that there is hope;
> do not be a willing party to their death. (Prov 19:18)[44]

The most popular one is:

> Whoever spares the rod hates their children,
> but the one who loves their children is careful to discipline them (Prov 13:24)

This is usually paraphrased as "Spare the rod, spoil the child." Cassiday-Shaw indicates how "tragic" it is to interpret this as parents beating the child as a way of discipline. When we read the word "rod" as it consistently appears in reference to discipline, we tend to assume that God is implying a literal rod that we beat children with. A thorough study on the original language of the biblical text tells us what God may have meant. "Rod" appears in the Bible many times. The original Hebrew word that has often been translated as "rod" is *shebet*. That same word has also been translated as "staff," "correction," "discipline," and most interestingly, as "tribe."

Cassiday-Shaw highlights how "beatest" has been used in place of punish in Proverbs 23:13 (KJV): "Withhold not correction from the child; for if thou beatest him with the rod, he shall not die." She argues "die" in the verse is referring to spiritual kind of death, hence, physical beating should not be the case. She opines indeed that God punishes and disciplines, however, the term "rod" should be envisaged as used in Psalm 23 where the rod and staff are also to bring comfort. Discipline must lead to bringing comfort and peace. It is relevant to note Paul's command to the church at Colossae, in Colossians 3:21: "Fathers, do not embitter your children, or they will become discouraged." I concur with Cassiday-Shaw that the above verses cannot justify domestic abuse. She further interprets the child's role of honouring and obeying parents which are not featured in this paper. The Bible cannot be used to reinforce violence against children. In fact, the father is to ensure that the child is not embittered; undoubtedly, domestic violence is one sure way of embittering children in the home. This must be flagged as a human right and criminal issue as spelt out in preliminary sections.

44. Cassiday-Shaw, *Family Abuse and the Bible*, ch. 4.

3.3 Spiritual Justification for Domestic Violence

Cassiday-Shaw[45] continues to assert that apart from general reasons like fear of leaving, the children, economic and emotional factors, Christian women stay in abusive marriages for spiritual reasons as confirmed by Acolatse[46] early on. Examples of Scriptures that form the basis of accepted abuse are Matthew 10:38, Matthew 16:24, Mark 8:34, Luke 9:23, and Luke 14:27. Luke 14:27 is where Jesus recorded that one "must carry his cross" to be a true disciple. In essence, abuse is seen as carrying one's cross and therefore endured. Cassiday-Shaw writes:

> Other Scriptures used to erroneously validate staying in an abusive relationship are ones that refer to the sufferings of being a Christian. Some of these are found in 1 Peter 3:13+. Peter writes: "But even if you should suffer for doing right, you are blessed" (1 Peter 3:14). What is right? He also writes: "It is better, if it is God's will, to suffer for doing good than for doing evil" (1 Peter 3:17). What is God's will? And finally, Peter writes: "Therefore, since Christ suffered in his body, arm yourselves also with the same attitude" (1 Peter 4:1). The attitude of suffering? Not exactly. Peter was referring to the attitude toward suffering, which the Lord adopted, and suffering because of ultimate submission to God's will. Suffering on the cross to be obedient to His father's will is the attitude that Peter refers to. Again, the theme is dying to self, and the inspired Word of God acknowledges that dying to self often requires some amount of suffering. God's will in and of itself does not mean we must suffer. Jesus demonstrated the ultimate act of submission and suffering through physical pain accompanied His submission. That obviously is no ordinary act. In fact, it is so unordinary that God reserved it for His Son. We, as Christians, do not have to suffer physical pain in order to be in submission to God's will. However, we must be willing to suffer if that is what God calls us to do.[47]

With the above indications and several other biblical texts on divorce, submission, and obedience, it is without doubt that domestic violence has a spiritual component which even compels victims to endure it as a way of serving the Lord. Abuse might then be perceived as a spiritual obligation.

45. Cassiday-Shaw, *Family Abuse and the Bible*, 55, 83.
46. Acolatse, "Christian Divorce Counselling in West Africa."
47. Cassiday-Shaw, *Family Abuse and the Bible*, 84.

This is confirmed by Phirias indicated above that 76 percent of the women who participated in her research experienced spiritual violence.[48] Acolatse likewise makes similar assertions by also highlighting the socio-cultural and psychological dimensions. The next section seeks to present a Christian response to domestic abuse.

4. A Christian Response to Domestic Violence

There are several ways to respond to domestic abuse, however the response to this pandemic is approached from a Christian dimension though not limited to Christian interventions. Many times, Christians have depended solely on the Bible as the only manual for life. The most disturbing part is when Scripture is misunderstood, misinterpreted and misapplied. It has been established that the Bible has been used to reinforce some sort of legitimacy for domestic violence. Contrarily, the Bible can still be proposed as an intervention. Since this vice is equally a legal (criminal), socio-cultural and engendered issue, appropriate responses in these contexts are also proposed. This is to say that Christians can respond to domestic violence in the following ways:

4.1 Biblical Response

The Bible remains the manual for Christian living. The following biblical principles are helpful to consider in conversations around domestic violence.

4.1.1 Love

The Christian has a responsibility to love unconditionally. Unconditional love would not make room for even a hint of violation. The subject of love in the Bible is so broad, touching every kind of relationship ranging from our relationship with God, spouses, children, subordinates, neighbours and even enemies. Simply put, Christianity is a religion or a way of life with love as a solid foundation. Hence, anything done outside of love is a sabotage to Christianity. Even discipline must be done in love. Domestic violence does not emulate love in any way so it must be abhorred.

4.1.2 Boldness and Responsibility

Cassiday-Shaw indicates even spiritual battles demand responsibility and accountability from the Christian. Although the Bible says God will fight for

48. Phiri, "Domestic Violence in Christian Homes," 94.

us, we have a part to play. For instance, we are expected to be strong and not timid in difficulties.[49] This means that we must stand tall and confront and address the issue rightfully. It is true that the devil fights us in all aspects of life including our marriages. It is needful for us to pray. God intervenes in several ways: our spouses may change through prayers and other interventions like counselling and mentoring.

On the other hand, it is God's will to deliver us from evil. I am not suggesting divorce as a quick fix for domestic abuse but in situations when other interventions have failed, the victims, especially women, must not accept abuse as a cross they must carry. As aforementioned, Acolatse highlights how the reformed theologies of John Calvin and Karl Barth about marriage and divorce have influenced West African Christian perspectives on divorce. To these reformers, marriage is for life and therefore divorce is not an option. Their theologies on the inferiority of the woman as against that of the man even further silences the woman who then succumbs to abuse as submission to authority. Phiri's findings affirm Cassiday-Shaw's emphasis on spiritual abuse as experienced by women who in the name of obedience to Scriptures remain in abusive relationships and environments. Keep in mind there may be health, emotional and psychological implications, it could even be lethal in severe cases. It is our responsibility to keep safe as Christians so lingering in constant abuse is not the best option either.

4.1.3 Repentance and Forgiveness

As Christians, we do not give up easily; when there is a problem and we commit it to God, we trust that he will come through. One of the ways is through repentance and forgiveness. The Christian faith is a call to repentance. This runs through the Old and New Testaments. From the Gospels, we see John the Baptist as the forerunner of the Messiah preaching repentance and baptism. Jesus Christ also preached repentance and commissioned us to preach the same.

It may be the desire of most stakeholders in domestic violence cases to salvage the relationship and at the same time ensure safety and security of victims. Even though to achieve both objectives are not usually a simple process, we must remember that God is at work in our lives. The Holy Spirit convicts us of sin and helps us to come to a place of total restoration if we let him. Cassiday-Shaw[50] proposes the need for both the abused and abuser to

49. As in 2 Timothy 1:7 which reads "the Spirit God gave us does not make us timid, but gives us power, love and self-discipline."

50. Cassiday-Shaw, *Family Abuse and the Bible*, 116.

repent. The need for the abuser to repent from abuse is key. However, even the abused need to repent from wrongfully accepting the situation perhaps due to some spiritual reason, and/or bitterness and unforgiveness must as well be dealt with if there is room for the relationship to be restored.

4.2 The Church's Response to Domestic Violence

It is important to note that the church as an institution has in many ways compounded the domestic abuse pandemic. Many have sought to protect the image of the church so they deny or hide instances of domestic abuse which may even be happening in the home of a church leader. As indicated earlier, the Bible has been used to justify various forms of abuse of household members.[51] In Africa, there is a double cause as culture reinforces biblical misinterpretations of Scripture to perpetuate domestic violence. The church has a moral responsibility as well as spiritual responsibility towards her members. It seems the focus has been only on the later. Perhaps, churches must review their policies, regulations and doctrines on sin and discipline. Should a church member be caught in fornication or adultery, there would be no disagreement on publicly disciplining the accused or demotion from leadership roles. It seems that while the church does not tolerate fornication or adultery, it tolerates abuse of people, especially where one person has been violated. Isn't this a double standard?

The church has a responsibility to provide support for domestic violence victims especially during a pandemic era where there are lockdowns and lots of people are working from home. Since the family stays a lot more together than usual, each family gets to experience family norms and values both positively and negatively. A happy family with a healthy environment will only enjoy more quality and joyous moments together while in households with domestic violence, it will only increase.

Churches must put programs in place where they can encourage victims to seek for help. Arrangements could be made to move the victim out of that situation, perhaps temporarily; if the victim is the mother for instance, arrangements should be made to support the children as well. I have been a minister for over two decades with first-hand information about domestic abuse in many Christian homes including that of pastors and church leaders.

51. Cassiday-Shaw, *Family Abuse and the Bible*; Acolatse, "Christian Divorce Counselling in West Africa"; Rosemary Isaacs, "Responding to Domestic Violence Biblical Reflections," *Domestic Violence and the Church* 52 (2019): 14–20.

A lot of wives who may have run to the pastor or the pastor's wife for refuge, may only get scolded for insubordination and forced back to endure more. This is a wake-up call for theological seminaries and churches to include domestic violence in their courses, trainings, and policies. Pastors and church leaders need holistic training on domestic violence from the biblical, legal, criminal, psychological and health perspectives.

It is important to take victim's reports in the first instance as serious, though it might seem very shocking. Many people who would report such cases might have endured for a long time or believed that they are to be blamed. It would take a lot of courage to voice this. Serious attention must be given to any hint of violence. Churches must seek professional interventions for victims if possible, and for perpetuators if they are willing.

The old adage "prevention is better than cure" must not be taken lightly. Premarital counselling is a norm in most African churches but not post-wedding counselling. When couples are preparing for marriage, they are excited and listen to whatever they are told. For many of the practical issues we deal with in the home we make no reference to our premarital counselling notes – that is if we even have some. This is to say that the church must look beyond and put in place post-wedding counselling and support for couples. Mentor couples could be assigned to newlyweds; regular marriage seminars and retreats could also be incorporated into the church's annual programs. Sound biblical hermeneutics must be encouraged rather than cultural bias teachings on authority and submission of wives and children.

If all interventions fail and the abuser is not willing to take responsibility, and/or both the victim and abuser are not willing for a fresh start, it is imperative that churches must not force the abused to remain in such a situation. In such cases Cassiday-Shaw, proposes approaching it from the sovereign will and permissive will of God dimensions. It is God's sovereign will that marriages remain intact and not be divorced, however if the situation becomes unsafe and the parties are unwilling to reconcile, then caution must be taken. The abused must not remain in an abusive relationship. Likewise other household members must not be forced to remain in abusive environments.

4.3 A Christian's Legal Response to Domestic Violence

Christians are expected to be law-abiding citizens. However, the most troubling part is godlessness, unethical and immoral considerations in our laws. As

Christians, we exercise biblical discretion in abiding to civil laws.[52] There are certain civil laws that are in contention with Christian belief systems. The issue of gender and homosexuality for instance is one of the recent unavoidable discourses. The argument here is that the law is meant to protect all citizens. If our constitutions, acts, and ramifications criminalize domestic abuse, and biblically, domestic abuse is a sin, then it automatically falls within those laws we as Christians need to uphold to maintain spiritual and moral sanctity in our households. This is to say victims of abuse must not be scared to make use of the law in such cases. In Ghana for instance, there is a rapid response number to report domestic abuse. There are several departments and legislation for domestic violence in different African countries. Seeking legal intervention for domestic abuse is not non-Christian as may be preached by some pastors.

4.4 A Socio-Cultural Response to Domestic Violence

It is assertively established above that domestic violence is a cultural issue with patriarchal orientations in the African socio-cultural context as a major causal factor. To this end, culture can at the same time be still proposed as an intervention. Culture is dynamic, we are now seeing women occupy major roles like presidents of nations and organizations, vice presidents, chief justices, ministers of states, members of parliament, pastors, chief executive officers, managers, and many other senior positions in society. Most cultures perceive women as incapable and weak, so must depend on the husband for livelihood while assuming the typical roles of wifehood and motherhood. Although patriarchal tendencies remain a drawback that even women in the positions mentioned above have to contend with, it is obvious that women are capable and not weak. As women gain financial independence and are allowed to contribute to the home and society, it boosts acceptance and responsibility which would also reduce patriarchal expectations from the husband. They shoulder the burdens, and the woman indeed becomes a helper as intended to be in this aspect among many other areas.

To the men who are perpetuators, please note that culture is dynamic, and a lot of things are changing, our mode of dressing has changed a lot. A lot of men have accepted new ways of doing things in society, they are quick to adopt to the use of mobile phones, new haircuts, and other trends. How about

52. David W. Norris, The Christian and the Civil Law 1, *Bible League Trust*, https://www.bibleleaguetrust.org/the-christian-and-the-civil-law-1/.

reconceptualizing masculinity in terms that does not take their authority away but also honouring to their spouses and other members of their household.

What about the few men who often fall victim to domestic abuse by their powerful and disrespectful wives? Enduring an abusive relationship for fear of exposure and ridicule does not in any way show masculinity. Do not respond violently but seek for appropriate means for support and rescue.

In Africa, children are to be seen and not heard, consequently they find it difficult to voice out their experiences of direct or indirect violence. Research proves that children who observe violence are equally violated as this may have psychological and/or attitudinal effects on them. This is not limited to only biological children but all other members of the household including relatives in the house. Children must not be afraid to seek help. Talk to adults you trust or to church leaders if abuse occurs from parents or guardians. If you are abused sexually or bullied by other relatives in the house, you must open up to your parents about it. Children who themselves are abusers of parents and others, this is not right, you must be willing to accept professional help so that you will not grow into a severe abuser which could land you in prison.

Generally, our stakeholders in our traditional settings like kings, queens, queen mothers and other traditional rulers must consider domestic violence among the social and traditional vices that are abhorred. Perhaps we must reconsider reflections on what is culturally wrong or right. For instance, someone caught stealing a goat could be punished or fined or in severe cases banished, why not domestic violence? Traditionally, the African is afraid of breaking a taboo. How about if we began to consider domestic abuse as a taboo? Some communities abhor sexual abuse, this could be taken further to include all forms of abuse.

4.5 An African Christian Woman's Response to Domestic Violence

As an African Christian woman who has been in pastoral ministry for over two decades with first-hand information on domestic abuse in Christian homes, this is how to respond to this pandemic called domestic violence. First of all, it is vital to make the following assertions:

- There are occurrences of domestic violence in many African Christian homes.
- The majority of Christian women in Africa experience some form of domestic violence hence domestic violence is engendered.

- Although there are occurrences of all forms of violence, spiritual violence is prevalent in many Christian homes especially in the household of pastors and church leaders. The untold stories and emotional torture of many pastors' wives remain hidden.
- Misinterpretations of scriptural verses on marriage, submission, honour, obedience, and divorce are the foundations of domestic abuse in Christian homes.
- Patriarchal orientations in most African cultures and societal structures justify domestic abuse as normal.
- Most women and children accept and remain in abusive relationships and/or environment.
- Many pastors have not been helpful in addressing domestic abuse cases due to their over-emphasis on spirituality and lack of professional counselling skills.
- Churches do not have structures in place to support domestic abuse victims.

In responding to the issues, these recommendations should be considered:

- Sound biblical sermons should be often preached in our churches.
- Engage Christian professionals for marriage workshops and seminars.
- Churches should not limit marriage counselling to pre-marital counselling, but post-wedding counselling must also take place. Couple mentors can be assigned to newlyweds.
- Churches should have a support system for domestic abuse victims.
- That women work towards gaining some sort of financial independence if possible (over dependence on husband may trigger abuse).
- That parents treat their children and other household members with respect, dignity, humility, and love.
- That abusers repent and make the efforts to seek help for change.
- That victims forgive and not wallow in bitterness (even if the relationship could not be salvaged).
- That victims, especially women, should seek support.
- Victims must make use of legal interventions.
- Both victims and perpetuators should seek both spiritual and professional support.
- We must endeavour to pray to God, depend on his guidance and allow the Holy Spirit to bring convictions, repentance, and healing.

- Above all we must let Christ reign in our homes as we follow Jesus's servant-leadership model.

5. Conclusion

The chapter sought to present a Christian response to domestic violence in Africa. In the wake of the COVID-19 pandemic, perhaps we must flag that, COVID-19 is not the only pandemic at the moment. Domestic violence has been a lingering global disease which is also triggered by the COVID-19. The chapter established that domestic violence is engendered; it is not limited to only intimate partners but extends to other members of the family. Domestic abuse occurs in various forms namely: physical, verbal, economical, emotional, psychological, and spiritual. It is relevant to highlight that it could as well be lethal. African cultural values and norms mostly enshrined in patriarchy validate domestic abuse as normal, compelling especially women and children to suffer in silence. A significant focus has been on how Christians have used the Bible to reinforce domestic abuse due to misinterpretations, misconceptions, and misapplication of biblical texts on marriage, obedience, discipline, submission, and authority. Since domestic violence is a public and societal, legal, criminal, and human rights issue, victims must make use of legal and societal interventions that are in place. Churches must move beyond spiritualizing domestic violence to put proper interventions in place to support victims. African women must stand up and not accept abuse as a norm. As Christians, we must allow the unconditional love of God to rule in our hearts and homes while we follow Jesus's model of servant-leadership. If these recommendations are considered closely, there is the possibility to reduce domestic violence in our homes.

Bibliography

Acolatse, Esther E. "Christian Divorce Counselling in West Africa: Seeking Wholeness Through Reformed Theology and Jungian Dreamwork." *Journal of Pastoral Theology* 21 no. 1 (2011): 1–18. https://doi.org/10.1179/jpt.2011.21.1.002.

Aizer, Anna. "The Gender Wage Gap and Domestic Violence." *The American Economic Review* 100 no. 4 (2010): 1847–59. http://www.jstor.org/stable/27871277.

Amenyedzi, Seyram. "We are Forgotten: The Plight of Persons with Disability in Youth Ministry." *Scriptura* 120 no. 1 (2021): 1–17. https://dx.doi.org/10.7833/120-1-1459.

———. "Equity and Access for Persons with Disability in Theological Education, Ghana." PhD Thesis, Department of Practical Theology and Missiology, Faculty of Theology, Stellenbosch University (2016).

———."The Lady Pastor: Reflections on Women in Ministry in Ghana." Paul's Theology on Men and Women Webinar, *South African Theological Seminary* (2019).

———. "Leadership Roles for Indigenous Ghanaian Women: The Case of Prof. Jane Naana Opoku Agyemang as Vice-Presidential Candidate for the National Democratic Congress (NDC)." *African Thought: A Journal of Afro-Centric Knowledge* 1 no. 1 (2021): 169–91.

Baffoe, Michael. "Stigma, Discrimination & Marginalization: Gateways to Oppression of Persons with Disabilities in Ghana, West Africa." *Journal of Educational and Social Research* 3 no. 1 (2013): 187–98.

Bettinger-Lopez, Caroline, and Alexandra Bro. "A Double Pandemic: Domestic Violence in the Age of COVID-19." *Domestic Violence Report* 25 no. 5 (2020): 85–86. https://www.cfr.org/in-brief/double-pandemic-domestic-violence-age-COVID-19; https://www.civicresearchinstitute.com/online/article_abstract.php?pid=18&iid=1444&aid=9391.

Boonzaier, Floretta, and Taryn van Niekerk. "Psychology and Domestic Violence against Women." In *The Routledge International Handbook of Domestic Violence and Abuse*. Edited by John Devaney, Caroline Bradbury-Jones, Rebecca J. Macy, Carolina Øverlien and Stephanie Holt, 27–39. New York: Routledge, 2021.

Bunston, Wendy. "The Impact of Domestic Violence and Abuse on Infant Mental Health." In *The Routledge International Handbook of Domestic Violence and Abuse*. Edited by John Devaney, Caroline Bradbury-Jones, Rebecca J. Macy, Carolina Øverlien and Stephanie Holt, 113–27. New York: Routledge, 2021.

Cassiday-Shaw, Aimee K. *Family Abuse and the Bible: The Scriptural Perspective*. New York: Routledge, 2012.

Chataika, Tsitsi. "Cultural and Religious Explanations of Disability and Promoting Inclusive Communities in South Africa in Theology and Disability: Changing the Conversations in Disability." Pages 117–128 in *Searching for Dignity: Conversations on Human Dignity, Theology and Disability*. Edited by Julie Claassens, Leslie Swartz and Len Hansen. Stellenbosch: Sun Media, 2013.

Collins, Patricia Hill. "What's in a Name? Womanism, Black Feminism, and Beyond." *Black Scholar*, 26 no. 1 (1996). Published online in 2015. https://doi.org/10.1080/00064246.1996.11430765.

Douglas, Carol Anne. "Gender Violence in Africa: African Women's Response." *Off Our Backs: A Women's News Journal* 30 no. 3 (2000): 9–19. http://www.jstor.org/stable/pdf/20836570.pdf.

Fantuzzo, John W., and Wanda K. Mohr. "Prevalence and Effects of Child Exposure to Domestic Violence." *Future of Children* 9 no. 3 (1999): 21–32. https://doi.org/10.2307/1602779.

Freedman, Jane. "Domestic Violence through a Human Rights Lens." In *The Routledge International Handbook of Domestic Violence and Abuse*. Edited by John Devaney, Caroline Bradbury-Jones, Rebecca J. Macy, Carolina Øverlien and Stephanie Holt, 68–78. New York: Routledge, 2021.

Groves, Betsy McAlister. "Mental Health Services for Children who Witness Domestic Violence." *Future of Children* 9 no. 3 (1999): 122–32. https://doi.org/10.2307/1602786.

Herring, Jonathan. "The Mystery of Domestic Abuse." *National Law School of India Review* 30 no. 1 (2018): 37–50.

Holt, Amanda. "Adolescent-to-Parent Abuse as a Form of 'Domestic Violence': A Conceptual Review." *Trauma, Violence, and Abuse* 17 no. 5 (2016): 490–99. https://doi.org/10.1177/1524838015584372.

Hudson-Weems, Clenora. *Africana Womanism: Reclaiming Ourselves*. London: Routledge, 2019. https://doi.org/10.4324/9780429287374.

Isaacs, Rosemary. "Responding to Domestic Violence Biblical Reflections." *Domestic Violence and the Church* 52 (2019): 14–20.

Jakobsen, Hilde. "What's Gendered about Gender-Based Violence? An Empirically Grounded Theoretical Exploration from Tanzania." *Gender and Society* 28 no. 4 (2014): 537–61. https://doi.org/10.1177/0891243214532311.

Kapilashrami, Anuj. "Tackling Domestic Violence and Abuse using a Rights-Oriented Public Health Lens." In *The Routledge International Handbook of Domestic Violence and Abuse*. Edited by John Devaney, Caroline Bradbury-Jones, Rebecca J. Macy, Carolina Øverlien and Stephanie Holt, 79–95. New York: Routledge, 2021.

Kasturirangan, Aarati, Sandhya Krishnan, and Stephanie Riger. "The Impact of Culture and Minority Status on Women's Experience of Domestic Violence." *Trauma, Violence, & Abuse* 5 no. 4 (2004): 318–32. https://doi.org/10.1177/1524838004269487.

Kertesz, Margaret, Larissa Fogden and Cathy Humphreys. "Domestic Violence and the Impact on Children." In *The Routledge International Handbook of Domestic Violence and Abuse*. Edited by John Devaney, Caroline Bradbury-Jones, Rebecca J. Macy, Carolina Øverlien and Stephanie Holt, 128–40. New York: Routledge, 2021.

Kigame, Reuben. "Cultural Barriers to the Disabled People's Participating in Church Life." Pages 121–37 in *Disability, Society and Theology: Voices from Africa*. Edited by Samuel Kabue, Esther Mombo, Joseph Galgalo and C. B. Peter. Limuru: Zapf Chancery, 2011.

Kohlenberger, John R. *The NIV Exhaustive Bible Concordance*. Grand Rapids: Zondervan, 2015.

Lintvelt, Mia. "Disability and Gender: Twofold Discrimination." Pages 285–305 in *Living with Dignity: African Perspectives on Gender Equality*. Edited by Elna Mouton, Gertrude Kapuma, Len Hansen and Thomas Togon. Stellenbosch: EFSA (2015).

Marshall, Katherine. “Religious Responses to Domestic Abuse During the COVID-19 Pandemic.” https://berkleycenter.georgetown.edu/posts/religious-responses-to-domestic-abuse-during-the-COVID-19-pandemic.

Naisiko, Tabitha. “The Paradox of Love and Violence against Women in Families: A Loophole in the Agents of Socialization?” *East African Journal of Traditions, Culture and Religion* 5 no. 2 (2022): 12–23. https://doi.org/10.37284/eajtcr.5.2.611.

Noble-Carr, Debbie, Tim Moore and Morag McArthur. “Children’s Experiences and Needs in Relation to Domestic and Family Violence: Findings from a Meta-Synthesis.” *Child & Family Social Work* (2019). Doi: 10.1111/cfs.12645.

Norris, David W. “The Christian and the Civil Law 1.” *Bible League Trust*. https://www.bibleleaguetrust.org/the-christian-and-the-civil-law-1/.

Phiri, Isabel Apawo. “Domestic Violence in Christian Homes: A Durban Case Study.” *Journal for the Study of Religion* 14 no. 2 (2001): 85–101.

Shiriko, Joseph. “Disability: Social Challenges and Family Responses.” Pages 168–96 in *Disability, Society and Theology: Voices from Africa*. Edited by Samuel Kabue, Esther Mombo, Joseph Galgalo and C.B . Peter. Limuru: Zapf Chancery (2011).

Sikweyiya, Yandisa, et al. “Patriarchy and Gender-Inequitable Attitudes as Drivers of Intimate Partner Violence against Women in the Central Region of Ghana.” *BMC Public Health* 20 no. 1 (2020): 1–11. https://doi.org/10.1186/s12889-020-08825-z.

Sinyo, Joseph. “Gender and Disability Challenges Within the Church.” In *Disability, Society and Theology: Voices from Africa*, edited by Samuel Kabue, Esther Mombo, Joseph Galgalo and C.B . Peter, 209–219. Limuru: Zapf Chancery (2011).

Takyi, Enock. “Barriers to Mainstream Participation of Persons with Disabilities: A Qualitative Study of Persons with Physical Disabilities in Techiman, Ghana.” Masters Thesis, Department of Psychology, Norwegian University of Science and Technology (2013).

United Nations. “COVID-19 Response: What is Domestic Violence?” https://www.un.org/en/coronavirus/what-is-domestic-abuse (n.d.).

———. “Policy Brief: The Impact of COVID-19 on Women” (2020). https://www.un.org/sites/un2.un.org/files/2020/04/policy_brief_on_covid_impact_on_women_9_apr_2020_updated.pdf.

Usdin, Shereen, Nicola Christofides, Lebo Malepe and Aadielah Maker. “The Value of Advocacy in Promoting Social Change: Implementing the New Domestic Violence Act in South Africa.” *Reproductive Health Matters* 8 no. 16 (2000): 55–65. http://www.jstor.org/stable/3775271.

VAWnet. “Impact of Domestic Violence on Health.” https://vawnet.org/sc/impact-domestic-violence-health.

Walby, Sylvia, et al. “Different Forms of Violence.” Pages 57–102 in *The Concept and Measurement of Violence*, 1st ed., edited by Sylvia Walby et al. Bristol University Press, 2017. http://www.jstor.org/stable/j.ctv47w5j0.9.

11

Christianity and the African Traditional Gods

Joseph Byamukama

PhD candidate in New Testament Studies, Ridley College, Australia, and RZIM Speaker

Abstract

Questions of young Africans move beyond the classical question of God's existence to a consideration of the relationship of the God revealed in Christ compared to African traditional gods. While the Christian faith proclaims the one God who self-identifies as the God of Abraham and self-manifests in the incarnate Jesus of Nazareth, Christ's relationship with the African gods is a poignant, pressing, and personal question to several people. Many pan-Africanists see the Christian god as white and foreign. This chapter compares the doctrine of God in the Bible with the concept of God in African Traditional Religions (ATRs). This chapter notes that the relational nearness of God in the Old Testament, the monotheistic concept of God in the Bible and the revelation of God in Jesus of Nazareth, distinguish the Judeo-Christian worldview from the ATRs. The contribution of this chapter is that God is therefore not foreign as in the emerging naturalistic worldviews but he is also close, in a way that protects Africans from the fearful God-concept in some polytheistic strands of ATRs.

Keywords: God, Supreme Being, Creator, Relational, Gods, African, Traditional, Christianity

1. Introduction

"What does the coming of Christ mean for traditional African gods?"

A student in his early twenties posed this question during a 2016 apologetics workshop. I had discussed the uniqueness of Christ and Christianity, among other religions. But this student's question bulldozed its way to the practical consequence of Christianity's proclamation of the one God who self-identifies as the God of Abraham and self-manifests in the incarnate Jesus of Nazareth. Christ's relationship with the African gods is a poignant, pressing, and personal question to several people. Many a pan-Africanist sees the Christian's God as white and foreign. For some, embracing Christianity seems to intrinsically entail a rejection of our fathers' gods and, to an extent, African-ness. Thus, the clamour to return to nativity concerns more than traditional herbalists and folklore. It regards a return to the gods of the land, the guardians of our ancestral clans. And those who advocate this anticipate either a total rejection or redefinition of Christianity. But one must wonder about the nature of gods in the African Traditional Religions (ATR) and their place in our ancestors' praxis. How do the exclusive claims of Christianity concerning YHWH relate to the traditional understanding of gods and their role in the African's life? And can one embrace Jesus as their only Saviour and God without forsaking their African-ness or suffering from spiritual schizophrenia? These and many more questions are the subject of this chapter.

2. Concept of God in Christianity and ATR

2.1 A Strangely Familiar God

The Hebrew Scriptures present a strangely familiar God, a transcendent God who is "not far from any one of us" (Acts 17:27). Jacob captures this well when he awakes from his theophanic dream, exclaiming: "surely the LORD is in this place, and I was not aware of it" (Gen 28:16). Jacob dreams of a ladder connecting earth to heaven, with God standing atop (vv. 12–15). But that the God of his fathers – Abraham and Isaac – exists beyond Canaanite borders surprises Jacob. The Lord was already wherever Jacob went, yet Jacob knew it not. Indeed, God's transcendence means that no single culture can domesticate him – not even the Jews. And as Bolaji Idowu notes, "God cannot be localized or pinned down to any particular race or culture."[1] The Lord has always been forever present in all places, and he is familiar to all people groups. But the Greek altar "[t]o an unknown god" (Acts 17:23) reminds us that this familiar

1. Bolaji Idowu, "God or Idol?," *The Journal of Religious Thought* 27 no. 3 (1970): 13–28.

and omnipresent God tends to also be unknown or hidden to the peoples. Though all cultures know his existence, there exists an unfamiliarity between him and the peoples of every gentile nation – a sort of strangeness. He is in every place, yet his people do not know. As John the evangelist writes, "he was in the world, and the world was made through him, yet the world did not know him" (John 1:10). Thus, the Bible presents a strangely familiar God to all peoples.

This chapter will discuss Christianity and the African concept of the gods. First, I will discuss God's transcendent presence in the traditional African consciousness. I will note that the knowledge of the supreme being as creator is pervasive in African cultures without respect to geographical borders, making God familiar to Africans. Then, I will talk about the transcendent nature of this supreme deity that removed him from the daily lives of many Africans, making him strange to many. Though Africans knew that the supreme God created the world, he remained relationally distant and unknown. Here, I will note the role of other divinities in traditional African life. Finally, I will tackle God's relational self-revelation in Scripture and ultimately in Jesus, which the Christian proclamation embodies. Under this, I will discuss God's confrontation with the nations' gods – African ones included. I will also note how Jesus bridges the relational gap between the supreme deity and humans, the bridging that ultimately removes the need for intermediary divinities in African cultures.

2.2 Concepts of God(s) in Africa

Even before missionaries, God has always been in Africa, for no one can bring anywhere the everywhere-God. We noted how Jacob learned that God is not geographically bound like we are. Paul's proclamation in Athens assumed that God was present there in some revelatory sense before Paul's arrival (Acts 17:23–31). Before Athens and while speaking among the idolatrous people of Iconium, the apostle Paul insisted that in every place, God "has not left himself without testimony" (Acts 14:17). If it is true that God is the creator of heaven and earth (Acts 17:24) who leaves himself a witness in every culture, it must follow that he transcends the geographical boundaries and timelines of all earth-dwellers. Presuming this to be the case, we would expect some concept of the supreme creator in Africa before the arrival of missionaries.

John Mbiti's careful survey of "over two hundred seventy different peoples (or tribes)"[2] records the pervasive knowledge of God's existence reflected in African folklore, poems, songs, proverbs, and mythologies. For example, to the Lotuko of Sudan, Ajok is traditionally the supreme God and creator of the world.[3] The supreme God is Akongo to the Ngombe of DRC, Ruhanga in Ankole and Katonda to the Baganda of Uganda. He is Chuku to the Igbo and Chido to the Jukun of Nigeria. The Khoisan and Khoikhoi of South Africa knew him,[4] and so did the Akamba in Kenya.[5] And after studying the Pygmies, Wilhelm Schmidt was "struck by one very remarkable fact above all others. That is, the clear acknowledgment and worship of the supreme being. He is everywhere the creator and sovereign Lord of the whole world."[6] We may still prove this point by how the God that Christianity proclaims is not called by new names in many cultures – because he is not new here.[7] Africans have known and named God, who has always been in their spiritual consciousness. The examples given should show that knowledge of the existence of the supreme being as creator of all things is ubiquitous here. In Africa, belief in God's presence is a given, and faith in the supreme being is not foreign. As P. H. Coetzee and A. P. J. Roux state, "African metaphysics is holistic in nature" and "God, the creator, and source of all vital forces is at the apex."[8]

Though named differently, Africans know God as the creator of everything who transcends them all, geographical and ethnic boundaries included. We saw that Schmidt raised this point in his study of the Pygmies. Jacob K. Olupona too speaks of how the Yoruba call God *òrìṣà agbaye*, doubly meaning "universal god" and "god of the universe."[9] Joyce Mlenga also notes that the Ngonde

2. John S. Mbiti, *Concepts of God in Africa* (Southampton: The Camelot Press Ltd, 1970), xiii.

3. Patricia Ann Lynch, *African Mythology A-Z* (New York: Chelsea House Publishers, 2010), 6.

4. David Chidester et al., *African Traditional Religion in South Africa* (Connecticut: Greenwood Press, 1997), 68–69.

5. Mbiti, *Concepts of God in Africa*, 45.

6. Wilhelm Schmidt, *The Origin and Growth of Religion*, trans. H. J. Rose (London: Methuen & Co Ltd, 1935), 191.

7. Bolaji Idowu, "God" in *Biblical Revelation and African Beliefs*, ed. Kwesi A. Dickson and Paul Ellingworth (London: Lutterworth Press, 1969), 24, though careful about building theology on names and their etymologies nevertheless argues that "God is real to Africans and that is why Africans call Him by names which are descriptive both of His nature and of His attributes."

8. P. H. Coetzee and A. P. J. Roux, *The African Philosophy Reader* (London: Routledge, 2003), 196.

9. Jacob K. Olupona, *African Religions: A Very Short Introduction* (New York: Oxford University Press, 2014), 21.

conceive the supreme being "as the creator or maker of all things" and as one who "owns and knows everything, both visible and invisible."[10] Africans have known that the whole universe is God's theatre and artwork. But while it is easier to see how Africans know the supreme deity as creator, one wonders whether scholars assign attributes like omnipresence and omniscience to the supreme deity anachronistically. Given the fading memory of the pre-Islam/Christian African oral tradition, it is hard to know how far this extends. But Mbiti surveys the supreme God's non-moral attributes in African cultures: eternality, omnipotence, omniscience, omnipresence, transcendence, infinity, self-existence, and immutability. He finds these qualities in many African cultures.[11]

Mbiti also muses over moral attributes such as mercy, love, goodness, righteousness, and holiness, which he finds common among many African tribes, with varying significance. Speaking of God's goodness, Mbiti notes that in some African tribes, God is good as far as he is removed from human affairs. Mbiti does not discuss the extent to which the belief in God's immanence or nearness is pervasive in Africa. But in cultures where God is believed to be near, his closeness tends to be perceived as dangerous.[12] If this is so, it seems logical, and perhaps a matter of survival, for these African cultures to keep the supreme deity at a distance. Indeed, Molefi Kete Asante and Ama Mazama argue that the African supreme being is traditionally removed from human affairs.[13] Such a god is deistic: an uninvolved creator in his works. Jacob K. Olupona states the same, arguing that a "remote or absent creator god is a common trope in African creation stories."[14] Peter R. McKenzie too notes that the spiritual beliefs of the Ovimbundu of Angola centre "around the mythical supreme being Suku," who they consider "too remote for everyday worship

---

10. Joyce Mlenga, *Dual Religiosity in Northern Malawi: Ngonde Christians and African Traditional Religion* (Project MUSE: Mzuni Press, 2016), 15.

11. Mbiti, *Concepts of God in Africa*, 19, discusses the Bacongo (people of Congo) who speak of God as one who "is made by no other, no one beyond him is." The Bambuti see God as "the First, who had always been in existence and would never die." God's self-existence and aseity exists among the Banyarwanda, and the Zulu who say that God is "He who is of himself." Mbiti cites the Pygmy hymn which declares: "In the beginning was God, today is God, tomorrow will be God. Who can make an image of God? He has no body . . ." The Langi, Lugbara, Bambuti, speak of the invisibility of God, the Maasai and Ngombe of his unknowability.

12. Mbiti, *Concepts of God in Africa*, 16–17.

13. Molefi Kete Asante and Ama Mazama, *Encyclopaedia of African Religion* (California: Sage Publications Inc, 2009), 136, 238, 284, 287, 422, 445, 447, 585.

14. Olupona, *African Religions*, 20.

and even for mention in conversation."[15] Mbiti helpfully notes many African stories narrate God's initial relational closeness to the people he made, lost when humans sinned against God.[16]

Whatever the cause of the separation, the supreme being's absence from daily human affairs created a religious and relational vacuum in the traditional African spiritual consciousness, a gap then occupied by lesser divinities. There seem to be two intermediate categories of deities: deified humans and personified natural phenomena.[17] Olupona argues that the "African pantheons of gods, goddesses, spirits and other nonhuman beings are varied in number and complex in character."[18] The Baganda have Lubaale – lesser gods who are revered men and guardians over the kingdom. Such guardians include Mukasa, the god of the seas and lakes; Kibuka and Nnende, the gods of war; Musoke, the god of weather and space; and Walumbe, the god of death. Besides these, the Baganda have Misambwa, the spirits for rivers, mountains, forests, and other natural phenomena. The Banyankore have emandwa, "the spirits of the deified Bacwezi," and emizimu, which are the spirits of relatives.[19] The Egyptian Pharaoh "ruled the land as a god, as the Son of Re, or as the Horus, or as the incorporation of the deities of Upper and Lower Egypt."[20] Robert K. Ritner also notes that the Egyptian Pyramid Texts "provide the precedents for other aspects of human divinization" where the "deceased king is equated not only with Osiris but with a wide range of traditional deities."[21] Mbiti himself discusses the existence of earth goddesses in the legends of the Lozi, Madi, Nkum, and Konjo, and "a pantheon of divinities" among the Ashanti, Bakene, Banyoro, Barundi, Basoga, and Dinka, among others. Perhaps fascinating is

15. Peter R. McKenzie, "John Mbiti's Work on African Religion as Reflected in the Perceptions of Students in a British University," in *Religious Plurality in Africa: Essays in Honour of John S. Mbiti* edited by Jacob K. Olupona and Sulayman S. Nyang, 319–40 (New York: Walter de Gruyter & Co., 1993), 328.

16. Mbiti, *Concepts of God in Africa*, 171–77.

17. D. A. Hughes, "Polytheism," in *New Dictionary of Theology: Historical and Systematic*, ed. Martin Davie et al., (London; Downers Grove: Inter-Varsity Press; InterVarsity Press, 2016), 687.

18. Jacob K. Olupona, *African Religions*, 19.

19. Yoramu K. Bamunoba, *The Cult of Spirits in Ankole* (Independently Published). Kindle Edition.

20. James B. Prichard, *Ancient Near Eastern Texts Relating to the Old Testament* (New Jersey: Princeton University Press, 1969), 431.

21. Robert K. Ritner, "Divinization and Empowerment of the Dead" in *The Book of the Dead: Becoming God in Ancient Egypt*, edited by Foy Scalf (Illinois: The Oriental Institute of the University of Chicago, 2018), 110.

how the Yorubas alone have "over one thousand seven hundred divinities,"[22] also called "*orisa*, meaning 'legion.'"[23]

The existence of such mediatory divinities complicates the argument for strict monotheism. For example, Benno van den Toren notes how "the line of separation between what is divine and what is not is not clear-cut."[24] For Toren, the many intermediary beings between the supreme God and humanity "are more or less close to the creator, more or less divine and more or less sacred."[25] Ritner also mentions how "the boundaries of divinity are notoriously fluid in ancient Egypt." Granted, these gods existed "under" the supreme being as his manifestations, servants, or agents concerned with the day-to-day governance of the world. But the fact that there is no natural distinction between these intermediary divinities and the supreme being makes Toren wonder whether the Mbiti's[26] and Bolaji's[27] argument for monotheism – modified as it may be – holds.

Moreover, these intermediary divinities are the direct recipients of ordinary people's sacrifices and prayers, making them more prominent in the African consciousness. In "the urgent business of daily living,"[28] the supreme deity is suppressed and subordinated to intermediary gods. It seems that where it most matters, in the daily lives of Africans, the supreme being is not supreme, remaining "unknown" in this regard, making it hard to hold to strict monotheism, if at all.

Yet Asante and Mazama, for their part, argue that "the question of monotheism or polytheism is not an African question" but a "profoundly Western" one.[29] They define polytheism as "several super-deities responsible for

22. Ritner, "Divinization," 114.

23. James Kombo, "The Trinity in Africa," *Journal of Reformed Theology* 3 (2009): 125–43.

24. Benno van den Toren, "The Christian God and Human Authority: A Theological Exploration with Reference to Africa's Principal Worldviews," in *Africa Journal of Evangelical Theology* 23 no. 2 (2004): 169.

25. van den Toren, "The Christian God and Human Authority," 169.

26. Mbiti, *Concepts of God in Africa*, 29, argues that "every African people recognize one God" before insisting that the other divinities are "mainly the personification of God's activities" or "deified national heroes."

27. Bolaji Idowu, "God," 18, believes that the "Supreme Being of the primitive culture is a genuinely monotheistic Deity, described as Father, Creator, eternal, completely beneficent, ethically holy, and creatively omnipotent."

28. A phrase Idowu uses in his critique of what he considered a culturally conditioned and classroom-defined missionary concept of God, a god who "cannot give spiritual satisfaction to man in the urgent business of daily living." See Idowu, "God or Idol?"

29. Molefi Kete Asante and Ama Mazama, *Encyclopaedia of African Religion* (California: Sage Publications Inc, 2009), xxiv.

human society" and argue that such a concept is absent in Africa. Asante and Mazama try to explain the existence of one supreme being and the "pantheon of divinities," saying that "the nature of the divinity is one, but the attributes of the one are found in the numerous manifestations of the one as the many."[30] What they don't do is deny that these divinities exist in their own right, whether under or as manifestations of the supreme deity. But if Africa traditionally had many gods or guardians, it does not immediately follow that Africans are not polytheistic. Polytheism is the idea that the one divine nature is shared by more than one being, other beings that may even exist under the supreme deity. Asante and Mazama's definition of the divine nature in African religious consciousness is precisely what polytheism is. In his excellent book *Great is the Lord*, Ron Highfield insists that polytheism prioritizes substance over person. For Highfield:

> The Greek religion distributed religious devotion among many gods. Like all ancient non-biblical religions, however, it assumed that the individual gods derive from and depend on a vast ocean of divinity. The gods are gods by virtue of their participation in this more fundamental nature, and this divine nature itself is not a person. Thus, deep within Greek religion lies the intuition that nature or substance has priority over person or freedom.[31]

Thus, Polytheism neither denies the existence of the supreme being nor asserts the natural equality between those beings and the creator but prioritizes divine nature than restricting divinity to particular persons. Many Ancient Near Eastern (ANE) and Greco-Roman cultures had the concept of the supreme being. Mary Beard et al. remind us that many Roman cults "proclaimed the superiority of one single supreme deity" such as Jupiter, Isis, or Mithras,[32] but the Roman empire remained polytheistic.[33] Zeus of the Greeks (Jupiter to the Romans) ruled supreme over all gods[34] and was "the preeminent personal god of the Greek residents of Thessaly" well before the times of Homer.[35] Prichard

30. Asante and Mazama, *Encyclopaedia of African Religion*, xxv.

31. Ron Highfield, *Great Is the Lord: The Theology for the Praise of God* (Grand Rapids: Eerdmans, 2008), 247.

32. Mary Beard, John North and Simon Price, *Religions of Rome*, Vol. 1 (Cambridge: Cambridge University Press, 1998), 286.

33. Beard et al., *Religions of Rome*, 212.

34. Chad Brand and Eric Mitchell, eds, *Holman Illustrated Bible Dictionary* (Nashville: B&H Publishing Group, 2015), 658.

35. "Zeus," in *Baker Encyclopaedia of the Bible* (Grand Rapids: Baker Book House, 1988), 2197.

shows how two Nineteenth Dynasty (1350–1:100 BC) manuscripts depicted Re as the Egyptian supreme god with many names, "one of which was hidden and was thus a source of supremacy."[36] Tablet Seven of the Akkadian Creation Epic displays Tutu as "supreme in the Assembly of the gods," adding that "no one among the gods is his equal." Just as in Africa, the existence of these supreme deities in various ancient cultures did not exclude other lesser gods, deified humans, or personified nature. It is thus not clear whether Asante and Mazama would ever conceive of a culture whose concept of the supreme deity fits their definition of polytheism. We cannot define polytheism as denying the nature of a supreme deity under whom other lesser divinities exist.

3. Judeo-Christianity in Confrontation with Polytheism

Judeo-Christianity was born in polytheistic cultural contexts. Biblical monotheism – the belief that only YHWH is God – is not held without knowing multiple deities among cultures around or even in Israel. The pantheon of divinities that African theologians and anthropologists find in African cultures prevailed in the ANE, the Roman Republic, and the Greek religious heritage. Philip Jones also argues that "ancient Mesopotamia knew a multiplicity of divine beings that fulfilled a wide variety of different roles."[37] YHWH insists on his exclusivity and utter otherness, always on the background of belief in other gods, whether conceived as rivals or intermediaries to the supreme being. The biblical authors do not entertain the idea of YHWH as the supreme deity under whom other deities exist. The God of Abraham asserted his supremacy over such gods whom he declared to be nothing.

But before discussing YHWH's contest against idols, we may recall that God is primarily known among Africans as the maker of heaven and earth. This understanding agrees with the biblical account (Gen 1:1; 2:4; Isa 37:16; 42:5; 45:8, 18; Neh 9:6; Ps 33:6). The Lord made the "great sea creatures" and every living creature that moves (Gen 1:21) and humanity too (1:26; 5:1, 2; 6:7; Deut 4:32; Isa 45:12; Mal 2:10; Eccl 12:1). YHWH alone made the ends of the earth (Isa 40:28) and everything there is (Rev 4:11), and he alone stretches out the heavens (Job 9:8–9). As such, God is the most high and supreme (Job 22:12; Gen 14:19, 20, 22; Num 24:16; Deut 32:8; 2 Sam 22:14; Ps 7:17; 47:2; 57:2; 82:6; 91:1; Dan 4:17). Before him, all nations are like "a drop in a bucket"

36. James B. Prichard, *Ancient Near Eastern Texts Relating to the Old Testament*, 12.

37. Philip Jones, "Divine and Non-Divine Kingship" in *A Companion to the Ancient Near East*, edited by Daniel C. Snell (Massachusetts: Blackwell Publishing Ltd, 2005), 330.

and "regarded as dust on the scales" (Isa 40:15). Indeed, "Before him all the nations are as nothing; they are regarded by him as worthless and less than nothing" (v. 17). The description of YHWH as both the creator and most high reminds us of the supreme being in African traditional religious conception, regarded as the maker of all there is. The Bible confirms the sensibilities of the African people about the creator's existence.

Yet, the designation of God as sole creator necessarily opens an ontological gap between him and everything he made. God has no equal and is incomparable (Isa 40:18, 25; 44:7). He alone is the first and the last, and there is no other god (Isa 44:6, 8). The Lord alone is "the true God; he is the living God, the eternal King" (Jer 10:10). In contrast, the nations' gods did not make the heavens, earth, or anything in them (Ps 96:5; Jer 10:11). Here, the assertion is that the title "God" only belongs to the creator of heaven and earth. To pass as "true God," one must necessarily pass the "creator" test. But the natural gap between the one creator and the rest means that as created, the gods of the nations are not what they claim to be. They are nothing (Isa 41:24), mere idols (Isa 40:19–20; 41:6–7), unable to foretell the future or do good or harm (Isa 41:23). Those who follow them are nothing, just like the gods they fashion (Isa 44:9–20; Jer 10:14–15). The ontological gap between the creator and everything else means that nothing should claim divine status, and no one should devote themselves to anything else that claims to be what it is not.

The Bible does not assert YHWH's exclusivity in the absence of gods. Bible authors such as Moses, Isaiah, and Jeremiah were familiar with the cultural polytheism of the nations among which Israel existed. Nathaniel Levtow notes how Jeremiah 10:1–16, for example, displays a "detailed familiarity with Mesopotamian iconic rituals" and functions "as an early crystallization of the icon parody genre."[38] But rather than accommodating polytheistic persuasions, such biblical texts leave no room for a continuum of divinities with fluid boundaries inherent in polytheism. "The literary and ideological structure [of Jer 10:1–16] is a set of privileged binary oppositions: life and death, strength and weakness, wisdom and foolishness, truth and falsehood." Levtow finds more of these iconic parodies in Isa 40:18–20; 41:5–7, 21–29; 42:8, 17; 44:9–20; 45:16–17, 20–21; 46:1–7; and 48:5. In all these texts, there does not exist among biblical authors the idea that God is the apex of divinity below whom other lesser divinities rightfully exist. The texts entertain no idea

38. Nathaniel Levtow, *Images of Others: Iconic Politics in Ancient Israel* (Winona Lake: Eisenbrauns, 2008), 50, 55.

that other gods exist as personifications of the supreme deity. For the biblical authors, only the creator is God by nature, and he alone is worthy of devotion.

4. God's Relational Nearness in the Old Testament

One striking characteristic of YHWH in the Old Testament is his gracious relational nearness to his people, which sharply contrasts with the concepts of the supreme being we found in Africa. We noted already the supreme being's absence from daily human affairs created a religious and relational vacuum in the traditional African spiritual consciousness, a gap then occupied by lesser divinities. We also saw that this absence itself arose out of human sin. Africans seem to have gone about this separation either by working their way towards God (as Mbiti notes among the Ashanti and Bambuti) or making other gods to save them, as we already mentioned.

In Scripture, YHWH resolves this sin-caused separation by his gracious divine presence. God's graciousness towards his people responds to our human impulse to work ourselves to God, while the divine presence satisfies the longing for intimacy with God, a yearning onto which idols latch. Only God can bridge the gap between him and humans, and he must do so graciously by his presence. Thus, Moses notes a peculiar closeness YHWH has with Israel which does not exist elsewhere and musingly asks: "What other nation is so great as to have their gods near them the way the Lord our God is near us whenever we pray to him?" (Deut 4:7). The inevitable and expected response is "none!" Moses acknowledges the relational distantness of the supreme deity among the many other nations and is fascinated at the Lord's gracious stooping down to relate with Israel. The gracious relational presence of the God of Abraham who covenants with his people is a significant theme of the Hebrew Scriptures. It begins from the temple-like Eden where the Lord walked with Adam and Eve (Gen 3:8) and even cared about what interpersonal choices Cain made (Gen 4:9–16). Both Enoch and Noah are said to have "walked with God" (Gen 5:22; 6:9), an indication of relational intimacy. Moreover, in Israel's wilderness trials, God promised to "dwell among the Israelites and be their God" (Exod 29:45) and to do so despite his people's idolatry (Exod 32–34).

Thus, while it is true that the Lord who made the heavens and the earth is above all things, this God "is in this place" (Gen 28:16), "is not far from any one of us" (Acts 17:27) and is intimate with his people – by grace. The benevolent relational nearness of the God of Abraham to his people positively resolves the traditional African concept of the supreme deity's distantness or malevolent nearness. To be sure, YHWH draws near in judgement – against those who forsake or forget him in favour of those things which are not by nature gods. But if idols are nothing, then to pursue that which by nature is nothing is to become what we follow – nothing. Idolatry, by nature, degrades those who set their heart to it.[39] (The intermediate divinities in Africa were fickle, manipulatable, and often malevolent.[40]) Thus, even in judgement, God draws near for the good of his people who would be destroyed by pursuing nothingness. This way, the divine presence is a blessing to God's people who serve him alone.

But suppose the pursuit of other gods – which are not gods by nature – is born out of hearts longing for relational intimacy that the distant supreme being did not provide for Africans. In that case, we could say then that the nearness of the God of Abraham removes the need for such traditional gods. Hence, not ancestors and intermediary divine beings, but YHWH was the centre of Israel's rituals and religious consciousness. YHWH's centrality in Israel's worship contrasts with Africa, where deified humans and natural phenomena were central to their rituals. YHWH removes the necessity for lesser gods and ancestors by intimate presence with his people. Israel's history is of a God who meets his people not only on a mountain but dwells in a tabernacle. But while the Old Testament proclaimed a God who makes his tent with his people, God's presence is no more concrete than in Jesus of Nazareth.

5. And the Supreme Deity Became Flesh

We noted in the beginning how John stated that the creator "was in the world, and though the world was made through him, the world did not recognize him" (John 1:10). John referred to Jesus as "full of grace and truth" (1:14). By declaring Jesus as the maker of the world, John sees him as the God of Israel, YHWH, and thus also the supreme being of the Africans. John had begun his written account by asserting the transcendent divine status of Jesus as God through whom all things were created (John 1:1–5). That Jesus is the creator of heaven and earth is confirmed in various places and ways in the New Testament. Paul himself insists that by him, "all things were created . . . visible and invisible," including thrones and dominions and rulers, so that "all

39. Idowu, "God or Idol?," argues that "the tragedy of idolatry is that an idol is not a mere nothing. It is, in fact, a very dangerous and destructive nothing, simply because it is a violation of the basic principle of life."

40. Mbiti, *Concepts of God in Africa*, 117, speaks of the Barundi who hold to the existence of Imana Mbi or "bad divinity" who kills children.

things have been created through him and for him" (Col 1:16). Jesus is the one Lord "through whom all things came and through whom we live" (1 Cor 8:6). Christ is the supreme being and creator of all things.

But John 1:14 remarkably states that the supreme creator became flesh and dwelt – or made his tent among us. The language John uses of Jesus tabernacling among his people echoes the Old Testament Exodus story where YHWH dwelt in a tabernacle with Israel. In Christ, YHWH crystalizes his relational intimacy with his people. In Jesus, God is gracious with humans as one of them. Thus, the incarnation – God becoming flesh – removes doubt about divine immanence and deals with non-relational deistic transcendence. The birth of Christ eradicates the need for divine intermediaries or gods whose existence is predicated on the perceived ontological and relational gap between the supreme being above and the fated humans below. By proclaiming the forgiving God who shares the fate of his creatures, the gap necessarily disappears, and so does the need for the gods. In Christianity, the God who became human replaces the humans who became gods.

The birth of Christ reminds us that God is not seated on a high mountain or standing on top of Jacob's ladder, waiting for us to approach him through intermediaries. We do not work our way towards God. Instead, the God of Abraham laid swaddled in a manger has descended upon Jacob's ladder into the world of creatures to dwell with them in Christ (John 1:51). Christianity, at the core, speaks of what God has done to relationally be with us, as opposed to what we can do to get good things from him. This way, Christianity confirms, corrects, clarifies, and confronts every cultural belief about God and his dealings with the world he made. Jesus is Immanuel, the "with us God." We proclaim him alone as God and Saviour because he alone united humanity and God, banishing the relational gap in his body. The other gods, though truly human, are not truly divine and cannot lead us to God. Only the supreme being can unite humanity to himself. And Christianity proclaims that this possibility and need is actualized and met in Jesus. The birth of Christ is both revelational and relational.[41]

41. In stating the above, I move beyond Idowu, "God," 22, who asserts that "It is because of the very weakness of our perception that God in His infinite love and mercy caused the Word to become flesh and pitch His tent among us." My departure from Idowu here is that relational unity and fellowship lies at the heart of the incarnation as much as revelational value is. Even without perceptive weaknesses, God would have united himself to creation, if for nothing else but that as creation existed from God, its end is to be united to him. The incarnation is the beginning point where God and creation are united in the one person of God the Son. Apart from this, I would still differ from Idowu's assertion that "nowhere is the concept of God clear

6. Conclusion

So, given the above, there are three things to note concerning Christ's coming and the African traditional gods. First, his coming confirms the ubiquitous African sensibilities that a supreme being is the creator of all things and through whom everything came. In establishing such beliefs, the Bible rejects the notion that Christianity is foreign and colonialist.[42] Christianity took root here in its early days because, among many other factors, it announced the same supreme God and creator always present in Africa and the religious consciousness of Africans. In the words of Paul, "you are ignorant of the very thing you worship – and this is what I am going to proclaim to you" (Acts 17:23). It is no surprise that Paul chiefly identifies this "unknown god" by his creative acts (v. 24). To embrace Christianity is not to reject all "African gods" but to acknowledge that only the creator of all things – whatever name we call him – only this one is truly God. In no way, therefore, does our worship of the God of Abraham make us less African, for Africans knew that God by nature has the entire universe as his domain. YHWH is the God of our ancestors whom they worshipped "as unknown" and whom Christianity now proclaims to our kin. Faith in the God of Abraham makes us part of a global family by grace. But it doesn't make us un-African.

Secondly, Christ corrects and clarifies the idea that God is relationally distant and directly uninvolved in his creation. Christianity rejects the idea that God does not care enough about his creation to feel its pain and redeem its brokenness. God, in Christ, unites humanity to himself and suffers as we do, even dying the worst form of death. The maker of all things banishes death in his body, which no traditional African god ever did or dared to do. The deified African guardians died their death, but their demise could not end death for all. The God who historically becomes human and dies for his people is uniquely Christian. But Christ's humanity and death mean that he is there, he is near, and he cares for each African in ways Africans never conceived of the supreme god. And while intermediary divinities were humans by default and then gods by elevation, Jesus was God by nature who voluntarily became human to share our afflictions. In so doing, he corrects and clarifies our idea of who God is and his goodness towards us. Thus, to reject Christ is to refuse this transcendent but immanent goodness.

---

in an absolute sense." Jesus Christ has revealed God truly and absolutely (John 1:18), and the biblical eyewitness accounts attest to this.

42. As elsewhere argued in this book, Christianity's African history is centuries older than the first colonialist on the continent. See especially Mugambi's chapter.

Thirdly, Christ confronts the notion that we need other gods to relate with the supreme being or bridge the presumed ontological gap between God and us. Christianity asserts that if such a gap exists, it owes to our idolatry – the pursuit of other gods in rejection of the true God – and not to the fact that God is by nature relationally distant. Christianity insists that God directly meets the longing for the human heart to relate. Thus, to search for satisfaction from anything else is to pursue nothingness and death.

Bibliography

Asante, Molefi Kete, and Ama Mazama. *Encyclopaedia of African Religion*. Thousand Oaks: Sage Publications Inc, 2009.

Bamunoba, Yoramu K. *The Cult of Spirits in Ankole* (Independently Published). Kindle Edition.

Beard, Mary, John North and Simon Price. *Religions of Rome*, Vol. 1. Cambridge: Cambridge University Press, 1998.

Brand, Chad, and Eric Mitchell, eds. *Holman Illustrated Bible Dictionary*. Nashville: B&H Publishing Group, 2015.

Chidester, David, Chirevo Kwenda, Robert Petty, Judy Tobler and Darrel Wratten, eds. *African Traditional Religion in South Africa: An Annotated Bibliography.* Westport: Greenwood, 1997.

Coetzee, P. H., and A. P. J. Roux. *The African Philosophy Reader*. London: Routledge, 2003.

Elwell, Walter A., and Barry J Beitzel, eds. "Zeus." In *Baker Encyclopaedia of the Bible*. Grand Rapids: Baker Book House, 1988.

Highfield, Ron. *Great Is the Lord: The Theology for the Praise of God*. Grand Rapids: Eerdmans, 2008.

Hughes, D. A. "Polytheism." In *New Dictionary of Theology: Historical and Systematic*. Edited by Kevin J. Vanhoozer, David Emmanuel Singh and Roland Chia. Downers Grove: InterVarsity Press, 2016.

Idowu, Bolaji. "God." In *Biblical Revelation and African Beliefs* edited by Kwesi A. Dickson and Paul Ellingworth, 17–29. London: Lutterworth Press, 1969.

———. "God or Idol?" *The Journal of Religious Thought* 27 no. 3 (1970): 13–28.

Jones, Philip. "Divine, and Non-Divine Kingship." In *A Companion to the Ancient Near East*. Edited by Daniel C. Snell. Oxford: Blackwell, 2005.

Kombo, James. "The Trinity in Africa." *Journal of Reformed Theology* 3 (2009): 125–43.

Levtow, Nathaniel. *Images of Others: Iconic Politics in Ancient Israel.* Winona Lake: Eisenbrauns, 2008.

Lynch, Patricia Ann. *African Mythology A–Z*. New York: Chelsea House Publishers, 2010.

Mbiti, John S. *Concepts of God in Africa*. Southampton: The Camelot Press Ltd, 1970.

McKenzie, Peter R. "John Mbiti's Work on African Religion as Reflected in the Perceptions of Students in a British University." In *Religious Plurality in Africa: Essays in Honour of John S. Mbiti* edited by Jacob K. Olupona and Sulayman S. Nyang, 319–40. New York: Walter de Gruyter & Co., 1993.

Mlenga, Joyce. *Dual Religiosity in Northern Malawi: Ngonde Christians and African Traditional Religion*. Project MUSE: Mzuni Press, 2016.

Olupona, Jacob K. *African Religions: A Very Short Introduction.* Oxford: Oxford University Press, 2014.

Pritchard, James B. *Ancient Near Eastern Texts Relating to the Old Testament*. Princeton: Princeton University Press, 1969.

Ritner, Robert K. "Divinization and Empowerment of the Dead." In *The Book of the Dead: Becoming God in Ancient Egypt* edited by Foy Scalf, 109–16. Chicago: The Oriental Institute of the University of Chicago, 2018.

Schmidt, Wilhelm. Trans. by H. J. Rose. *The Origin and Growth of Religion.* London: Methuen & Co Ltd, 1935.

Van den Toren, Benno. "The Christian God and Human Authority: A Theological Exploration with reference to Africa's Principal Worldviews." *Africa Journal of Evangelical Theology* 23 no.2 (2004): 16–186.

Part IV

Practical Issues

12

Ministry in Light of New Age Movements in Africa

Daniël Maritz, PhD

Ratio Christi, University of Pretoria, South Africa

Abstract

It has been said by many scholars that one of the major difficulties in discussing the New Age movement lies in the attempt to locate, capture and define it. Some have compared New Age spirituality to a jelly-like substance. The moment you think you have grasped New Age spirituality, it takes on another form and slips through your fingers. The New Age movement has, nevertheless swept across the U.S.A., Europe, Asia, and is penetrating the continent of Africa to the point of being alive and well in South Africa. It has also managed to infiltrate Christian churches in some of the major cities of Africa. Pastors and ministers, knowingly or unknowingly, are teaching New Age ideas, cloaked with Bible verses removed from their proper context. The New Age movement certainly poses a covert threat to the churches in Africa, and the only question left for us to answer is: How can we do God-honouring apologetics to counter the New Age movement and point people to Jesus Christ, the only true mediator between God and humanity?

Keywords: Apologetics, Cults, New Age

1. Introduction

It has been said that "world religions and other forms of 'faith,' even the vague mix-and-match varieties of spirituality," are becoming far more notable on a global level than secularism.[43] Why is this happening, you might wonder. Although secular humanism has proven to be very influential in many parts of the world, it has also proven itself to be insufficient and ultimately inadequate.[44]

With secularism's rejection of God's existence and its ideological suppression of humanity's inherent religiosity, it is bound to end up in nihilism[45] where it is forever unable to pull itself up by its own metaphysical bootstraps. Humanity has always "been incurably religious" and shares an irreducible and irremovable "religious heritage."[46] As image bearers of God, we are made

---

43. William Edgar and K. Scott Oliphint, *Christian Apologetics Past & Present: A Primary Source Reader*, Volume 1 (Wheaton: Crossway, 2009), 5. The word "secular" can have many different connotations. The way in which I am using the word here is mainly to refer to a sceptical position towards or an outright denial of the existence of God, and the supernatural beyond the natural world. The word "secular" would therefore typically refer to positions like atheism, agnosticism and scepticism.

44. Timothy Keller diagnoses this observation as follows: "Strict secularism holds that people are only physical entities without souls, that when loved ones die they simply cease to exist, that sensations of love and beauty are just neurological-chemical events, that there is no right or wrong outside of what we in our minds determine and choose. Those positions are at the very least deeply counterintuitive for nearly all people, and large swaths of humanity will continue to simply reject them as impossible to believe. Many ask: Why do people feel they need religion? Perhaps now we see that the way this question is phrased doesn't explain the persistence of faith. People believe in God not merely because they feel some emotional need, but because it makes sense of what they see and experience. Indeed, we have seen that many thoughtful people are drawn toward belief somewhat unwillingly. They embrace religion because they think it is more fully true to the facts of human existence than secularism is." See Timothy Keller, *Making Sense of God: An Invitation to the Skeptical* (New York: Viking, 2016), 23.

45. James W. Sire helpfully defines nihilism in the following way: "Nihilism is more a feeling than a philosophy, more a solitary stance before the universe than a worldview. Strictly speaking, nihilism is a denial of any philosophy or worldview – a denial of the possibility of knowledge, a denial that anything is valuable. If it proceeds to the absolute denial of everything, it even denies the reality of existence itself. In other words, nihilism is the negation of everything – knowledge, ethics, beauty, reality. In nihilism no statement has validity; nothing has meaning. Everything is gratuitous, de trop – that is, just there." See James W. Sire, *The Universe Next Door: A Basic Worldview Catalog*, 6th ed. (Downers Grove: IVP Academic, 2020), 84.

46. Norman L. Geisler and Winfried Corduan, *Philosophy of Religion* (Eugene: Wipf & Stock Publishers, 2003), 26. The observation from Geisler and Corduan that being religious is part of what it means to be human, finds its foundation in Genesis 1:27: "So God created man in his own image, in the image of God he created him; male and female he created them" (ESV). Since God created human beings in his image, they will always have what John Calvin (1509–1564) referred to as an "awareness of divinity" by natural instinct (John Calvin, *Institutes of the Christian Religion*, I.3.1, trans. and ed. J. T. McNeill (Louisville: Westminster John Knox Press, 2011), 43. Of course, Calvin did not invent this category, but borrowed it from the Roman philosopher and statesman, Cicero (106–43 BC). See John V. Fesko, *Reforming Apologetics: Retrieving the Classical Reformed Approach to Defending the Faith* (Grand Rapids: Baker Academic, 2019), 49–69.

to know and worship him and to experience and share the gifts and joys of his creation. To find meaning and purpose in knowing God is part of what it means to be human.

The world created by secularism, however, leaves humanity without any sense of ultimate meaning and purpose. The moment God, as humanity's ultimate end, is removed from the picture, people will feel as if they are all alone in this big universe.[47] People will start experiencing a restlessness within their hearts[48] which is exactly why the "inadequacy of secular humanism made people crave for something more – something divine, something sacred."[49] In many places, unfortunately, it is not the truth of Christianity that has stepped in to fill the restless void left behind by secularism, but rather the New Age. As a "vague mix-and-match" spirituality, the New Age, as we will see, is a worldview based on an attempt to seek and find God in all the wrong places.[50]

During the last couple of decades, New Age movements have moved across the continents of North America, Europe and Asia. Alas, the continent of Africa and its churches have not remained untouched by its ideas and practices.[51] The New Age worldview has indeed managed to reach the shores of Africa and in 2007, Christina Steyn, a South African scholar, announced that the "New Age is alive and flourishing in South Africa."[52] Although the New Age movement has

---

47. Ron Rhodes, *The Challenge of the Cults and New Religions* (Grand Rapids: Zondervan, 2001), 138.

48. This is a reference to Saint Augustine's famous words: "Thou hast formed us for Thyself, and our hearts are restless till they find rest in Thee." See Augustine of Hippo, *The Confessions of St. Augustine*, I.1, in *A Select Library of the Nicene and Post-Nicene Fathers of the Christian Church*, First Series, ed. Philip Schaff (Buffalo: Christian Literature Company), 45.

49. Rhodes, *The Challenge of the Cults*, 138.

50. See Herman Bavinck, *Reformed Dogmatics: Sin and Salvation in Christ*, Volume 3 (Grand Rapids: Baker Academic, 2006), 491. According to Bavinck the human heart is created for God and in one sense seeks God. However, because of humanity's fallen nature, God is never sought in the right manner or in the right place.

51. A. K. A. Chepkwony, "New Age Movement: A Challenge to the Church in the 21st Century," *African Ecclesial Review* 48 no. .4 (2006): 313.

52. H. Christina Steyn, "A New Look at New Age in South Africa," *Religion & Theology* 14 (2007): 265. Elsewhere Steyn also discusses certain New Age trends and concludes that "to a large extent the new religious movements that have been discussed are movements which originated in the United States or were established there by their founders, and which spread from there to the European continent and also, in time, to South Africa." See Chrissie Steyn, *Worldviews in Transition: An Investigation into the New Age Movement in South Africa* (Pretoria: The University of South Africa, 1994), 121. It is also important to recognize that there are "points of convergence" between New Age ideas and practices, and traditional African religions that has already been present in South Africa before the "arrival" of the New Age movement on the African continent. See H. Christina Steyn, "Where New Age and African Religion Meet in South Africa: The case of Credo Mutwa," *Culture and Religion* 4 no. 1 (2003): 67–68.

made countless headlines and quickly became a hot topic between the 1970s and the 1990s, it almost seemed to have disappeared over the last few years. This "disappearing act," however, should not fool anyone. It is not a matter of the New Age disappearing from the cultural and religious scene, but only a matter of the New Age adapting and becoming more and more acceptable to more and more people, culturally and religiously.

It is very often the case that the "most powerful influences come from worldviews that emerge from culture."[53] Underneath the radar of conscious thought, hidden in plain sight, these worldviews manage to infiltrate our minds and hearts. In this manner New Age thinking has filled the thoughts of many people through popular movies like *X-Men*, *Star Wars*, and more recently, *Doctor Strange*.[54] The *Oprah Winfrey Show* also had its fair share of influence in this regard. Furthermore, best-selling books from New Age authors like Rhonda Byrne,[55] Eckhart Tolle and Deepak Chopra are consumed by the young as well as the old to the extent that their ideas have been preached from Christian pulpits.

Christians cannot assume that non-Christian ideas and practices will always remain on the other side of the church door.[56] Although the church has received many warnings about the New Age, there has not always been an adequate response. The result, unfortunately, is that whenever "the church has failed to defend the faith and expose what is wrong, false doctrines and heretical teachings have plagued us."[57]

Since the New Age movement, with its different ideas and practices, will be with us for some time to come, we must now raise the basic question, "What is the New Age?"

---

53. Steve Wilkens and Mark L. Sanford, *Hidden Worldviews: Eight Cultural Stories that Shape Our Lives* (Downers Grove: IVP Academic, 2009), 12.

54. See L. Russ Bush, "Christ in the New Age," in *Passionate Conviction: Modern Discourses on Christian Apologetics*, ed. Paul Copan and William Lane Craig (Nashville: B&H Academic, 2007), 177–79.

55. Since there are so many New Age authors with tremendous influence around the world today, it is impossible to consult all of them. Accordingly, I have picked Rhonda Byrne's works as a primary source in this chapter to use as an example of New Age spirituality. The reason for this choice is because she seems to have been the most influential in my direct context here in South Africa.

56. Wilkens and Sanford, *Hidden Worldviews*, 11.

57. Walter Martin, *The Kingdom of the Cults: The Definitive work on the Subject* (Grand Rapids: Bethany House, 2019), 406.

2. What Is the New Age?

The New Age movement can be somewhat difficult to identify and define. Some have said that an attempt to define the New Age is "like trying to nail Jell-O to a wall."[58] Because of its jelly-like substance, the moment you think that you have captured the New Age, it might just take on a new form and slip right through your fingers.

Because of this challenge, and because different definitions emphasize different aspects of the New Age Movement, it will be beneficial to consider more than one definition that has been given for this movement over the years. I will especially consider four of those definitions here.

The first definition is given by Walter Martin (1928–1989) and goes as follows: "The New Age movement is a millennium without God where man enthrones himself as the sovereign over all, and in the process dethrones or demotes God."[59] This definition is helpful because it underlines the main aspiration of the New Age worldview. The driving propeller behind New Age ideas and practices is, for the most part, the dethronement of God and the enthronement of humans. To many of you this might sound like a familiar attempt given that the serpent, in Genesis 3, already seduced humanity with the words: "you will be like God" (Gen 3:5 ESV). Ever since that day, the false promise of becoming like God has proven to be fallen humanity's biggest temptation, and it seems to remain one of the reasons why the New Age will stay a distorted replacement for Christianity.[60]

The second definition comes from Douglas Groothuis who explains that "[t]he *New* Age movement is not new; it is the most recent repeat of the second oldest religion, the spirituality of the serpent. Its impulse is foreign to none of us. The appeal is ancient indeed; its rudiments were seductively sold to our first parents in the garden. Human pride was tickled, and it jumped."[61] Besides also emphasizing the dethronement of God as an essential part of New Age thinking, this definition is relevant since it lays to rest any claim that the New

58. Wilkens and Sanford, *Hidden Worldviews*, 120–21.

59. Walter Martin, "The New Age Movement – Dr. Walter Martin," YouTube video, https://www.youtube.com/watch?v=KQse-4xTptg. Martin also states elsewhere that the "New Age sought, from the very beginning, to undermine Christianity and destroy the revelation of God as it is given to us in the Old and New Testament" (Walter Martin, *The Kingdom of the Occult*, eds. Jill Martin Rische and Kurt Van Gorden [Nashville: Thomas Nelson, 2008], 190–91).

60. According to Steyn the New Age must inevitably be seen as a "search for spirituality and meaning that is in contrast to prevalent mainstream religious or scientific beliefs." See Steyn, *A New Look at New Age*, 266.

61. Douglas Groothuis, *Confronting the New Age: How to Resist a Growing Religious Movement* (Downers Grove: InterVarsity Press, 1988), 17.

Age is actually *new*. Here it is rather described as a version of the "second oldest religion" which was established by the serpent in Genesis 3. The spirituality with which the New Age pull and lure its adherents is therefore an "ancient" one. This means that the philosophical foundations of the New Age movement in both the East and the West, can be traced far back to centuries before Jesus Christ.[62]

The third definition is from L. Russ Bush when he explains that the New Age should not mainly be thought of through popular culture, but rather "through following the loss of absolutes."[63] In its simplest expression, he says, "New Age thought is postmodern in its essence." Moreover, it "has roots in the ancient world, in the occults, and in the paganism of the ancients. It draws its power from the passion its ideas generate." Apart from also commenting on the ancient roots of the New Age and the momentum this movement generated with its alluring ideas, this definition is noteworthy for its philosophical diagnosis of New Age thinking. It identifies the New Age as a product of relativism and postmodernism. In fact, some reckon that it is because of the New Age movement that relativism has received such a great boost in modern times.[64] Such a philosophical approach allows you to not only discuss the philosophical ideas that gave rise to the New Age, but also to level a thorough philosophical critique against this movement based on a metaphysical inquiry into reality.

The fourth and final definition is given by Ron Rhodes who claims that the best and easiest way to understand the New Age, is as "a loosely structured network of individuals and organizations who share a common vision of a new age of enlightenment and harmony." He goes on to explain that these individuals and organizations, although diverse and independent in many ways, still "subscribe to a common set of religious and philosophical beliefs."[65] This definition is valuable because it reminds us that the label "New Age" is a loose umbrella term. There is no fixed dogma or supreme leader which

62. David K. Clark and Norman L. Geisler, *Apologetics in the New Age: A Christian Critique of Pantheism* (Eugene: Wipf & Stock Publishers, 1990), 117. I take note of Christina Steyn who says that it is "trite to say that there is nothing new in New Age." See Steyn, *A New Look at New Age*, 266. One must remember, however, that this claim is made with a great deal of justification. This will become clearer as we proceed further with this discussion.

63. Bush, "Christ in the New Age," 179.

64. Rhodes, *The Challenge of the Cults*, 44–45. In the light of the New Age Movement's adoption of relativism, Rhodes goes on to observe that "if all truth is relative, then one person's 'truth' is just as good as another person's 'truth.' This ultimately means that any religion's 'truth' – and any cult's 'truth' – is as good as Christianity's truth."

65. Rhodes, *The Challenge of the Cults*, 130.

characterizes the New Age. It is vast and diverse and can include cults, sects, and even certain denominations, however, it cannot be limited to any one of these.[66] Yet, in its chaotic diversity, there is certain commonly held beliefs and tenets which does allow us to meaningfully discuss the New Age as a worldview.[67]

3. The Major Beliefs and Tenets of the New Age Worldview

The New Age has been referred to as "a worldview[68] in its late adolescence."[69] Although the New Age movement will still undergo many developments and changes in the future, it seems as if it will not mature any further because of its intrinsic eclectic approach. Nonetheless, this worldview has taken form and can be effectively analyzed by considering the following major New Age tenets and beliefs.[70]

3.1 An Emphasis on Eastern and Occult Mysticism

When Christian culture started to disappear in the West, and secularism undoubtedly failed to provide a satisfying alternative, many people went to the East in search for answers to the big questions of life, meaning, and purpose. In 1973, Os Guinness for example observed that because of Christianity's decay in the Western world, the East might still be the East, "but the West is no longer the West."[71]

66. See Groothuis, *Confronting the New Age*, 18.

67. The scholar Jack Finnegan provides a helpful definition which also emphasizes this final aspect of the New Age Movement: "[The New Age is] an extremely vast and widespread, but loosely structured, mega-network of individuals, groups and organizations, who share common values and ideas characterized by mysticism and monism, and a common vision of a coming age of peace and mass enlightenment. In this sense the New Age movement is rather a loose umbrella term that refers to a variety of people, organizations, events, practices and ideas. Although this movement includes cults, sects, and even denominations it cannot be restricted to only one of these." See Jack Finnegan, "The New Age Movement – A New Religion?" *The Furrow* 43 no. 6 (1992): 353.

68. It is beyond the scope of this chapter to go into the finer details of the term "worldview" and what it means. For a nuanced approach to this concept see Daniël Maritz and Karnu Van Heerden, "The Truth about Worldviews (Part 1)," https://ratiochristi.co.za/the-truth-about-worldviews-part-1/.

69. Sire, *The Universe Next Door*, 157.

70. To be sure, there are more than just these tenets and beliefs which are held within the New Age Movement. Due to limited space, only a limited number of tenets can be meaningfully discussed here.

71. Os Guinness, *The Dust of Death* (Bedford Square: Inter-Varsity Press, 1973), 195.

During the 1960's many people were convinced that the ancient Eastern religions with its antirationalism and syncretism provided a better way forward.[72] This subsequently led to a massive rediscovery of Eastern thought in the Western world. Indeed, "[t]he West welcomed the East and tasted its mysteries as a flood of gurus, yogis and swamis swarmed society."[73] Suddenly, both Hindu and Buddhist Scriptures became a cherished source of authority for Westerners.[74] Even here in South Africa the Hindu Scriptures known as the *Bhagavad-Gita* and Buddhist meditation groups became very popular at a certain point in time.[75] The New Age was, to a large extent, therefore shaped by Eastern traditions and although "Eastern 'guruism'" have since faded away again, the teachings and ideas of the gurus have not. According to Groothuis "[w]hat was once on the esoteric periphery has moved into the spotlight. Much of what used to be underground is seeping – if not rushing – into the mainstream, as a plethora of New Age teachers, practices, and events contend for our souls."[76]

This arrival of Eastern philosophies and religions in the West resulted in a strong eclectic syncretism between Eastern and Western ideas. Despite the big influence of, and emphasis on Eastern religions, the New Age worldview cannot be reduced solely to Hinduism or Buddhism. Like a massive "cosmic sponge" the New Age have soaked up and mixed different ideas and practices from other world religions and ancient traditions.[77] Three examples of these mystical traditions are commonly held to be Hermeticism, Kabballah, and Gnosticism.[78] These early movements were all, in one way or another, characterized by mystical experiences, paganism and occultic practices that are now being revived through the spirituality of the New Age. It explains why practices like divination or channelling, a search for secret knowledge, and an obsession with natural objects like trees and the sun endure in this esoteric

72. Sire, *The Universe Next Door*, 135.

73. Groothuis, *Confronting the New Age*, 19.

74. Sire, *The Universe Next Door*, 135.

75. Steyn, *Worldviews in Transition*, 111–13.

76. Groothuis, *Confronting the New Age*, 19. The scholar, James A. Herrick also helpfully states that "ancient Eastern traditions have shaped the new spirituality even more dramatically than have ancient Middle Eastern ones. Buddhist influence is evident virtually everywhere on the contemporary scene." See James A. Herrick, *The Making of the New Spirituality: The Eclipse of the Western Religious Tradition* (Downers Grove: InterVarsity Press, 2003), 24–25.

77. Rhodes, *The Challenge of the Cults*, 131.

78. More details on Hermeticism, Kabballah, and Gnosticism will be given as we continue to discuss the main beliefs and tenets of the New Age worldview.

worldview.[79] There is indeed a "tremendous fascination with the mysterious and the unknown,"[80] which flourishes in the New Age.

After the mixture of ideas between the East and the West was completed, the product that emerged is a mystical spirituality with many "inner tensions" and "flat-out contradictions."[81] The New Age worldview can consequently be viewed as a "hybrid spirituality."[82] The motivation behind this eclectic syncretism is the belief that "a common truth underlies all religions"[83] and that the truth is big enough to include Buddha, Confucius, Krishna, Mohammad, Jesus, and many other teachers, sages, and gurus through the centuries.[84]

This inherent eclectic syncretism means that New Age proponents will always have the luxury of mixing and matching their sources until the result is a spiritual product that feels right and works for them. The catchphrase often used to describe this phenomenon is *cherry-picking*. This is clearly observable in Rhonda Byrne's book, *The Secret*, wherein she appeals to sources as far and wide as Winston Churchill (1874–1965), Jesus Christ, Buddha, and Albert Einstein (1879–1955) to substantiate her spiritual and metaphysical positions.[85] Within the New Age ideology there are different "paths to enlightenment" and everyone is encouraged to explore and find their own way to it. This phenomenon also gives the New Age its fair share of a Western "individualistic tone."[86]

Herman Bavinck (1854–1921) described this well when he explained the way the culture in which he found himself has come to view religion. It is such that people seem to borrow certain elements "from occultism and theosophy, from spiritism and magic. And everything is then made into an object of religious veneration, both world and humanity, heroes and geniuses, science and art, state and society, the world of spirits and the power of nature. Each

---

79. Clark and Geisler, *Apologetics in the New Age*, 11.

80. Martin, *The Kingdom of the Occult*, 1.

81. Sire, *The Universe Next Door*, 157.

82. Douglas R. Groothuis, *Unmasking the New Age: Is There a New Religious Movement Trying to Transform Society?* (Downers Grove: InterVarsity Press, 1986), 131.

83. Steyn, *A New Look at New Age*, 268.

84. Martin, *The Kingdom of the Occult*, 192–93. Martin goes on to explain that the New Age, "under the auspices of tolerance," deemed all religions to be equally true and therefore equally valid. This notion has come to be "memorialized in their theme of 'unity in diversity'" (193). This, of course, ties back to the prevalence of relativism within the New Age Movement.

85. See Rhonda Byrne, *The Secret* (New York: Beyond Words Publishing, 2006), 36, 54, 73, 91.

86. Wilkens and Sanford, *Hidden Worldviews*, 123.

has its own divinity." The horrible consequence is that "religion has become, for many, a private matter, which they arrange to their own liking.[87]

3.2 A Pantheistic Monistic View of the Universe

Because of the Eastern and occultic influences, New Age spirituality can typically be classified as a pantheistic monistic worldview. The two keywords here is clearly "pantheism," which means "all is God," and "monism," which means "all is one."[88] This may seem like a strange combination, but when we consider the broader definitions of these words it might become clear how they are held in tension within New Age circles.

If pantheism is unpacked in more detail, it means that "God pervades all things, contains all things, subsumes (includes) all things, and is found within all things. Nothing exists apart from God, and all things are in some way identified with God." It follows then that the world is God and God is the world. To put it shortly, "all is God and God is all. Nothing exists that is not God."[89] In its turn monism can be more thoroughly defined as the notion that "nothing that exists is really distinct from anything else that exists – which is just to say, in the final analysis, only one thing exists. And that one thing – call it 'the universe,' 'reality,' 'the One,' or whatever you like – cannot be divided or decomposed into more fundamental parts or constituents."[90] In the New Age understanding of the universe therefore, "God is all in all," and "all is one."[91]

Reality is not only fundamentally *one*, but also fundamentally *divine* since God is all there is. The ultimate oneness that undergirds everything and is within everything is God and anything in this world that seems to be separate from the whole, or diverse from the one, will consequently be explained as an "illusory manifestation" of the one single divinity.[92] In certain contexts, this tenet of the New Age worldview has also come to be known as *holism* where it

87. Herman Bavinck, *Christian Worldview* (Wheaton: Crossway, 2019), 26.

88. Pantheism comes from the Greek words *pan* (meaning: "all") and *theos* (meaning: "God"). In its turn, monism comes from the Greek word *monos* (meaning: "one"). See Rhodes, *The Challenge of the Cults*, 131–32.

89. Norman L. Geisler and William D. Watkins, *Worlds Apart: A Handbook on Worldviews*, 2nd ed. (Grand Rapids: Baker Book House, 1989), 75–76.

90. James N. Anderson, *What's Your Worldview?: An Interactive Approach to Life's Big Questions* (Wheaton: Crossway, 2014), 71.

91. Martin describes the New Age as an "all-pervasive, all-encircling philosophy birthed from Theosophy and Hinduism. New Age groups comprise a united syncretistic religion; everything comes together under one philosophy" (Martin, *The Kingdom of the Occult*, 193).

92. Wilkens and Sanford, *Hidden Worldviews*, 128.

is used to dismiss as illusions the real existence of dualisms like good and evil for example. Holism, once again, serves to emphasize the ultimate unity of all things and rejects any distinctions between God and the world, the world and humanity, and finally, between God and humanity.[93]

Slightly different from pantheism, the New Age worldview has also been associated with the position known as *panentheism* which means "all in God." Everything in the world is still seen as inherently divine and identical with God, however, there is an aspect of the divine which still transcends the world.[94] God's relationship to the world can be thought of as the way in which a mind is related to a body. The world is God's body and exists as one pole of the divine, while the mind is that pole of the divine which still goes beyond the world.[95]

It would be a mistake to limit this worldview of pantheistic monism to the East. It has been observed that from the East, with its mysticism and Hindu sages, to the West, with its extreme rationalism, "pantheism has always found advocates."[96] Moreover, the ancient magical tradition of Hermeticism maintained some form of paganistic pantheism which "found divinity in everything."[97] One of the main similarities between New Age thought and traditional African religions[98] also seems to be "the holistic world view in which the inter-relationship and interdependence of all the dimensions of a person and of the humans, nature and the Divine are emphasised."[99] Given the size and diversity of the New Age movement, this divine oneness will not always be understood or explained in exactly the same way and can appear to be modified between the many different manifestations of New Age spirituality.

Rhonda Byrne expresses this view of the universe by claiming that the "greatest teachers and avatars described the Universe . . . by saying that all that

---

93. Wouter J. Hanegraaff, *New Age Religion and Western Culture: Esotericism in the Mirror of Secular Thought* (Leiden, The Netherlands: E. J. Brill, 1996), 119.

94. Wilkens and Sanford, *Hidden Worldviews*, 122.

95. Geisler and Watkins, *Worlds Apart*, 108.

96. Geisler and Watkins, *Worlds Apart*, 76. Geisler and Watkins especially considers the ideologies of Parmenides (515 BC), Plotinus (AD 205–270), Benedict de Spinoza (1632–1677), and G. W. F. Hegel (1770–1831) to be examples of Western versions of pantheism. See Clark and Geisler, *Apologetics in the New Age*, 75–114.

97. Herrick, *The Making of the New Spirituality*, 39.

98. In time, the New Age movement became characterized by its interest in Native American spirituality. This trend eventually expanded to other indigenous religions of different countries across the world, including the traditional African religions of South Africa. Steyn observed for example that there is much in the traditional African worldview "that is attractive to the ideal-typical New Ager." See Steyn, *A New Look at New Age*, 272.

99. Steyn, *Where New Age and African Religion*, 78.

exists is the One Universal Mind, and there is nowhere that the One Mind is not. It exists in everything." This One Universal Mind is everywhere and in everything without any diversity, individuality, or composition. If this One Universal Mind is everything, and everything is one, and "the whole of it exists everywhere, then it is all in You!" She goes on to explain that everything in the universe is connected and that "we are all part of the One Energy Field, or the One Supreme Mind, or the One Consciousness, or the One Creative Source. Call it whatever you want, but we are all One."[100]

One of the major implications of pantheistic monism is not only that "opposites like good and evil coalesce in God," but that God ends up being an impersonal force or presence, much like the force which keeps the balance in and between everything in the story of *Star Wars*. Since this worldview abandons any notion of duality, diversity, or distinctions, there can be no personal God. To live personally there must be a distinction between at least two "somebodies" who can consequently communicate with each other on a personal level. However, there are no distinctions or individuality within this worldview and so everything collapses into a great sea of absurdity. The God of pantheistic monism transcends the category of "personal" and will forever remain impersonal.[101]

3.3 The Deification of the Self

The New Age movement has long been characterized by the idea that humanity is on the way to reaching a higher consciousness about the nature of time, the purpose of human beings in the universe, and the nature of reality.[102] The vision that this scenario sketches is one of a great spiritual awakening and mass enlightenment. We are all destined to partake in a monumental spiritual evolutionary process which will advance and reach its climax in the dawning of a "New Age." When as many people as possible have reached a higher spiritual consciousness the "cosmic history's future" which is finally foreseen "as the arrival of the New Man, the New Woman and the universal New idyllic Age," will be realized.[103] Many envision this event as the ultimate deification

100. Byrne, *The Secret*, 160, 162.

101. Clark and Geisler, *Apologetics in the New Age*, 118–19.

102. Bush, *Christ in the New Age*, 170.

103. Sire, *The Universe Next Door*, 196.

of humanity. People will gain a "divine identity that rivals that possessed by Christ himself."[104]

Although this grand vision of a "New Age" was very common during the earlier stages of the movement, it has become less evident among New Age proponents in recent years.[105] However, one thing that did not fade away or lose its emphasis in New Age circles is the idea of the deification of the self. Once a pantheistic monistic view of reality is granted, things quickly tumble into the inherent godhood of every individual. If "God is all in all," and "all is one," then the divine is manifested in everything. This is analogous to a large lake with many different streams flowing from it. In the same way as the water in each stream is of the same essence as the water in the large lake, each individual person is of the same essence as the divine.[106]

Once again, the idea of the self being or becoming a god in some sense cannot be limited to the Eastern forms of pantheism. Ancient Hermeticism, Kabbalah, and Gnosticism have cherished a similar stance for centuries. Hermeticism stressed your mental or spiritual experience in life over your physical body which is stuck in space and time. Only after you mastered certain secret spiritual techniques could your mind gain control over time, space, and your body. Ultimately, the goal of "Hermetic spirituality is the individual's divinity."[107] Enlightenment by means of spiritual advancement therefore changed you into a god of some kind.

Kabbalah, on the other hand, refers to a collection of mystical Jewish writings which was supposedly given, in secret, to Moses on mount Sinai. He was ordered to only reveal these writings to an elite group of elders. In this way, Kabbalah was meant to be a system to help you advance spiritually, but only if you were part of the spiritual elite who were ready to receive these secret insights. This tradition inverted the relationship in Judaism between God and his creation by "rendering human beings virtually divine." They also had the ability "to control and even create God rather than the other way around."[108]

Gnosticism was a very influential movement which found itself in constant conflict with Christianity. The name Gnosticism comes from the Greek word meaning "one who knows." What a gnostic typically knows would then be

---

104. Bush, *Christ in the New Age*, 170.

105. Steyn, *A New Look at the New Age*, 268.

106. William Honsberger and Dean C. Halverson, "The New Age Movement," in *The Compact Guide to World Religions*, ed. Dean C. Halverson (Minneapolis: Bethany House, 1996), 164.

107. Herrick, *The Making of the New Spirituality*, 38–39.

108. Herrick, *The Making of the New Spirituality*, 40–41.

called *gnosis*.[109] The gnostics got rid of the true historical Jesus,[110] "choosing instead to pursue self-salvation through secrets that come from beyond the earthly and historical scheme of things." This secret knowledge was only available to the "spiritually capable" with the potential to free them from their embodied existence. In this context various means were used to reach alternate states of consciousness through which salvation can be achieved and your own divinity realized.[111]

New Agers today have expressed this belief in the deity of the self in many ways and in many different contexts. Rhonda Byrne is very explicit about it when she claims for example that "You are God in physical body. You are Spirit in the flesh. You are Eternal life expressing itself as You. You are cosmic being. You are all power. You are all wisdom. You are all intelligence. You are perfection. You are magnificence." She ends her attempt to dethrone God and enthrone humanity by asserting that "You are the creator, and you are creating the creation of You on this planet."[112]

---

109. Rodney Stark, *Cities of God: The Real Story of How Christianity Became an Urban Movement and Conquered Rome* (New York: Harper Collins, 2006), 143–44.

110. It is worth mentioning that the typical view of the person and the work of Jesus Christ within the modern New Age environment is still very much influenced by ancient Gnosticism. Some streams of Gnosticism held to a "separation christology." This refers to a separation between "Jesus" and "the Christ" as two different entities. This separation serves to explain "what happened to Jesus after his baptism: the heavenly Christ descended on him in the form of a dove and proclaimed the unknown Father." On the occasion of his baptism, Jesus, a mere man, was therefore "adopted by God as his son (the Christ)." See Birger A. Pearson, *Ancient Gnosticism: Traditions and Literature* (Minneapolis: Fortress Press, 2007), 37. This was especially a trait of the early christological heresy known as adoptionism which seem to have been hijacked by the New Age movement as well. According to Norman Geisler and Ron Rhodes "New Agers typically argue that Jesus was a mere human vessel who embodied the Christ – a cosmic, divine entity." See Norman L. Geisler and Ron Rhodes, *Conviction Without Compromise: Standing Strong in the Core Beliefs of the Christian Faith* (Oregon: Harvest House Publishers, 2008), 54. Furthermore, Groothuis explains that the New Age movement generally understands the Christ to be a "universal Presence" and an "impersonal cosmic process or principle." See Douglas Groothuis, *Revealing the New Age Jesus: Challenges to Orthodox Views of Christ* (Downers Grover: InterVarsity Press, 1990), 221–23. In this context Jesus was also only a mere man, and he, "along with many others, deserves the highest praise as a god-realized man." In "Mind Science" cults such as Christian Science "Jesus and Christ are not the same person . . . Jesus is the man, while Christ is the spiritual idea or element of God," H.W . House and G. Carle, *Doctrine Twisting: How Core Biblical Truths are Distorted* (Downers Grove: InterVarsity Press, 2003), 74. One example of this can be seen in the works of Ernest Holmes (1887–1960), the founder of The Church of Religious Science. He wrote that Jesus is "the name of a man" which must be distinguished "from the Christ." The point is that the "man Jesus became the embodiment of the Christ, as human gave way to the Divine idea of Sonship," Ernest Holmes, *The Science of Mind: The Complete Edition* (New York: Penguin, 2010), 285.

111. Herrick, *The Making of the New Spirituality*, 179–80.

112. Byrne, *The Secret*, 164.

This belief of the New Age is why so many of its practices are based on building your own reality. If you are a god, you should be able to manipulate your world and "create in your own image."[113] Very often this can be done by using your thoughts and words to perform the act of speaking something into existence. This idea of creating your own reality has been described as a "base premise" of the New Age worldview and especially refers to the different ways in which you can come to know your own divine potential.[114] This aspect of New Age thinking has managed to not only spread widely within popular culture, but has also subtlety infiltrated the Christian church.

3.4 An Infiltration of Society and the Church

With a massive social agenda and a widespread influence, the New Age has been able to propagate its ideas on many different levels of society. It is not just the spiritual and religious domain, but psychology, health, medicine, sociology, anthropology, science fiction, entertainment, the arts, and in some cases politics.[115] Herrick strikingly explains that the New Age spirituality "has now moved into the lecture hall and the classroom, the movie theatre and the surgical theatre, the corporate office and the Oval office."[116]

This observation certainly emphasizes the influential nature of the New Age movement. Unfortunately, however, the church cannot be excluded from the list of all the things that has been infiltrated by this worldview. Pastors and ministers, knowingly or unknowingly, are teaching New Age ideas, cloaked with Bible verses removed from their proper context. Consequently, the New Age spirituality has indeed revealed the "unpaid bills" of Christianity.[117]

The New Age, with its tributary manifestations,[118] gave rise to what came to be known as the Word of Faith movement. The Word of Faith movement

---

113. I am here making a reference to Genesis 1:27.

114. Groothuis, *Confronting the New Age*, 24.

115. See Sire, *The Universe Next Door*, 163–68.

116. Herrick, *The Making of the New Spirituality*, 18.

117. See Jan Karel Van Ballen, *The Chaos of Cults: A Study in Present-day Isms*, 4th ed. (Grand Rapids: Eerdmans, 1962), 390.

118. One of the forerunners of the New Age movement is known as the New Thought Movement. This movement was inspired by Phineas Parkhurst Quimby (1802–1866). Among other things, Quimby argued that since the source of all sickness lies in the mind, the source of all healing also resides there, Steyn, *Worldviews in Transition*, 105. According to David W. Jones and Russel S. Woodbridge the New Thought movement believes that "God is a force; spirit or mind is ultimate reality; people are divine; disease originates in the mind; and thoughts can create and/or change reality." See David W. Jones and Russel S. Woodbridge, *Health, Wealth &*

goes by different names of which the name, "Prosperity Gospel," is probably the most popular. Some have referred to the Word of Faith as "'Christian' occultism" given the fact that it borrows heavily from the New Age worldview and yet claims to be Christian.[119] According to Hank Hanegraaff many of the doctrines that are prevalent in the Word of Faith are so "unbiblical" that they "boggle the mind." He goes on to say that "these concepts find their genesis in the kingdom of the cults; in other cases, they are firmly rooted in the world of the occult."[120]

One of the reasons why this movement is called the "Word of Faith" is because it highlights the power of your *words*. The teachers of the Word of Faith movement views faith as a force which you can tap into and consequently speak faith-filled words. By speaking these faith-filled words you can direct a force at God to manipulate him or somehow equip him to deliver to you whatever it is you want.[121] Thus, this practice, known as "positive confession," becomes a way of manipulating reality using thoughts and words.[122] It is a "spiritual activation" which sets into motion the spiritual laws that governs the universe.[123] Besides the teaching of positive confession, the Word of Faith movement is also known for its "little gods doctrine." In a very explicit manner, it is taught in "Christian" churches that people are in fact little gods.[124] Although these teachings are taught by many Word of Faith teachers in the Western world today, it is also taught locally here in South Africa.[125]

Happiness: Has the Prosperity Gospel Overshadowed the Gospel of Christ? (Grand Rapids: Kregel, 2011), 27.

119. Richard G. Howe, "'Christian' Occultism: The Word of Faith Movement," *PowerPoint Slide Deck*, http://www.richardghowe.com/index_htm_files/OccultWordofFaithShort16x9.pdf.

120. Hank Hanegraaff, *Christianity in Crisis: 21st Century* (Nashville: Thomas Nelson, 2009), 94.

121. Jones and Woodbridge, *Health, Wealth & Happiness*, 87–88. Hank Hanegraaff for example explains that the Word of Faith teachers "define faith as a force and claim that words are the containers of the force . . . the 'God' of the Faith movement is not the true God at all. He is a pathetic puppet governed by the impersonal force of faith." Hanegraaff, *Christianity in Crisis*, 94.

122. For a brief overview of the teaching of Positive Confession within the Word of Faith movement see Dima Rozet, "The Word of Faith Movement and Positive Confession,": https://ratiochristi.co.za/the-word-of-faith-movement-and-positive-confession/.

123. Daniël J. Maritz and Henk G. Stoker, "Does the Christian Worldview provide a place for the Law of Attraction? (Part 1): An Apologetic evaluation of the roots of this doctrine," *Verbum et Ecclesia* 37 no. 1 (2016): 6.

124. See Hanegraaff, *Christianity in Crisis*, 131–66.

125. Maritz and Stoker, *Does the Christian Worldview*, 7.

A well-known pastor, At Boshoff, for example explains that you must always change from the negative to the positive because just as your faith can be seen and heard, your unbelief can also be seen and heard. God is not able to override the positive or negative power that is within you. Once you open your mouth to speak, you can invite God into the equation or leave him out of it. If there is a "no" in your words, God cannot intervene on your behalf.[126] Elsewhere, Boshoff preaches to his church about the practice known as the "Law of Attraction." He explains that everyone is always "sending out a force, a power, an energy, that either attracts good things and good people into your life, or it repels good things and good people."[127] Whether you like it or not, Boshoff says, "you live by the simple law of attraction . . . you are attracting things into your life, good or bad, wanted, or unwanted. You attract what is at the core of your heart." Boshoff spends a couple of sermons trying to show that "the Bible says" whatever "is in your heart you are attracting into your life all the time."[128] Moreover, in one of his church's manuals, titled *Releasing the Power*, it is said that after being born again "you receive the nature of God" and consequently also "receive the power and ability of God."[129]

Rhonda Byrne's book *The Secret* is mainly focussed on explaining what the Law of Attraction is and how it works. In fact, *The Secret* that she is busy unpacking throughout her book *is* the Law of Attraction. The Law of Attraction, according to her "determines the complete order in the Universe, every moment of your life, and every single thing you experience in your life." This law is constantly forming your life she says, and this "all-powerful law" is achieving this "through your thoughts." The law receives your thoughts and then reflects those thoughts back into your life. It basically "gives you whatever it is you are thinking about."

It would seem, therefore, as if many ideas from the New Age worldview have been welcomed in many churches across the world, also here in South Africa. A phenomenon like this is too important to leave unaddressed. At

126. At Boshoff, *Live a Yes! Life: Become All that you Possibly can Be* (Cape Town: Struik, 2008), 40–41.

127. At Boshoff, "The Law of Attraction Part 1 – 1/3," YouTube video, https://www.youtube.com/watch?v=Ed9F38bjLy8.

128. At Boshoff, "The Law of Attraction Part 2 – 01 of 03," YouTube video, https://www.youtube.com/watch?v=gmMqKNbZM50. Given that the space here is limited, it is not possible to work through At Boshoff's sermons in more detail. However, I have done an analysis of his sermons which can be found here: Daniël J. Maritz and Henk G. Stoker, "Does the Christian Worldview provide a place for the Law of Attraction? (Part 2): An Apologetics evaluation of the way the Bible is used in Promoting this Idea," *Verbum et Ecclesia* 37 no. 1 (2016): 1–9.

129. Christian Revival Church, *Releasing the Power*, 40–41.

Boshoff's sermons and his church's discipleship manual rather appear to be a subtle compromise, one which seems to fit comfortably with New Age thought.

4. What Is There to Redeem in the New Age?

Although space is limited, any critical analysis of anything, should include, if warranted, a consideration of redeemable matters. In other words, one should ask whether there are features of the New Age spirituality that might be true and useful?[130]

First, New Age spirituality gives some kind of priority to the spiritual dimension of reality. Both New Agers and Christians are critical of a naturalistic stance to reality wherein any form of transcendence or religion is dismissed as a mere superstition or a psychological coping mechanism.

Secondly, the New Age movement reminds one of problems with organized religion. Many people who have joined some stream of New Age thought shared their stories of how they were victimized and abused by the church. It doesn't follow from this that Christianity is false, but in many cases, it does warrant a sincere apology from the church. Unfortunately, the church is not perfect.

Finally, New Age Spirituality has correctly questioned Enlightenment rationalism. Christianity is based on nothing less than human reason. However, it is based on far more than just naked human reason. Although the anti-intellectualism of the New Age is not desirable, there should be a place for mystery and a realization of the limits of reason. There should never be place for absurdity on the other hand.[131]

---

130. Wilkens and Sanford provide some features that can be viewed as positive within the New Age worldview. This brief discussion will focus on their list of positive aspects. See Wilkens and Sanford, *Hidden Worldviews*, 130–32.

131. The distinction between something that lies beyond the reach of natural reason, and something that contradicts natural reason is always helpful to keep in mind. A mystery within Christian theology, like the doctrine of the Trinity for example, must therefore be described, not as *irrational*, but rather as *suprarational*. Applying this distinction would mean that the Trinity is a truth that lies "above and beyond . . . human discovery and comprehension," but does not contradict human reason. So, although it transcends natural reason, it nevertheless does not violate it. See Travis James Campbell, "Van Til's Trinitarianism: A Reformed Critique" in *Without Excuse: Scripture, Reason, and Presuppositional Apologetics*, edited by David Haines (The Davenant Press, 2020), 297–98. In fact, when discussing the Trinity, Harold O.J. Brown for example insists that "God does not require a *sacrificium intellectus*, a 'sacrifice of the intellect' as part of faith. Because the sacrifice of the intellect is a violent affront to the integrity of one's soul, it is always dangerous and certainly is a poor way to begin to love God with all one's heart, soul, and mind," Harold O. J. Brown, *Heresies: Heresy and Orthodoxy in the History of the Church*, 152. This approach stands in stark contrast to New Age thinking where, in many contexts, the "sacrifice of the intellect" is encouraged and even required to attain enlightenment.

5. What are the Cracks in the New Age Worldview?

Despite the redeemable aspects of the New Age worldview, it is ultimately irreconcilable with reality and consequently, the gospel of Jesus Christ. Daniel Strange strikingly states that "the gospel of Jesus Christ stands as the subversion, antithetical contradiction, confrontation, condemnation and crisis of all manifestations of the religious Other."[132] The real Christ will differ drastically from the "redeemers and saviours" which "the religions of man" evoke. Indeed, the true gospel of Jesus Christ is the condemnation of "such human fancy and speculation."[133] The true gospel will always contradict other false ideological systems like the one found within the New Age.

Mitch Horowitz, a New Age adherent, writes in an article that he wants his friends in the New Age movement to engage more seriously with the "intellectual inquiry" levelled against the New Age. He explains that he cannot conclude that the critics of the New Age worldview are right. According to him, he has "seen too many instances where the therapeutic and spiritual ideas and methods that emerge from New Age culture prove meaningful in the lives of a wide range of people."[134] Horowitz desperately wants to defend the New Age movement in all its finer details. I, for one, am not convinced that this movement is ultimately defensible. Here are some of the reasons why.

5.1 Spiritualism versus Realism

The New Age worldview replaces a one-sided naturalism, found in secular cultures, with a one-sided spiritualism, or at least a very low view of "the real." Although Christianity and the New Age agree about the existence of the supernatural, created reality cannot be lost altogether.[135] The major influence from the East which has turned the world into a mere illusion, combined with

132. Daniel Strange, *Their Rock is not like Our Rock: A Theology of Religions* (Grand Rapids: Zondervan), 269.

133. J. H. Bavinck, *An Introduction to the Science of Mission* (Phillipsburg: P&R), 136.

134. Mitch Horowitz, "In Defense of New Age," https://medium.com/s/real-magic/in-defence-of-new-age-4e55f8dadcc2. Notice that Horowitz does not attempt to defend the New Age worldview because it is true, but only because it is "meaningful." It seems as if he is working with a pragmatic theory of truth in the sense that if the New Age *works* and is therefore meaningful, it is true. Christianity, on the other hand, has always claimed that something is true when it corresponds to reality. When Christians therefore attempt to defend the gospel of Jesus Christ, it is not first and foremost because it works or because it is meaningful, but because it is *true* and as such, corresponds with what is real.

135. Wilkens and Sanford, *Hidden Worldviews*, 132–33.

occultic practices and rituals aimed to manipulate the spiritual, has separated this worldview from reality-anchored truths.

In New Age thought, truth is not a matter of correspondence to anything real anymore, but only internal coherence, which is only tested by your own personal, subjective experiences. In some cases, this also leads to the abandonment of the sensory faculties. Any knowledge that depends on our senses becomes irrelevant and is sometimes considered misleading.[136] Ironically, science is still held in high regard, but these kinds of irreconcilable differences are only an example of cherry-picking your sources of authority. Sire explains that some New Agers will just accept all the different languages of reality, that of "sorcery and science, of witchcraft and philosophy, of drug experience and waking reality, of psychosis and normality."[137] This eclecticism eventually leads to epistemological nihilism, since nobody can really know what is true. You can only know your own mystical experience. The New Age fails to see the importance of grounding reasoning and especially experiences in reality, even though whatever is not based on reality is un-reality or unreal.

The major concern when it comes to the New Age, therefore, is the loss of reality. For Christians "reality is what dictates the method, and not the method which defines reality."[138] We must always "seek to lay bare the metaphysics that God has woven into reality" and never attempt to manipulate reality to obey our feelings.[139] This, of course, assumes clear and undistorted access to reality with a true knowledge thereof. Accordingly, Bavinck reminds us that "[t]he Christian religion thus shows its wisdom primarily in this, that it knows and preserves truth as an objective reality, which exists independent of our consciousness and is displayed by God for us in his works of nature and grace." He continues to say that "each person proceeds spontaneously on the basis of the conviction that the objective world exists outside him and that it exists as he has come to know it in clear perception."[140]

In John 14:6 Jesus says, "I am the way, and the truth, and the life." Of all the things Jesus might be saying in this verse, one thing he is claiming is to be the authority and ultimate reference point for truth – that which is real. He uttered perfect truth, expressed perfect truth, lived perfectly in the truth, and

136. Clark and Geisler, *Apologetics in the New Age*, 122.

137. Sire, *The Universe Next Door*, 200.

138. Etienne Gilson, *Methodical Realism: A Handbook for Beginning Realists* (San Francisco: Ignatius Press), 86.

139. Gustav Portig as quoted by Bavinck, *Christian Worldview*, 47.

140. Bavinck, *Christian Worldview*, 33.

corresponded perfectly to the truth. In John 8:32 he also added that "you will know the truth, and the truth will set you free." Rather than seeking alternative states of consciousness or practicing rituals to detach his mind from what is real, Jesus found God's hand in the real world. To him, the lilies of the field reveal God's care (Luke 12:27). The heavens and the skies pour forth "speech and knowledge" of God says the Psalmist (Ps 19). In Romans 1:20 the apostle Paul writes that certain invisible attributes of God are clearly seen in the visible, real world.[141]

Reality is indeed a "gateway to a deeper mystery."[142] It is "a mirror . . . of invisible things."[143] It is "a school for attaining the knowledge of God" for through "visible and perceptible objects it provides guidance to the mind for the contemplation of the invisible."[144] Grounded in reality is God's revelation of himself and reality is therefore known to be a revelatory gift mediating knowledge of God's invisible attributes. Moreover, the fact that Jesus was raised back to life in the same physical body with flesh and bones, and not some mystical or ghostly body, indicates that Jesus is saying "yes" to this world and confirms the importance of physical reality. The point is that we do not need to enter alternate states of consciousness and detach ourselves from this world to arrive at spiritual truths.

5.2 Gnosis versus Logos

The New Age worldview leads to logical absurdities. In its quest to plumb the depths of the universe in search of secret, ancient, and hidden knowledge, or *gnosis*, it arrives at untenable conclusions. If subjective experience is all there is, how can you know whether anything corresponds to the universe that other people also inhabit? If the divine reality is but an impersonal force, why is the only way to evaluate divine reality through a personal, subjective experience? Since certain experiences can mislead you, on what grounds do you make a distinction between deception and truth? If two sources blatantly contradict each other, which one is true and how do you know that? If our true identity is

141. See J. Gresham Machen, *Christianity and Liberalism* (Grand Rapids: Eerdmans), 48.

142. John Nerness, "Theological Examination of Nihilism and the Eucharist Applied to Missions and Apologetics," PhD Thesis, NWU, South Africa, 85.

143. John Calvin, *Commentary on the Epistle of Paul the Apostle to the Romans* (Bellingham: Logos Bible Software), 70.

144. Gerald Bray, ed., *Romans* (Revised), Ancient Christian Commentary on Scripture (Downers Grove: InterVarsity Press), 37.

that of a god, how can one avoid the conclusion that the divine can also make mistakes and undergo changes?[145]

Christianity certainly grants mysteries that are beyond reason,[146] but not absurdities that contradict sound reason. It seems that the New Age has sacrificed sound reason for a supposed secret *gnosis* of the world and humanity. In many cases, this sacrifice, and an embrace of the absurd[147] is encouraged as a precondition for achieving the hidden secrets of the world. This relentless search for hidden knowledge has also led to what Sire calls an "esoteric interpretation" of the Bible. Apparently, this esoteric tradition has a long history which claims that "the Bible – and many other religious and nonreligious texts – contains a secret, hidden, inner meaning that can only be spiritually discerned."[148] This means that only those who are spiritually enlightened can interpret the Bible to uncover its true meaning. In this process logic is untethered from hermeneutics[149] and additional revelations from the "Other side" are sought to supplement the biblical text.[150]

In John 1:1 we read: "In the beginning was the Word [*logos*], and the Word [*logos*] was with God, and the Word [*logos*] was God." *Logos* is the Greek word from which we get the word logic. "God is more than a rational being . . . Nonetheless, God is rational, and the principles of good reason do flow from his very nature. Consequently, learning the rules of clear and correct reasoning is more than an academic exercise. For the Christian, it is also a means of

145. Wilkens and Sanford, *Hidden Worldviews*, 132–33.

146. Like the doctrine of the Trinity or the Hypostatic Union of Christ for example.

147. The word "absurd" is a loaded term. Here it is only used to refer to cases where plain and clear contradictions are upheld as true, while it violates the law of noncontradiction.

148. James W. Sire, *Scripture Twisting: 20 Ways the Cults Misread the Bible* (Downers Grove: InterVarsity Press), 107. Geisler also unpacks such a stance towards the Bible where the true meaning of the text is not sought in the text but beyond or behind it: "The meaning is not found beyond the text (in God's mind), beneath the text (in the mystic's mind), or behind the text (in the author's unexpressed intention); it is found in the text (in the author's expressed meaning). For instance, the beauty of a sculpture is not found behind, beneath, or beyond the sculpture. Rather, it is expressed in the sculpture." Norman L. Geisler, *Systematic Theology: Volume 1: Introduction, Bible*, 174.

149. For a brief overview of basic hermeneutics and also the role of logic and metaphysics therein, see Daniël Maritz, "How to Read your Peculiar Bible," https://ratiochristi.co.za/how-to-read-your-peculiar-bible/.

150. There is a reason why H. Wayne House and Gordon Carle say that "the Christian should be educated not only in biblical knowledge but also in systematic theology (the systematic study of God and related concepts), apologetics (the branch of theology dealing with the defence of the faith), hermeneutics (the art of interpretation) and logic (correct thinking or reasoning)." H. Wayne House and Gordon Carle, *Doctrine Twisting: How Core Biblical Truths are Distorted*, 13.

spiritual service."[151] When we pursue good and coherent logical arguments for our positions, we are "in a limited and analogical way, reflecting what God is like."[152] Sound logic is our best tool for arriving at truth, and to abandon it for absurdities is absurd.

5.3 Moral Preference versus Moral Obligations

Although the New Age worldview has a strong social agenda, in different levels of society with the aim to do good, it cannot justify any moral categories. In a pantheistic, monistic worldview, good and evil, right, and wrong, are just divisions that restrain you. There is no real difference between them. One must rather transcend these categories and realize that they collapse into the oneness of ultimate reality. Good and evil has no meaning in the New Age, and consequently there is no obligation to pursue the good and to avoid evil. Rather, since "God is within, we do not need artificial moral dogmas. We simply need to be our true selves."[153] Morality only becomes a personal preference based on one's personal experience.

The history books are filled with utopian visions that failed miserably in their striving for equality, elimination of poverty, enhanced health, democracy etc. Although social upliftment is good, it would be wise to base such an agenda on something more solid than mere illusions, preferences and experiences. This is exactly the reason why Christians started hospitals, schools, universities, and programs to help the poor throughout history. They went out of their way to raise orphans left for dead and show love and charity towards their neighbours. For many of the early Christians "[t]here was no reach of the fallen world so dark . . . that it could not be illumined by the light of heaven"[154] as they pursued to help all image bearers of God.

Why did they do it, you might ask? Because, in Matthew 22:37–39, their Lord and God once said, "Love the Lord you God with all your heart and with all your soul and with all your mind . . . and . . . love your neighbour as yourself." The very nature of the Christian God is love. And love is not a shallow emotion that comes and goes, it is a desire to will the good of the other. Hence,

151. Norman L. Geisler and Ronald L. Brooks, *Come, Let Us Reason: An Introduction to Logical Thinking* (Grand Rapids: Baker Book House, 1990), 6.

152. Travis James Campbell, "Van Til's Trinitarianism," 303.

153. Clark and Geisler, *Apologetics in the New Age*, 131.

154. Tom Holland, *Dominion: How the Christian Revolution Remade the World* (New York: Basic Books, 2019), 178.

this motivation to do good, for Christians, is based on something solid, the immutable and eternal nature of God.

5.4 Occultic Animism versus Christian Theism

A big concern that arises from New Age spirituality is its involvement in the occult and animism. Nicole Watt, a former New Ager, testifies that, "as the doorway to the demonic realm swung open, terrifying incidents occurred." She adds that "although Christians often associate New Age philosophies with crystal balls, Ouija boards, and séances, most New Agers regard these activities as dime-store knockoffs of more mature paths of self-discovery."[155]

Sire explains that in certain New Age circles there are "a host of demigods, demons and guardians who inhabit the separate reality, or the inner spaces of the mind." Whatever people end up calling them, "projections of the psyche or spirits of another order of reality," they are haunting "the New Age and must be placated with rituals or controlled by incantations." In this sense, the

> New Age has reopened a door closed since Christianity drove out the demons from the woods, desacralized the natural world and generally took a dim view of excessive interest in the affairs of Satan's kingdom of fallen angels. Now they are back, knocking on university dorm-room doors, sneaking around psychology laboratories, and chilling the spines of Ouija players.[156]

There is a reason why Christianity closed this door long ago (see Deut 18:9–14 for example). Although Christianity maintains the existence of good angels under the command of God, and fallen angels under the command of Satan, Christians should not contact them or attempt to mobilize their aid. You see, God alone should be the Christian's source of power, wisdom, and strength. Martin seriously warns that "if you turn the handle of the unopened door of a forbidden dimension, what will come through is satanic power of enormous proportions."[157] In Mark 5:1–20 Jesus casts out the demons from the Gerasene demoniac. These demons were real beings and not just a projection of the man's psychosis. They used language to deceive and plan and they entered a herd of

155. Nicole Watt, "I was a New-Age healer. Then I realized I wasn't the one doing the healing," https://www.christianitytoday.com/ct/2020/may-june/nicole-watt-reiki-master-new-age-healing.html?utm_source=&utm_medium=Newsletter&utm_campaign=2013&utm_term=28967654&utm_content=708417743.

156. Sire, *The Universe Next Door*, 198.

157. Martin, *Kingdom of the Occult*, 222.

pigs once they were cast out. But they were still inferior to Jesus. Jesus, being God in the flesh, has complete control over them, and it is in that truth that the Christian finds hope.[158]

6. Conclusion: Are we Gods, or are we God's?[159]

All the attempts from New Agers to seek and find God inevitably expose their desire for salvation and mediatorship between God and humans. Strange asserts that "[t]here is a relationship between the disastrous dream [the New Age] and glorious reality [the true gospel of Jesus Christ]. Biblically speaking," he says, "the cracked cisterns of idolatry that bring only disillusionment, despair and unfulfilled desires are wonderfully fulfilled and surpassed in the fount of living water, Jesus Christ the Lord."[160]s

It seems like the ancient lie, from the serpent, that we can be "like God" (Gen 3:5) is here to stay. Given our human nature, we should expect it to. G. K. Chesterton said that "of all the horrible religions the most horrible is the worship of the god within."[161] It is a horrible religion, for it is deeply seated within our "sinful desires." It seems as if the waters of this religion are sweet and pleasant. That its cup is "spiritually intoxicating" for fallen human beings.[162] New Age beliefs clearly underestimate the effect of sin on us as humans, and the world. While New Agers believe they can save themselves with their advanced secret *gnosis*, inherent godhood, and upper spiritual awareness, Christians maintain that, because of sin, we are ultimately unable to save ourselves from

---

158. Sire, *The Universe Next Door*, 198. Martin informs one on the occult saying that "[f]rom Jesus we learn, then, that demonic spirits can inhabit human beings. Rather than experiment with the occult and New Age practices, where the person unwittingly opens the soul to demons, it is much better to close the door and refuse participation." Martin, *The Kingdom of the Occult*, 194.

159. Take note that the title of the conclusion is not my own use of words. It creatively comes from Wilkens and Sanford's chapter on the New Age. See Wilkens and Sanford, *Hidden Worldviews*, 120.

160. Strange, *Their Rock is not Like Our Rock*, 270–71.

161. G. K. Chesterton, *Orthodoxy* (New York: John Lane Company, 1909), 138.

162. Abraham Kuyper, *The Work of The Holy Spirit* (New York: Funk & Wagnalls, 1900), 328. Kuyper goes on to helpfully reminding us of the distinction between the creator and the creature: "To escape from the witchery of these pantheistic charms, one needs to be aroused by bitter experience. And once awakened, the soul is alarmed at the fearful danger to which this siren had exposed it. No; the contrast between God and man must not cease; the contrast between heaven and earth may not be placed upon the same line with that of Jew and Gentile; the contrast between the infinite and finite must not be effaced by the Mediator; time and eternity must not be made identical" (328).

within. Our source of salvation lies outside of ourselves because we don't belong to ourselves. We are God's.

Clark and Geisler describe the answer to this problem vividly:

> The Christian message of the cross is this: the hope for genuine personal transformation, social revolution, and cosmic reconciliation comes not from us but from God. Through the cross of Christ, the evil we all experience and long to overcome has already been defeated. Through the cross, human values can be enhanced and human redemption achieved. In Jesus Christ, the living Water, the thirst for peace and hope that drives the New Age will be quenched.[163]

Bibliography

Anderson, James N. *What's Your Worldview? An Interactive Approach to Life's Big Questions*. Wheaton: Crossway, 2014.

Augustine of Hippo. *The Confessions of St. Augustin*. In *A Select Library of the Nicene and Post-Nicene Fathers of the Christian Church*, First Series, edited by Philip Schaff. Buffalo: Christian Literature Company, 1886.

Bavinck, Herman. *Christian Worldview*. Wheaton: Crossway, 2019.

———. *Reformed Dogmatics: Sin and Salvation in Christ*, Volume 3. Grand Rapids: Baker Academic, 2006.

———. *An Introduction to the Science of Mission*. Phillipsburg: P&R, 1960.

Boshoff, At. *Live a Yes! Life: Become All that you Possibly can Be*. Cape Town: Struik, 2008.

———. "The Law of Attraction Part 1 – 1/3." YouTube video, https://www.youtube.com/watch?v=Ed9F38bjLy8.

———. "The Law of Attraction Part 2 – 01 of 03." YouTube video, https://www.youtube.com/watch?v=gmMqKNbZM50.

Brown, Harold O. J. *Heresies: Heresy and Orthodoxy in the History of the Church*. Peabody: Hendrickson, 1988.

Bush, L. Russ. "Christ in the New Age." Pages 170–86 in *Passionate Conviction: Modern Discourses on Christian Apologetics*. Edited by Paul Copan and William Lane Craig. Nashville: B&H Academic, 2007.

Byrne, Rhonda. *The Secret*. New York: Beyond Words Publishing, 2006.

Calvin, John. *Commentary on the Epistle of Paul the Apostle to the Romans*. Bellingham: Logos Bible Software, 2010.

———. *Institutes of the Christian Religion*. Trans. and ed. John T. McNeill. Louisville: Westminster John Knox Press, 2011.

163. Clark and Geisler, *Apologetics in the New Age*, 235.

Campbell, Travis James. "Van Til's Trinitarianism: A Reformed Critique." Pages 295–322 in *Without Excuse: Scripture, Reason, and Presuppositional Apologetics*. Edited by David Haines. Landrum: Davenant Press, 2020.

Chepkwony, Adam K. A. "New Age Movement: A Challenge to the Church in the 21st Century." *African Ecclesial Review* 48 no. 4 (2006): 312–31.

Chesterton, G. K. *Orthodoxy*. New York: John Lane Company, 1909.

Christian Revival Church. *CRC Bible Training Center: Releasing the Power. Church Training Manual.*

Clark, David K., and Norman L. Geisler. *Apologetics in the New Age: A Christian Critique of Pantheism*. Eugene: Wipf & Stock, 1990.

Edgar, William, and K. Scott Oliphint. *Christian Apologetics Past & Present: A Primary Source Reader Volume 1*. Wheaton: Crossway, 2009.

Fesko, John V. *Reforming Apologetics: Retrieving the Classical Reformed Approach to Defending the Faith*. Grand Rapids: Baker Academic, 2019.

Finnegan, Jack. "The New Age Movement: A New Religion?" *The Furrow* 43 no. 6 (1992): 351–59.

Geisler, Norman L. *Systematic Theology: Volume 1: Introduction, Bible*. Minneapolis: Bethany House, 2002.

Geisler, Norman L., and Ronald L. Brooks. *Come, Let Us Reason: An Introduction to Logical Thinking*. Grand Rapids: Baker Books, 1990.

Geisler, Norman L., and Winfried Corduan. *Philosophy of Religion*. Eugene: Wipf & Stock, 2003.

Geisler, Norman L., and Ron Rhodes. *Conviction Without Compromise: Standing Strong in the Core Beliefs of the Christian Faith*. Eugene: Harvest House Publishers, 2008.

Geisler, Norman L., and William D. Watkins. *Worlds Apart: A Handbook on Worldviews*, 2nd ed. Grand Rapids: Baker Books, 1989.

Gilson, Etienne. *Methodical Realism: A Handbook for Beginning Realists*. San Francisco: Ignatius Press, 1990.

Groothuis, Douglas R. *Confronting the New Age: How to Resist a Growing Religious Movement*. Downers Grove: InterVarsity Press, 1988.

———. *Unmasking the New Age: Is There a New Religious Movement Trying to Transform Society*? Downers Grove: InterVarsity Press, 1986.

———. *Revealing the New Age Jesus: Challenges to Orthodox Views of Christ*. Downers Grove: InterVarsity Press, 1990.

Guinness, Os. *The Dust of Death*. Downers Grove: InterVarsity Press, 1973.

Hanegraaff, Hank. *Christianity in Crisis: 21st Century*. Nashville: Thomas Nelson, 2009.

Hanegraaff, Wouter J. *New Age Religion and Western Culture: Esotericism in the Mirror of Secular Thought*. Leiden: Brill, 1996.

Herrick, James A. *The Making of the New Spirituality: The Eclipse of the Western Religious Tradition*. Downers Grover: InterVarsity Press, 2003.

Holland, Tom. *Dominion: How the Christian Revolution Remade the World*. New York: Basic Books, 2019.

Holmes, Ernest. *The Science of Mind: The Complete Edition*. New York: Penguin, 2010.
Honsberger, William, and Dean C. Halverson. "The New Age Movement." In *The Compact Guide to World Religions*, ed. Dean C. Halverson, 160–81. Minneapolis: Bethany House, 1996.
Horowitz, Mitch. "In Defense of New Age." https://medium.com/s/real-magic/in-defence-of-new-age-4e55f8dadcc2.
House, H. Wayne, and Gordon Carle. *Doctrine Twisting: How Core Biblical Truths are Distorted*. Downers Grove: InterVarsity Press, 2003.
Howe, Richard G. "'Christian' Occultism: The Word of Faith Movement." PowerPoint Slide Deck accessed December 30, 2021. http://www.richardghowe.com/index_htm_files/OccultWordofFaithShort16x9.pdf.
Jones, David W., and Russel S. Woodbridge. *Health, Wealth & Happiness: Has the Prosperity Gospel Overshadowed the Gospel of Christ?* Grand Rapids: Kregel, 2011.
Keller, Timothy. *Making Sense of God: An Invitation to the Skeptical*. New York: Viking, 2016.
Kuyper, Abraham. *The Work of The Holy Spirit*. New York: Funk & Wagnalls, 1900.
Machen, J. Gresham. *Christianity and Liberalism*. Grand Rapids: Eerdmans, 1923.
Maritz, Daniël. "How to Read your Peculiar Bible, Website Article." https://ratiochristi.co.za/how-to-read-your-peculiar-bible/.
Maritz, Daniël, and Karnu Van Heerden. "The Truth about Worldviews (Part 1)." https://ratiochristi.co.za/the-truth-about-worldviews-part-1/.
Maritz, Daniël J., and Henk G. Stoker. "Does the Christian Worldview provide a place for the Law of Attraction? (Part 1): An Apologetic evaluation of the roots of this doctrine." *Verbum et Ecclesia* 37 no. 1 (2016): 1–9.
Martin, Walter. *The Kingdom of the Cults: The Definitive Work on the Subject*. Grand Rapids: Bethany House, 2019.
———. *The Kingdom of the Occult*. Edited by Jill Martin Rische and Kurt Van Gorden. Nashville: Thomas Nelson, 2008.
———. "The New Age Movement – Dr. Walter Martin." YouTube video, https://www.youtube.com/watch?v=KQse-4xTptg.
Nerness, John. "Theological Examination of Nihilism and the Eucharist Applied to Missions and Apologetics." PhD thesis at the North-West University, South Africa, 2020.
Pearson, Birger A. *Ancient Gnosticism: Traditions and Literature*. Minneapolis: Fortress Press, 2007.
Rhodes, Ron. *The Challenge of the Cults and New Religions*. Grand Rapids: Zondervan, 2001.
Rozet, Dmitry. "The Word of Faith Movement and Positive Confession." https://ratiochristi.co.za/the-word-of-faith-movement-and-positive-confession/.
Sire, James W. *The Universe Next Door: A Basic Worldview*, 6th ed. Downers Grove: IVP Academic, 2020.

———. *Scripture Twisting: 20 Ways the Cults Misread the Bible*. Downers Grove: InterVarsity Press, 1980.

Stark, Rodney. *Cities of God: The Real Story of How Christianity Became an Urban Movement and Conquered Rome*. New York: Harper Collins, 2006.

Steyn, H. Christina. "A New Look at New Age in South Africa." *Religion & Theology* 14 (2007): 265–83.

———. "Where New Age and African Religion Meet in South Africa: the case of Credo Mutwa." *Culture and Religion* 4 no. 1 (2003): 67–91.

———. *Worldviews in Transition: An Investigation into the New Age Movement in South Africa*. Pretoria: The University of South Africa, 1994.

Strange, Daniel. *Their Rock is Not Like Our Rock: A Theology of Religions*. Grand Rapids: Zondervan, 2014.

Van Baalen, Jan Karel. *The Chaos of Cults: A Study in Present-day Isms*, 4th ed. Grand Rapids: Eerdmans, 1962.

Watt, Nicole. "I was a New-Age healer. Then I realized I wasn't the one doing the healing." https://www.christianitytoday.com/ct/2020/may-june/nicole-watt-reiki-master-new-age-healing.html?utm_source=&utm_medium=Newsletter&utm_campaign=2013&utm_term=28967654&utm_content=708417743.

Wilkens, Steve, and Mark L. Sanford. *Hidden Worldviews: Eight Cultural Stories that Shape Our Lives*. Downers Grove: IVP Academic, 2009.

13

Apologetics and Cults in Africa

Rev. Rodgers Atwebembeire

Director, Africa Center for Apologetics Research

Abstract

Across sub-Saharan Africa, evangelical Christians face a growing challenge from imported and local missionary groups promoting "another Jesus . . . a different spirit . . . a different gospel" (2 Cor 11:4 ESV) – a challenge unprecedented in its scale and impact. The present chapter will focus on east Africa, with references to the broader situation in west and southern Africa and will propose the relevance of apologetics as a reponse. Though not intended to be exhaustive, it will explore key dimensions of this much-neglected problem and propose practical, long-term responses.

Keywords: History of Apologetics, New Religious Movements, New Testament Apologetics, Post-New Testament Apologetics

1. Introduction

1.1 Scriptural Precedents

The Bible repeatedly warns believers to beware of false teachers and false teachings – not only in the Old Testament, but in every book of the New Testament (except Philemon). Such deceivers endanger individual believers and the body of Christ as a whole in every age and in every place. Yet strangely, today's local church often avoids proactively and constructively responding to the threat and safeguarding its members by using the means that God provides in his word.

1.2 Historical Precedents

The early church fathers found themselves needing to defend the faith against the errors of aggressive Judaizers and gnostics. Ecumenical councils gathered to define Christian essentials in response to the threat of divisive and destabilizing movements like Arianism, docetism, and sabellianism. Together, they have left us a legacy in the form of timeless, universal affirmations of truth like the Apostles' Creed, Athanasian Creed, Niceno-Constantinopolitan Creed, and Definition of Chalcedon. Centuries later, the Protestant Reformers also resolutely confronted error with the truth of Scripture and the force of reason, and we must emulate their example.

1.3 The Present Situation

In 2002, the great missiologist David J. Hesselgrave (1924–2018) wrote:

> During the era of modern missions, evangelical missionaries have focused on adherents of the major religions and, especially, on folk religionists. As we enter a new century and new millennium it is becoming increasingly apparent that we must also focus on millions who are being caught up in new religious movements emanating from both East and West. They constitute not only a new "mission field," but also one of our most aggressive competitors for the allegiance of multiplied millions who are turning away from the faiths of their fathers.[1]

Today it can truly be said that counterfeit Christian groups are going *from* everywhere *to* everywhere. This multi-pronged assault is unprecedented in its scale and diversity. Cultic missionary movements are taking maximum advantage of inexpensive travel and powerful technology to promote their false doctrines and make spiritual captives. This is especially true in sub-Saharan Africa, where millions – perhaps most – of those who profess to be followers of Jesus have only a superficial knowledge of the gospel and Scripture, leaving them vulnerable to deception.

In majority-Christian nations of sub-Saharan Africa, most imported missionary cults are still working primarily in Western colonial-era languages (English, French, Portuguese) and focusing their "on the ground" missionizing in urban centres. One could rightly describe them as both *predatory* and

1. Hesselgrave, "New and Alternative Religious Movements – Some Perspectives of a Missiologist," https://www.apologeticsindex.org/cpoint12-1.html.

parasitic since the primary targets of their proselytizing are already professing Christians. But as they steadily spread to villages of the interior in search of new converts, the threat grows greater.

Our direct experience at the Africa Centre for Apologetics Research (ACFAR) is with cultic groups operating in East Africa – that is to say, the seven partner states of the East African Community (EAC) as of 2022: Kenya, Uganda, Tanzania, DR Congo, Rwanda, Burundi, and South Sudan. More than a decade of interdenominational, "on the ground" ministry has shown us that the heart-breaking harm caused by spiritual counterfeits is both deep and wide.

2. Definitions and Characteristics

2.1 Cult (from Latin Cultus, "worship")

A cult of Christianity is a group of people who claim to be Christian yet hold to "a particular doctrinal system" set forth by a leader, group of leaders, or organization which "denies . . . one or more of the central doctrines of the Christian faith as taught in the sixty-six books of the Bible."[2] There is no one, universal definition of the word "cult." Although popular media frequently use the word in a reckless and sensationalistic way, it has not lost its value. We have found that the best serious working definitions acknowledge two dimensions – behavioural and theological.

2.1.1 Behavioural Dimension of Cults

Sociologist John Lofland has described cults as "little groups" which break off from the "conventional consensus and espouse very different views of the real, the possible, and the moral."[3] Another sociologist, Benjamin Zablocki, explains that a cult is "an ideological organization held together by charismatic relationships and demanding total commitment."[4] Based on such criteria, "cults" are not only religious in nature, but can sometimes be political, commercial, or even "therapeutic." At the most basic level, most secular definitions of "cult" are grounded in perceptions of *deviance* and *harm*.

---

2. Alan W. Gomes, *Unmasking the Cults* (Grand Rapids: Zondervan, 1995), 7.

3. Cited by Ronald Enroth, *A Guide to New Religious Movements* (Downers Grove: InterVarsity Press, 2005), 17.

4. Herbert L. Rosedale and Michael D. Langone, "On Using the Term 'Cult,'" *ICSA Today* 6 no. 3 (2015), https://www.icsahome.com/articles/onusingtermcult.

2.1.2 Theological Dimension of Cults

Theological – evangelical apologist and cult researcher Robert M. Bowman, Jr. defines a cult as "A religious group originating as a heretical sect and maintaining fervent commitment to heresy." He adds that a heresy is "a teaching which opposes the essentials of the Christian faith, so that true Christians must divide themselves from those who hold it."

2.2 Heresy (from Greek hairesis, "party," "grouping")

The theologian Alister McGrath observes that heresy "is a Trojan horse, a means of establishing (whether by accident or design) an alternative belief system within its host. Heresy appears to be Christian, but it is actually an enemy of faith that sows the seed of faith's destruction."[5] Some other scholars have differentiated amongst different types of heresy. For instance, Bowman helpfully highlights six types of heresy most often promoted today:[6]

1. Revelation – teachings that distort, deny, or add to Scripture in a way that leads people to destruction; and false claims to apostolic or prophetic authority.
2. God – teachings that promote false gods or idolatrous distortions of the true God.
3. Christ – denials of his unique lordship, his genuine humanity, his true identity.
4. Salvation – teaching legalism or licentiousness; denying or distorting the gospel of Christ's atoning death and bodily resurrection; etc.
5. The church – deliberate attempts to lead people away from the fellowship of true Christians; and utter rejection of the church.
6. The future – false predictions for which divine authority is claimed; claims that Christ's return has already taken place; and so on.

What kinds of cultic groups are undermining the gospel and afflicting the body of Christ in Africa? Some are headquartered overseas, while others are very local indeed. There are dozens of such missionary movements, and the following brief descriptions highlight several of the most significant ones.

---

5. Alister McGrath, *Heresy: A History of Defending the Truth* (New York: HarperOne, 2009), 34.

6. Robert M. Bowman, Jr., *Orthodoxy & Heresy: A Biblical Guide to Doctrinal Discernment* (Grand Rapids: Baker, 1992), 79.

But we must avoid superficial generalizations. For example, although some cultic groups (like the Jehovah's Witnesses) deny or distort many points of biblical doctrine, others (like the United Pentecostal Church) target only a few. Likewise, some cultic groups are known to exploit and abuse their followers, subjecting them to extreme mental and emotional manipulation, whereas others do not. (Please note that the availability and reliability of membership statistics varies greatly from one group to the next.)

3. Cults in Africa

3.1 Cultic Groups from North America

Jehovah's Witnesses[7]

Adherents: 21.36 million worldwide; roughly 5 million in Africa (2021)[8]

Distinctive teachings and practices:

- Denial of the Trinity. Jehovah (God the Father) is the only true God. Jesus is a created being associated with Michael the Archangel who did not die on a cross and did not rise bodily from the dead. Jesus already returned invisibly to earth in 1914. The "holy spirit" is an impersonal force.
- Works-based salvation. Only Watchtower members can be saved (144,000 in the "anointed" class go to heaven, while all others – the "great crowd" – hope to live forever in paradise on earth). Human beings have no immortal soul or spirit, and there is no hell (conscious eternal punishment) for the unsaved.
- The Watchtower Society is Jehovah God's one true organization, the only channel of divine truth and correct Bible understanding. All other churches are "apostate Christendom." The cult's message is mainly promoted through its website and *Watchtower* and *Awake!* magazines, along with its own deceptive *New World Translation* of the Bible.
- Most proselytizing is done by lay members ("publishers") who actively seek converts by going from house to house and distributing literature in public places.

---

7. See "Theocratic Instrumentalities" in *1980 Yearbook of Jehovah's Witnesses*, 257, https://wol.jw.org/en/wol/d/r1/lp-e/301980006#h=2.

8. See "2021 Grand Totals," https://www.jw.org/en/library/books/2021-service-year-report/2021-grand-totals/ and "2021 Country and Territory Reports," https://www.jw.org/en/library/books/2021-service-year-report/2021-country-territory.

- The Watchtower Society officially forbids its members to vote; sing national anthems; join political parties; run for elected office; serve in the military; receive blood transfusions; and celebrate birthdays, Christmas, and Easter.

Africa facts: The cult has gone far beyond any other group in its translation efforts, with printed and online teaching materials in dozens of African languages (including sign languages for the deaf). Large following in west (especially Nigeria, Ghana) and southern Africa (especially Angola, Malawi, and Zambia).

Controversies: The *Watchtower* has repeatedly promoted false dates for the end of the world, besides changing other teachings. In the 1960s and 70s the government of Malawi drew worldwide attention for severely persecuting Jehovah's Witnesses who refused to buy a required political-party card.

Mormonism[9]

Adherents: 16.8 million worldwide (2021)[10]

Distinctive teachings and practices:

- Denial of the Trinity. God the Father is an exalted man of flesh and bone with at least one wife ("Heavenly Mother"). Jesus is the literal first-born of God and his wife and was not born of a virgin on earth (his heavenly Father having had sexual relations with Mary to produce Jesus's body).
- Works-based salvation. God the Father was once a human being, and like him human beings can progress to an "exalted" state of godhood in the celestial kingdom through church membership and righteous living. Two other heavenly realms (the "terrestrial" and "telestial" kingdoms) await those who are less righteous, and the worst of sinners are sent to "outer darkness." Temple rituals are required of those who seek exaltation; baptisms are performed on behalf of the dead.
- The Church of Jesus Christ of Latter-day Saints is the one true and living church on earth, "restored" – along with its ancient priesthood

9. Formally known as "The Church of Jesus Christ of Latter-day Saints." See Russell M. Nelson, "The Correct Name of the Church," https://www.churchofjesuschrist.org/study/general-conference/2018/10/the-correct-name-of-the-church?lang=eng.

10. "Facts and Statistics," https://newsroom.churchofjesuschrist.org/facts-and-statistics.

authority – via Joseph Smith (1805–1844) beginning in 1820. All other churches are "apostate." The cult is governed by a hierarchy led by a living prophet and subordinates including twelve apostles. It has three volumes of Scripture in addition to the King James Version of the Bible: The Book of Mormon, Doctrine and Covenants, and Pearl of Great Price. These and other church materials are available in at least two dozen African languages, including Swahili and Zulu.

- Most proselytizing is done by pairs of full-time missionaries ("elders" and "sisters") who actively seek converts by going from house to house and raising awareness through public-service projects.

Africa facts: 736,700 adherents in Africa (2021).[11] The cult operates two Missionary Training Centres (in Ghana and South Africa) and maintains 39 missions across the continent. Additionally, there were 16 temples (not meetinghouses, but special ritual sites) operating, under construction, or announced for Africa as of March 2022. Well-established in Nigeria and Ghana, with especially strong growth in DR Congo and Cape Verde.

Controversies: Until 1978 the cult denied African males full access to its priesthood and temple privileges, stating that they were under a divine curse.[12] This ban limited its African missionary presence to Rhodesia and South Africa.

Seventh-day Adventist Church (SDA)
Adherents: 21.91 million in over 200 countries (2021)[13]

Distinctive teachings and practices:

- Contemporary Adventism indicates that God the Father possesses a physical body. Jesus begged the Father to be the Saviour and did not know whether he would rise from the dead after his crucifixion. He is also associated with Michael the Archangel. Most early Adventist leaders strongly denied the deity of Christ.
- Works-based salvation. Jesus's sacrifice on the cross did not complete the atonement; instead, since 1844 he has been applying his blood

11. "Facts and Statistics" at https://newsroom.churchofjesuschrist.org/facts-and-statistics.

12. See, for example, Bill McKeever and Eric Johnson, *Mormonism 101: Examining the Religion of the Latter-day Saints* (Grand Rapids: Baker, 2015), 268–77.

13. "Seventh-day Adventist World Church Statistics 2021" at https://www.adventist.org/statistics/seventh-day-adventist-world-church-statistics-2021/.

in heaven in an ongoing "investigative judgment."[14] Seventh day (Sabbath) observance is the sign of the seal of God; Sunday worship is the "mark of the beast." Human beings have no immortal soul or spirit; at the final judgement, the lake of fire will annihilate the wicked.

- The Seventh-day Adventist Church considers itself God's special, end-time remnant. The prophetess Ellen G. White (1827–1915) is God's unique last-days messenger; her revelations and numerous books (such as *The Great Controversy* and *Desire of Ages*) shape Adventist doctrine and Bible interpretation.
- Proselytizing takes many forms, including missionary work, literature distribution, and extensive health outreaches (with numerous hospitals and clinics). Extensive use of radio and television.
- The church officially forbids its members to use tobacco products, or to drink alcohol, coffee, or tea.

Africa facts: 9.94 million in sub-Saharan Africa (2021).[15] Especially strong presence in east and southern Africa, with over 1 million adherents in Zambia alone.

Controversies: Ellen G. White made false prophecies and committed extensive plagiarism. Adventists are taught that a "time of trouble" is coming when those who worship on Sunday will hunt and kill Sabbath-keepers.

United Pentecostal Church International (UPCI)

Adherents: nearly 3 million in 197 countries[16]

---

14. For a detailed description and critique, see Dale Ratzlaff, "No Reason to Exist Without the Central Pillar," *in Proclamation!* magazine 14 no. 1 (Spring 2013), online version at https://www.lifeassuranceministries.org/proclamation/2013/1/ratzlaff.html.

15. Total based on individual country statistics in "2021 Annual Statistical Report, Volume 3," https://documents.adventistarchives.org/Statistics/ASR/ASR2021.pdf.

16. For UPCI membership estimate, see Todd M. Johnson and Gina A. Zurlo, *Introducing Spirit-Empowered Christianity: The Global Pentecostal & Charismatic Movements in the 21st Century* (Tulsa: ORU Press, 2020), 82. The authors explain that "Oneness Pentecostalism emerged after 1914 from the Assemblies of God by individuals who challenged traditional Trinitarian doctrine and baptismal practice. They advocated for a modalistic view of God, a "Jesus-only" doctrine and rebaptism in the name of the Lord Jesus Christ." They further note that "the worldwide Oneness [Pentecostal] movement is estimated to have nearly 19 million followers." For countries in which the UPCI is present, see "About the UPCI," https://www.upci.org/about/about-the-upci.

Distinctive teachings and practices:

- Denial of the Trinity is central to the cult's identity. UPCI teaches that Jesus is the Father, the Son, and the Holy Spirit. Being baptized "in the name of Jesus" (Acts 2:38) – instead of the triune formula in Matthew 28:19 – is required for salvation.

Brahmanism

Voice of God Recordings, Cloverdale Bibleway, other "Message" groups

Adherents: No statistics available

Distinctive teachings and practices:

- William Marrion Branham (1909–1965) is God's special end-time prophet, the "angel of the Laodicean church" age (Rev 3:14) sent to correct errors in the church so the bride of Christ will be prepared for Christ's return.[17] His spoken-word sermons are considered as authoritative as Scripture, and the Bible can only be properly understood through his teachings.
- Denial of the Trinity. Branham's teachings on the godhead are confused and contradictory, though at times they resemble a form of Oneness Pentecostalism.
- Branhamite organizations distribute millions of his books and booklets (primarily *An Exposition of the Seven Church Ages*) and audio recordings translated into many African languages. Much innovative use of technology, including the "The Table app" and "Agapao Tablet" to disseminate teachings.
- No single, centralized organization. Local "Message" churches have a variety of names, many including words such as "eagle," "tabernacle," and "Bible believers." Much proselytizing targets traditional Pentecostals and charismatics.

---

17. Dwight J. Wilson, "Branham, William Marrion," in *The New International Dictionary of Pentecostal and Charismatic Movements* Revised and expanded, ed. Stanley M. Burgess and Eduard M. van der Maas (Grand Rapids: Zondervan, 2002), 440–41.

3.2 Cultic Groups from Europe

New Apostolic Church (NAC)

Adherents: 9.12 million in nearly 190 countries as of 2021[18]

Distinctive teachings and practices:

- Despite its affirmation of the traditional Apostles' Creed, the NAC maintains various divisive and unorthodox beliefs. For example, it emphasizes the necessity of living apostles (hundreds at this time), especially the Chief Apostle – considered the highest spiritual authority in the Christian church today. It also requires that for salvation, "those baptised with water must receive the Holy Spirit through an apostle, to obtain the childhood in God, whereby they become incorporated as members in the body of Christ."[19] In the words of theologian Victor Kuligin, the role of the NAC Chief Apostle "cannot be over-estimated. He has the power and authority to lead, as the only representative of Jesus on earth, and he has the authority to forgive sins and hence save. In short, his word is law."[20] The Lord's supper (eucharist) was not properly administered until the restoration of living apostles in the nineteenth century.
- In the NAC's doctrine of "divine services for the departed" it is said that its apostles dispense the church's three sacraments "to living proxies for the blessing and benefit" of the dead. Former members report that apparitions of spirits resembling deceased relatives are known to occur on such occasions.
- The church uses the Old and New Testaments plus 15 apocryphal books. New revelations can be declared "binding doctrine."

Africa facts: As of 2016, about 80% of the NAC's global membership was in Africa – close to 8 million followers, mainly in east and southern Africa.[21]

18. New Apostolic Church, "2021–01–01 Facts and figures," downloadable PDF at https://nak.org/api/media/33360/process?attachment=1&token=f3b2a7797597de5543e4c1ae8e890640%3A1685520042%3A5137627.

19. "The New Apostolic Creed Ten Articles of Faith," http://nac-hongkong.org/our-creed. Accessed on May 30, 2022.

20. Victor Kuligin, "The New Apostolic Church," *Africa Journal of Evangelical Theology* 24 no. 1 (2005), 70.

21. New Apostolic Church, "2021–01–01 Facts and figures," downloadable PDF at https://nak.org/api/media/33360/process?attachment=1&token=f3b2a7797597de5543e4c1ae8e890640%3A1685520042%3A5137627.

Controversies: Although the NAC acknowledges that no one knows the exact time of Christ's return (Mark 13:32), its apostles have repeatedly claimed to know the approximate time of Christ's return and have been proven wrong. Famously, in 1951 Chief Apostle J. G. Bischoff (1871–1960) predicted that he would not die before Christ's return.[22]

3.3 Cultic Groups from Middle East

Bahá'í Faith

Adherents: more than 5 million in over 200 countries as of 2020[23]

Distinctive teachings and practices: Bahá'ís preach that God has sent a series of nine "manifestations" (prophets) – one of whom was Jesus – culminating in Bahá'u''lláh (1817–1892), the last and greatest of them all.[24] Other manifestations included Moses, Krishna, Buddha, and Mohammed – spiritual leaders whose belief systems cannot be reconciled with one another. Christ's deity, atonement, bodily resurrection, and unique role in salvation are all denied.

Africa facts: According to one source "In 1952, there were probably fewer than 200 Bahá'ís in all of Africa."[25] But as of 2010, the combined Bahá'í membership in just six African countries (Kenya, DR Congo, Zambia, South Africa, Tanzania, Uganda) was reportedly 1.47 million.[26]

Other imported cultic and controversial groups now active in Africa include:

- Universal Church of the Kingdom of God (Brazil)
- World Mission Society Church of God (South Korea)
- Shincheonji Church of Jesus (South Korea)
- Good News Mission (South Korea)
- Church of Almighty God, *aka* Eastern Lightning (China)

---

22. See, for example: Frederick O. Burklin, "The New Apostolic Church," in *Dynamic Religious Movements: Case Studies of Rapidly Growing Religious Movements Around the World*, ed. David J. Hesselgrave (Grand Rapids: Baker, 1978), 70.

23. See "Statistics," https://news.bahai.org/media-information/statistics.

24. See, for example Francis Beckwith, "The Bahá'í World Faith," in *A Guide to New Religious Movements.* Edited by Ronald M. Enroth, pp. 155–68. Downers Grove: InterVarsity Press, 2005.

25. See "Establishing a New Religious Movement, 1952–1962: The Bahá'í Faith in Africa," https://international.ucla.edu/institute/event/9491.

26. See "Countries with the Largest Bahá'í Populations," https://www.worldatlas.com/articles/countries-with-the-largest-baha-i-populations.html.

Note that many of the above groups practice their own form of "apologetics" against biblical Christianity with varying degrees of sophistication.

3.4 Indigenous Cultic Groups

In East Africa one finds twentieth-century African Instituted (or Initiated) Churches with ethnic or Roman Catholic roots that have gathered followers beyond their country of origin. These include Legio Maria and "mightiest prophet" David Owuor's Ministry of Repentance & Holiness (Kenya); the Faith of Unity and the Universal Apostles Fellowship Church of Righteousness (Uganda); and largest of all, the Church of Jesus Christ on Earth by his Special Envoy Simon Kimbangu (Democratic Republic of the Congo), which reportedly claims 22 million adherents.[27]

Numerically speaking, in southern Africa the religious scene is dominated by Zionist (amaZioni) sects; the Nazareth Baptist Church (amaNazaretha) of Isaiah Shembe; and various "apostolic" groups (such as those founded by Johane Maranke and Johane Masowe) – with combined adherents estimated to be in the tens of millions. Also significant are the Tocoístas and Luz do Mundo (an Adventist offshoot) in Angola.

In west Africa, one notes "Aladura" groups and other assorted independent movements such as the Celestial Church of Christ, Brotherhood of the Cross and Star, and Cherubim and Seraphim (Nigeria), as well as the Musama Disco Christo Church (Ghana). (Note that the term "cult" is widely used in Nigeria to refer to "confraternities" and criminal secret societies sometimes operating on university campuses.)

Overall, new religions derived from Buddhism, Hinduism, and other traditional Far East belief systems have gained comparatively few adherents and often maintain only a token presence in Africa. For instance, the Japanese neo-Buddhist cult Happy Science, led by self-proclaimed god-man Ryuho Okawa, poured money into Uganda in 2012 in an attempt to win converts, but with no lasting results. Similarly, groups rooted in Western occultism (such as Rosicrucianism, the Grail Message, and Anthroposophy) have also had limited success, as have "mind science" and "new thought" cults (such as Christian Science and Unity School of Christianity), although scholars have described

27. See Marc Jourdier, "Au Berceau du Kimbanguisme, cette religion Congolaise aux 22 million de Fidèles" (At the cradle of Kimbanguism, this Congolese religion with 22 million followers), https://africa.la-croix.com/berceau-kimbanguisme-cette-religion-congolaise-aux-22-millions-de-fideles.

New Age activity in Nigeria and South Africa.[28] Likewise high-profile Western "human potential" groups such as Scientology have had little impact.

3.5 The Problem of False Teachers

Besides the challenge of overtly cultic movements from abroad and at home, African Christians suffer from an even wider (and equally dangerous) problem of neo-Pentecostal "pastorpreneurs" and heretical "fellowships" that teach false doctrine and often exploit their followers based on supposedly biblical pretexts. One of the most popular passages is Luke 6:38 (KJV), "Give, and it shall be given unto you; good measure, pressed down, and shaken together, and running over, shall men give into your bosom. For with the same measure that ye mete withal it shall be measured to you again." Unethical pastors guarantee that congregants who contribute sacrificially to the ministry of the "man of God" will see their finances flourish in no time, based on what is characterized as "Jesus' promise." Such self-appointed "apostles" and "prophets" also abuse Acts 4:34b–35a (". . . those who owned land or houses sold them, brought the money from the sales and put it at the apostles' feet . . ."), exhorting followers to sell cars and properties and empty their bank accounts for the sake of the kingdom, surrendering the proceeds to their church leaders in order to receive an even greater blessing. Peter cautions believers about such false teachers, who "in their greed . . . will exploit you with false words" and on whose account "the way of the truth will be maligned" (2 Pet 2:1–3 NASB). One chapter later he adds to his warning about such Scripture-twisting "men of God," who he characterizes as "untaught," "unstable," and "unscrupulous" (2 Pet 3:16–17 NASB). I have personally known the victims of such scams.

Locally grown, self-appointed apostles and prophets emulate heretical Western televangelists like Kenneth Copeland and Benny Hinn and west African prosperity-gospel preachers like T. B. Joshua and David Oyedepo, advocating extreme forms of "health and wealth" doctrine and "deliverance." Operating without accountability or restraint, many use intimidation and claims of supernatural authority to gain control over followers' property and more. Conrad Mbewe has drawn convincing parallels between their beliefs

---

28. See, for example Chrissie Steyn, *Worldviews in Transition: An Investigation into the New Age Movement in South Africa* (Pretoria: University of South Africa, 1994), with an update by Steyn in "A New Look at the New Age in South Africa," *Religion and Theology* 14 no. 3 (November 2007), 265–83; and Rosalind I. J. Hackett, "New Age Trends in Nigeria: Ancestral and/or Alien Religion?" in *Perspectives on the New Age*, edited by James R. Lewis and J. Gordon Melton (Albany: State University of New York Press, 1992), 215–31.

and those of traditional African religions, condemning superstitious and syncretistic teachings often promoted by such preachers. Common examples are the concept of "spirit husbands and wives" and the devilish influence of "marine spirits" like "mami wata."

In Uganda, charismatic "men of God" promote themselves via high-energy, media-savvy "fellowships" that operate parallel to established churches. The result is that young believers (often urban professionals) unwittingly smuggle the doctrinal errors promoted at mid-week rallies into their traditional churches when they return on Sundays, thereby infecting others. Prime examples of this phenomenon are the fast-growing Phaneroo International Ministries led by Grace Lubega and Zoe Fellowship led by Elvis Mbonye.

4. Responses/Solutions to Cults

> . . . when false teachers increase, the most appropriate long-term strategy is to multiply the number of true teachers, who are equipped to rebut and refute error. We need to be convinced that this is possible.[29]

What is to be done? Again, our starting point is God's word. We propose the following three-point approach.

4.1 Equipping Pastors

As the apostle Paul told the elders of Ephesus, it is the duty of pastors to "be on guard," both for themselves and for all the flock (Acts 20:28–31). Indeed, a proven ability to "encourage others by sound doctrine and refute those who oppose it" so as to safeguard the sheep is built into their job description (Titus 1:9–16). Neglect of this duty naturally leads to vulnerability, division, and confusion, and for this reason cults have rightly been called "the unpaid bills of the church."

The fact that vast numbers of African pastors have little or no formal preparation for their work and only a minimal knowledge of Scripture puts the congregations under their care at great risk. Seminaries, Bible colleges, and informal training programs all need to ensure that instruction on cults

29. John Stott, *The Message of 1 Timothy and Titus* (Downers Grove: InterVarsity Press 2021): Loc. 20 of 29. Perlego e-dition. https://www.perlego.com/book/1470580/the-message-of-1-timothy-and-titus-pdf.

and defending the gospel are incorporated into their curriculum. This author and his colleagues conducted informal surveys in 2015 and 2021 and found only a handful of African institutions offering such courses.[30] Pastors must understand that equipping both young and old to biblically discern between truth and error is a goal of Christian discipleship and spiritual maturity and actively pursue this objective (Eph 4:14–16; Heb 5:11–14).

4.2 Equipping Lay Believers

Mass evangelism without discipleship has been a recipe for disaster. Lay believers in Africa suffer from a lack of basic Bible knowledge, the ability to interpret and apply Scripture in its proper context, the fundamentals of the gospel, and biblical tools to detect deception (2 Tim 2:15). Christians need to be taught both *what* they believe and *why* at the earliest opportunity, lest they easily be led astray by those who are untaught, unstable, and unprincipled (2 Pet 3:14–18 NASB). Understanding what Scripture says about error not only prevents harm but inspires compassion for victims of deception. Believers also need to know why the Bible is uniquely authoritative and trustworthy. Indeed, such knowledge builds confidence in evangelism and gives strength and comfort in trials.

Pastors can encourage an awareness of spiritual danger by simple, memorable teaching and preaching through key apologetics-themed passages from the Gospels and epistles (e.g. Matt 7:15–27; 1 Thess 5:19–22, "test all things"). Topical preaching on themes such as how to biblically test those who claim to be prophets can also build awareness and discernment. Additionally, pastors can use ancient or contemporary statements of faith, such as the Apostles' Creed or the New City Catechism, to give disciples a firm foundation in essential doctrine. Pastors should emphasize that discernment is literally a spiritual survival skill in our day, and that the believer can only gain by knowing how to spot cultic groups and leaders by their beliefs, motives, and methods. It is also appropriate to warn vulnerable Christians by selectively naming divisive and deceptive teachers and cults, as the apostles did (e.g. Hymenaeus, Philetus,

30. Results of the East Africa survey are found in the author's 2015 master's thesis, "Christian Apologetics Education in Theological Institutions in Uganda," (Department of Mass Communications, Uganda Christian University). References to the southern Africa survey can be found in "Contending for the Faith in Theological Education," recorded at the 2021 Theological Education Association of Southern Africa conference in Pretoria (online at https://www.youtube.com/watch?v=Y4Opt-sPDtY).

Alexander, and Diotrephes). In addition, special priority must be given to inoculating and equipping two especially vulnerable groups:

i. **Students and youth** are easy prey for cultic missionaries who proselytize on university and secondary-school campuses. They are passionate and hungry for knowledge, but shallow in their theology. Youth are easy to hook with new teachings and claims of revelation, open to manipulation with offers of financial help or exciting overseas travel. And they typically have enough time on their hands to mobilize and spread the cult's false message, whether in hostels or on social media.

ii. **Women** are a majority in virtually every congregation. False teachers tend to take advantage of the spiritual, emotional and psychological vulnerabilities of all people, including women.[31] By doing this, they are also able to uniquely infiltrate homes.

In our experience, there may be some resistance at first. Some Christians balk at the suggestion that they are personally in danger from false teachers and teachings, like the Corinthians – 2 Cor 11:3–4, thinking that only "other people" are weak and easily deceived. Some fall back on excuses, misunderstanding and misapplying biblical warnings and commands – for example, not to "judge" (Matt 7:1–5) or "cast the first stone" (John 8:7); not to "touch the Lord's anointed" (Ps 105:13–15); not to "wrangle about words" (2 Tim 2:14); and not to "gossip" (Prov 20:19). Others protest that such matters are too difficult ("I'm not a student") or "not my place" ("I'm not a pastor"). But such objections can be patiently addressed.

For such instruction to be effective, congregations need to observe in their shepherds – in both word and deed – what Paul explains and exemplifies in Acts 20:18–21, 26–27, 33–35. He demonstrates faithfulness, transparency, and accountability in ministry, giving him the credibility to warn against those who seek to infiltrate, deceive, and exploit.

31. See Kevin Muriithi Ndereba, "New Religious Movements in Kenya: An Overview," Special Lecture delivered at the Biblical Equity Africa Conference held on 25th October 2023. Accessed on 3rd November 2023 from https://www.researchgate.net/publication/374951393_New_Religious_Movements_in_Kenya_An_Overview.

4.3 The Role of Para-Church Ministries

In most of Africa, denominations and pastors, parachurch ministries and Christian workers, and lay believers in general lack a robust and reliable source of factually sound, biblically grounded information and analysis so they can identify, answer, and evangelize the wide range of false and defective religious groups that pose a constant challenge to the proclamation of the Gospel and the building of the church. Even the most dedicated pastors lack the time, tools, and training to investigate and evaluate the many new and controversial groups that constantly appear on the scene.

In response to this need, in 2010 the Africa Centre for Apologetics Research (ACFAR) was established in Kampala, Uganda as a nondenominational, non-profit, nongovernmental organization of evangelical Christian conviction. Its fundamental purposes are to:

- Monitor and continuously compile accurate data on new and controversial religious groups active in East Africa.
- Analyze the beliefs and practices of such groups in the light of Scripture, and develop practical, contextualized apologetic responses in English and local languages.
- Warn and inoculate the greatest possible number of lay believers against both indigenous and imported cults and aberrant Christian movements.
- Equip pastors, seminary and Bible college students, Christian workers, and lay believers with tools and training to enable them to recognize and respond effectively to such groups (both apologetically and evangelistically).
- Raise up African apologists who will model balanced, biblical reasoning and responses to the challenges posed by heretical movements.
- Maintain a specialized reference collection, consisting of a research library and files in its primary subject areas, for its own use and for consultation by qualified researchers.

ACFAR seeks to equip believers to respond to suspected cults in six ways:

- **Identify** the group based on common patterns of cultic teaching and behaviour.
- **Understand** its false claims and practices – and how they differ from biblical truth.
- **Answer** its false claims and practices based on Scripture and other evidence.

- **Evangelize** its followers sensitively and strategically (2 Tim 2:24–26).
- **Embrace** those who find Christ, and **integrate** them into a local church fellowship (because "out of the cult is not necessarily into the truth").

By God's grace, ACFAR is working in partnership with Christian organizations across the region, training believers through seminars and conferences, campus outreaches, radio and television, podcasts and more in six languages. The work to be done is so vast that we hope God will soon raise up similar agencies to assist Christians and win cultists to Christ across the continent.

5. Conclusion

Across Africa, many millions are trapped in counterfeit forms of Christianity – hoping to please God and know Jesus, but spiritually imprisoned by deception. Among them are multitudes pouring vast amounts of time and treasure into taking others captive to the same deception.

But it's not too late for the body of Christ to act. Scripture shows us the way forward, and God has blessed us with powerful tools by which we can specially equip pastors, and warn and disciple lay believers. Indeed, because "our struggle is not against flesh and blood" (Eph 6:12), let us beseech him to raise up gifted men and women to lead the way, modelling gracious and effective responses to cultic groups that seek to erase the truth and plunder the church. The stakes are high, and we cannot shrink back; may God grant us a measure of faith equal to the task.

> [C]onduct yourselves in a manner worthy of the gospel of Christ. Then, whether I come and see you or only hear about you in my absence, I will know that you stand firm in the one Spirit, striving together as one for the faith of the gospel without being frightened in any way by those who oppose you. (Phil 1:27–28)

The author gratefully acknowledges the special assistance of his colleagues at the Centres for Apologetics Research (USA).

Bibliography

The inclusion of a book here does not necessarily constitute an endorsement of all works by the authors or publishers listed, or of all of the positions they may take on a variety of debatable groups or issues.

Adeleye, Femi. *Preachers of a Different Gospel: A Pilgrim's Reflections on Contemporary Trends in Christianity*. Carlisle: HippoBooks, 2011.

Adogame, Afeosemime. *Celestial Church of Christ: The Politics of Cultural Identity in a West African Prophetic-Charismatic Movement*. Bern: Peter Lang, 1999.

Anderson, Allan. *Zion and Pentecost: The Spirituality and Experience of Pentecostal and Zionist/Apostolic Churches in South Africa*. Pretoria: Unisa Press, 2000.

Atebembweire, Rodgers. "Christian Apologetics Education in Theological Institutions in Uganda." Unpublished Master's Thesis, Uganda Christian University, 2015.

Barnes, Philip W., et al. *The Abandoned Gospel: Confronting Neo-Pentecostalism and the Prosperity Gospel in Sub-Saharan Africa*. AB316, 2021.

Beckwith, Francis. "The Bahá'í World Faith." In *A Guide to New Religious Movements* edited by Ronald M. Enroth, 155–68. Downers Grove: InterVarsity Press, 2005.

Beisner, E. Calvin. *"Jesus Only" Churches*. Grand Rapids: Zondervan Academic, 2016.

Blanes, Ruy Llera. *A Prophetic Trajectory: Ideologies of Place, Time and Belonging in an Angolan Religious Movement*. New York: Berghahn, 2014.

Bledsoe, David Allen. *Brazilian Neo-Pentecostalism and the IURD: A Missiological Case Analysis of the Igreja Universal do Reino de Deus*. Saarbrücken: LAP LAMBERT Academic Publishing, 2011.

Bowman, Robert M. *Orthodoxy and Heresy: A Biblical Guide to Doctrinal Discernment*. Grand Rapids: Baker, 1992.

———. *Jehovah's Witnesses*. Grand Rapids: Zondervan Academic, 1995.

———. *The Word-Faith Controversy: Understanding the Health and Wealth Gospel*. Grand Rapids: Baker, 2001.

Burklin, Frederick O. "The New Apostolic Church." In *Dynamic Religious Movements: Case Studies of Rapidly Growing Religious Movements Around the World* edited by David J. Hesselgrave, 67–84. Grand Rapids: Baker, 1978.

Challies, Tim. *The Discipline of Spiritual Discernment*. Wheaton: Crossway, 2007.

Duyzer, Peter M. *Legend of the Fall*. Independent Scholar's Press, 2014.

Enroth, Ronald. *A Guide to New Religious Movements*. Downers Grove: InterVarsity Press, 2005.

Gampiot, Aurélien Mokoko, and Cécile Coquet-Mokoko. *Kimbanguism: An African Understanding of the Bible*. University Park: Pennsylvania State University Press, 2017.

Gomes, Alan W. *Unmasking the Cults*. Grand Rapids: Zondervan, 1995.

Hackett, Rosalind I. J. "New Age Trends in Nigeria: Ancestral and/or Alien Religion?" In *Perspectives on the New Age*, edited by James R. Lewis and J. Gordon Melton, 215–31. Albany: State University of New York Press, 1992.

Hesselgrave, David J. *Dynamic Religious Movements: Case Studies of Rapidly Growing Religious Movements Around the World*. Grand Rapids: Baker, 1978.

———. "New and Alternative Religious Movements: Some Perspectives of a Missiologist." https://www.apologeticsindex.org/cpoint12-1.html.

Johnson, Todd M., and Gina A. Zurlo. *Introducing Spirit-Empowered Christianity: The Global Pentecostal & Charismatic Movements in the 21st Century*. Tulsa: ORU Press, 2020.

Jourdier, Marc. "Au Berceau du Kimbanguisme, cette Religion Congolaise aux 22 millions de Fidèles" (At the cradle of Kimbanguism, this Congolese religion with 22 million followers), https://africa.la-croix.com/berceau-kimbanguisme-cette-religion-congolaise-aux-22-millions-de-fideles.

Kayiso, Fulgencio. *The Origin and Impact of the Faith of Unity on People in the Kibaale District*. Kampala: CACISA, 2007.

Kgatle, Mookgo Solomon. *Pentecostalism and Cultism in South Africa*. London: Palgrave Macmillan, 2021.

Kroesbergen, Hermen, ed. *In Search of Health and Wealth: The Prosperity Gospel in African Reformed Perspective*. Eugene: Resource Publications, 2014.

Kuligin, Victor. "The New Apostolic Church." *Africa Journal of Evangelical Theology* 24 no. 1 (2005).

Langtry, Stephen. *Inside the New Apostolic Church*. Claremont, South Africa: Forum Project, 1999.

Mbugua, Ken, et al. *Prosperity? Seeking the True Gospel*. Nairobi: ACTS Kenya, 2016.

McGrath, Alister. *Heresy: A History of Defending the Truth*. New York: HarperOne, 2009.

McKeever, Bill, and Eric Johnson. *Mormonism 101: Examining the Religion of the Latter-day Saints*. Grand Rapids: Baker, 2015.

Ndereba, Kevin Muriithi. "New Religious Movements in Kenya: An Overview." Special Lecture delivered at the Biblical Equity Africa Conference held on 25th October 2023. Accessed on 3rd November 2023 from https://www.researchgate.net/publication/374951393_New_Religious_Movements_in_Kenya_An_Overview.

Oguti, Athanasius. *The Origin and Impact of the Legio Maria Religious Movement in Eastern Uganda*. Kampala: CACISA, 2006.

Ortlund, Gavin. *Finding the Right Hills to Die On: The Case for Theological Triage*. Wheaton: Crossway, 2020.

Ratzlaff, Dale. "No Reason to Exist Without the Central Pillar." *Proclamation* 14 no. 1 (Spring 2013).

———. *Cultic Doctrine of Seventh-day Adventism: An Evangelical Wake-Up Call*. Camp Verde: LAM Publications, 2009.

Rosedale, Herbert L., and Michael D. Langone. "On Using the Term 'Cult.'" *ICSA Today* 6 no. 3 (2015).

Steyn, Chrissie. "A New Look at the New Age in South Africa." *Religion and Theology* 14 no. 3 (November 2007): 265–83.

———. *Worldviews in Transition: An Investigation into the New Age Movement in South Africa*. Pretoria: The University of South Africa, 1994.

Stott, John. *The Message of 1 Timothy and Titus*. Downers Grove: InterVarsity Press 2021. Perlego e-edition, https://www.perlego.com/book/1470580/the-message-of-1-timothy-and-titus-pdf.

Van Wyk, Ilana. *The Universal Church of the Kingdom of God in South Africa: A Church of Strangers*. Cambridge: Cambridge University Press, 2014.
Vokes, Richard. *Ghosts of Kanungu: Fertility, Secrecy and Exchange in the Great Lakes of East Africa*. Suffolk: James Currey, 2009.
Williams, Russ. *Analyzing Bahá'í Beliefs*. Laguna Hills: GTO Publishing, 2003.
Wilson, Dwight J. "Branham, William Marrion." In *The New International Dictionary of Pentecostal and Charismatic Movements*. Edited by Stanley M. Burgess and Eduard M. van der Maas. Grand Rapids: Zondervan, 2002.

14

Atheism in Africa

Kevin Muriithi Ndereba, PhD

Lecturer at St. Paul's University, Kenya and Research Fellow Department of Practical Theology and Missiology, Stellenbosch University, South Africa

Abstract

Atheism in Africa is rising. While missiologists project an upward trajectory of growth in African Christianity, part of Christian engagement will involve responding to sceptics within the continent. In this chapter, I explore the roots of atheism in the intellectual history of the West, in key figures such as Feuerbach, Marx, Nietzsche and Freud. Secondly, I trace the impact of the New Atheist movement within the continent, as a result of globalization and the rise of new media. Third, I orient the reader to some of the issues raised by atheists including morality, doctrine of God as well as the faith and science dialogue. The last section of the paper considers the worldview differences behind scientific naturalism, which undergirds contemporary atheism, and closes by offering practical recommendations in apologetic and evangelistic engagement of atheists in Africa.

Keywords: African Christianity, Apologetics, Atheism, Worldviews

1. Atheists Rising

Twenty-first-century economists coined the phrase "Africa rising." From Western media shapers such as the *Financial Times*, *The Economist* and *Time* magazine, commentators used this title to describe the burgeoning economies of African countries after the year 2000. Borrowing the same thinking, we could argue that in contemporary Africa, "African atheism is rising." At the time of writing of this chapter, the world is recovering its stride after the staggering COVID-19 global pandemic. A new COVID-19 variant called Omicron is the subject of many headlines. What this pandemic has done is to bring to the surface worldview issues around the reality of God, the faith-science dialogue as well as responses to pain and suffering in the world. While Christians are navigating the possibility of pain and suffering with their caring and concerned Father, atheists are doubting the existence of such a "god" – a "god" who is all powerful yet unmoved by this remarkable pain and suffering. I found it striking how atheists responded to this global pandemic, as per the atheist's charge. One of the members on a Facebook platform observes:

> COVID-19 is a proof that we need more scientific research institutions and laboratories and maybe more equipped health care facilities and less churches, mosques and temples, or whatever you call that place you go to meet with your imaginary friends.[1]

This post reveals the various logical gymnastics atheists have to go round to assert their worldview. For one, there is an underlying false dichotomy between science and religion. Atheists insist that religious people should choose between one or the other. Fortunately, the historical evidence of the development of science reveals that the choice is a limited one. The third way is simply that science and religion have a level of compatibility. Secondly, one sees the shallow doctrine of God that atheists think they have compared to what Christians really believe. This strawman of "imaginary friend" never engages the evidence of God's existence offered by many a theologian or philosopher, or the distinction of being between the triune God and other concepts of God. In summary, one senses the perennial and underlying issues that are raised by atheists. These include the relationship between faith and science, the equality of different religions as well as the scepticism towards anything supernatural. While atheists in Africa have often said that "Christianity is a white man's religion," we could also challenge them that "Atheism is a white man's irreligion."

On the positive side, many theologians have debunked this myth in both popular and scholarly circles. For instance, the missiologist Tim Welch has engaged with numerous evidences of African people and places in the biblical account, revealing how central Africa is to the redemptive arc of God.[2] A

1. Atheists in Kenya, Facebook Post. https://www.facebook.com/groups/atheistsinkenya/.

2. Tim Welch, *Africans and Africa in the Bible: An Ethnic and Geographic Approach* (Oasis International, 2019).

famous Nigerian Old Testament scholar, David T. Adamo has also engaged the theme of Africa, with specific focus in the Old Testament.[3] Other African scholars who have engaged African culture, presence and interpretation in and of the New Testament are Ukpong, Togarasei and Loba-Mkole.[4] Elsewhere, Adamo notes that there are about 867 mentions of Africa and Africans in the Bible.[5] His approach has thus engaged biblical hermeneutics for the purposes of the transformation of African realities, by engaging European hegemony and uplifting African culture and tradition.[6]

More recently, Elizabeth Mburu has offered a "four-legged approach" to the task of biblical interpretation in Africa, which seeks to engage the biblical text inductively while utilizing African worldview thinking in its interpretation and application. Some theologians, such as Mofokeng, have resourced this rich heritage of Africa and Africans in the Bible, towards the task of liberation within the continent.[7] Within the context of Africans in the diaspora, the biblical scholar C. H. Felder had published an influential book for the context of African-Americans.[8] Most recently, the New Testament scholar Esau McCaulley has been well received through his book on African-American hermeneutics.[9] In terms of the histories of Christianity in Africa, the historians Elizabeth Isichei, Adrian Hastings and Ogbu Kalu have unpacked the rich heritage of Christian faith in the continent.[10] Consequentially, Christianity

---

3. David T. Adamo, *Africa and the Africans in the Old Testament* (Eugene: Wipf & Stock Publishers, 2001).

4. Justin S. Ukpong, "New Testament Hermeneutics in Africa: Challenges and Possibilities," *Neotestamentica* 35 no. 1/2 (2001): 147–67; Jean-Claude Loba-Mkole, "The New Testament and Intercultural Exegesis in Africa," *Journal for the Study of the New Testament* 30 no.1 (2007): 7–28; Lovemore Togarasei, "African Traditional Religion in the Study of the New Testament in Africa," in *African Traditions in the Study of Religion in Africa: Emerging Trends, Indigenous Spirituality and the Interface with other World Religions*, ed. Afe Adogame, Bolaji Bateye, and Ezra Chitando (2013): 205–18.

5. David T. Adamo, "The historical development of Old Testament interpretation in Africa," *Old Testament Essays* 16 no. 1 (2003): 9–33.

6. David T. Adamo, "The Task and Distinctiveness of African Biblical Hermeneutic(s)," *Old Testament Essays* 28 no. 1 (2015): 31–52.

7. Takatso Mofokeng, "Black Christians, the Bible and Liberation," *Journal of Black Theology* 2 no. 1 (1988): 34–42.

8. H. C. Felder, *The African American Guide to the Bible* (Meadville: Christian Faith Publishing, 2018).

9. Esau McCaulley, *Reading while Black: African American Biblical Interpretation as an Exercise in Hope* (Downers Grove: InterVarsity Press, 2020).

10. Adrian Hastings, *The Church in Africa: 1450–1950* (Oxford: OUP, 1994); Elizabeth Isichei, *A History of Christianity in Africa: From Antiquity to Present* (Grand Rapids: Eerdmans, 1995); Bengt Sundkler, *A History of the Church in Africa* (Cambridge: Cambridge University

can be understood as an African faith. In terms of the theological contribution of Africa to global Christianity, the Methodist theologian, Thomas Oden, has noted that Africa is the intellectual seedbed of the faith.[11] Thus, with regards to continental and diasporic African contexts, there has been much conversation around the place of Africa and Africans in the Bible. These proposals on biblical interpretation have focused on the transformation of African life and society in view of the continent's complex historical past. Clearly, these scholars have thoroughly engaged various issues raised by sceptics of the Christian faith in a manner that puts the argument of Christianity as a foreign religion to rest. The book chapter by Kyama Mugambi makes the case at length.

However, atheists in Africa seem to have bypassed this critical work by Christian scholars. The upward trajectory of statistics of Africans who are defining themselves as "nones," the growth of atheist societies in key African cities such as Cape Town, Nairobi and Lagos as well as their loudening cries on social media and in the public sphere reveal that atheism in Africa is linked to the rise of the New Atheists in the West. Recent research places "religious nones" in Africa at 30 million people.[12] This statistic does not align with the secularization thesis but argues that it is critical to consider this cohort of African people, particularly for the purposes of Christian mission. It is true that the rise of Christianity in Africa has rebutted the claim that with increasing modernization, the African continent would become more secular. Statistics such as the above, which collated results from Pew and Afrobarometer surveys from 2002–2018, continue to raise the focus on "nones," which is inclusive of those who identify as atheists, and seeks to understand them not only quantitatively but also qualitatively.

Other structural issues have to do with the religious backgrounds of African people as well as the violent responses to voices of descent in many

---

Press, 2000); Ogbu Kalu, *African Christianity: An African Story* (Trenton: African World Press, 2007).

11. See Thomas Oden's books, *How Africa Shaped the Christian Mind: Rediscovering the African Seedbed of Western Christianity* (Downers Grove: IVP Academic, 2010); *The African Memory of Mark: Reassessing an Early Church Tradition and Early Libyan Christianity* (Downers Grove: IVP Academic, 2011); *Uncovering a North African Tradition* (Downers Grove: IVP Academic, 2011).

12. Yonatan N. Gez, Nadia Beider and Helga Dickow, "African and Not Religious: The State of Research on Sub-Saharan Religious Nones and New Scholarly Horizons," *Africa Spectrum* (November 2021), https://doi.org/10.1177/00020397211052567. Other localised studies of "religious nones" include Thomas J. Farrar, Khanyisane A. Falake, Adriel Mebaley, Mandisi D. Moya and Ivor I. Rudolph, "A Mall Intercept Survey on Religion and Worldview in the Cape Flats of Cape Town, South Africa," *Journal for the Study of Religion* 32 no. 1 (2019): 1–30, https://dx.doi.org/10.17159/2413-3027/2019/v32n1a3.

African nations. These issues affect the statistics surrounding atheism in the continent.[13] The research reveals that most who identify as "religious nones" in Sub-Saharan Africa (SSA) tend to be young and male. In terms of age, the median age of SSA "nones" is twenty years and in terms of gender, 65 percent of SSA "nones" are male, compared to 35 percent female.[14] African atheists societies may be a good place to chart such a research agenda.[15] In Kenya, atheists in Kenya are the major organized society of atheists. They have been receiving popular airing on television and radio stations, for their seemingly "non-conventional" views. Additionally, they have been pushing for the retreat of religion from the public square. Yet what is clear from their interviews and our engagements with them is that they have merely imported a Western idea of irreligion or atheism. In Nigeria, atheists are organised under the Atheist Society of Nigeria and in South Africa, Atheist Movement of South Africa. Much more research is needed to clearly identify, understand and engage with religious nones in the continent, in light of cultural biases, freedom of religion as well as Christian mission.

2. The Historical Roots of Atheism

African traditional societies had a conception of God, even though their conceptions of God have received both sympathetic and critical comparison with the triune God of the Christian Scriptures. This *sensus divinitatis*, as per Calvin, was a given fact, which led one of the foremost scholars of African traditional religions, the late John Mbiti to portend that "Africans are religious."[16] Thus, within the history of religion in Africa, atheism is an import from the West. The South African theologian J. H. Van Wyk notes the rise of modern atheism in the eighteenth century as a result of the Enlightenment, although other scholars such as Sedley trace it to the Greco-Roman context of the ancient world in the writings of Socrates and others.[17] In a work edited by Bullivant

13. Gez, Beider and Dickow, 9–10.

14. Gez, Beider and Dickow, 12.

15. Atheists in Kenya webpage http://atheistsinkenya.org/; Atheist Society of Nigeria https://www.atheist.org.ng/; Atheist Movement of South Africa https://www.facebook.com/Atheist.Movement.South.Africa/.

16. John Mbiti, *African Religions and Philosophy*, 2nd ed. (Oxford: Heinemann, 1990).

17. J. H. Amie Van Wyk, "Calvinism, Atheism and Freedom of Religion: A South African Perspective," In *Skriflig* 48 no. 2 (2014): 1–12. Available from http://www.scielo.org.za/scielo.php?script=sci_arttext&pid=S2305-08532014000200005; David Sedley, "From the Pre-Socratics to the Hellenistic Age," in Stephen Bullivant and Michael Ruse eds., *The Oxford Handbook of Atheism* (Oxford: Oxford University Press, 2013).

and Ruse various authors also explore the philosophical, historical, sociological and religious perspectives around atheism.[18] For instance, they distinguish between negative atheism, which critiques organized religion, and positive atheism, which makes a case for atheism.[19]

At the heart of the Enlightenment was the idea that humans are a law unto themselves, and that reason is supreme. This double emphasis on human autonomy and rationality carried over into the Western thought of the nineteenth century in the works of Feuerbach, Marx, Nietzsche and Freud. Van Wyk summarises the various strands of atheism as follows:

- Ludwig Feuerbach (1804–1872) viewed the idea of God as wish fulfilment and a projection of the human mind.
- Karl Marx (1818–1883) argued that religion is the opium of the people.
- Friedrich Nietzsche (1840–1900) declared triumphantly that the (metaphysical) God is dead.
- Sigmund Freud (1856–1939) considered religious faith in God an illusion and a projection of infantile desires.

3. The New Atheist Movement

These views of God spilled into all fields of study and affected entire societies. The resurgence of atheism in contemporary life is a marker of the longstanding effects of the aforementioned thinkers. In the 2000s, a movement dubbed "New Atheism" gained momentum through the work of "The Four Horsemen" – Daniel Dennett's *Darwin's Dangerous Idea: Evolution and the Meaning of Life* (1995), Richard Dawkins' *The God Delusion* (2006), Sam Harris' *The End of Faith* (2004), and the late Christopher Hitchens' *God is not Great: How Religion Poisons Everything* (2007). Several researchers correlate the rise of the New Atheists with the rise of social media, which has aided them in their public voice as well as a sense of belonging and identity.[20] The underlying views of New Atheism are that evolution explains the origin of the world, while science and reason alone can deal with life's realities, as opposed to religion. On the

18. Stephen Bullivant and Michael Ruse, (eds)., *The Oxford Handbook of Atheism*.

19. Stephen Bullivant, "Defining Atheism," in Bullivant and Ruse (eds.), *The Oxford Handbook of Atheism*.

20. Richard P. Cimino and Christopher Smith, "How the Media Got Secularism – With a Little Help from the New Atheists," *Religion and Society*, 2014. DOI: 10.1093/oxfordhb/9780199935420.013.15.

contrary, Christian apologists have debunked the science-faith and reason-faith dichotomy, by proposing that there are many Christians who are scientists and many who value intellectual pursuits. The issue is not science or reason, but an underlying worldview or belief system that idolizes science with the consequence of a materialistic or a naturalistic perspective about life.[21]

4. The Common Arguments from Atheists

Generally, in their arguments, some atheists commit logical and historical fallacies. For instance, in *The End of Faith*, Sam Harris lumps Christianity and Islam in the same box when he equates "Jesus" to "Allah" as well as "Ram."[22] Yet an elementary understanding of both religions reveals differing views on the person and work of Jesus Christ. Harris also contends that past injustices, such as political executions, slavery and murders, have arisen as a result of religion.[23] He therefore advises that we should abandon religion. This has been the similar push by atheists in Kenya. Many of them consider the chequered history of colonialism in Africa and throw the baby with the bathwater. In their wholesale rejection of Christianity without nuance, they fail to distinguish between the missionary enterprise and the colonial enterprise – which were simultaneously distinct, yet with areas of overlap, in terms of the agenda to explore the interior of Africa.[24] Secondly, critiques of religions on the grounds of oppression also fail to consider the positive arguments for religions as a precursor of development as well as the negative effect of atheism in communist and post-communist societies.[25] These critiques beg the question. In summary, atheists have popularized several arguments which are similar to "flogging a dead horse," rather than exploring the intricate interrelationships of religion and society. Other popular arguments include the false dichotomy of faith and science and the question of morality.

---

21. John C. Lennox, *Gunning for God: Why the New Atheists are Missing the Target* (Oxford: Lion Books, 2011), 15; James Porter Moreland, *Scientism and Secularism: Learning to Respond to a Dangerous Ideology* (Wheaton: Crossway, 2018).

22. Sam Harris, *The End of Faith* (New York: W. W. Norton, 2005), 35.

23. Harris, *The End of Faith*, 26.

24. Zablon Nthamburi, "The Beginning and Development of Christianity in Kenya: A Survey." In Zablon Nthamburi, ed., *From Mission to Church: A Handbook of Christianity in East Africa* (Nairobi: Uzima Press, 1991).

25. Paul Gifford, *Christianity, Politics, and Public Life in Kenya* (New York: Columbia University Press, 2009); Tam Ngo and Justine Quijada, eds., *Atheist Secularism and its Discontents: A Comparative Study of Religion and Communism in Eurasia* (Basingstoke: Palgrave Macmillan, 2015), 2.

4.1 Faith vs. Science

The most popular, yet unfounded critique of Christianity, comes from the apparent antagonism between faith and science.[26] Termed the "conflict thesis," this antagonism between science and religion has received recent attention.[27] Atheists claim that access to science is limited to them, with Christians often caricatured as anti-science. This faulty conclusion reveals that rather than engaging with the real issues in the faith-science dialogue, atheists in Africa seem to parrot what is most popular on social media among the New Atheist Movement. By dichotomizing faith and science, they portray a shallow historical analysis. Their view that faith and science are incompatible falls flat in the face when we consider the impact of Christian scientists, or at least scientists with theistic beliefs, on the field of scientific development. Rebecca McLaughlin for example notes:[28]

> The importance of believers in the history of science is revealed by none other than Albert Einstein. Einstein kept pictures of three scientific heroes on the wall of his study: Isaac Newton, Michael Faraday, and James Clerk Maxwell. Newton (ca. 1642–1727) is one of the most influential scientists of all time, famous for formulating the laws of gravity and motion. While not an orthodox Christian, owing to his denial of the full divinity of Christ, Newton was an earnest believer in God and wrote more about theology than physics. Faraday (1791–1867) is best known for his work on electromagnetism, and his scientific contributions were so significant that he is considered one of the greatest experimental scientists ever. The Faraday constant is named after him, as is the Faraday effect, the Faraday cage, and Faraday waves. Faraday was a passionate Christian, deeply interested in the relationship between science and faith. Maxwell (1831–1879) has been credited with the second great unification of physics, bringing together electricity, magnetism, and light. He was an evangelical Presbyterian, who

---

26. I have provided a sociological analysis of how the faith and science incompatibility theory influences the non-religious or atheistic identity formation of Atheists in Kenya. See Kevin Muriithi Ndereba, "Faith, Science, and Nonreligious Identity Formation Among Male Kenyan Youth," *Zygon®: Journal of Religion and Science*, 58 no. 1 (2023): 45–63.

27. See for instance Michael N. Keas, "Evaluating Warfare Myths about Science and Christianity and How These Myths Promote Scientism," *Religions* 12.132 (2021): 1–13, https://doi.org/10.3390/rel12020132.

28. Rebecca McLaughlin, *Confronting Christianity: 12 Hard Questions for the World's Largest Religion* (Wheaton: Crossway, 2019).

> became an elder of the Church of Scotland. For these men, science and faith went hand in hand, and studying God's creation was an act of worship.

McLaughlin unpacks how the history and philosophy of science render the fault lines between faith and science as imaginary. In contemporary society, the sociologist Elaine Howard Ecklund has debunked this wrongly accepted wishful thinking by showing that more than 50 percent of 1,700 scientists in top universities are people of faith, even though her definition of faith is quite broad.[29] The influential philosopher, Alvin Plantinga, has noted that most respected scientists in history were people of faith – Nicholas Copernicus, Galileo Galilei, Isaac Newton, Robert Boyle, John Wilkins, Roger Cotes, and many others.[30] Plantinga reveals that the real issue is not the incompatibility of faith and science, rather it is the incompatibility of naturalism and faith. Thus, the Christian response to the problem posed by atheists, that they ought to choose between faith and science, should be answered as "No, I prefer to have both." The issue is that rather, faith and *naturalism*[31] are at odds.

4.2 No Place for Morality?

Another question of debate among atheists and Christian apologists is in the area of morality. Because atheism views the origin of the world from an evolutionary lens, it does not consider any inherent purpose in the universe. As the spacecraft, Voyager 1, was departing our planetary boundaries for the fringes of the solar system on 14th February 1990, it turned around and captured a picture of our observable world. At that point, 6.4 billion kilometres away, earth appears as a tiny dot, a point of light only 0.12 pixel in size. Carl Sagan, gazing on that miniscule moment in time, would come to write "The Earth is a very small stage in a vast cosmic arena."[32] Richard Dawkins, later amplifies Sagan's observation into a statement in *River Out of Eden* that reads this way: "The universe we observe precisely has the properties we should

29. Elaine Howard Ecklund, *Science vs. Religion: What Scientists Really Think* (Oxford: Oxford University Press, 2010).

30. Alvin Plantinga, *Where the Conflict Really Lies: Science, Religion, and Naturalism* (Oxford: Oxford University Press, 2011), 266.

31. Also used synonymously with scientific *materialism* – the belief that only matter exists – or *scientism* – the belief that only science is the valid way of interpreting reality.

32. Carl Sagan, *Pale Blue Dot*, 1994. See also planetary society "Pale Blue Dot" https://www.planetary.org/worlds/pale-blue-dot.

expect if there is, at bottom, no design, no purpose, no evil and no good, nothing but blind, pitiless indifference."[33]

Blind, pitiless indifference.

The logical end goal of atheism is nihilism – or in other words, oblivion. Consequently, some have suggested that atheists can thus have no basis of morality. If they do, their grounds of morality would be borrowing from the objective morality inherent in the Judeo-Christian worldview. Without a reference to a moral lawgiver or transcendent standard of right and wrong, as we find in the triune God, then atheists cannot make any value judgements on a societal wrong. In fact, it would seem that an atheistic underpinning to morality can lead to disturbing ethical practices. For example, the Princetonian atheist bioethicist Peter Singer has argued that it is acceptable to kill babies who have physical disabilities or that it is morally acceptable to rape disabled people. The latter view was made as a response to a case of Anna Stubblefield, a Rutgers University philosophy professor convicted of sexually assaulting her mentally disabled pupil and sentenced to twelve years in prison.[34] On the former ethical support for infanticide, Singer says:

> For me, the knowledge that my [hypothetical Down Syndrome] child would not be likely to develop into a person whom I could treat as an equal . . . would greatly reduce my joy in raising my child and watching him or her develop.[35]

Singer's moral fibre is based on a materialistic ethos rather than on the inherent dignity of persons, created in *imago dei.* Clearly, without a foundation of morality anchored in an unchanging God who has created all human beings with value, the end of moral reasoning is degeneration. It is evident that the question of morality is a shibboleth for atheists who would like to reason objectively yet are only threaded along by a shifting postmodern and relativistic ethical foundation. To them, rape is a possibility. With such hollow arguments from the false dilemma of faith and science as well as the problematic ethical issues surrounding the purposeless and subjective worldview, why has the atheist movement found a resonance with the emerging African generations?

---

33. Richard Dawkins, *River out of Eden: A Darwinian View of Life* (New York: Basic Books, 2008), 133.

34. Nathan J. Robinson, "Now Peter Singer Argues That It Might Be Okay to Rape Disabled People," *Current Affairs* (4 April, 2017), https://www.currentaffairs.org/2017/04/now-peter-singer-argues-that-it-might-be-okay-to-rape-disabled-people.

35. Peter Singer, "Twenty Questions," *Journal of Practical Ethics* 4 no. 2 (2016): 67–78. http://www.jpe.ox.ac.uk/papers/twenty-questions/.

5. African Millennials and Atheism

Three things are stimulating atheism in Africa. First, African atheism has been popularized by the rise of scientism through Western education and the social media phenomenon. Whereas such literature within the African context is lacking, a growing body of research in the West notes the correlation between social media and the rise in atheism.[36] Having attended a gathering of atheists in Kenya, it is clear that not only are new media platforms supporting the propagation of atheistic ideas, but they are also platforms for belonging in a digital world.

Secondly, caricatures of Christianity, such as the wealth and health gospel, have stimulated African atheism. These paint a distorted picture of God as well as the Christian faith. The majority expression of Christianity in Africa is Pentecostal or charismatic, of course with a wide variety of nuance. However, the excessive versions of these have portrayed God as an ATM machine or a modern day "Santa Claus." Based on this overemphasis on wealth and health, many Christians are not equipped with a robust theology that can deal with evil, pain and suffering in our world. Thus, when atheists critique Christianity, they critique a false representation of the triune God in Scripture, who is the sovereign lord of all.

Thirdly, African atheism is growing because of the retrieval of traditional African religions. This seems counter-intuitive. But with the resurgence of African millennials tracing their African identities in a postmodern and global world, African atheists are finding a vehicle for casting the age-old assertion that Christianity is at odds with African identity. Thus, African atheists continue to bemoan Christianity as a white man's religion. Fortunately, a growing body of work among African Christian leaders is responding to such issues within the African context.[37] Such work is responding to various critiques of Christian faith from within a biblical worldview that engages the questions of traditional religions, science, and comparative religions.

---

36. Patrick Brian Segaren Pillay, "The Emergence of Atheism in Post-Colonial South Africa," PhD dissertation (University of Kwa Zulu Natal, 2017), 50. See also Christopher R. Cotter, Philip Andrew Quadrio and Jonathan Tuckett, eds. *New Atheism: Critical Perspectives and Contemporary Debates* (Dordrecht: Springer, 2017).

37. See The Gospel Coalition Africa, Apologetics series. https://africa.thegospelcoalition.org/series/african-apologetics/.

6. The Worldview Clash – Atheism vs Biblical Worldview

At a more foundational level, the clash of faith and atheism is a clash of worldviews. Atheism is made up of two words: "a" and "theism." "A" is a negation. And "theism" is "belief in God." Thus, atheism can be defined as a lack of belief in the existence of God or gods. Some atheists have expanded on this simple definition. For instance, some suggest that atheism is a lack of belief in God due to the absence of evidence for God's existence. However, such arguments focus on the conceptualizations of knowledge and attendant notions of evidence and justification. This strand of atheism, for example, grounds unbelief in the fact that there is no "evidence, or enough evidence, for that [Christian] belief."[38] Plantinga has engaged these strands of atheism based on philosophical arguments on the concepts of justification in knowledge to claim that contrary to what people say, Christian faith is warranted on the account of its facts being properly basic. He builds on Calvin's concept of *sensus divinitatis*, whereby belief in God, according to Plantinga, is in a sense "innate" although it flourishes within particular conditions, here we would say for example, personal experiences of grace and special revelation.[39] Plantinga puts it this way: "what one has from his mother's womb is not this knowledge of God, but a capacity for it." Expanding this, he says:

> People in grave danger instinctively turn to the Lord, asking for succor and support. (They say there are not atheists in foxholes.) On a beautiful spring morning (the birds singing, heaven and earth alight and alive with glory, the air fresh and cool, the treetops gleaming in the sun) a spontaneous hymn of thanks to the Lord – thanks for your circumstances and your very existence – may arise in your soul. According to the model, therefore, there are many circumstances, and circumstances of many different kinds, that call forth or occasion theistic belief.[40]

What the Christian philosopher Alvin Plantinga has been able to do is to unpack the concept of evidence. Christian belief, he argues, can be supported by evidence, for instance arguments for the existence of God. However, such beliefs are not the ground of Christian faith. A Christian may become a Christian before grasping these sophisticated arguments. In this sense,

---

38. Alvin Plantinga, *Knowledge and Christian Belief* (Grand Rapids: Eerdmans, 2015) [Kindle edition].

39. Plantinga, *Knowledge and Christian Belief.*

40. Plantinga, *Knowledge and Christian Belief,* ch. 6. Loc: 7 of 15.

Christian faith "resembles the faculties of perception, memory and *a priori* knowledge." Christian belief,

> will ordinarily be basic, in the sense that it is not accepted on the evidential basis of other propositions. The same goes for memory. You ask me what I had for breakfast; I think for a moment and then remember: pancakes with blueberries. I don't argue from the fact that it seems to me that I remember having pancakes for breakfast to the conclusion that in fact I did; rather you ask me what I had for breakfast and the answer simply comes to mind.[41]

Atheism is conflicted when it comes to both the quality and quantity of "evidence" that atheists expect. Plantinga has engaged these arguments to show that the rejection of Christianity based on justification of knowledge, is, to some extent, a clutching after a straw. The reality is not that there is insufficient evidence. In fact, archeologists, philosophers, theologians, historians have marshalled up various strands of evidence. Rather, the issue is what people do with this evidence. It boils down to contrasting worldviews in how we look and respond to this evidence (Ps 19; Rom 1).

In terms of demographics, although small, there is an increase in the population of atheists in Kenya – currently standing at 1.6% percent according to the 2019 Kenyan population census. Similar and growing trajectories have also been noted in South Africa as well as in Nigeria. However, behind the tag "atheist" or "atheism" lies an underlying view of the world, called scientific naturalism; that only what is tangible exists. Or stated negatively: that the supernatural does not exist. As has been argued in the previous paragraphs, other "softer" versions of atheism would critique some of these simplistic definitions by arguing that atheism arises from the lack of evidence that God exists. However, what is interesting is that theists claim to have plenty of evidence for God's existence.

Imagine yourself, after COVID-19 ends, sitting on a sandy beach. You are there with your friend, and she has her sunglasses on. Both of you are gazing into the beautiful horizon of the ocean. You begin a conversation about the color of the ocean. You say the blue of the ocean fits very nicely with the bright blue sky. She says "actually, the green color of the ocean contrasts better with the blue sky." You see blue. She sees green, a darker shade, because of the sunglasses. You are both looking at the same ocean. Why the difference?

41. Plantinga, *Knowledge and Christian Belief*, ch. 6. Loc: 7 of 15.

The difference is likely because of the sunglasses that add a different perspective to the reality. In reality, the ocean is blue. But because of the lens through which you are both gazing through, it may appear different. This is basically the concept of worldview. Whether you realize it or not, whether you've rationalized it or not, a worldview is a lens through which you view the world. The concept of worldview is therefore not only for the basis of Christian discipleship but also for evangelistic and apologetics engagement. The concept of *worldview* has been defined as follows in shorthand:

- Assumptions or presuppositions we hold about reality.[42]
- Foundational and comprehensive beliefs about the world and which are embodied in a story.[43]
- Interconnected systems of beliefs.[44]
- Framework of thought.[45]

These shorthand definitions reveal that the concept of worldview is a foundational way in which we look at life, the interconnected thought systems and values we hold, and how those orient us in our pursuit of the good life. I find Sire's longer definition a good way to both expand and synthesize all these concepts of worldview:

> a commitment, a fundamental orientation of the heart, that can be expressed as a story or in a set of presuppositions (assumptions which may be true, partially true, or entirely false) which we hold (consciously or subconsciously, consistently or inconsistently) about the basic constitution of reality, and that provides the foundation on which we live and move and have our being.[46]

From this vantage point, atheism and Christianity, and any other religion for that matter, operate on different worldviews. These worldviews have different ways of answering the deepest human questions: where do we come from? What is our meaning in life? What happens after we die? Atheism operates from a view that holds that "only what can be measured is real" –

42. James Sire, *Naming the Elephant: Worldview as a Concept* (Downers Grove: InterVarsity Press, 2004), 22.

43. Michael W. Goheen and Craig G. Bartholomew, *Living at the Crossroads: An Introduction to Christian Worldview* (Grand Rapids: Baker Academic, 2008).

44. Richard DeWitt, *Worldviews: An Introduction to the History and Philosophy of Science* (Hoboken: John Wiley & Sons, 2018), 7.

45. Diphus C. Chemorion, *Introduction to Christian Worldview* (Nairobi: Nairobi Academic Press, 2014), 2.

46. James Sire, *The Universe Next Door*, 5th ed., 18–24.

scientific naturalism or materialism. Christianity operates from a Judeo-Christian worldview, which includes the revealed truths of a powerful and personal God, beauty and the corruption of sin, good and evil, and heaven and hell, among others.

6.1 Biblical View of Atheism

To understand atheism by necessity means understanding how atheists identify as atheists. The verb "identify" in the previous sentence is helpful. For the biblical view is that God's existence is clear to all of humanity (Ps 19; Rom 1:20). Thus, the issue is not so much the existence of God but whether or not we acknowledge it.

According to Scripture, atheism is not the absence of God but the rejection of God (Rom 1:18, 21–23). Throughout the Bible, there are only two responses to God: acknowledgement or rejection. The problem is that sin, as a distortion of what is good and true, including coming to the reasonable conclusion of God's presence, casts its net far into the recesses of the heart. Atheism, as a rejection of God, is not so much a lack of evidence but the suppression of it.

This is evident in a person's lifestyle (Rom 1:18). The New Testament usually draws a parallel between thinking and living. In the case of those who acknowledge the reality of God through the person of Jesus Christ, their minds are renewed and they live uprightly (Rom 12:1–2; Col 3:1–3; 1 Thess 4:1–3). In the case of those who deny God's existence, their understanding is darkened and their living rebels against God's wise rule (Eph 4:17–18; 1 Pet 4:1–3).

Within the Reformed tradition, theologians and apologists utilize the concept of regeneration to describe how different people respond to the things (or for our case, knowledge) of God. Without the work of the Holy Spirit through the living word of God to renew the hearts of sinners, any evidence offered to the unbeliever will always be rejected, no matter how compelling they are. Thus, in Christian apologetics, it is important that our apologetic engagements take the word of God as presuppositional or axiomatic or foundational to the entire apologetic enterprise, even though we may make use of extra-biblical evidence.[47] Therefore, atheism is not an intellectual problem but a spiritual problem. This spiritual problem affects one's view of the world, and how we ought to live in it. But what is the atheistic worldview?

---

47. John Frame, *Apologetics: A Justification of Christian Belief* (Phillipsburg: P&R Publishing, 2015), 53–57.

6.2 Differences between the Atheistic and Biblical Worldviews

Atheism claims that science, especially the "big bang," accounts for the origin of the universe. The biblical worldview assumes God as the source of the universe, creating from nothing or *ex nihilo*. According to special revelation, this understanding is received by faith (Gen 1:1; John 1:1; Heb 11:3). Christians have taken different perspectives regarding how to square this understanding of creation with the scientific proposals. But in all these views, the understanding of God as creator is central.

The atheistic worldview attaches no inherent purpose to existence. Therefore, meaning is elusive, while it also lacks an objective standard for morality. The common view among atheists is that morality is conditioned by society. However, when push comes to shove, few of us readily accept responsibility for wrong actions. For while we easily identify the evil in the holocaust or genocides, individually our consciences are ignored or downplayed. A biblical worldview assumes the fallenness of creation. But there is redemption of creation through Jesus Christ. The character of God is the norm of morality and he provides meaning in life (Exod 20:1–17; Prov 3:5–6; Titus 2:11–14; 1 Pet 1:16).

Atheism and Christian faith additionally differ on the question of destiny. What happens after death? Is there life after death? The atheistic worldview rejects the idea of eternity, while a biblical worldview views eternity as real and spent either in eternal fellowship with God or without God in eternal damnation (John 3:16; Heb 9:27–28; Rev 22:12–15). Although atheists view the progression of the world in evolutionary terms of chance, Christians acknowledge the sovereignty and providential nature of God moving the entire creation towards his distinct purposes.

7. Practical Advice for Engaging Atheists

African Christians should be concerned with engaging the major issues of the prosperity gospel, issues arising from traditional religious worldviews and also postmodernism. For we see these challenges presently and anticipate them for the next generation. But Africans must also be ready to give an answer when engaging atheists.

When one looks at the responses by Christians on the Atheists in Kenya (AIK) Facebook page, for instance, the responses are usually more emotive than reasonable. Their responses lacked righteous reason. However, the reality is that as we engage with atheists, eventually we have in mind the gospel message of Christ. Even if our arguments engage some of the aforementioned issues, eventually the intellectual engagement reduces the barriers in order to expose the gospel. In an online seminar on morality hosted by AIK, the hosts gave the following condition to responders: "please do not preach." But how do we preach without preaching?

In answer to that question, I will conclude this chapter with four ways to engage atheists:

7.1 Learning the Art of Answering Questions

Asking questions is such a helpful tactic in apologetic engagement.[48] Asking questions helps one, in a gentle and wise way, to go beneath the questions asked and explore the motives, plausibility and orientation of the questioner. By doing this, one is able to explore the deeper presuppositions that underlie particular ideologies and through the Word of God, "take every thought captive to Christ" (2 Cor 10:5).

7.2 Loving the Person Behind the Question

At the end of the day, atheists are human beings created in the image of God. Yet many atheists are informed by negative personal experiences of both life and the church. Because they will either live with God forever – or without him – we must graciously love them. So, as we engage with atheists let us do so with "gentleness and respect" (1 Pet 3:15–16). Apologists are known to say that "love is the greatest apologetic."

7.3 Considering the Heart Behind the Person

It has been said many times in pulpits that "the heart of the problem is the problem of the heart." For rejecting God is never merely an intellectual choice. It is spiritual. Therefore, we need to humbly depend on God in any and every engagement with unbelievers of all stripes. There is a need to rely on the Holy Spirit to engage the heart issue behind every question, as he has the power to transform the most sophisticated unbeliever.

---

48. To my knowledge, one of the best books that discusses some of these tactics at length is Gregory Koukl, *Tactics: A Game Plan for Discussing your Christian Convictions* (Grand Rapids: Zondervan Reflective, 2019).

7.4 Convincing the Person Using God's Gospel

However, the truth is that some atheists will completely reject God. The task of preaching the gospel, in love and truth, is to witness to Christ. The changing of the heart is God's prerogative. The pattern for God's people has been to proclaim the life, death, resurrection and ascension of Christ to all nations. After all, the gospel is the power of God unto salvation (Rom 1:16). Thus, we must remember, it is only the Spirit of God working through the word of God that can birth a child of God.

Bibliography

Adamo, David T. *Africa and the Africans in the Old Testament*. Eugene: Wipf & Stock, 2001.

———. "The Historical Development of Old Testament Interpretation in Africa." *Old Testament Essays* 16 no. 1 (2003): 9–33.

———. "The Task and Distinctiveness of African Biblical Hermeneutic(s)." *Old Testament Essays* 28 no. 1 (2015): 31–52.

Bullivant, Stephen, and Michael Ruse, eds. *The Oxford Handbook of Atheism*. Oxford: Oxford University Press, 2013.

Chemorion, Diphus C. *Introduction to Christian Worldview.* Nairobi: Nairobi Academic Press, 2014.

Cimino, Richard P., and Christopher Smith. "How the Media Got Secularism – With a Little Help from the New Atheists." *Religion and Society*, 2014. DOI: 10.1093/oxfordhb/9780199935420.013.15.

Cotter, Christopher R., Philip Andrew Quadrio and Jonathan Tuckett, eds. *New Atheism: Critical Perspectives and Contemporary Debates*. Dordrecht: Springer, 2017.

Dawkins, Richard. *River out of Eden: A Darwinian View of Life*. New York: Basic Books, 2008.

Dawkins, Richard, and Lalla Ward. *The God Delusion*. Boston: Houghton Mifflin Company, 2006.

DeWitt, Richard. *Worldviews: An Introduction to the History and Philosophy of Science.* Hoboken: John Wiley & Sons, 2018.

Ecklund, Elaine Howard. *Science vs. Religion: What Scientists Really Think*. Oxford: Oxford University Press, 2010.

Farrar, Thomas J., et al. "A Mall Intercept Survey on Religion and Worldview in the Cape Flats of Cape Town, South Africa." *Journal for the Study of Religion* 32. no. 1 (2019): 1–30. https://dx.doi.org/10.17159/2413-3027/2019/v32n1a3.

Felder, H. C. *The African American Guide to the Bible*. Meadville: Christian Faith Publishing, 2018.

Frame, John. *Apologetics: A Justification of Christian Belief*. Phillipsburg: P&R Publishing, 2015.

Gez, Yonatan N., Nadia Beider and Helga Dickow. "African and Not Religious: The State of Research on Sub-Saharan Religious Nones and New Scholarly Horizons." *Africa Spectrum* (November 2021). https://doi.org/10.1177/00020397211052567.

Gifford, Paul. *Christianity, Politics, and Public Life in Kenya*. New York: Columbia University Press, 2015.

Goheen, Michael W., and Craig G. Bartholomew. *Living at the Crossroads: An Introduction to Christian Worldview*. Grand Rapids: Baker Academic, 2008.

Harris, Sam. *The End of Faith*. New York: W. W. Norton, 2005.

Hastings, Adrian. *The Church in Africa: 1450–1950*. Oxford: Oxford University Press 1994.

Isichei, Elizabeth. *A History of Christianity in Africa: From Antiquity to Present*. Grand Rapids: Eerdmans, 1995.

Kalu, Ogbu. *African Christianity: An African Story*. Trenton: African World Press, 2007.

Keas, Michael N. "Evaluating Warfare Myths about Science and Christianity and How These Myths Promote Scientism." *Religions* 12.132 (2021): 1–13. https://doi.org/10.3390/rel12020132.

Koukl, Gregory. *Tactics: A Game Plan for Discussing your Christian Convictions*. Grand Rapids: Zondervan Reflective, 2019.

Lennox, John C. *Gunning for God: Why the New Atheists are Missing the Target*. Oxford: Lion Books, 2011.

Loba-Mkole, Jean-Claude. "The New Testament and Intercultural Exegesis in Africa." *Journal for the Study of the New Testament* 30 no. 1 (2007): 7–28.

Mbiti, John S. *African Religions and Philosophy* 2nd ed. Oxford: Heinemann, 1990.

McCaulley, Esau. *Reading while Black: African American Biblical Interpretation as an Exercise in Hope*. Downers Grove: InterVarsity Press, 2020.

McClendon III, John H. "Nkrumah's Consciencism: Philosophical Materialism and the Issue of Atheism Revisited." *Journal on African Philosophy* 4 (2012). https://www.africaknowledgeproject.org/index.php/jap/article/view/1644.

McLaughlin, Rebecca. *Confronting Christianity: 12 Hard Questions for the World's Largest Religion*. Wheaton: Crossway, 2019.

Mofokeng, Takatso. "Black Christians, the Bible and Liberation." *Journal of Black Theology* 2 no. 1 (1988): 34–42.

Moreland, James Porter. *Scientism and Secularism: Learning to Respond to a Dangerous Ideology*. Wheaton: Crossway, 2018.

Ndereba, Kevin Muriithi. "Faith, Science, and Nonreligious Identity Formation Among Male Kenyan Youth." *Zygon®: Journal of Religion and Science*, 58 no. 1 (2023): 45–63.

Ngo, Tam, and Justine Quijada, eds. *Atheist Secularism and its Discontents: A Comparative Study of Religion and Communism in Eurasia*. Basingstoke: Palgrave Macmillan, 2015.

Nthamburi, Zablon. "The Beginning and Development of Christianity in Kenya: A Survey." In *From Mission to Church: A Handbook of Christianity in East Africa*. Edited by Zablon Nthamburi. Nairobi: Uzima Press, 1991.

Oden, Thomas. *How Africa Shaped the Christian Mind: Rediscovering the African Seedbed of Western Christianity*. Downers Grove: IVP Academic, 2010.

———. *The African Memory of Mark: Reassessing an Early Church Tradition and Early Libyan Christianity*. Downers Grove: IVP Academic, 2011.

———. *Uncovering a North African Tradition*. Downers Grove: IVP Academic, 2011.

Pillay, Patrick Brian Segaren. "The Emergence of Atheism in Post-Colonial South Africa." PhD dissertation, University of Kwa Zulu Natal, 2017.

Plantinga, Alvin. *Knowledge and Christian Belief*. Grand Rapids; Cambridge, UK: Eerdmans, 2015. Perlego e-edition, https://www.perlego.com/book/2015628/knowledge-and-christian-belief-pdf.

———. *Where the Conflict Really Lies: Science, Religion, and Naturalism*. Oxford: Oxford University Press, 2011.

Robinson, Nathan J. "Now Peter Singer Argues That It Might Be Okay to Rape Disabled People." *Current Affairs* (4 April, 2017). https://www.currentaffairs.org/2017/04/now-peter-singer-argues-that-it-might-be-okay-to-rape-disabled-people.

Sagan, Carl. *Pale Blue Dot*, 1994. See also planetary society "Pale Blue Dot" https://www.planetary.org/worlds/pale-blue-dot.

Sedley, David. *From the Pre-Socratics to the Hellenistic Age*. Oxford: Oxford University Press, 2013.

Singer, Peter. "Twenty Questions." *Journal of Practical Ethics* 4 no. 2 (2016): 67–78. http://www.jpe.ox.ac.uk/papers/twenty-questions/.

Sire, James. *Naming the Elephant: Worldview as a Concept*. Downers Grove: InterVarsity Press, 2004.

Sundkler, Bengt. *A History of the Church in Africa*. Cambridge: Cambridge University Press, 2000.

Togarasei, Lovemore. "African Traditional Religion in the Study of the New Testament in Africa." Pages 205–18 in *African Traditions in the Study of Religion in Africa: Emerging Trends, Indigenous Spirituality and the Interface with other World Religions*. Edited by Afe Adogame, Bolaji Bateye and Ezra Chitando (Farnham: Ashgate, 2012).

Ukpong, Justin S. "New Testament Hermeneutics in Africa: Challenges and Possibilities." *Neotestamentica* 35 no. 1/2 (2001): 147–67.

Van Wyk, J. H. Amie. "Calvinism, Atheism and Freedom of Religion: A South African Perspective." In *Skriflig* 48 no. 2 (2014): 1–12. http://www.scielo.org.za/scielo.php?script=sci_arttext&pid=S2305-08532014000200005.

Welch, Tim. *Africans and Africa in the Bible: An Ethnic and Geographic Approach*. Chicago: Oasis International Publishing, 2019.

15

Christian-Muslim Apologetics

History and Contemporary Practice

Judy Wanjiru Wang'ombe, PhD
Lecturer at Africa International University, Kenya

Abstract

Living in a "global village" has enabled Christians and Muslims to interact in contemporary times especially in Africa. People can no longer ignore each other as they rub shoulders in different spheres of life. This chapter seeks to discuss religious encounter between Christians and Muslims with a specific focus on the apologetics. Apologetics differ from polemical engagements that have tended to characterize Christian-Muslims relations in Africa. Negative polemics are unbiblical because they go against the call to give a gentle and respectful answer to anyone who asks for an explanation of the Christian faith (1 Pet 3:15). This chapter aims at giving suggestions for constructive apologetics between Christians and Muslims. To do this, a global historical overview of how Christians engaged with Muslims will be provided. This overview will include a section on the apologetics that has been played out in different parts of Africa with specific attention on the East African context. Finally, the chapter will culminate with practical suggestions of how to engage appropriately especially using a Scriptural Reasoning (SR) approach that seeks to understand the textual basis of apologetical engagements. SR is an appropriate venture that points to the need to understand the "Other" from their textual religious affiliations. It is suitable because it commences with a respectful stance where participants are willing to painstakingly read scriptural texts of the "Other" without prior biases. The advantage of starting from such a premise is that it ensures there is striving to understand the textual "Other" from an emic (insider's) perspective.

Keywords: Christian-Muslim Relations, Christian-Muslim Apologetics, Interreligious Dialogue, Scriptural Reasoning

1. Introduction

The world of John of Damascus resembles the contemporary times only in terms of the heightened interfaith interactions between Christians and Muslims. John wrote his famous treatises, *Heresy of the Ishmaelites*, as an apologetical response to Islam, which he classified as a Christian heresy. The Christian world today is more enlightened in the understanding of Islam, not as a heresy, but a religion that has ardent followers who defend it to the core. Such a defence was illustrated by the infamous 9/11 incidents that awakened the world to a need to understand Muslims as people and Islam as a religion. Myriad books and articles have been written about Islam. Institutions have established departments that teach Islamic studies. Christian organizations have been founded to help people interact better with Muslims. All these endeavours indicate how pertinent the topic under study in this book, and this chapter, is to contemporary times.

The topic of Christian-Muslim relations is as broad as it is pertinent to the world in contemporary times. This chapter narrows down to a discussion on the Christian-Muslim apologetics, which has been studied from various approaches. Apologetics can be examined as a literary genre, or from a historical perspective that shows how Christians have defended their faith before Muslims. Other scholars have examined the topic from a religious perspective, while others from an anthropological angle. All these bring out a rich tapestry of information that helps current scholarship to advance their research and writing efforts.

This chapter provides a historical and contemporary overview of Christian-Muslim apologetics in the different historical epochs in various locations including the African context. As a way forward, the chapter also suggests some practical thoughts on contemporary engagements between Muslims and Christians. These suggestions align with the Scriptural Reasoning (SR) approach and are deemed to be an amicable way that contrasts with the popular polemical approach that has pitted Christians against Muslims in many African countries.

2. Overview of Historical Eras in Apologetics

John of Damascus, mentioned above, was the first apologist to Muslims, according to Daniel Janosik.[1] Yet, it is important to note that Christians and Muslims began to engage in apologetics even before John of Damascus' treatises. This section gives a brief overview of the history of Christian-Muslim relations, with a specific focus on apologetical engagements. Scholars who delve specifically into the historical discussions on apologetics divide the eras as follows:

1. Early beginnings (Late Antiquity, AD 610–650)
2. Early apologetics of Middle Ages (AD 650–1000)
3. Later apologetics (AD 1100–1300)
4. Modern apologetics (AD 1400–to date)

2.1 The Early Beginnings (AD 610–650) and Middle Ages Apologetics (AD 650–1000)

The Early beginnings of apologetics date back to the establishment of Islam and how Muhammad and his companions (*Ṣaḥābah*), interacted with Christians in the Hijaz (Arabian Peninsula) region. Muhammad tried very hard to convert Christians and Jews to his "monotheistic" religion, since he perceived that they worshipped "three gods" when they talked about the Trinity. The Qur'an gives tacit evidence to the polemical debate that may have ensued when Muhammad denounced some of the religious beliefs of both Jews and Christians of his day.

The Early apologetics feature dialogues between leading theologians and Muslims like Caliph al-Mahdi with Patriarch Timothy 1's discussion in 781 AD. The famous apologist, John of Damascus' engagement with Muslims is a significant treatise that has left an indelible mark over the centuries. John's perception of Muhammad and Islam are worth noting. He considered Muhammad a false prophet and a "forerunner of the anti-Christ."[2] In his treatise, *Heresy of the Ishmaelites*, John refers to Muhammad as "Mamed" who knew the Old and New Testaments only superficially and may have learnt the contents from an Arian monk.[3] John further considered Islam as a heresy rather

1. Daniel J. Janosik, *John of Damascus: First Apologist to the Muslims* (Eugene: Pickwick Publications, 2016).

2. Hugh Goddard, *A History of Christian-Muslim Relations* (Chicago: New Amsterdam Books, 2000), 39.

3. Janosik, *John of Damascus: First Apologist to the Muslims*, 99.

than a false religion that was leading its adherents astray. As a "church father" John saw his obligation to counter heresies like the Arianism (319–336), which split the fourth-century church on the *homoi-ousios* (similar substance) versus *homo-ousios* (same substance) stance about Jesus. John therefore saw Islam as an aberration from the true Christian religion. According to him, Muslims were Ishmaelites (also called Saracens and Hagarenes), who had distorted what the other two monotheistic religions espoused.

As much as John of Damascus is esteemed as a Christian apologist, it is important to note that his apologetics had limitations in order to learn and not repeat similar mistakes in contemporary times. For instance, it would be unfortunate for any Christian in the contemporary world to consider Islam as a Christian heresy. When John considered Islam as heretical, he never saw anything good in it; he did not acknowledge any vestiges of God in Islam.

Another shortcoming was that John did not intend to instruct Christians on how to witness to Muslims. His main intention was to refute the heresy that had infiltrated Christianity. He especially was eager to prove the superiority of Christianity over Islam, which appealed to the Christians of his days. His approach was popular for a long time as Christians tried to prove their supremacy over Muslims. However, this approach was to be proved unviable especially with the global realities of inter-religious interactions.

2.2 Later Apologetics (AD 1100–1300)

The Later apologetics era was marked by the infamous twelfth-century Crusades. It is well noted that despite the Crusades, the *Convivencia* period "evokes an aura of tolerance, coexistence, and open-mindedness," as Wang'ombe and Wang'ombe narrate.[4] Even though *Convivencia* was not a "fixed and settled entity" according to Wheatcroft,[5] its significance cannot be underestimated. There were noteworthy exchanges between Christians and Muslims scholars who sought to understand each other's religion. Christians in Al-Andalus adopted the Arabic culture including language, dress, literature,

4. Judy Wang'ombe and Harun Wang'ombe, "Re-Reading Spanish Medieval Convivencia," in *Forgiveness, Peacemaking, and Reconciliation*, ed. David Ngaruiya and Rodney Reed (Carlisle, Cumbria, England: Langham Global Library, 2020), 129.

5. Andrew Wheatcroft, *Infidels: A History of the Conflict between Christendom and Islam* (New York: Random House, 2003), 73.

and poetic interest without really converting to Islam.[6] The fanatical Cordoba martyrdom movement however tainted the Al-Andalus *Convivencia* when Christians publicly insulted Islam, which led to the execution of several of them. The precursor to these fateful events was the apocalyptic reading of the Bible particularly by two Christians in Cordoba, one a priest called Eulogius, and the other a layperson called Paul Alvarus. Goddard recounts that these two appealed to the biblical apocalypse to interpret the entrance of Islam, identifying Muhammad as the antichrist.[7] The result of such scriptural interpretation in Cordoba was the execution of Christians including Eulogius who was decapitated. The negativity against Islam was to be propagated in the West and which gave rise to the eleventh-century Crusades.

Amidst the negative image of Islam, which prompted the Crusades, there were alternative perceptions of Islam by a few noted Christians. Peter the Venerable (c. 1092–1156), who was the abbot of the monastery of Cluny in Burgundy, preferred to study Islam comprehensively using Islamic sources. By then, the first translation of the Qur'an from Arabic to Latin had been effected in 1143, which thus made things easier for Peter the Venerable. He even travelled to Spain with the aim of accessing other Islamic and apologetic materials like al-Kindi's *Apology*. Peter not only read these materials, but he also wrote treatises on Islam. These treaties included calling Muslims to salvation by saying: "Loving, I write to you; writing, I invite you into salvation."[8]

Another notable person with such a "loving" outlook towards Muslims was Francis of Assisi (1181–1226) who travelled to Egypt in 1219 during the fifth Crusade. He is regarded as one of the models of irenicism because of the peaceful nature of engaging with Muslims that contrasted sharply with the crusading Christians. He accompanied the crusaders to Egypt and sought an audience with the Sultan of Egypt, al-Malik al-Kamil, which was granted. Francis was able to preach to the Sultan about Christianity. There are varied accounts about this encounter that have been written over the years, yet suffice it to mention, Francis' apologetics was contrary to the negative attitude of the Crusade, which earned him the title, "apostle of love."[9]

---

6. Lindsey Marie Vaughan, "Convivencia: Christians, Jews, and Muslims in Medieval Spain" (University of Tennessee Honors Thesis Projects, Knoxville, USA, University of Tennessee, 2003), 9.

7. Goddard, *A History of Christian-Muslim Relations*, 82–83.

8. Goddard, 95.

9. Francis of Assisi's different attitude to Muslims also prompted Pope Paul II to select Assisi as the location for the Global Day of Prayer for Peace that was held in 1986 and was attended by people from different religions.

We cannot exit from this Later apologetics epoch without mentioning the contributions of Ramon Llull/Lull (c. 1232–1316), who is believed to be the first Christian missionary to Muslims. It is intentional that Annemarie Mayer entitles her book chapter, "The Future of Interreligious Dialogue in the Light of Ramon Llull's Contribution to the Encounter of Religions."[10] Mayer discusses Llull's dialogical contributions to interfaith encounters, highlighting some of Llull's endeavours including his renowned book, *The Book of the Gentile and the Three Wise Men* (c. 1274). The book includes an interesting allegorical illustration of three men, a Jew, Christian, and Muslim, who are confronted by a Gentile seeking to know which is the way to eternal salvation. The story illustrates Llull's irenic approach to interreligious dialogue that has been termed as a milestone especially for its "spirit of fairness and openness."[11]

Llull was intentional in his preparation for ministry. He spent nine years studying Arabic, and at the age of sixty years, he went to Tunis in 1291 to debate with Muslim scholars. Goddad recounts that Llull told the Muslims that,

> (H)e had studied the laws of Christians and now wished to learn Islam, promising that if it were better, he would become Muslim, but his answers to the questions which he was asked were so challenging that his life was threatened, and he was forced to flee.[12]

Llull fled but soon returned to Tunisia with a different approach. He decided to try the confrontational way where he stated publicly that the Christian laws were true unlike the Muslims' ones, which were false. This led to his imprisonment, and he was released after some European merchants pleaded for him. He later moved to Algiers where he was stoned to death after he made some inflammatory comments against Islam.

Llull's life displays a paradox when it comes to Christian-Muslim apologetics. No wonder he earned the title, "the fool of love" who had dreamed of dying as a martyr. On a positive note, one of the contributions that Mayer highlights about Llull's life is his desire to move from the negative polemics of

10. Annemarie C. Mayer, "The Future of Interreligious Dialogue in the Light of Ramon Llull's Contribution to the Encounter of Religions," in *The Past, Present, and Future of Theologies of Interreligious Dialogues*, ed. Terrence Merrigan and John Friday (Oxford: Oxford University Press, 2017), 47–63.

11. Goddard, *A History of Christian-Muslim Relations*, 115.

12. Goddard, *A History of Christian-Muslim Relations*, 115.

his day to a dialogue approach. Mayer further outlines three convictions that Llull held as he engaged in dialogue with Muslims:[13]

1. Non-Christians are human beings like Christians (*infidels sunt homines sicut et nos*).
2. Non-Christians do not pay heed to Christian authorities such as Councils, Church Fathers, or Holy Scripture (*infidels non stant ad auctoritates fidelium*).
3. Non-Christians do not want to exchange one uncertain faith for another equally unproven belief, but to exchange believing for understanding (*nolunt dimittere credere pro credere, sed credere pro intelligere*).

Armed with such convictions, Llull had the audacity to approach King Frederick III of Sicily in 1312, four years before his death. He suggested to the king to allow an interreligious exchange. He envisioned Muslim and Christian scholars who were knowledgeable in their religions and in Arabic entering each other's spaces to discuss their respective tenets so that each may understand the other's religion and hence have peaceful coexistence. Such a quest will be seen to be revived using the Scriptural Reasoning (SR) approach that will be suggested later in this chapter as an alternative to the polemical stance that has dominated the East African Christian-Muslim context.

2.3 Modern Era Apologetics (1400–to date)

Ramon Llull's contributions to interreligious dialogue ushered in a modern approach to apologetics as well as to contemporary Christian mission to Muslims. This endeavour was further enhanced by the events of the sixteenth-century Protestant Reformation, which witnessed more concerted efforts towards mission to Muslims. Before discussing the apologetics of the Reformation, it is expedient to underline the participation of some of the Roman Catholics who engaged with Muslims.

The Dominicans (or Order of Preachers) founded in 1216, followed Thomas Aquinas, and ventured into the Islamic world with the same notion of combating Islam as a heresy. A number of the friars went to Tunis to study Arabic, and many other priests were sent on diplomatic missions to rulers of

13. Mayer, "The Future of Interreligious Dialogue in the Light of Ramon Llull's Contribution to the Encounter of Religions," 53–54.

different parts of the Islamic lands. For example, Pope Innocent IV (1243–1254) sent a Franciscan monk, John de Carpini, to the Mongol ruler at Karakorum in 1245 to undertake a diplomatic mission. Apparently, the Franciscan mission was established in 1345 in the Holy Land, although it was aimed at safeguarding the Christian holy places. By this time, the Ottoman Empire had expanded and captured Constantinople in 1453. It was within this epoch that we also find the great figures of the sixteenth-century Protestant Reformation, who also formulated their response to the Islamic world.

The Protestant Reformation that resulted into the great fissure between the Roman Catholics and Protestants allowed the latter group to expand rapidly over the years. This expansion further brought major divisions among the Protestant Christians who undertook interfaith dialogue and apologetics in diverse ways. Generally, the encounters with Muslims during this period were motivated by fear as well as ignorance. While previous decades of Christians perceived Islam as a Christian heresy, the Reformation Christians chose to see Islam as a deception from Satan. They also considered Muhammad as a "degraded moral character, often associated with the Antichrist, and Muslims as being sexually depraved on the grounds that they permitted polygamy."[14] The Reformation leaders thus saw their mandate to guide the church on how to respond to Muslims.

An example is how the German reformer, Martin Luther (1483–1546) took time to study Islam. He particularly read the Qur'an for himself because he realized that much of what he read about Islam from a Christian perspective was distorted ideas about Muslims. For him, Muhammad was not the final Antichrist, but Islam was a major force to reckon with. Luther was convinced that Islam was a "positive instrument of God in judgment on the corrupt practices of the Christians."[15] Goddard further explains that Luther responded to Islam from a political and religious perspective. He saw the advance of Islam against Christendom and thus wrote treatises to encourage Christians. Luther condemned the idea of the Crusades, particularly refuting the call for the final Crusade against the Ottoman Turks.

14. Richard John McCallum, "A Sociological Approach to Christian-Muslim Relations: British Evangelicals, Muslims and the Public Space" (PhD Dissertation, University of Exeter, UK, 2011), 134.

15. Kenneth Crandall, *The Impact of Islam on Christianity* (New York: American Friends of the Middle East, Inc., 1952), 7.

2.4 Apologetics of the Twentieth Century (Modern Mission Era)

The modern mission era of the nineteenth–twentieth centuries was birthed during the Enlightenment period (seventeenth–nineteenth centuries), a period that emerged from the "Age of Reason" (seventeenth–eighteenth centuries). Mission work to non-Christian people during this period was therefore influenced significantly by the ideologies of the Enlightenment era. Such ideologies upheld the primacy of reason and the exercise of human senses in gaining knowledge that informed practice. Christian responses to Islam were therefore influenced accordingly. It was also within this epoch that Islamic geopolitical dominance declined considerably as the balance of power continued to tilt towards the Western powers, culminating with European imperialism. Christian mission witnessed great expansions during this period, which also saw heighted outreach to Muslims to such places like India and the Middle East. Sharkey surmises that it was not until the early 1880's that British and American missionaries engaged in "aggressive evangelization of Muslims."[16] Two significant missionaries sent to Islamic areas are worth noting: Samuel Zwemer and Temple Gairdner, who belonged to the nineteenth-century Christian missionary expansion periods.

Dutch American Samuel Zwemer (1867–1952) popularly referred to as the "Apostle to Islam" founded the Arabian Mission in 1889 under the Reformed Church of America. He worked as a missionary in the Gulf region as well as in Egypt for a number of years. He perceived Islam as a dying religion, which was bound to collapse. His triumphalist attitude is further noted in the titles of two of the books he wrote about Islam: *The Disintegration of Islam* and *The Cross above the Crescent*.

Zwemer's writing and ministry to Muslims was influenced by his perception that Islam was antithetical to Christianity and thus there should be no compromise when addressing it. At least he separated Islam from Muslims since he was more sympathetic to the latter than the former, which to him was the system to confront. Zwemer's confrontational strategies included entering Al-Azhar university mosque in Egypt to distribute a polemical tract that attacked the Qur'an, according to the Muslims. This event happened in 1928 and caused a stir in the city. It prompted Muslim religious scholars to establish a "Society for the Defense of Islam" that was known to lash out against Christian missionaries including Zwemer, who was seen as a threat to Islam.[17] In 1930,

16. Heather J. Sharkey, "Empire and Muslim Conversion: Historical Reflections on Christian Missions in Egypt," *Islam and Christian–Muslim Relations* 16 no. 1 (2005): 43–60, 45.

17. Sharkey, "Empire and Muslim Conversion," 47.

two years after this event, Zwemer was inaugurated to the chair of Professor of History of Religion and Christian Missions at Princeton Theological Seminary.

Zwemer's thinking influenced other writers like W. A. Rice, who was a missionary with the Church Missionary Society (CMS) in Iran. Rice wrote a book *Crusaders of the Twentieth Century*, which outrightly showed an antagonistic attitude against Islam. Apparently, after the British occupation of Egypt of 1882, there seemed to have been a renewed call for a "modern crusade to produce spiritual as well as territorial conquest and envisioned a contest against Islam in the race to convert sub-Saharan Africans especially."[18] It is within this context that in 1910 Rice called his fellow missionaries the "crusaders of the twentieth century" who were called to expand Christendom.[19]

Temple Gairdner (1873–1928), on the other hand, was less confrontational than Zwemer or Rice. Gairdner was a British missionary who worked in Egypt with the Anglican CMS. Like Zwemer, he saw the importance of learning Arabic language in order to reach the educated Muslims with the Christian message. Like Zwemer, Gairdner produced pamphlets, books, and newspapers about the message that needed to be taken across. Unlike Zwemer, Gairdner was more sympathetic to Islam and saw,

> [M]uch good in Islam, particularly in the writings of the Sufis and of al-Ghazālī and viewed Islam not as the antithesis of Christianity but rather Christianity as a kind of fulfilment of Islam, with Islam as a kind of preparation for Christianity.[20]

Gairdner's position about Islam displayed a clear demarcation from the polemical stance that characterized the nineteenth-century imperialistic position even against Islam. This positivity was influenced by the thought that there was "spiritual richness of Muslim life."[21] His book, *The Reproach of Islam*, published in 1909 by the Baptist Missionary Society in London, shows how he perceived Islam as a divine reproach to the failure of the church. Nonetheless, he took time to learn Islam and got the courage to debate publicly with Muslim scholars at al-Azhar university using Arabic. As he engaged in such debates, he became more convinced that the living exemplification of the Christian brotherhood was what was needed for the redemption of Islam. The testimony

18. Sharkey, "Empire and Muslim Conversion," 46.

19. Sharkey, "Empire and Muslim Conversion," 46.

20. Goddard, *A History of Christian-Muslim Relations*, 124.

21. Daniel Madigan, "Christian-Muslim Dialogue," in *The Wiley-Blackwell Companion to Inter-Religious Dialogue*, ed. Catherine Cornille,. 244–60 (Malden: John Wiley & Sons, Ltd., 2013), 250.

of his approach to Islam is summed herein: "Other teachers taught us how to refute Islam; he taught us how to love Muslims."[22]

Constance Padwick wrote a biography of Gairdner, which she entitled, *Temple Gairdner of Cairo*.[23] In the book, published in 1929, she comments that Gairdner found the Christian literature that were used to respond to Islam to be very mechanical. The literature had turned Christians into "argumentative machinery" expending all their crucial strength with unnecessary arguments instead of wooing Muslims with love. Padwick, apart from writing about Gairdner, also attempted to respond to Islam by seeking to understand Islam and Muslims through the eyes of prayers. She wrote the classic, *Muslim Devotions: A Study of Prayer Manuals in Common Use*, published in 1961, in which she tries to understand how Muslims devote themselves to prayer and the value they accrue from this act.[24]

Other Protestant missionaries, who offered their evangelical responses to Islam, include Constance Padwick, Henry Martyn (1781–1813), Karl Pfander (1803–1865), and Kenneth Cragg (b. 1913). One common aspect of the apologetics performed by these missionaries was their irenic attitude towards Islam and Muslims. They preferred friendly engagements as opposed to polemical debates that aroused the anger of Muslims. These missionaries further wrote treatises that were popularly used by Christian apologists of later years even in the African contexts.

3. Africans in Christian-Muslim Apologetics

Andrew Walls wrote an article that was published in 1999, which was titled "Africa as the Theatre of Christian Engagement with Islam in the Nineteenth Century."[25] Walls recognized the significance of African Christians' engagement with Muslims. Such realization came in the wake of a rapidly growing church in the continent, which seems to compete with the growth of Islam as well. This section will highlight some key contributions of African Christians in apologetics.

22. Colin Chapman, *Cross and Crescent: Responding to the Challenge of Islam* (Downers Grove: InterVarsity Press, 2003), 220.

23. Constance Padwick also wrote a biography of Henry Martyn entitled, *Henry Martyn: Confessor of the Faith,* London: Inter-Varsity Fellowship, 1963.

24. Chapman, *Cross and Crescent: Responding to the Challenge of Islam*, 71.

25. Andrew Walls, "Africa as the Theatre of Christian Engagement with Islam in the Nineteenth Century," *Journal of Religion in Africa* 29 no. 2 (1999): 155–74.

The West African context offers a unique contribution to Christian-Muslim relations in Africa. There were liberated slaves who chose to spread Christianity after their emancipation, for instance Samuel Ajayi Crowther (1807–1891) from Nigeria. In spite of his humiliation by Western imperialists, Crowther made a massive contribution to Christianity and Christian-Muslim relations in West Africa. Born as a Yoruba man in today's Ogun state, Nigeria, Crowther converted to Christianity and later trained to be a missionary. He was consecrated in 1864 as the first African bishop of the Anglican Church. As a linguist and translator, he wrote the first Yoruba dictionary and the Yoruba Bible. Solihu reports that as Crowther prepared to write the dictionary and the Bible, he "contacted Yoruba Muslims and traditional worshippers whose religious dialect had become part of the spoken Yoruba language."[26] Crowther intentionally reached out to Yoruba Muslims as he did his clergy work. In 1872, Crowther visited the Ilorin emirate in Western Nigeria, and encountered Muslims there. This enabled him to encourage Christians to engage with Muslims instead of avoiding them. He particularly advocated that missionaries working among Yoruba Muslims engage in scriptural dialogue with Muslims. Crowther not only urged these missionaries, but also gave some guidelines towards the same, as Solihu notes:

> The Qur'an's recognition of some key Biblical doctrines and historical figures is what he [Crowther] considered to be the "vulnerable parts" of the Qur'an which missionaries must exploit to wage "good warfare in support of the great Christian doctrine of the Trinity, which the Koran flatly denies." Yorubaland then became the centre of serious engagement between Muslims and Christians.[27]

Crowther saw the importance of learning Arabic, and he urged missionaries to learn it in order to engage with the Muslims more intelligibly. Andrew Walls (1999) recounts Crowther's encounters with Muslims and remarkably points out his success and failures. One incident that Crowther lived to regret was when he once tried to debate with Muslims in Sierra Leone but suffered humiliation. This encounter was instigated when Crowther found a Muslim student wearing a charm. He cut it off and told the boy that superstition was not allowed in the Christian school. The father of the boy complained angrily, and

26. Abdul Kabir Hussain Solihu, "The Earliest Yoruba Translation of the Qur'an: Missionary Engagement with Islam in Yorubaland," *Journal of Qur'anic Studies* 17 no. 3 (2015): 14.

27. Solihu, "The Earliest Yoruba Translation of the Qur'an," 15.

Crowther responded by calling other Muslim elders for a public rebuttal. He went with his Bible and a copy of George Sale's Qur'an. Walls reports Crowther's humiliation: "All his well-marshalled arguments were useless. For Muslims, there was only one argument: "God did not have a son."[28]

Crowther realized the futility of public debates where Christians shouted, "Jesus is the Son of God" while Muslims respond, "He is not." This encounter changed his approach to Islam and to Muslims from confrontational polemics to a more apologetic and respectful approach.[29] Walls recounts how Crowther's approach turned to seeking for common themes in the Qur'an and the Bible particularly on Jesus. A valid example was when Crowther went to the palace at Ilorin in 1872. This account is chronicled in Crowther's book, *Experiences with Heathens and Mohammaedans in West Africa*. Walls also provides a summary of the dialogue that ensued between Crowther and the Muslims who had gathered at the palace. Some key things to note include:

- Usage of the Bible to answer Muslims' questions.
- Asking Muslims some related questions to prompt them to think further.
- Displaying the Yoruba and English Bibles and openly reading from them.
- Acknowledging the commonality between the biblical and Quranic accounts.
- Allowing Muslims to ask questions.
- Avoiding confrontational answers to such questions like whether Muhammad was prophesied in the Bible (Crowther answered that Muhammad was born many years after Christ and after the Bible, hence the latter is silent about it).
- Avoid using the Bible against the Qur'an.

Walls further explains that during the same session, Muslims requested Crowther to pray. He chose the "prayer for the Queen's Majesty," which was used commonly in the Anglican church. He explained that for the Christians living outside the Queen's dominion, they are allowed to replace the name of the Queen and instead pray for the ruler of the specific place. Crowther

28. Walls, "Africa as the Theatre of Christian Engagement with Islam in the Nineteenth Century," 161.

29. John Azumah, "Patterns of Christian-Muslim Encounters in Sub-Saharan Africa," in *The Character of Christian-Muslim Encounter: Essays in Honour of David Thomas* edited by Douglas Pratt, Jon Hoover, John Davies and John A. Chesworth, 381–400 (Leiden, Boston: Brill, 2015), 393.

therefore mentioned that Christians prayed for the Emir, which everyone present consented. This experience enabled Crowther to say:

> There was no argument, no dispute, no objection made, but the questions were answered direct from the Word of God . . . After many years of experience, I have found that the Bible, the sword of the Spirit, must fight its own battle, by the guidance of the Holy Spirit.[30]

Crowther's experience made him acknowledge the supremacy of the Bible in apologetics. He therefore advocated that Christians should be familiar with the Scriptures and if possible, the Bible in the common language that Muslims use. He used both the English and Yoruba Bibles in answering the questions posed. Walls asserts that Crowther's approach differed considerably from that of Pfander's approach even if the latter was already a leading missionary to Muslims in his time.[31]

4. Christian Apologetics in Eastern Africa

4.1 Christian Apologetics in East Africa in History

Christian-Muslim engagement in eastern African region goes back to the early years of the founding of Islam. Muslim sources aver that in 615 Muhammad sent a group of his followers (forty or eighty) to Aksum in Abyssinia to escape the persecution from the Quraysh tribesmen of Mecca. Historians further narrate that after the departure of these Muslims, Quraysh leaders sent two envoys to convince the Abyssinian king (Negus the Ge'ez title for King) to send the Muslims back. The king made a fair judgement and invited the Muslims to give their defence. Muhammad's cousin, Ja'far, who was the spokesman and leader, narrated their conversion to Islam and when the king asked for scriptural reference, Ja'far narrated the story of the annunciation and the virgin birth of Jesus from Surah 19 (Maryam). The king is said to have wept, "until his beard was wet, and the bishops wept until their scrolls were wet" when they heard this narration. Negus exclaimed that: "This and what Jesus brought have come from the same niche."[32] He allowed the Muslim to take refuge in his kingdom, where they remained for several years. Some of them later returned

30. Walls, "Africa as the Theatre of Christian Engagement with Islam in the Nineteenth Century," 163.

31. Walls, "Africa as the Theatre of Christian Engagement with Islam in the Nineteenth Century," 163–64.

32. Azumah, "Patterns of Christian-Muslim Encounters in Sub-Saharan Africa," 382–83.

to Mecca, while others moved to Medina after Muhammad settled there. It is believed that there were some of the refugees who preferred to stay in Abyssinia after converting to Christianity. The Abyssinian model of "host-guest" was replicated in other parts of Africa like in the Sudan.[33] Other places welcomed missionaries who sought to engage with the Muslims especially along the coast.

European missionaries like Johann Ludwig Krapf, Johannes Rebmann, and David Livingstone found several Muslims along the East African coast. There was intensive Islamic resistance from the Muslim leaders like Sultan of Oman as well as the locals who had converted to Islam. Johann Ludwig Krapf (1810–1881) became the first Protestant missionary along the East African coast. He arrived in 1844 and served under the auspices of the Church Missionary Society (CMS) in Mombasa. Krapf learnt Kiswahili and translated the New Testament into Kiswahili in 1846. Together with his teammate Rebmann, Krapf interacted with Muslims both in Mombasa and also in the interior mainland among the Mijikenda of Rabai. In 1848, Krapf went to Digoland where he found Digo people who had already become Muslims. He interacted with a Digo leader, Chief Muhensano, who received him in a friendly way allowing him to share the gospel with the Digo villagers. These Digo Muslims debated with Krapf on different issues including matters about food. Krapf responded by speaking against Muhammad as he narrates:

> I seated myself under a tree, when a crowd of old and young Wadigo assembled round me, who behaved themselves very decorously and respectfully . . . I narrated to them the fall of Adam, and spoke of the atonement through Jesus Christ, the Son of God. When they asked me whether we ate pork and the flesh of beasts slaughtered by the Wanika I was obliged to answer in the affirmative; upon which Bana Kheri (a Muslim) was so provoked that he called me a Mkafiri, unbeliever, like the Wanika, so by way of reproof of this and his attempts to ride rough-shod over my Wanika, I told him that in many respects the Suahili were worse than the heathen. I then showed him that Mohammed was an impostor, who had stolen from the Bible of the Christians everything good taught in the Koran, and who had spread his religion by the sword. The Wanika, who listened attentively, were delighted that I had thus driven the proud Mohammedan into a corner.[34]

33. Azumah, "Patterns of Christian-Muslim Encounters in Sub-Saharan Africa," 384.

34. Johann Ludwig Krapf, *Travels, Researches, and Missionary Labours* (London: Frank Cass and Company Ltd., 1968), 273–74.

From Krapf's narration above, he employed a polemical approach that had a competitive element to outwit Muslims. One wonders whether such an approach contributed to very minimal conversions of Digo Muslims to Christianity when Krapf and Rebmann's mission in East Africa came to an end in 1875.

Apart from Kraft's initial encounters with the Digo Muslims, there were other missionaries who tried to engage the Digo Muslims along the coast. Julius Gathogo reports that there was already a "heavy Islamic and African religious presence in Digo land" which made it difficult for "missionaries to conquer Digo land."[35] In spite of the difficulties encountered in the Digo Mission, one CMS missionary recounts how they interacted with Muslims. George W. Wright went for an evangelistic trip to Digo land in 1912 and narrated how he visited a town called Vanga, along the Kenyan coast. Wright refers to the town as a "Mohammadan town" governed by a *liwali* (local chief). When the chief asked what they had come to do, Wright boldly announced that they had gone to teach people about God, to which the administrative leader responded by saying: "We are all slaves of God." Wright then made a rejoinder saying: "This is just the difference; we are here to tell you all that we are 'sons of God.'" Reading the New Testament to the Muslims substantiated this claim. It seems that this dialogue had an amicable outcome because the local leader took Wright for a walk to the town as he showed him where to sleep. They shared "a cup of tea and sweet rice cakes and an appointment for the next morning when the people might gather together to hear more of our teaching. In the meantime, our men were selling portions of Scripture," recounts Wright.[36] There was indeed a subsequent meeting held the following morning at the marketplace, where Wright "reasoned" with the Muslims from Scriptures, although he does not mention whether he used the Qur'an or not. It can be deduced that this second public meeting was also amicable because the local leader even offered to provide a guide for the Christian entourage asking them to go back again to establish a hospital and a school if possible.[37]

35. Julius Gathogo, "Challenges and Prospects in Digo Mission," in *The Digo Mission of the Anglican Church of Kenya: Essays in Commemoration of 114 Years of Mission Work in Kwale County (1904–2018)*, edited by Julius Mutugi Gathogo, 109–24. (Wilmore, Kentucky: First Fruits Press, 2020), 109.

36. George Wright, "Itineration in the Digo Country: July 16–28, 1912," in *The Digo Mission of the Anglican Church of Kenya*, edited by Julius Gathogo, pp. 1–10 (Wilmore: First Fruits Press, 2020), 5.

37. Wright, "Itineration in the Digo Country," 5.

Two other missionaries, William Ernest Taylor (1856–1927) and Godfrey Dale (1861–1941) left an indelible mark on the East African coast in terms of apologetic engagement with Muslims. Both wrote materials on Islam for Christians and Muslims as well. Taylor was sent by CMS and settled in Mombasa from 1880–1897, choosing to live with the Muslims instead of staying at the mission compound in Frere Town to spend ample time with the local Muslims. He employed various evangelistic approaches to engage with Muslims. He wrote evangelistic tracts, which he gave out while treating patients in his medical dispensary. He also learnt Kiswahili and used it while preaching in the marketplace. Taylor also composed evangelical songs using the local tunes, which made him earn respect from some of the local Muslims, even though others ridiculed him.[38]

The Universities' Mission to Central Africa (UMCA) sent Godfrey Dale to Zanzibar in 1902. Prior to that, Dale took time to study Arabic and Islam, which qualified him to go to the Island as a specialist in Islam. Such knowledge and language expertise gave him confidence to engage in public discussions with both Arab and African Muslims in Zanzibar. He wrote tracts in Kiswahili, *Khabari za Dini ya Kiislamu* (News about the Religion of Islam), and *Maisha ya Muhammad* (The Life of Muhammad), which were published in 1909. Dale also wrote books on Islam like *Darkness or Light*, published in 1912 and *Islam and Africa: An Introduction to the Study of Islam for African Christians* (1925). Apart from the tracts and books that he wrote on Islam, Dale made a significant contribution by writing a Kiswahili translation of the Qur'an, which he titled *Tafsiri ya Kurani ya Kiarabu* (Translation of the Arabic Qur'an), published in London in 1923.

A germane question would be: What motivated Dale to produce all these literatures especially the Kiswahili version of the Qur'an? Was he offering a polemical rebuttal against Muslims and Islam? Chesworth, from whom much of this information about Taylor and Dale has been derived, assesses Dale's motivation as tending towards a polemical stance. According to Chesworth, Dale sought to provide materials, including the Kiswahili Qur'an, so that Christians would know what Islam is and that the "Koran actually does teach on subjects as slavery, polygamy, divorce; and will compare it with Christian teachings. And as Christian teaching has largely prevailed on these subjects

38. John Chesworth, "Fundamentalism and Outreach Strategies in East Africa: Christian Evangelism and Muslim Da'wa," in *Muslim-Christian Encounters in Africa* edited by John Hunwick, Rüdiger Seesemann and Knut Vikør (Leiden: Brill, 2006), 161–62.

in the past, why should we doubt whether it will prevail in the future?"[39] Chesworth further notes that Dale's translation of the Qur'an in Kiswahili was "viewed with suspicion" by the Muslims, albeit the Kiswahili script that Dale used did not meet the later language standards set up by the Kiswahili language committee.[40] Furthermore, Chesworth affirms the polemical tendency with which Dale wrote his works when he quotes Frankl who asserts that the 140 pages of the comments appearing as endnotes in Dale's Kiswahili Qur'an, "reveal a biased turn of mind" and hence an inclination towards being polemical.[41]

Both Taylor and Dale played their parts and served their generations, as they deemed appropriate. Evidently, they were both keen to learn about Islam as well as the language of the people (Kiswahili) and religion (Arabic), respectively. They left indelible marks even though the twentieth and twenty-first centuries Christians in East Africa may not be conversant with their names. Yet would it be appropriate to state that their combative public engagement with Muslims laid a foundation that has continued to the present twenty-first century? An affirmative answer would negate Kamau's assertion (quoting Mutei) that the public debates (*mihadhara*) were "introduced in Kenya around 1987 (Mutei 2006)."[42]

4.2 Christian-Muslim Apologetics in the Twenty-first Century in East Africa

The contemporary Christian-Muslim relations in East Africa, particularly in Kenya, are steeped with public debates, *mihadhara*, that have become quite popular. These debates have been termed as the "modi operandi of Muslim outreach to Christians."[43] However, it is not only Muslims who employ these public debates; Christians have also taken these as a popular way of engaging with Muslims, as evident from the historical account in the previous section

39. John Chesworth, "The Use of Scripture in Swahili Tracts by Muslims and Christians in East Africa" (PhD Thesis, University of Birmingham, UK, 2007), 145.

40. Chesworth, "Fundamentalism and Outreach Strategies in East Africa," 180.

41. P. J. L. Frankl, "Tarjama ya al-Muntakhab Katika Tafsiri ya Qur'ani Tukufu by Ali Muhsin al-Barwani: Review," *British Journal of Middle Eastern Studies* 25 no. 1 (1998): 191–93 cited in Chesworth, "The Use of Scripture in Swahili Tracts," 145.

42. Patrick Mburu Kamau, "Christian-Muslim Dialogue with Particular Reference to Pentecostals and Muslims in Nairobi North District, Nairobi County, Kenya" (PhD Thesis, Kenyatta University, 2013), 16.

43. Nelson Kahumbi Maina, "A History of Christian-Muslim Relations in Kenya, 1963–2015," in *Christian Responses to Terrorism: The Kenyan Experience*, ed. Gordon Heath and David Tarus, 12–32 (Eugene, Oregon: Pickwick Publications, 2017), 19.

above. One significant difference between the African Christian participants of these *mihadhara* and the white missionaries mentioned above is that most of them are not proficient in Arabic or Islam as Taylor and Dale. The prevalent strategy employed by both Christians and Muslims during *mihadhara* debates is using each other's scriptural passages to disparage the other. Kamau reports that Pentecostal Christians engage in the debates, which have unfortunately ended in "open physical confrontation between Muslims and Christians, leading to injury, loss of property and death."[44] Maina also notes the negative outcome of these debates when he cites how some church leaders have spoken ill of Islam and the result was violence.[45] Karuku and Wang'ombe similarly recount the antagonism that has been witnessed between Muslims and Christians due to an exclusivist approach employed by Christians in Nairobi.[46]

The negative apologetics that ensues when adherents of different religions take such exclusivist positions has led to polemical engagements that are unwarranted. Loss of life, destruction of property, community polarization and other negative outcomes has necessitated the dire need for Christians especially to seek for alternative ways of engaging Muslims. Some Christian leaders have resorted to spread Islamophobia by warning their congregants to be wary of Muslims who perpetrate violence in the name of religion. The heated debate about Kadhi's courts during the Kenyan Constitutional review process in 2005 showed the extent of Islamophobia by Christians. Such reactions continue to propagate negative apologetics among Christians as they engage with Muslims. A clarion call seems to be sounded in the recent years to counter such negativity for the sake of peaceful coexistence in the region. One of the main strategies being propagated is the interfaith dialogue between Muslims and Christians. A number of scholars have formulated theories about interfaith dialogue in a bid to enhance tolerance and peaceful religious coexistence.

An example of a theory on interfaith dialogue has been suggested by Kamau, which he has named Integrated Inclusivism Conceptual Model (IICM).[47] This model aims at finding constructive Christian-Muslim dialogue

44. Kamau, "Christian-Muslim Dialogue with Particular Reference to Pentecostals and Muslims in Nairobi North District, Nairobi County, Kenya," 16–17.

45. Maina, "A History of Christian-Muslim Relations in Kenya, 1963–2015," 20.

46. Harun Karuku and Judy Wang'ombe, "Religious Territoriality in a Socio-Economic Context: A Case of Christian-Muslim Relations in Kiamaiko Slum, Nairobi-Kenya," *Impact: Journal of Transformation* 3 vol. 2 (2020): 100–113, 110.

47. Patrick Mburu Kamau, "Christian-Muslim Dialogue with Particular Reference to Pentecostals and Muslims in Nairobi, Kenya," *International Journal of Peace and Development Studies* 9 no. 5 (2018): 60–65, 62.

that integrates crucial aspects of a society, which can bring adherents of the two religions together. Among the aspects included in the IICM, is the call to consider the shared theological concepts and values in Islam and Christianity as basis of interfaith dialogue. Muslims and Christians would be required to listen to each other from both verbal dialogue and reading each other's Scriptures. Such interfaith dialogue is deemed to have the capacity to transcend negative apologetics and instead create an amicable socio-religious atmosphere devoid of the violence instigated by religious conflicts.

The IICM mentioned above is a viable theory that should be publicized in order to offer an alternative approach beyond the popular *mihadhara* polemics. The advantage of IICM over the *mihadhara* debates is that the former advocates for "religious equality in interfaith relations."[48] Equality here means that both Muslims and Christians who engage in interfaith dialogue based on IICM should consider each other as equal partners and that none is more superior to the other. Such a standpoint is further elaborated in another model that bears similar ethos as the IICM, but which is perceived to offer more practical steps towards positive apologetics. The suggested model is termed Scriptural Reasoning (SR).

5. Contextualizing Scriptural Reasoning as a Model for African Apologetics

Scriptural Reasoning (SR) is a model developed for engaging in interfaith dialogue. It was originally established for Jews, Christians, and Muslims to study each other's texts. The analogy used to explain the ethos of SR is that of inviting guests into a house and sharing a pertinent aspect of life together. The dimension of hospitality cannot be undermined when discussing the concept of SR. Hospitality is a significant virtue in African contexts, which can be leveraged for the sake of fruitful interfaith dialogues on the continent.

SR originated from Textual Reasoning within a Jewish university context that aimed at discussing crucial issues in Judaism. Later, the concept of SR was adapted within an interfaith context that was intended to bring mutual understanding among adherents of the three Abrahamic religions. Moseley narrates that in the mid-1990s, David Ford of the Cambridge Interfaith Programme, adapted the principles of Textual Reasoning to an interfaith setting when Christians joined the ongoing Jewish textual reasoning. The inclusion of the study of Islamic texts later changed the SR scenario as an "epistemologically

48. Kamau, "Christian-Muslim Dialogue," 64.

valid practice,"[49] which has been employed to engage adherents of the three Abrahamic faiths in religious conversations. Such deliberations are not intended to find commonality or agreements, although there may be some, but they are envisioned to help people learn how to disagree respectfully.[50] In the early 1990's, SR was originally confined to the Western hemisphere (Britain and North America). Gradually, the movement has continued to expand to other parts of the world. The fast growth is occasioned by the flexibility of the practice to allow for contextual integration and thus evolve in a variety of different styles and forms. This adaptability allows SR to be tried out in the African context where the virtue of guest-host is prominent.

Maniraj Sukdaven calls for a possibility of including African traditional religion(s) in a "reimagined scriptural reasoning model."[51] His plea is based on the fact that SR is a textual engagement yet ATRs do not have any written texts that serve as Scriptures. Sukdaven's argument for inclusion of ATR(s) in the SR conversations is constructed on the redefining religion in a materialistic way (material religion).[52] Such a call to apply SR and to include ATR(s) in the SR conversation is appropriate here as it gives an idea that Africans are considering SR model in the interreligious conversations. This chapter advances this call to embrace SR as an alternative to the negative polemics that have been the basic engagements between Muslims and Christians in the African context. Detailed accounts of such an engagement may not be appropriate for this chapter but it will be discussed in forthcoming articles as more people embrace the SR model. For now, this chapter concludes by listing some aspects of how SR would look like in African contexts where Muslims and Christians engage with each other.

5.1 Leveraging on African Hospitality

The model of SR builds on mutual hospitality where strangers become friends and walk together as they seek to understand each other despite their religious differences. The African contexts are basically known for the hospitality virtue

49. Anne Moseley, "An Inquiry into the Development of Intercultural Learning in Primary Schools Using Applied Scriptural Reasoning Principles" (PhD Thesis, University of Warwick, UK, 2018), 27.

50. Marianne Moyaert, "Scriptural Reasoning as Inter-Religious Dialogue," in *The Wiley-Blackwell Companion to Inter-Religious Dialogue*, ed. Catherine Cornille, 64–86 (Hoboken: Wiley-Blackwell, 2013), 73.

51. Maniraj Sukdaven, "Exploring the Possibility for African Traditional Religion to Be Included in a Reimagined Scriptural Reasoning Model," *HTS Teologiese Studies/Theological Studies* 74 no. 3 (2018): 1–6.

52. Sukdaven, "Exploring the Possibility," 5.

that has been mentioned in various African philosophies like Ubuntu. The famous Zulu proverb: *Umuntu ngumuntu ngabantu* which means "a person is a person because of/by/through other people,"[53] captures the essence Ubuntu philosophy. This philosophy has become a bedrock of Pan-Africanism, and which can also be adapted as part of the contextualized SR in African contexts.

Ubuntu philosophy contains three aspects of hospitality that are pertinent to a contextualized SR model, namely: "welcoming, accommodating, sharing and sustaining human relations and behaviour."[54] In the contextualized SR, welcoming one another into a physical and religious space is crucial. The physical space can be a neutral place that is neither a mosque nor a church setting. Alternatively, there can be an interchange of venue for the Scriptural discussions. Accommodation within the physical/religious space entails that each participant comes with an unbiased religious stance that accommodates the "Other" as fellow human beings made in the image of God despite different religious affiliations. Accommodation comes with sharing. Both Muslims and Christians share their textual discourses for better understanding of the "Other."

5.2 Leveraging on African Pragmatism

The Ubuntu philosophy is a lived-out concept that does not remain confined to books in the library. Africans are pragmatic and thus the SR model is ideal since it involves actions. Marianne Moyaert is emphatic when she asserts that SR "is not a theory that is turned into practice but rather a practice about which one can theorize."[55] As Christians and Muslims meet together, there are some SR ground rules that have been suggested by David Ford:

i. Need to acknowledge the sacredness of the others' Scriptures to them (Other) without necessarily acknowledging its authority on oneself. Christians should therefore acknowledge that the Qur'an is a sacred text to Muslims, while Muslims should recognize that the Bible is a sacred text to Christians.

53. Andani Thakhathi and T. G. Netshitangani, "Ubuntu-as-Unity: Indigenous African Proverbs as a 'Re-Educating' Tool for Embodied Social Cohesion and Sustainable Development," *African Identities* 18 no. 4 (2020): 407–20, 409.

54. Thembisile Molose, "The Experience of Ubuntu to a Hospitality Organization: Scale Development and Validation," *Journal of Advances in Humanities and Social Sciences* 5, no. 3 (2019): 113–28.

55. Moyaert, "Scriptural Reasoning as Inter-Religious Dialogue," 72.

ii. Need to actively listen to each other respectfully as each acknowledge that the respective Scriptures are a public asset that can be read by anyone. Each person therefore acts like a guard or a gatekeeper for their own scriptural tradition, which makes it imperative to know their own texts.

iii. The ethos of contextualized SR is not about aiming to achieve a consensus. The aspect of competition is therefore absent and instead the aim is to attain a "hermeneutic diversity" that contributes to societal harmony.

iv. Christians and Muslims as guests of each other should aim at deepening their relationships with each other. David Ford sees the value of spending "time with people of other religions, talking about scriptural texts they really care about . . . often lead to friendship."[56]

6. Conclusion

This chapter concludes by asking: Is a contextualized SR Practice doable in Africa? It is possible to adapt and adopt SR in the different African contexts as an alternative to the popular *mihadhara* debates especially in the Kenyan context. Irrefutably, SR emerged from a Western context with the aim of bringing religion into the public space where the Abrahamic faiths can dialogue with each other for amicable coexistence. The aim of this chapter has been to provide a historical overview of apologetics as an interfaith dialogue between Christians and Muslims over the different epochs and especially highlighting the African context. The focus on the Africa setting was intentional. This chapter has underscored the polemical nature of the public debates that have elicited negative responses including violence and loss of life. The contemporary African contexts, and specifically the Kenya one, are becoming increasingly fatigued with the polemical approach. The time is ripe to seek an alternative particularly in light of the fact that Muslims and Christians are increasingly sharing space.

---

56. David F. Ford, "Scriptural Reasoning: Its Anglican Origins, its Development, Practice and Significance," *Journal of Anglican Studies* 11 no. 2 (2013): 147–65, 154.

Bibliography

Azumah, John. "Patterns of Christian-Muslim Encounters in Sub-Saharan Africa." In *The Character of Christian-Muslim Encounter: Essays in Honour of David Thomas* edited by Douglas Pratt, Jon Hoover, John Davies and John A. Chesworth, 381–400. Leiden: Brill, 2015.

Chapman, Colin. *Cross and Crescent: Responding to the Challenge of Islam*. Downers Grove: InterVarsity Press, 2003.

Chesworth, John. "Fundamentalism and Outreach Strategies in East Africa: Christian Evangelism and Muslim Da'wa." In *Muslim-Christian Encounters in Africa* edited by John Hunwick, Rüdiger Seesemann and Knut Vikør, 159–86. Leiden: Brill, 2006.

———. "The Use of Scripture in Swahili Tracts by Muslims and Christians in East Africa." PhD Thesis, University of Birmingham, UK, 2007.

Crandall, Kenneth. *The Impact of Islam on Christianity*. New York: American Friends of the Middle East, Inc., 1952.

Ford, David F. "Scriptural Reasoning: Its Anglican Origins, its Development, Practice and Significance." *Journal of Anglican Studies* 11 no. 2 (2013): 147–65.

Gathogo, Julius. "Challenges and Prospects in Digo Mission." In *The Digo Mission of the Anglican Church of Kenya: Essays in Commemoration of 114 Years of Mission Work in Kwale County (1904–2018)* edited by Julius Mutugi Gathogo, 109–24. Wilmore, Kentucky: First Fruits Press, 2020.

Goddard, Hugh. *A History of Christian-Muslim Relations*. Chicago: New Amsterdam Books, 2000.

Janosik, Daniel J. *John of Damascus: First Apologist to the Muslims*. Eugene: Pickwick Publications, 2016.

Kamau, Patrick Mburu. "Christian-Muslim Dialogue with Particular Reference to Pentecostals and Muslims in Nairobi North District, Nairobi County, Kenya." PhD Thesis, Kenyatta University, 2013.

———. "Christian-Muslim Dialogue with Particular Reference to Pentecostals and Muslims in Nairobi, Kenya." *International Journal of Peace and Development Studies* 9 no. 5 (2018): 60–65.

Karuku, Harun, and Judy Wang'ombe. "Religious Territoriality in a Socio-Economic Context: A Case of Christian-Muslim Relations in Kiamaiko Slum, Nairobi-Kenya." *Impact: Journal of Transformation* 3 no. 2 (2020): 100–13.

Krapf, Johann Ludwig. *Travels, Researches, and Missionary Labours*. London: Frank Cass and Company Ltd., 1968.

Madigan, Daniel. "Christian-Muslim Dialogue." In *The Wiley-Blackwell Companion to Inter-Religious Dialogue*, edited by Catherine Cornille, 244–60. Malden: John Wiley & Sons, Ltd., 2013.

Maina, Nelson Kahumbi. "A History of Christian-Muslim Relations in Kenya, 1963–2015." In *Christian Responses to Terrorism: The Kenyan Experience*, ed. Gordon Heath and David Tarus, 12–32. Eugene: Pickwick Publications, 2017.

Mayer, Annemarie C. "The Future of Interreligious Dialogue in the Light of Ramon Llull's Contribution to the Encounter of Religions." In *The Past, Present, and Future of Theologies of Interreligious Dialogues*, ed. Terrence Merrigan and John Friday, 47–63. Oxford: Oxford University Press, 2017.

McCallum, Richard John. "A Sociological Approach to Christian-Muslim Relations: British Evangelicals, Muslims and the Public Space." PhD Dissertation, University of Exeter, UK, 2011.

Molose, Thembisile. "The Experience of Ubuntu to a Hospitality Organization: Scale Development and Validation." *Journal of Advances in Humanities and Social Sciences* 5 no. 3 (2019): 113–28.

Moseley, Anne. "An Inquiry into the Development of Intercultural Learning in Primary Schools Using Applied Scriptural Reasoning Principles." PhD Thesis, University of Warwick, UK, 2018.

Moyaert, Marianne. "Scriptural Reasoning as Inter-Religious Dialogue." In *The Wiley-Blackwell Companion to Inter-Religious Dialogue*, edited by Catherine Cornille, 64–86. Hoboken: Wiley-Blackwell, 2013.

Padwick, Constance. *Henry Martyn: Confessor of the Faith*. London: Inter-Varsity Fellowship, 1963.

Sharkey, Heather J. "Empire and Muslim Conversion: Historical Reflections on Christian Missions in Egypt." *Islam and Christian–Muslim Relations* 16 no. 1 (2005): 43–60.

Solihu, Abdul Kabir Hussain. "The Earliest Yoruba Translation of the Qur'an: Missionary Engagement with Islam in Yorubaland." *Journal of Qur'anic Studies* 17 no. 3 (2015): 10–37.

Sukdaven, Maniraj. "Exploring the Possibility for African Traditional Religion to Be Included in a Reimagined Scriptural Reasoning Model." *HTS Teologiese Studies/ Theological Studies* 74 no. 3 (2018): 1–6.

Thakhathi, Andani, and T. G. Netshitangani. "Ubuntu-as-Unity: Indigenous African Proverbs as a 'Re-Educating' Tool for Embodied Social Cohesion and Sustainable Development." *African Identities* 18 no. 4 (2020): 407–20.

Vaughan, Lindsey Marie. "Convivencia: Christians, Jews, and Muslims in Medieval Spain." University of Tennessee Honors Thesis Projects, Knoxville, USA, University of Tennessee, 2003.

Walls, Andrew. "Africa as the Theatre of Christian Engagement with Islam in the Nineteenth Century." *Journal of Religion in Africa* 29 no. 2 (1999): 155–74.

Wang'ombe, Judy, and Harun Wang'ombe. "Re-Reading Spanish Medieval Convivencia." In *Forgiveness, Peacemaking, and Reconciliation*, edited by David K. Ngaruiya and Rodney L. Reed. Carlisle: Langham Global Library, 2020.

Wheatcroft, Andrew. *Infidels: A History of the Conflict between Christendom and Islam*. New York: Random House, 2003.

Wright, George. "Itineration in the Digo Country: July 16–28, 1912." In *The Digo Mission of the Anglican Church of Kenya* edited by Julius Gathogo, 1–10. Wilmore: First Fruits Press, 2020.

16

Apologetics in a Digital Age[1]

Incarnating the Gospel for Africa's Next Gens

Kevin Muriithi Ndereba, PhD

Lecturer at St. Paul's University, Kenya and Research Fellow Department of Practical Theology and Missiology, Stellenbosch University, South Africa

Abstract

Applying apologetics in the continent involves engaging with the largest demographic of people in the continent. Unfortunately, apologetics is seen as an abstract endeavour that does not reach the grassroots. This chapter considers the apologetic engagement of young people in the continent. It conceptualizes young people in their worldview divergences as well as their socio-economic and ethnic uniqueness. Specifically, it locates young people within the digital media culture that shapes them as persons in three major areas. First, it leads to a shift in the areas of knowledge and certainty. Hence, young people are sceptical of claims to authority or pursuit of objective truth, as is found in the person and work of Jesus Christ for instance. Second, it leads to isolation and attendant mental health issues. The apologetic implications are that engagement with young people must be a holistic approach, which is both cognitive and affective. Third, digital media culture provides a bridge for engaging popular

1. Originally published in *Global Missiology*, www.globalmissiology.org, October 2021..

culture's philosophical and religious ideas that are propagated by new media. This chapter proposes that, to counter digital isolation or assimilation, Christian leaders are called to "wise-engagement" modelled after Paul's apologetic in Acts 17. The chapter offers practical considerations for engaging in the apologetic task among Africa's next gens.

Keywords: Apologetics, Digital media, Next Gens, Practical Theology, Youth Ministry

1. Laying the Groundwork

As numerous scholars have noted, the African continent plays a prominent role in God's mission to the world today.[2] A majority of the population, approximately 77%, are young by definition.[3] Thus, if God's mission today is to be relevant to the continent's distinct makeup, this mission must be targeted to this burgeoning demographic. However, this task by necessity involves a cross-cultural engagement of the complexities of cultures, especially in key cosmopolitan cities in Africa such as Nairobi, Cape Town, Abuja, and Tunis. Christians must negotiate a plurality of worldviews and religions in engaging the next generations in Africa. It is to this mandate of cross-cultural and worldview engagement that apologetics is necessary.

The task of apologetics is an intellectual engagement of questions posed to Christian faith and takes either an offensive or defensive approach.[4] In its traditional approach, apologetics has used different methodologies in handling a variety of questions.[5] William Lane Craig has for instance explored the philosophical foundations for the existence of God as well as theories on the atonement, Gary Habermas has assessed the evidential claims surrounding Jesus Christ's resurrection, and J. P. Moreland has explored the intersection

2. Lamin Sanneh and Joel A. Carpenter, eds., *The Changing Face of Christianity: Africa, the West, and the World* (Oxford: Oxford University Press, 2005).

3. Bandar Hajjar, "The Children's Continent: Keeping up with Africa's Growth," *World Economic Forum* website, Jan 13, 2020, https://www.weforum.org/agenda/2020/01/the-children-s-continent/.

4. John M. Frame, *Apologetics to the Glory of God* (Phillipsburg: P&R Publishing, 1994); William Lane Craig, *Reasonable Faith: Christian Truth and Apologetics* (Wheaton: Crossway, 2008).

5. Stephen Cowan and Stanley Gundry, *Five Views on Apologetics* (Grand Rapids: Zondervan Academic, 2010).

of science and religion.[6] These continue to be necessary areas in the task of classical apologetics, and will not be easily replaced.

Though different apologetic schools emphasize particular aspects of the apologetic task, in general, to engage in apologetics is a biblical command for all Christians. First, apologetics is part of ordinary Christian discipleship. *Apologia* is the Greek word for making a case for something. Peter is writing to dispersed Christians in the early Christian communities, instructing them, and us, that *apologia* is something that every Christian should be conversant with (1 Pet 3:15). Given the context of suffering and persecution that defines his letter, Peter shows us how "giving a reason for the hope that you have" is part of everyday Christian witnessing. Second, apologetics is not an "unspiritual" intellectual diatribe but a spiritual task of Christian formation. Paul writes, "For though we walk in the flesh, we are not waging war according to the flesh. For the weapons of our warfare are not of the flesh but have divine power to destroy strongholds" (2 Cor 10:3–4 ESV). Intellectual strongholds are barriers that present themselves up against a worshipful knowledge of Christ. The task of apologetics is therefore to offer credible reasons for believing in Christ, while also critiquing faulty arguments against Christian belief.[7] Third, transformative apologetic engagement may make use of extra-biblical evidence such as theistic proofs and archaeological findings, but these are grounded in God's revelation in Scripture. It is precisely because God has made an intelligible world in the first place that we can engage in logical argument and scientific development.[8] In other words, reason, arguments, and evidence are subordinate to Scripture. God has provided the evidence all people need. The issue is people's "suppression of the truth" (Rom 1:18–20; Acts 17:31). How exactly the apologetic task should be practiced in missional engagement with Africa's young people is the central question this chapter addresses.

---

6. William Lane Craig, "The Existence of God and the Beginning of the Universe," *Truth: A Journal of Modern Thought* 3 (1991): 85–96; Gary R. Habermas, "The Minimal Facts Approach to the Resurrection of Jesus: The Role of Methodology as a Crucial Component in Establishing Historicity," *Southeastern Theological Review* 3, vol. 1 (2012): 15–26; William Lane Craig, *The Atonement* (Cambridge: Cambridge University Press, 2018); James Porter Moreland, *Scientism and Secularism: Learning to Respond to a Dangerous Ideology* (Wheaton: Crossway, 2018).

7. Frame, *Apologetics to the Glory of God*.

8. Frame, *Apologetics to the Glory of God*, 21–25.

2. An Insider's Perspective

My own pilgrimage is that I am a fourth generation of Christians in my family and was nurtured in a Christian home. Having made a profession of faith at 16 years old, during my campus years I came across international students from other philosophical and religious backgrounds – including some students with no particular commitments. My prominent question at this time concerned the uniqueness of Jesus Christ in light of other religions. Some would merely retort, "just believe." However, this response was not sufficient for my theological and philosophical issues surrounding the exclusivist view of truth.

My initial encounter with Christian apologetics was interacting with the works of William Lane Craig, Hugh Ross, and C. S. Lewis on digital platforms. Here was a stream of Christianity that appealed to both faith and reason. In my earlier twenties, upon reading the letter of 1 John, I had a deeper spiritual experience of the reality of sin and the offer of the grace of God in the gospel, and eventually yielded my life to Christ. My intellectual barriers were really cushioned in spiritual antagonism to the claims of Christ. In other words, unbelief is usually a holistic issue that not only affects the head (thinking), but also involves the heart (affections) and the hands (volition) (Eph 4:17–19). Many emerging Africans have these tensions of Christian faith and the critical questions being asked.

However, the questions of young Africans regarding the Christian faith are more nuanced than Western apologetic approaches can address. While traditional apologetics methods have engaged Westerners' typical questions about God's existence and the problem of evil and suffering, apologetics engagement in interreligious contexts such as in African cities raises different questions.[9] As practical ministry experience shows, young Africans are raising questions surrounding Christianity's acquiescence to the hostile colonial enterprise, the place of the Bible in shaping Africa's socio-economic challenges, and the reality of God in the presence of widespread suffering. In addition, the author's initial engagement in corporate life as an engineer, his pastoral ministry in the Presbyterian Church of East Africa, postgraduate theological education at the University of South Africa, and experience as a lecturer at the St. Paul's University inform this chapter's awareness of questions that young Africans are asking.

9. Harold Netland, "Evangelical Missiology and Theology of Religions: An Agenda for the Future," *International Journal of Frontier Missiology* 29 (2012): 11.

3. African Youth Are Not Monolithic

The "youth bulge" that is characteristic of the continent is varied in its definition. Young Africans are not monolithic but can be described through many different lenses. Rural and urban, traditional and postmodern, economically marginalized and privileged, plus religious and non-religious are just some of the categories taken up by the censuses of different countries. Further, there are rising communities of atheists in different parts of Africa, including the author's own city and country, Nairobi (Kenya), and other cities and countries like Lagos (Nigeria) and Cape Town (South Africa), among other prominent African cities. My practical ministry experience shows there is a rising generation of young Africans who demystify the "Africans are religious" tagline commonly proposed by religious scholars.[10] Given these varied cultural identifications and worldviews, how might apologetics engagement be a handmaid of transformative ministry to young Africans?

The COVID pandemic has raised the salience of digital technology in our everyday life as well as in Christian ministry. An oft-repeated statement in ministry engagement during the 2020–2021 COVID context has been that "the world is online, but the church is offline" or that "the church's evangelists must not answer the questions that they are asking but the questions that the next generation is asking." Clearly there is a role that digital culture is playing in popular youth culture, with attendant consequences for apologetic engagement.

4. The Apologetics Landscape and Research Gap

Apologetics ministries in Africa include Ratio Christi South Africa, the Africa Center for Apologetics Research (Uganda), the Institute of Christian Apologetics Studies (Ghana), and Apologetics Kenya, among others.[11] Ratio Christi is based on integrating a philosophical approach to the articulation of Christian faith and focused on campus students and professors. In Africa, the local chapters can be found in universities such as Potchefstroom and Pretoria. Centres for Apologetics Research can be found in many countries worldwide, with the African office located in Uganda and engaged particularly in counter-cult research and evangelistic engagement in Africa. The Institute of Christian Apologetics Studies (ICAS) engages in evangelism and training, for the apologetics task in Ghana, West Africa. Apologetics Kenya is a national

10. John S. Mbiti, *African Religions & Philosophy* (Oxford: Heinemann, 1990).

11. Apologetics Kenya 2021; Ratio Christi 2021; The Africa Center for Apologetics Research 2021.

ministry whose purpose is "to engage sceptics and to equip believers"[12] to respond to questions asked within a postmodern and postcolonial African context. They have a vibrant digital ministry and host annual conferences.

The research gap relative to African youth is that, while apologetics ministries in Africa are doing a commendable work in creating apologetic content, there is more that can be done in engaging digital natives in Africa. The digital age has shaped youth cultures deeply and in various ways, and apologetic engagement has not approached the unique issues raised by the changes in new media – especially within African contexts.

What follows comes from research the author has conducted into digital cultures and next generations ("gens") within the fields of youth studies and youth ministry.[13] Part of the research studies how young people are engaging with new media, how that engagement shapes youth cultures, and implications for discipleship. The research was a qualitative study among fifteen young people in the Presbyterian Church of East Africa (PCEA), a Kenyan denomination, among its urban congregations in Nairobi. The article also includes other studies among young people within the fields of digital culture, youth studies, and adolescent development in order to broaden the approach. The following section unpacks arising themes and exegetes Acts 17 as a model of practical apologetic engagement.

5. Three Approaches to Digital Media

In terms of the assumptions that underlie various analyses of digital media among young people, two extreme approaches can be taken. Both are based on critical approaches to digital media. Topf, for example, critiques the modern technological reality as a form of the Tower of Babel in how social media companies have become disproportionately wealthy as well as how the cyber-world negatively impacts human anthropology.[14] Although he does not then propose that we should be techno phobic, Topf's approach to digital culture and social media exemplifies an isolationist perspective. In addition to the aforementioned issues, an isolationist perspective considers the rising research in the area of how digital media has led to the increase in sexual deviant

12. Apologetics Kenya: www.apologeticskenya.org.

13. Kevin Muriithi Ndereba, "The Influence of Youth Cultures on Faith Formation of Youth in Nairobi: A Practical Theological Approach" (PhD thesis, University of South Africa), 2021.

14. Daniel Topf, "Technology as a Modern-Day Tower of Babel: The Garden of Eden as an Alternative Vision for Missionally Engaging a Media-Saturated Culture," *Global Missiology* 18 no. 2 (2021): 1–10.

behaviour or negatively affected mental health issues, for example, and proposes that digital media should be abandoned.[15] The second perspective gives rise to what can be called an assimilative approach. This approach considers the benefits of digital media in communication, learning, and entertainment and proposes that we should uncritically assimilate new media in all that we do. This chapter proposes a middle approach of "wise-engagement" of digital culture if we are to use it for the purposes of Christian ministry – and, more specifically, for apologetics engagement.[16]

6. Three Effects of Digital Culture among African Next Generations

The need for "wise-engagement" arises from the fact that digital media culture has shaped Africa's next gens in three important ways. First, it has affected them in the area of knowledge and certainty. With the ubiquitous nature and availability of technological adaptation, young people have access to a barrage of information and knowledge. The reality of "influencers" challenges the traditional notions of experts and institutions of learning, for instance. Fake or merely fascinating news has created a reality that conflicts with balanced, creative and critical thinking.

On the other hand, technology has been a handmaid of globalization and the attendant multi-lateral flows of ideas. The rising phenomenon of atheist societies in Africa's major cities can be correlated to access to the New Atheist movement through the digital content of such proponents as Dawkins and Hitchens. A similar argument on the universality of digital media can be made for the rise of Christian apologetics in the country as a result of digital access to the ministries of William Lane Craig and John Njoroge, among other influential apologists. One effect of these changes in knowledge production and movement is that young people have a lower level of trust for "traditional institutions" as well as experts and may innocently imbibe hostile ideologies, especially in an age of "keyboard warriors." Another effect is that young people are now more acquainted with conflicting arguments, so it takes greater effort to engage them, especially given the digital context of postmodernity.

15. Inge Tamburrino, Elijah Getanda, Michelle O'Reilly and Panos Vostanis, "'Everybody's Responsibility': Conceptualization of Youth Mental Health in Kenya," *Journal of Child Health Care* 24 no. 1 (2020): 5–18.

16. David C. Ononogbu and Nathan Chiroma, "Social Media and Youth Ministry in Nigeria: Implications and Christological Thrust," *International Journal of Humanities Social Sciences and Education* 5 no. 1 (2018): 48–54.

Second, whereas digital culture has connected young people, it has also isolated them. Fascinating research by the psychologist Jean Twenge explores how digital media has affected the healthy transitions of young people into adulthood.[17] She expands on work done in the area of emerging adulthood, which reveals how adolescence is extending into the mid-twenties.[18] For instance, Twenge correlates how more screen time means more isolation and eventually more loneliness.[19] She unpacks a study conducted between 1991–2015 and reveals that "31% more 8th and 10th graders felt lonely in 2015 than 2011, along with 22% more 12th graders."[20] Although some critique the correlation of increased screen time with mental health challenges, similar negative consequences have been shown in the African context, including issues to do with addiction and cyber-crime.[21] The negative impact of social media on young people in Nigeria, such as loss of identity, self-esteem, and interpersonal skills, has also been noted.[22] Apologetics must therefore also take an affective approach in addition to the cognitive approach that characterizes much of traditional apologetics. I have argued at length about what such an approach should look like, by taking the critical voices of youth workers in Nairobi city as dialogue partners from practical ministry engagement.[23]

Third, digital media creates an opportunity for engagement with secular and religious ideas. Rather than withdrawing from digital media, Christian apologists must take the Pauline approach of Acts 17 to create meaningful engagement with pop cultural ideas – whether those have to do with African traditional ideas, the question of identity, or the question of truth. The South African practical theologian Anita Cloete has engaged with youth issues at the intersection of digital media and religion. From her research with young

17. Jean Twenge, *iGen: Why Today's Super-Connected Kids are Growing up Less Rebellious, More Tolerant, Less Happy and Completely Unprepared for Adulthood and what that Means for the Rest of Us* (New York: Simon and Schuster, 2017).

18. Jeffrey J. Arnett, "Emerging Adulthood(s): The Cultural Psychology of a New Life Stage," in *Bridging Cultural and Developmental Approaches to Psychology: New Syntheses in Theory, Research and Policy*, ed. Jeffrey Arnett (Oxford: Oxford University Press, 2011), 255–75.

19. Twenge, *iGen*, 98.

20. Twenge, *iGen*, 97.

21. Rea Alonzo, Junayd Hussain, K. Anderson and Saverio Stranges, "Interplay between Social Media Use, Sleep Quality, and Mental Health in Youth: A Systematic Review," *Sleep Medicine Reviews* 56.101414 (2020): 1–12; Philip E. Ephraim, "African Youths and the Dangers of Social Networking: A Culture-Centred Approach to using Social Media," *Ethics and Information Technology* 15 no. 4 (2013): 275–84.

22. Ononogbu and Chiroma, "Social Media and Youth Ministry in Nigeria," 52.

23. Kevin Muriithi Ndereba, "Ubuntu Apologetics in Faith Formation: An Ethnography of Youth Ministry in Nairobi," *Journal of Youth and Theology* 1 (2021): 1–16.

people, she reveals that young people utilize religious and philosophical ideas in digital film and other media in worldview construction.[24] Thus, meaningful missional engagement with young people necessitates the appropriation of films, TV series, music, and other media so as to unpack worldview issues at play and how to engage them with the biblical worldview and gospel.

7. Engaging Africa's Next Gens: Paul's Model in Acts 17

Growing up with digital culture has contributed to rising generations of Africans' marked differences from older generations. In Africa, whereas postmodernity is definitive of global youth culture, there are certain cultural identities and practices unique to the next generations in Africa's cities. In practical ministry, these complexities can be seen in youth double denominational belonging or the dabbling in African traditional cultural practices.[25] Those involved in youth ministry must therefore exegete African youth cultures even as they seek to exegete the Word. Paul's various approaches in his defences in the book of Acts reveal how he uses different methodologies for different audiences. When engaging with a largely Jewish audience, Paul engages and confronts their Jewish understanding based on the common knowledge he has with them of the Old Testament and its ultimate fulfilment in Christ (see Paul in Salamis in Acts 13:5; in Thessalonica in Acts 17:1–3). When he engages with the Gentiles, particularly the Epicurean and Stoics in Acts 17:16–34, Paul uses their religious knowledge as a point of missional contact and moves forward to commend the gospel to them.

7.1 Compassion as the Starting Point of Engagement

Paul's model reveals Jesus's heart for engaging with people from a place of compassion (Matt 11:28–30; Luke 7:13; John 11:34–38). Unfortunately, apologetics has been caricatured as an enterprise of winning an argument rather than winning a person. Even more worrisome is a widespread distorted

24. Anita Cloete, "Religious Function of Film: A Viewer's Perspective," *Interdisciplinary Reflections on the Interplay between Religion, Film and Youth*, ed. Anita Cloete (Stellenbosch: Sun Press, 2019), 65.

25. Marc Sommers, "Urban Youth in Africa," *Environment and Urbanization* 22 no. 2 (2010): 317–32; Lawrence N. Okwuosa, Favour C. Uroko, Michael Mokwenye, Uchechukwu Monica Agbo and Stella Chinweudo Ekwueme, "Double Denominational Belonging among Youths in Nigeria: Implications on Christianity," *Journal of Youth and Theology* 19 no. 1 (2020): 95–114; Kingsley Ikechukwu Uwaegbute, "Christianity and Masquerade Practices Among the Youth in Nsukka, Nigeria," *African Studies* 80 no. 1 (2021): 40–59.

vision of young people. Older people can easily make value judgements about young people based on surface-level cultural issues rather than engaging the deep-level cultural issues involved.[26] Rather than engaging the symbols of youth culture (for example, dreadlock hairstyles, contemporary fashion styles, hip-hop sub-cultural realities), ministry leaders often push young people away. Paul reveals how compassion is the starting point of engagement. After all, we who are followers of Jesus are called to apologetic engagement from a place of "gentleness and respect" (1 Pet 3:15b). Paul is "provoked" – literally stirred, stimulated, irritated (see also 2 Pet 2:8) – by the idol worship of the Athenians (Acts 17:16). It is compassion that drives him to engage them rather than to abandon them.

7.2 Connecting Point in the Culture

Apologetic engagement with youth culture, rather than being an uncritical dumping of information, is a sensitive engagement with the values behind popular cultural symbols and ideas. This is what it means to connect with what young people value, whether they do it knowingly or unknowingly, and engaging the assumptions behind their value systems. We who serve young people must be present in their lives. Paul reasons "in the synagogue with the Jews and devout persons, and in the marketplace every day . . ." (Acts 17:17). One-time evangelistic contacts may work in some circumstances, but with the contemporary cultural complexities there is need to make use of our relationships for the sake of missional engagement. Additionally, connecting with young people means noting their religious and cultural symbols. Paul observes the altar's inscription "to an unknown God" and uses it as a point of apologetic engagement (Acts 17:23). Paul uses the altar as a cultural bridge to move the Athenians from where they are to where they should be – that is, from an unknown God to the living God. Finally, Paul's knowledge of the culture's influencers – Epimenides (Acts 17:28a) and Aratus (Acts 17:28b) – is exemplary for how apologetic engagement must be aware of and engage with the influencers of Africa's next generations.

Within the Kenyan context, ministering to young people may thus mean engaging with the ideas behind Sauti Sol's music or sensitively discerning Caroline Mutoko's lifestyle hacks among urban Kenyans. Sauti Sol's music articulates a combination of plural religious values, a contemporary and global

26. Walt Mueller, *Engaging the Soul of Youth Culture: Bridging Teen Worldviews and Christian Truth* (Downers Grove: IVP Books, 2006).

appeal within the Afro-pop music subculture and an aesthetic of postmodern African identity. These songs navigate both global youth culture as well as its localized elements of Kenyan youth cultures and sub-cultures, evident from the language to the turns of phrases in the lyrics. Such music presents an urban Kenyan contemporary culture which is conversant with a global youth culture, thereby revealing how seamlessly religion, popular culture, and postmodernity intertwine.[27] Caroline Mutoko is a popular radio host-cum-digital influencer who is the image of an articulate feminist voice, aware of the key dialogues happening in the culture and offering wisdom that is palatable to the working-class urban Kenyan.[28] Together, Sauti Sol and Mutoko unpack how postmodernity, new-age philosophical ideals, glocalized youth cultures and subcultures, and lived realities of young people in African cities can present common points of contact with the gospel. After all, the aspects of truth, identity, and multiculturalism find their nexus and fulfilment in the gospel of Jesus Christ.

7.3 Conviction with the Gospel

Although some Christians drive a wedge between apologetics and evangelism, these approaches to people outside of Christ are always held in a symbiotic relationship within the biblical canon. Apologetics is a handmaid of evangelism, so that when the intellectual barriers are removed Christ can be presented with clarity. Paul takes this approach in his engagement with the people of Athens. After he shows Christ-like compassion and then connects with them, the Spirit convicts them with Paul's message of the gospel. Paul's progression is not an undirected presentation of the gospel, but he begins carefully with a deep engagement with their worldviews about divinity and reality. By beginning with the doctrine of God and making a case for his spiritual nature, his self-sufficiency, his sovereignty, and his immanence, Paul directly engages with the Greco-Roman conceptualizations of divinity – particularly their polytheism and Hellenistic philosophy.[29] Once he clears the way, Paul then calls the people to "repentance," the normative call of all the preachers of the New Testament,

27. Mwenda Ntarangwi, *East African Hip Hop: Youth Culture and Globalization* (Urbana and Chicago: University of Illinois Press, 2009).

28. Wanjiru M. Gitau, "The Transformation of a Young Continent: Dimensions of Africa Rising," *Contemporânea-Revista de Sociologia da UFSCar* 9 no .2 (2019): 411.

29. Joshua W. Jipp, "Paul's Areopagus Speech of Acts 17:16–34 as both Critique and Propaganda," *Journal of Biblical Literature* 131 no. 3 (2012): 567–88; Clare K. Rothschild, *Paul in Athens: The Popular Religious Context of Acts 17* (Tübingen: Mohr Siebeck, 2014).

including Jesus and the other apostles (Mark 1:15; John 1:12–14; 3:5; Acts 2:38–39; 2 Pet 3:9). At the end of the day, it is faith in the good news of Jesus Christ that is the heart of true transformation.

The gospel message is presented within particular cultural and inter-religious contexts. While postmodernity allows us to consider different cultural contexts from our own, thereby revealing our subjective interpretations of reality, it also creates a conflicting climate for the truth claims of Christ.[30] In today's digital age, tolerance is often confused with blind acceptance of contradictory truth claims. Entertainment is preferred to intellectual engagement. *Ad-hominems* are a favourite strategy for keyboard atheists and apologists rather than long-term conversations. We must seek to answer the age-old questions surrounding issues to do with justification in knowledge as well as objectivity in truth, as well as attendant theories such as the non-contradictory laws of logic, which are a hallmark of any reasonable defence of the Christian faith. Eventually, however, those discussions must only serve to offer Christ to Africa's next generations.

8. Holistic Apologetics in a Digital Age

With the now accepted COVID-shaped reality of our world, and with many transitions in the life milestones of young people, apologetic engagement must holistically consider youth contexts. The COVID context is a "low hanging" fruit for engaging such classical questions of apologetics as the problem of pain, evil and suffering, or particular Christian doctrines, including eschatology. The author suggests that, as important as it is to engage in these conversations, how we go about them is just as crucial. Digital cultures are affecting young people in distinct ways. A holistic apologetic methodology must engage the head, the heart, and the hands. Gould describes such a holistic approach as a "re-enchantment of the reason, the conscience, and the imagination."[31]

Digital cultures shift how we consume and critique knowledge claims. Without a careful consideration of how such claims shape the lives of young people, we who seek to serve them may be engaging in discourses that are detached from their lived realities. This chapter has considered how digital culture shapes young people in three key areas: knowledge, mental health, and popular culture. By exploring Paul's engagement in the context of Athens in

30. Mueller, *Engaging the Soul of Youth Culture*, 62.

31. Paul M. Gould, *Cultural Apologetics: Renewing the Christian Voice, Conscience, and Imagination in a Disenchanted World* (Grand Rapids: Zondervan Academic, 2019), 32.

Acts 17, this chapter has proposed critical tools for incarnating the gospel for "igens," that is, African youth who are digitally native. First, we must engage digital cultures with compassion. Second, we must consider common points of popular cultural contact with young people. Third, we must offer Christ clearly in light of the apologetics task within the varied postmodern, modern, and traditional worldviews and interreligious climate of Africa's key cities.

Bibliography

The Africa Center of Apologetics Research. Facebook page. https://www.facebook.com/ACFAR/.

Alonzo, Rea, Junayd Hussain, K. Anderson and Saverio Stranges. "Interplay between Social Media Use, Sleep Quality, and Mental Health in Youth: A Systematic Review." *Sleep Medicine Reviews* 56.101414 (2020): 1–12.

Apologetics Kenya. "Apologetics Kenya" Facebook page, https://www.facebook.com/ApologeticsKenya.

Arnett, Jeffrey J. "Emerging Adulthood(s): The Cultural Psychology of a New Life Stage." Pages 255–75 in *Bridging Cultural and Developmental Approaches to Psychology: New Syntheses in Theory, Research and Policy.* Edited by Jeffrey Arnett. Oxford: Oxford University Press, 2011.

Cloete, Anita. "Religious Function of Film: A Viewer's Perspective." In *Interdisciplinary Reflections on the Interplay between Religion, Film and Youth* edited by Anite Cloete, 65–74. Stellenbosch: Sun Press, 2019.

Cowan, Stephen, and Stanley Gundry. *Five Views on Apologetics*. Grand Rapids: Zondervan Academic, 2010.

Craig, William L. "The Existence of God and the Beginning of the Universe." *Truth: A Journal of Modern Thought* 3 (1991): 85–96.

———. *Reasonable Faith: Christian Truth and Apologetics*. Wheaton: Crossway, 2008.

———. *The Atonement*. Cambridge: Cambridge University Press, 2018.

Ephraim, Philip E. "African Youths and the Dangers of Social Networking: A Culture-Centred Approach to using Social Media." *Ethics and Information Technology* 15 no. 4 (2020): 275–84.

Frame, John M. *Apologetics to the Glory of God*. Phillipsburg: P&R Publishing, 1994.

Gitau, Wanjiru M. "The Transformation of a Young Continent: Dimensions of Africa Rising." *Contemporânea-Revista de Sociologia da UFSCar* 9 no. 2 (2019): 401–30.

Gould, Paul M. *Cultural Apologetics: Renewing the Christian Voice, Conscience, and Imagination in a Disenchanted World*. Grand Rapids: Zondervan Academic, 2019.

Habermas, Gary R. "The Minimal Facts Approach to the Resurrection of Jesus: The Role of Methodology as a Crucial Component in Establishing Historicity." *Southeastern Theological Review* 3 no. 1 (2012): 15–26.

Hajjar, Bandar. "The Children's Continent: Keeping up with Africa's Growth." *World Economic Forum* website, Jan 13, 2020. https://www.weforum.org/agenda/2020/01/the-children-s-continent/.

Institute of Christian Apologetics Studies (ICAS). Facebook page, https://www.facebook.com/Institute-for-Christian-Apologetics-Studies-ICAS-331535666866436/.

Jipp, Joshua W. "Paul's Areopagus Speech of Acts 17:16–34 as both Critique and Propaganda." *Journal of Biblical Literature* 131 no. 3 (2012): 567–88.

Mbiti, John S. *African Religions & Philosophy*. Oxford: Heinemann, 1990.

Moreland, James Porter. *Scientism and Secularism: Learning to Respond to a Dangerous Ideology*. Wheaton: Crossway, 2018.

Mueller, Walt. *Engaging the Soul of Youth Culture: Bridging Teen Worldviews and Christian Truth*. Downers Grove: IVP Books, 2006.

Ndereba, Kevin Muriithi. "The Influence of Youth Cultures on Faith Formation of Youth in Nairobi: A Practical Theological Approach." PhD Thesis, University of South Africa, 2021.

———. "Ubuntu Apologetics in Faith Formation: An Ethnography of Youth Ministry in Nairobi." *Journal of Youth and Theology* 1 (2021): 1–16.

Netland, Harold. "Evangelical Missiology and Theology of Religions: An Agenda for the Future." *International Journal of Frontier Missiology* 29 (2012): 5–12.

Ntarangwi, Mwenda. *East African Hip Hop: Youth Culture and Globalization*. Chicago: University of Illinois Press, 2009.

Okwuosa, Lawrence N., Favour C. Uroko, Michael Mokwenye, Uchechukwu Monica Agbo and Stella Chinweudo Ekwueme. "Double Denominational Belonging among Youths in Nigeria: Implications on Christianity." *Journal of Youth and Theology* 19 no. 1 (2020): 95–114.

Ononogbu, David C., and Nathan Chiroma. "Social Media and Youth Ministry in Nigeria: Implications and Christological Thrust." *International Journal of Humanities Social Sciences and Education* 5 no. 1 (2018): 48–54.

Ratio Christi South Africa. Ratio Christi website. https://ratiochristi.co.za/.

Rothschild, Clare K. *Paul in Athens: The Popular Religious Context of Acts 17*. Tübingen: Mohr Siebeck, 2014.

Sanneh, Lamin O. and Joel A. Carpenter, eds. *The Changing Face of Christianity: Africa, the West, and the World*. Oxford: Oxford University Press, 2005.

Sommers, Marc. "Urban Youth in Africa." *Environment and Urbanization* 22 no. 2 (2010): 317–32.

Tamburrino, Inge, Elijah Getanda, Michelle O'Reilly and Panos Vostanis. "'Everybody's Responsibility': Conceptualization of Youth Mental Health in Kenya." *Journal of Child Health Care* 24 no. 1 (2020): 5–18.

Topf, Daniel. "Technology as a Modern-Day Tower of Babel: The Garden of Eden as an Alternative Vision for Missionally Engaging a Media-Saturated Culture." *Global Missiology* 18. no. 2 (2021): 1–10.

Twenge, Jean. *iGen: Why Today's Super-Connected Kids are Growing up Less Rebellious, More Tolerant, Less Happy and Completely Unprepared for Adulthood and what that Means for the Rest of Us*. New York: Simon and Schuster, 2017.

Uwaegbute, Kingsley Ikechukwu. "Christianity and Masquerade Practices Among the Youth in Nsukka, Nigeria." *African Studies* 80 no. 1 (2021): 40–59. DOI: 10.1080/00020184.2021.1886049.

List of Contributors

DANIËL MARITZ, PhD (South Africa) After school, Daniël pursued his studies in theology at the North West University in Potchefstroom. In 2015 he started his master's degree on the New Age movement's infiltration of the church and consequently enrolled for a PhD in theology which he completed in 2020. He is a pastor at the Reformed Church Brooklyn in Pretoria and on the leadership of a church plant group called Dialogue. He established the Ratio Christi chapter at the University of Pretoria in 2018. Daniël married Ansie, who is a lecturer in linguistics, in 2015. They currently live in Pretoria.

ELIZABETH MBURU, PhD (Kenya) was the first woman to gain a PhD from Southeastern Baptist Theological Seminary, North Carolina, USA. She is an associate professor of New Testament and Greek at International Leadership University, Africa International University and Pan-Africa Christian University in Nairobi, Kenya. Dr. Mburu is on the board of the *Africa Bible Commentary* and is the editorial coordinator and New Testament editor for its revision. She is also the Anglophone Africa Regional Coordinator for Langham Literature. Professor Mburu is also the author of *Qumran and the Origins of Johannine Language and Symbolism* (T&T Clark, 2019).

JOSEPH BYAMUKAMA (Uganda) is the founder and team leader at Veracity Fount, a ministry in Uganda that aims at researching and resourcing for church renewal. He is a PhD New Testament candidate at Ridley College, Melbourne under Dr. Brian Rosner. His research focuses on the "Witness" language in the Acts of the Apostles on the backdrop of YHWH's contest against the gods of the nations in Isaiah. Joseph is married to Daphne, and together they have a son – Abaho.

JOSEPH OKELLO, PhD (Kenya/USA) is professor of philosophy of Christian religion. Dr. Okello received a ThB from Scott Theological College , Kenya, 1994; a MDiv (1999) and MA in church music (2000) at Asbury Seminary; and a MA (2004) and PhD (2007) in philosophy at the University of Kentucky. While he was a student at Asbury Seminary, he earned the Frank Bateman Stanger award for excellence in preaching and the Philosophy and Christian apologetics award. Dr. Okello has served as a pastor and choral director at Africa Inland Church. He has published several articles and books, including *Revisiting God: A Commonsense Approach to Theism* (Xulon Press, 2008).

JUDY WANJIRU WANG'OMBE, PhD (Kenya) is a lecturer at the Africa International University. She has been serving as a cross-cultural missionary since 1992 and is involved in children's ministry in her local church. She holds a BSc Agricultural Economics (Egerton University, 1991), MDiv Biblical Studies (NEGST/AIU, 2001), MTh Missions (Islamic Emphasis) (AIU, 2007) and a PhD Interreligious Studies (AIU, 2019).

KEVIN MURIITHI NDEREBA, PhD (Kenya), is a lecturer and head of department of Practical Theology at St. Paul's University, Kenya and research fellow in the Department of Practical Theology and Missiology, Stellenbosch University, South Africa. For ten years, he has served in the Presbyterian Church of East Africa and holds a PhD in Theology from the University of South Africa. His educational background includes a BSc in Electrical & Electronics Engineering and an MA in Biblical and Theological Studies. He has a certificate in Christian Apologetics from Talbot School of Theology, Biola University, and is chairperson of Apologetics Kenya. He has also participated as a summer seminar fellow with Discovery Institute's center for Science and Culture. Kevin serves in the executive board of the International Association for the Study of Youth Ministry, is the current vice-chair of the Africa Society of Evangelical Theology, writes for The Gospel Coalition Africa and is also working on a monograph tentatively titled *Youth Ministry after the Pandemic: A Practical Theology from the Global South.* He is married to Jessica and father to Noah.

KYAMA MUGAMBI, PhD (Kenya/USA) is assistant professor of World Christianity at Yale Divinity School, Connecticut, USA. He was previously at Africa International University, where he has been serving as a senior researcher and faculty member at the university's Centre for World Christianity. He specializes in ecclesial, social, cultural, theological and epistemological themes within African urban Christianity. His book, *A Spirit of Revitalization: Urban Pentecostalism in Kenya* (Baylor University Press, 2020), which traces the history of Pentecostalism in Kenya, has been hailed as a singular contribution to the fields of mission studies, world Christianity, and intercultural theology. He also served as the editorial manager of African Theological Network Press, an initiative advancing theological discourse among academics and church workers. He is a member of the editorial boards of the Dictionary of African Christian Biography [www.dacb.org] and Missio Africanus. He remains connected to the local church having served as a pastor for more than twenty years.

MIHRETU GUTA, PhD (Ethiopia/USA) teaches philosophy at Biola University, Azusa Pacific University, and Addis Ababa University. Dr. Guta completed his PhD in Philosophy at Durham University, UK under the supervision of Professor E. J. Lowe and Professor Sophie Gibb. Dr. Guta subsequently worked as a postdoctoral research fellow within the Durham Emergence Project (funded by the John Templeton Foundation), where he researched the nature of the emergence of consciousness from the standpoint of metaphysics, philosophy of mind, neuroscience and quantum physics. In the past, Dr. Guta served as an assistant to the academic dean and lecturer at the Evangelical Theological College in Addis Ababa, Ethiopia. Dr. Guta also served as a member of the preaching team at the Redeemer Church in La Mirada, California, USA.

PRIMROSE MUYAMBO (South Africa) has a master's degree from George Whitefield College in Cape Town, South Africa. She is passionate about issues related to marriage especially in African context. Her honours thesis looks at "oppressive challenges faced by Shona women due to traditional understanding of headship and submission." Her master's thesis looks at "Adultery in Matthew 5:27–32 in the context of discipleship in the Sermon on the Mount." Primrose and her husband are currently serving in youth ministry at St Mark's church Plumstead in Cape Town. Previously, she was serving in student ministry at the University of Zimbabwe with FOCUS Zimbabwe.

ROBERT FALCONER, PhD (South Africa) holds degrees in architecture and theology. After having practiced architecture in Scotland and South Africa, he and his wife were called to Kenya as missionaries. He currently works at the South African Theological Seminary as the MTh and PhD coordinator. His primary research interests are Architectonic Theology, African Philosophical-Theology, Architecture and Theology, Soteriology and Eschatology.

REV. RODGERS ATWEBEMBEIRE (Uganda) is a PhD candidate at North-West University, South Africa. He serves as the East Africa Director of the Africa Centre for Apologetics Research (ACFAR) and pastor of New City Community Church in Kampala, Uganda. Rodgers is much in demand as a conference speaker on apologetics, cults and related topics, and his teaching ministry includes radio and television programs and a podcast. He is also a frequent contributor to The Gospel Coalition – Africa.

SAMUEL WAJE KUNHIYOP, PhD (Nigeria) is professor of Theology and Ethics at Jos ECWA Theological Seminary (JETS), where he previously served as Provost. Prior to that, he served as head of the Postgraduate School, South African Theological Seminary. He holds a BA (JETS), MAET (Western Seminary, Oregon), and PhD (Trinity International University, Illinois) He is an ordained minister with the Evangelical Church of West Africa (ECWA).

SEYRAM B. AMENYEDZI, PhD (Ghana) holds an MSc in Christian Education from the Life Christian University, USA and PhD in Missiology (disability research) from Stellenbosch University (2016) where she also pursued several courses in research methodology at the African Doctoral Academy. She is an ordained minister and has been in ministry for over twenty-three years. Seyram is currently a postgraduate supervisor at the South African Theological Seminary where she was a full-time senior lecturer for over five years. She is a research fellow with the International Research Training Group, *Transformative religion: Religion as situated knowledge in processes of social transformation*, funded by the South African National Research Foundation (NRF) and the German Research Foundation (DFG), and is stationed at the University of Western Cape. She has developed a number of research methodologies for doing Afrocentric Research.

Index

Milton Keynes UK
Ingram Content Group UK Ltd.
UKHW011951020224
437175UK00012B/1345

9 781839 736629